8/01

The Critical Response to John Steinbeck's *The Grapes of Wrath*

Recent Titles in
Critical Responses in Arts and Letters

The Critical Response to John Steinbeck's *The Grapes of Wrath*

Edited by
Barbara A. Heavilin

Critical Responses in Arts and Letters, Number 37
Cameron Northouse, Series Adviser

Greenwood Press
Westport, Connecticut • London

Library of Congress Cataloging-in-Publication Data

The critical response to John Steinbeck's The grapes of wrath / edited by Barbara A. Heavilin.
    p. cm.—(Critical responses in arts and letters, ISSN 1057–0993 ; no. 37)
    Includes bibliographical references and index.
    ISBN 0-313-29990-0 (alk. paper)
    1. Steinbeck, John, 1902–1968. Grapes of wrath. 2. Migrant agricultural laborers in
literature. 3. Rural families in literature. 4. Labor camps in literature. 5. Depressions in
literature. 6. California—In literature. I. Heavilin, Barbara A., 1945– II. Series.
PS3537.T3234 G8472 2000
813'.52—dc21   00–022322

British Library Cataloguing in Publication Data is available.

Library of Congress Catalog Card Number: 00–022322
ISBN: 0-313-29990-0
ISSN: 1057–0993

First published in 2000

Greenwood Press, 88 Post Road West, Westport, CT 06881
An imprint of Greenwood Publishing Group, Inc.
www.greenwood.com

Printed in the United States of America

The paper used in this book complies with the
Permanent Paper Standard issued by the National
Information Standards Organization (Z39.48–1984).

10 9 8 7 6 5 4 3 2

COPYRIGHT ACKNOWLEDGMENTS

The editor and publisher gratefully acknowledge permission for the use of the following material:

Charles Lee, "'The Grapes of Wrath': The Tragedy of the American Sharecropper," *Boston Herald*. 22 April 1939, Sec. A, p. 7.
-----, "'The Grapes of Wrath' Tops Year's Tales in Heart and Art," *Boston Herald*. 17 June 1939, Sec. A, p. 9.

Fritz Raley Simmons, "Farm Tenancy Central Theme of Steinbeck," *Greensboro Daily News*, 16 July 1939, Sec. D, p. 6.

Robert DeMott, *Steinbeck's Typewriter: Essays on His Art*, Troy, N. Y.: The Whitson Publishing Company, 1996.

Woodburn O. Ross, "John Steinbeck, Naturalism's Priest," *College English*. May 1949. Reprinted by permission of the National Council of Teachers of English.

Joseph Fontenrose, Chapter 6 "*The Grapes of Wrath*" from *John Steinbeck: An Introduction and Interpretation*. American Authors and Critics Series. New York: Barnes and Noble, 1963. Reprinted by permission of HarperCollins Publishers.

Peter Lisca, "Steinbeck and Hemingway: Suggestions for a Comparative Study," *Steinbeck Quarterly*. Spring 1969. Reprinted by permission of author and Dr. Tetsumaro Hayashi, editor and copyright owner.

Colin Matton, "Water Imagery and the Conclusion to *The Grapes of Wrath*," *Northeast Modern Language Association Newsletter*. Vol. 2, 1970.

George Henderson, "John Steinbeck's Spatial Imagination in *The Grapes of Wrath*: A Critical Essay," *California History*. Vol. 68, Winter 1989/90. Reprinted by permission.

Louis Owens and Hector Torres. "Dialogic Structure and Levels of Discourse in Steinbeck's *The Grapes of Wrath*." Reprinted from *Arizona Quarterly: A Journal of American Literature, Culture and Theory*, 45:4 (1989): 75-94, by permission of the Regents of the University of Arizona.

To Mother

Gladys Aileen Lackey Coalson

Contents

Contents

Series Foreword

Critical Responses in Arts and Letters is designed to present a documentary history of the highlights in critical reception to the body of work of writers and artists and to individual works that are generally considered to be of major importance. The focus of each volume in this series is basically historical. The introductions to each volume are themselves brief histories of the critical response an author, artists, or individual work has received. This response is then further illustrated by reprinting a strong representation of the major critical reviews and articles that have collectively produced the author's, artist's, or work's critical reputation.

The scope of *Critical Responses in Arts and Letters* knows no chronological or geographical boundaries. Volumes under preparation include studies of individuals from around the world and in both contemporary and historical periods.

Each volume is the work of an individual editor, who surveys the entire body of criticism on a single author, artist, or work. The editor then selects the best material to depict the critical response received by that author or artist over his/her entire career. Documents produced by the author or artist may also be included when the editor finds that they are necessary to a full understanding of the materials at hand. In circumstances where previous isolated volumes of criticism on a particular individual or work exist, the editor carefully selects material that better reflects the nature and directions of the critical response over time.

In addition to the introduction and the documentary section, the editor of each volume is free to solicit new essays on areas that may not have been adequately dealt with in previous criticism. Also, for volumes on living writers and artists, new interviews may be included, again at the discretion of the volume's editor. The volumes also provide a supplementary bibliography and are fully indexed.

While each volume in *Critical Responses in Arts and Letters* is unique, it is also hoped that in combination they form a useful, documentary history of the critical response to the arts, and one that can be easily and profitably employed by students and scholars.

Cameron Northouse

Preface

This book on the critical response to John Steinbeck's *The Grapes of Wrath* is divided into two parts, with the first part looking back on the first fifty years, 1939-1989 and the second looking forward to a new millennium. The rationale for such an arrangement is to an extent logistical and logical and to another extent hopeful. That is, the volume must have divisions of some kind, and, since the occasion of the anniversary of this novel's first fifty years received much deserved celebration—with a major conference, new editions, critical attention, and recognition as one of the top ten of the hundred best novels of the century list—the end of the inclusive years 1939-1989 seems an appropriate dividing point.

There is also a rationale for devoting the second part of the book to the nineties, looking forward to a new millennium. For the most part, the critical responses of Steinbeck scholars have included an apologia as a nod of recognition to those critics who denigrate him and his fiction. Jackson J. Benson, for example, writes the opening chapter, entitled "John Steinbeck: The Favorite Author We Love to Hate," for Donald R. Noble's 1993 *The Steinbeck Question: New Essays in Criticism.*

Critics in the later nineties, though, seem to be breaking free from such an oxymoronic mix of emotive and unsure responses to the Steinbeck aesthetic. To illustrate, in *Parallel Expeditions: Charles Darwin and the Art of John Steinbeck*, Brian E. Railsback best epitomizes these new critics in his depiction of the "vindictive style" of Leslie Fiedler as he assaulted and damned Steinbeck "at an international conference, '*The Grapes of Wrath*, 1939-1989: An Interdisciplinary Forum,' held at San Jose State University in California." Neither angry nor defensive, Railsback points out that Fiedler "had little new to say" and that he seemed "somewhat confused." After a brief overview of other chief

Steinbeck detractors—among them Arthur Mizener, Donald Weeks, and Harold Bloom—Railsback concludes that these critics, like Fiedler, "wander about slightly baffled." (1-3) Such an assured, confident tone bodes well for future Steinbeck scholars. And this tone of confidence and anticipation is characteristic of recent scholarship, which is well represented in this volume's introductory essay and in articles and reviews in part two. Steinbeck studies, then, can look forward to the new millennium in a mood similar to that of John Milton's *Lycidas*: "Tomorrow to fresh woods and pastures new."

I am grateful for all of those who have made this book possible: journal and book editors and publishers, those whose articles have been reprinted here; those whose original contributions were generously and thoughtfully written; the Dean of Academic Affairs , Dr. Dwight Jessup, and the Faculty Personnel Committee of Taylor University for a January leave; my mentors, Dr. Tetsumaro Hayashi, Dr. Roy Simmonds, and Dr. John Ditsky, whose advice, encouragement, assistance, time, and patience were invaluable; my student, Juliana Menges, who helped more than she realized by typing the manuscripts; and most of all my husband, Charles, who is always long suffering, encouraging, and helpful.

Chronology

1902	On February 27 born John Ernst Steinbeck to Olive Hamilton Steinbeck, former schoolteacher, and John Ernst Steinbeck, miller and later treasurer of Monterey County.
1919-24	Graduates from Salinas High School and attends Stanford University sporadically, publishing "Fingers of Cloud" and "Adventures in Arcademy" in *The Stanford Spectator*.
1925-26	Leaves Stanford without a degree, moves to New York and works for the *American*, writes short stories but finds no publisher, returns to California where he continues to write and has several jobs, among them caretaker of a lodge at Lake Tahoe.
1927	*Cup of Gold* published.
1930	Marries Carol Henning.
1932	Moves to Los Angeles, publishes *The Pastures of Heaven*.
1933	Returns to Pacific Grove, publishes *To a God Unknown* and parts one and two of *The Red Pony*.

1934   "The Murder" chosen as an O. Henry Prize Story, and his
            mother, Olive Hamilton Steinbeck, dies.

1935   His father dies, and he publishes *Tortilla Flat* and is
            awarded the Commonwealth Club of California
            Gold Medal.

1936   Publishes *In Dubious Battle* and "The Harvest Gypsies,"
            articles on migrants, for *San Francisco News.*

1937   Publishes *Of Mice and Men*, to become a bestseller and a
            Book-of-the-Month Club selection, and also *The Red
            Pony* in three parts. *Of Mice and Men* play production
            wins the Drama Critics Circle Award.

1938   Publishes *The Long Valley* and *Their Blood Is Strong* (a
            reprint of the migrant articles plus a postscript).

1939   Publishes *The Grapes of Wrath* (which becomes number
            one national bestseller) and is elected to the National
            Institute of Arts and Letters.

1940   Receives the Pulitzer Prize for *The Grapes of Wrath*, is
            elected to the National Institute of Arts and Letters,
            writes *The Forgotten Village*, a film script.

1941   With Edward F. Ricketts, publishes *Sea of Cortez.*

1942   Publishes *The Moon Is Down* (also a play) and *Bombs
            Away* and is divorced from Carol Henning.

1943   Marries Gwendolyn Conger, moves to New York, and
            serves as a war correspondent for New York *Herald
            Tribune*.

1944   Writes an unpublished film story for *Lifeboat*, and his
            first son, Thom, is born.

1945   Publishes *Cannery Row*, *The Red Pony* (with a fourth
              part included), "The Pearl of the World" (*The Pearl*), and
              a story for film, *A Medal for Benny*.

1946   Is awarded King Haakon Liberty Cross in Norway for
              The Moon Is Down, and his second son, John IV, is born.

1947   Publishes *The Pearl* and *The Wayward Bus* and visits
              Russia with photographer Robert Capa.

1948   With Robert Capa publishes *A Russian Journal* and is
              elected to American Academy of Arts and Letters.
              Ricketts dies as a result of an automobile accident, and
              Steinbeck is divorced from Gwendolyn Conger.

1950   Publishes *Burning Bright*, writes *Viva Zapata!* for film,
              and marries Elaine Scott.

1951   Publishes *The Log from the Sea of Cortez*, including
              a tribute to Ricketts.

1952   Publishes *East of Eden*.

1954   Publishes *Sweet Thursday*.

1955   *Pipe Dream*, a musical comedy based on *Sweet
              Thursday*, is produced by Rodgers and Hammerstein.

1956   Publishes *The Short Reign of Pippin IV*.

1958   Publishes *Once There Was a War*.

1961   Publishes *The Winter of Our Discontent*.

1962   Publishes *Travels with Charley in Search of America* and
              is awarded the Nobel Prize for Literature.

1964   Receives Presidential Medal of Freedom.

1965-1966   Publishes "Letters to Alicia," based on his travels for
                 Newsday in Europe and the Middle East.

1966   Publishes *America and Americans*.

1966-1967   Continues to publish "Letters to Alicia," based on
                 his travels in Vietnam.

1968   Dies at home of cardiorespiratory failure.

*Journal of a Novel: The"East of Eden" Letters, Steinbeck: A Life in
Letters, The Acts of King Arthur and His Noble Knights, Working Days:
The Journals of "The Grapes of Wrath,"* and *Zapata* have all been
published posthumously.

Introduction

"Here ye the voice of the Bard!
Who Present, Past, and Future sees"
--William Blake, "Introduction," *Songs of Experience*

In a letter to his editor, Pascal Covici, on January 16, 1939, John Steinbeck defends the artistic merit of the final tableau in *The Grapes of Wrath*, a scene in which Rose of Sharon--her baby dead, placed in an apple box by Uncle John, and sent down stream as a mute testimony to "tell" the tragic story of dispossession--nurses a starving old man in a deserted barn (446-53).[1] In the process he sets forth his intentionality not only in thus ending *GW* as some critics complain, inconclusively,[2] but also in creating a story with the affective power "to rip a reader's nerves to rags." Concerning the reader, Steinbeck further asserts: "I don't want him satisfied" (178).[3] Refusing to change this ending, he insists that the "design and balance" are there and that readers must discover the implied climax for themselves:

> The reader must bring the implication to it. If he doesn't, it wasn't a book for him to read. Throughout I've tried to make the reader participate in the actuality, what he takes from it will be scaled entirely on his own depth or hollowness. There are five layers in this book, a reader will find as many as he can and he won't find more than he has in himself. (*SLL* 178-79)

By implication at least, this letter takes into consideration, delineates, and prescribes the relationships among writer, reader, critic, text, and the literary and social context.

In effect, in this letter Steinbeck himself models the behavior of the writer as the creator of the fictional world, as one who must maintain artistic integrity if the work is to be well envisioned, well grounded, and well made. On this ground of integrity, then, when Covici objects to such an "abrupt" ending, suggesting that "the incident needs leading up to, so that the meeting with the starving man is not so much an accident or chance encounter, but more an integral part of the saga," Steinbeck insists that he cannot change this ending: "To build this stranger into the structure of the book would be to warp the whole meaning of the book" (*SLL* 177-78).

His concern for "meaning" here is classical, importing from Aristotle the persuasion that poetry is truer than history because history deals in facts whereas the poetic arts deal in universals. Integrity demands, therefore, that the text remain "true" to the artistic vision of the human condition--with the ultimate purpose that the reader "participate in the actuality." In eighteenth-century terms, Steinbeck holds the mirror so that readers may see themselves and their society as they actually are, warts and all, in the hope that there will be reform and a return to right reason in governing human affairs.

In thus holding the mirror, Steinbeck's role is at once idealistic and pragmatic, and it places him squarely in a persona of the bardic tradition in his relationship to text and reader. In this role he is the one who sees and understands the heritage of the past--both good and bad--the turmoil of the present, the bleak hope for a better future. His voice is that of a Merlin who tries to advise an adolescent Arthur, here an Every American, whose dream of and search for Camelot/Eden/Paradise is now tarnished and forever flawed.

As Merlin is to Arthur, then, so Steinbeck is to his readers--peering over shoulders in the interchapters, guiding responses, assuring an empathic, participatory involvement with "the actuality." He states bluntly and a bit gruffly of the reader who does not want to participate: "It wasn't a book for him to read." In this Merlin-like role, too, he is part companion or fellow-traveler; part guide, or authority figure; part prophet/bard/ preacher. And this bardic persona[4] is very much present in *GW*, his ethos permeating and pervading, especially in the interchapters but also, on occasion, in his characters, one of them so real and so much an alter ego that, as Robert DeMott points out, "he imagined that Tom Joad actually entered the novelist's work space, the private chamber of his room: 'Tom! Tom! Tom! I know. It wasn't him. Yes, I think I can go on now. In fact, I feel stronger.

Much stronger. Funny where the energy comes from. Now to work, only now it isn't work any more,' he recorded in his journal on 20 October (*WD*, 91)" (186).[5]

In a sense, therefore, Steinbeck is himself a participant, held by the evocative power of his own story. He is compelled to tell it and intends to compel the reader to hear and understand it not only with the intellect but with the heart as well.[6] Perhaps it is the bard-like voice or the closeness and intimacy of this writer/reader/text hug dance that has led some critics to label and to dismiss this novel on the basis of sentimentality--a most damaging, even though undeserving, assessment, especially in the view of the coolly detached American critic who may not wish to be drawn into a story in which a strong empathic involvement is demanded as essential to a right reading. However this may be, in this 1939 January 16 letter to Covici, Steinbeck has provided critics and readers with both the literary ingredients that are in his novel and those that are not there. Some of these points may overlap, but it is instructive to consider each, beginning with those characteristics of *GW* that are either explicit or implicit:

- *GW* has a "casual" ending that Steinbeck maintains he "cannot change."[7]
- If there is a symbol in the final tableau, "it is a survival symbol, not a love symbol."
- The ending must have "an accident" and "a stranger," and "it must be quick."
- It has a "meaning" that would be warped if the stranger were not built into the structure.
- The "emphasis" is on "the fact that the Joads don't know him, don't care about him, and have no ties to him."
- It has the "design and balance" that Steinbeck intends for it to have.
- "Every incident has been . . . carefully chosen and its weight judged and fitted."
- It has a strong empathic element, designed to leave the reader dissatisfied, "to rip . . . nerves to rags."
- It is written "the way lives are being lived."
- "A strong deep climax" is there by "implication" only.
- The reader is integral to the text and "must bring the implication to it."[8]
- "The reader must participate in the actuality."
- Further, this book is entrenched in this "actuality." For it foreshadows a larger social context than the plight of dispossessed "Okies" in

California in 1939 and the inexorable forces against which they have no weapons --setting forth also a long-range concern for the American psyche and its penchant for greed and materialism.[9]

- What readers discover will depend on their "own depth or hollowness."
- It has "five layers." A reader will not "find more than he has in himself."

And to underscore and emphasize his strong sense of purpose and design, Steinbeck has provided as well the ingredients that are **not** present in *GW* because they neither fit into its "design" nor contribute to its "balance":

- "There is no fruity climax."
- The climax "is not more important than any other part of the book."
- The stranger cannot be built into the book's structure.
- "The giving of the breast has no more sentiment than the giving of a piece of bread."
- The story is not "new" because "there are no new stories."
- It is not intended to be "a satisfying story."
- It is not written "the way books are written."
- It does not have the usual "strong deep climax."
- The text is not autonomous, standing alone in the making of meaning.[10]

In letters to editors and friends and in *Working Days: The Journals of "The Grapes of Wrath,"* Steinbeck has thus generously and clearly set forth his intentions in writing *GW* and has provided as well guidelines for reading it.

But like the clues in a mystery game, these intentions and guidelines are subject to interpretation and dependent upon the perceptiveness of the reader and critic. And the question of how well or not these authorial intentions translate into art remains to be answered. It is the purpose of this introductory essay on the critical response to *GW* to explore this evidence of Steinbeck's intentions and the question of his artistic fulfillment, placing them in a perspective and context by considering them among other related and necessary questions, as follows:

1. What is the relationship between Steinbeck and his reader/critic? How well or not do his intentions inform, or guide, this relationship? How well or not have critics through the decades discovered, sought, or taken into account his intentions for *GW*?

2. How well or not do Steinbeck's intentions translate into art in *GW* ?

3. Might not the source of some of the negative critical responses to *GW* over the years lie in its presentation of an image of an Every American[11] that some critics do not want to acknowledge (or that may be too close for some to see)? What does Steinbeck have to say to America today? How should Steinbeck criticism--both popular and critical--be evaluated? How should this criticism be educated, and where does it go from this point? These questions, then, comprise the direction of this introductory essay on the critical response to *GW*--an exploration that will finally conclude that, in large part because of its empathic appeal, its careful design, and artistic balance, the critical response to Steinbeck's *GW* shows that this novel goes from story, to art, and then beyond art to myth as a part of the living heritage of America and the creation of the national identity.

1
"Steinbeck has seen clearly, felt intensely, written passionately.
As a result, the reader is absorbed, shaken, and convinced."
--Charles Lee in a 1939 review for *The Boston Herald*

"Steinbeck's participatory aesthetic, based on a circle of complicity
which linked 'the trinity' of writer, text, and reader
to ensure maximum affective impact,
helps explain the book's runaway popularity--each reader had a stake in it,
each reader feels somehow that the book belongs to him or her."
--Robert DeMott in his 1996 *Steinbeck's Typewriter*

In "Suggestions for an Interview with Joseph Henry Jackson," a journalist of the *San Francisco Chronicle*, Steinbeck provides a paradigm for a professional relationship between writer and critic, one that centers on the text. His suggested questions for an interview, therefore, involve thematic issues; human concerns for "comfort," "security," and relationships; the evolution of American literature; and "the material the writer deals in." Steinbeck's own "materials" include his admiration of "the struggling poor," especially the migrants of his day (Lisca, Hearle 541). Such questions, he believes, are the province of the critic.

His view of the serious role of the writer and the bardic persona of the omniscient narrator in *GW* are reflected in his description of the writer's "province": "The province of the writer is to set down what is and what may come of it with as little confusion and as little nonsense as possible" (541-42). Here, then, he reveals the role and ethos of a writer/persona/seer who not only holds the mirror reflecting the social, spiritual, and economic woes of the present but also sees into the future and prophetically warns against "what may come" if there is no reform, no redemption, no reconciliation, no restoration of the humane and human ties that have been hastily, brutally severed.

Although Steinbeck's statement of his purpose in writing *GW*, his guidelines for reading it, and this paradigm of his view of the relationship among writer, critic, and text were not available for earlier reviewers and critics, they nevertheless provide a convenient means of discussing this relationship and considering the critical response across time to the artistic merits, or lack thereof, of *GW*.[12]

In "Editors' Introduction: The Pattern of Criticism" in their 1997 "*The Grapes of Wrath*": *Text and Criticism*, editors Peter Lisca and Kevin Hearle point out that "one of the most striking aspects of critical writing about *The Grapes of Wrath* in its first fifteen years was its assertive nature," that "there was little analysis or detailed explication" (*GW* 548).   This very assertiveness, however, frequently lends itself to an analysis of another kind--not textual, but one that reveals reviewers and critics responding to *GW* in the light of its affective powers, that is, more in the light of what it **does** rather than what it **is**.[13] Many of these early writers, both positive and negative, then, analyze the novel on the basis of an initial, affective reaction[14] and witness to its evocative drawing and its insistence on participatory involvement.   Such effects are exactly what Steinbeck intended: that readers "participate in the actuality" and that this experience leave them dissatisfied. The 1939 reviewer, Fritz Raley Simmons, from *Greensboro North Carolina Daily News*, for example, bluntly describes the effect of such participation in his own experience with the novel: "It gets you."[15]

Charles Lee writes two 1939 reviews of *GW* for *The Boston Herald*, one in April and the other in June.[16] The titles of both assert (to borrow Lisca's term) the novel's dramatic impact: "*The Grapes of Wrath*: The Tragedy of the American Sharecropper" and "*The Grapes of Wrath*" Tops Year's Tales in Heart and Art," both of which attest to the novel's persuasive power to draw a reader, even though unwillingly, into the story:

> The ordinary reader, like myself, . . . cannot help believing that things must be as Steinbeck has painted them. The fact that he does not want to believe and does demonstrates the emotional power of the book. Steinbeck has seen clearly, felt intensely, written passionately. As a result, the reader is absorbed, shaken, and convinced. (April, Sec. A, p. 7)

There is here a strong sense not only of the reader's compelled involvement with the text but also of the pervading ethos of the persona, the authoritative narrator, who does not permit readers "to miss the point. It is sledged home in . . . bursts of indignation, hymns almost, of hate against those 'who own the things people must have.'" Recognizing the involvement of the Every American in this novel, Lee hopes that the story will be read by "every congressman . . . and everybody in America who loves his country and fellowmen" (April, Sec. A, p. 7). And in June he again reminds readers that "Steinbeck's novel is one of the few perfectly articulated soarings of genius of which American literature can boast" (Sec. 1, p. 9).

The 1939 Greensboro reviewer, Fritz Raley Simmons, writes of *GW* and of Steinbeck similarly in accolades and superlatives, with the assertiveness and lack of analytical explication that Lisca has pointed out:

- "It is terrific writing that makes one think and think hard."
- "It is a vivid, living story."
- "There is no doubt left that John Steinbeck is one of the ablest if not the ablest writer on the present scene."
- "His characterizations are superb."
- "There is majesty in the alternate chapters of this book."

In a sense, these accolades do, however, analyze an aspect of *GW* that matters a great deal to Steinbeck--the interaction between reader and text. This particular reader/ reviewer has not only thought "hard" about this story, but he has also entered into its pages, participated in its story, and come away with something "vivid" and "living."[17] And when Simmons compares his initial reading of *GW* to listening to a sonata, he approaches an analysis of its affective domain, by analogy making the abstract experience more concrete:

> When we started reading the book somebody was playing a piano sonata over the radio. We couldn't identify the music, but the soft, insistent notes kept falling into the pool of silence with a cumulative effect that built up into a climax that was as powerful as it was subdued. And that is the first chapter of "The Grapes of Wrath." It is a sonata in a minor key. It gets you. (6)

Like Lee and Simmons, other 1939 reviewers attest to the novel's evocative power. John Selby, for instance, maintains that "the reader is lifted into the stream which flows from the author, and goes with it gladly.

This is not novel reading, but experience at living, and details do not matter."[18]

"The American's Book Shelf" in *Waterbury American*[19] also attests that *GW* "is a powerful voice rising against injustice and will leave a burning memory on all who read it" (4). And David H. Appel in "Books" for the *Cleveland News*[20] declares that "there are moments of tenderness, pathos and even harshness that are done with such burning intensity that one is left breathless in the wake of such power (12). Although these early reviewers offer "little analysis or detailed explication" that centers on the text itself, therefore, they do offer a glimpse of the process of the readers' own "education of the heart," to borrow French's depiction of the Joads' experience.

As Lisca maintains, those reviews and articles that view the novel in negative terms are also assertive in nature, but they, too, provide an analysis of sorts of the reader/text/author relationship. Strangely, those who protest *GW* most shrilly are also those who also acknowledge its power to engross and involve readers. Describing it as "amorphous in construction, loose in style and nauseating in matter" and condemning it as "a prolonged scream from Page 1 to Page 619," in "The Book of the Day" Bartlett Randolph,[21] to illustrate, writes that "the reader finds himself in the position of the bird hypnotized by the snake--he hates it but he cannot tear himself away from it" (17). Perhaps the most damaging criticisms of the novel are by those who find fault with its structure and characterization, assessments not well supported but, on occasion, delivered with a vehemence that reveals more about the emotional response of the critic than the aesthetic value of the text. For instance, in his April 17 review, "But . . . Not . . . Ferdinand," *Newsweek*'s Rascoe Burton[22] declares that "the book has beautiful and even magnificent passages in it; but it is not organized" (46)--an assessment he amends on May 1, to castigate *GW* more fully as "silly propaganda, superficial observation, careless infidelity to the proper use of idiom, tasteless pornographical and scatological talk" and to apologize to his readers "for hedging too much about a bad book" (38).

Similar to these early reviews and, like them, more impressionistic than substantive, is the chapter dealing with *GW* in Henry Thornton Moore's 1939 book, *The Novels of John Steinbeck: A First Study.*[23] Moore complains about a lack of organic unity in its structure, a "lack of force in the center of the story," a lack of "proportioned and intensified drama," and of "vital conflict" (68-69). "No conflict is created," Moore states, "because these trampled people don't fight back" (69). Thus guided by his own expectations for a rousing good story line, looking for a satisfactory "rounding off," or a resolution of "the issues that have been raised," he finds the ending "too quiet." But Moore reveals more about his own means of measuring literary merit ("force," "intensified drama," "vital conflict") than he does about *GW* itself.

Even in this first book-long study of Steinbeck's novels, however, at the edge of a reader's awareness, Moore begins to grasp what Toni Morrison calls "unspeakable thing unspoken" as he sees a national psyche beginning to unfold: "The incidents seem . . . part of a vast mythos" (68). And when he describes the impact of the scene in which Tom and Al encounter a one-eyed man, he affirms the affective impact of *GW*: "The whole scene floats in the mind like a piece of an epic" (71). Further, in grappling "with meanings that may be partly understood in terms of his previous tendencies," Moore perceives also that in this novel "there are new beginnings which may lead to future developments" by this writer who is becoming "the poet of our dispossessed" (70, 72).

In all of these 1939 views of *GW*, Steinbeck achieves a vital part of his intentions, for, whether the assessment is negative or positive, each critic or reviewer has in a sense been involved with "the actuality"--some of them "absorbed, shaken, and convinced" and others trapped, as though "hypnotized," unable to "tear . . . away from it."[24] In 1941 Frederic I. Carpenter in "The Philosophical Joads" also acknowledges "the narrative power of the book and the vivid reality of its characters" (563).[25] Unlike other early reviewers and critics, however, he does not dwell on its affective powers but offers a "theory of art" by which to evaluate *GW* against the backdrop of "great writers of American history." He defines art as a "moving picture" that offers a "criticism of life" and a "clearly suggested. . . abstract idea of life"--a world view (563).

Carpenter observes that *GW* "goes beyond" the dark Calvinist world view of sin and evil, "the revolt of the 'natural individual' against 'civilization,'" and the denunciations of "the narrow conventions of 'society' . . . to preach a positive philosophy of life and to damn that blind conservatism which fears ideas" (563). In this depiction he moves away from what *GW* **does**--that is, its powerful impact on readers--to what this novel **is**, carefully positioning it against a theory of art and against a backdrop of the works of Hawthorne, Melville, Twain, Sinclair Lewis, and Emerson. In "going beyond" these other world views with their themes of sin, or corruption, or individualism, or transcendental mysticism, *GW* strikes out into new territory with a more positive, optimistic tone of voice that unites "the mystical transcendentalism of Emerson, . . . the . . . democracy of Whitman, and the pragmatic instrumentalism of William James and John

Dewey" (Lisca/Hearle 563). In as much as this novel "preaches . . . and develops a new kind of Christianity. . . earthly and active," it places Steinbeck's persona in its Merlin-like, prophetic role and its readers in the role of captive listeners who must hear his message, with the implied obligation to act on it (571). Even though Carpenter has engaged *GW* on an intellectual as well as an affective level and has thus given a new dimension to its criticism, his diction--that is, the choice of the word "preaching"--still indicates his recognition of a design on readers, who may or may not respond positively to its "message."

In 1947 Chester E. Eisinger's "Jeffersonian Agrarianism in *The Grapes of Wrath*"[26] expands Carpenter's thesis that Steinbeck's ideas are essentially American--an amalgam of transcendental, democratic, and pragmatic philosophies--to include "Jeffersonian agrarianism" (149). While Eisinger, too, discusses his thesis and *GW* analytically and persuasively, he, too, enters into its affective domain, going beyond Carpenter to speak in the first person, as a representative American, recommending a course of action, or, with Steinbeck, preaching that "new kind of Christianity" that Carpenter suggests: "We must seek another road to the independence and security and dignity that we expect from democracy" (154).

In his 1949 "John Steinbeck: Naturalism's Priest," Woodburn R. Ross[27] looks beyond the art to its creator and his persona in the text. Ross surveys the role of an empathic, paradoxical Steinbeck persona who is actively, intuitively, and emotionally involved in "the world" of his text and analyzes this pervading ethos: "Steinbeck . . . is both rational and irrational: he accepts all that reason can tell him and permits his intuition and affections to add what they will to the world created by reason and to determine his position toward the universe as it then appears" (438). Ross recognizes the mythical and the mystical in the text, and, hence, the "message" of the text, and also the persona's priestly relationship with readers/critics, who take the layman's place as the Every American.

Such positive critical participation in *GW* does not run in a straightforward path. Throughout its critical history, there have been those who choose not to participate with the text, a decision that colors their final evaluation of the novel's merits. George F. Whicher's discussion of Steinbeck in "Proletarian Leanings" in Arthur Hobson Quinn's 1951 *The Literature of the American People: An Historical and Critical Survey*,[28] to illustrate, up to a point reads like a gathering of accolades: "In Ma Joad we encounter one of the great authentic people of fiction. . . . There is brilliant writing in *The Grapes of Wrath*, memorable description, episodes of moving power, forceful expression of social justice" (960). What Whicher gives with one hand, however, with the other he takes away with vehemence. Of the characters other than Ma Joad, he writes, "The rest are puppets with differentiating traits." And in his conclusions concerning the novel's merits, he writes: "Yet on reflection the final impression . . . is not of the author's indignation so much as his cleverness as a contriver of effects. . . . The reader can hardly avoid feeling let down" (960). The uneasiness, even depression, that Whicher reveals here attests to the fulfillment of Steinbeck's desire to leave the reader dissatisfied. But his "final impression" also serves to negate his overall appraisal, leaving in Limbo the questions of design, balance, artistic merit--a negation which some more recent critics also use.[29]

The prevailing critical emphasis on the powerful affective domain of *GW* only partially gives way over time to more analytical approaches that center on the novel as art. But, because this empathic aspect is intentionally a part of the novel's "design," it often is—and should be--considered alongside Steinbeck's careful "design and balance" in its more formal aspects of structure, characterization, and language. In 1957, to illustrate, Lisca's "*The Grapes of Wrath* as Fiction" addresses characterization, style, and structure. As an aside, he also discusses reader response: "The characters are so absorbed into the novel's 'basic situation' that the reader's response goes beyond sympathy for individuals to moral indignation about their social condition. This is, of course, precisely Steinbeck's intention" (Lisca/Hearle 578). In his conclusion, Lisca again melds analytical concerns with reader response: "Steinbeck's art encompasses but transcends its "materials," creating "a well-made and emotionally compelling novel out of materials which in most other hands have resulted in sentimental propaganda" (587).

Similarly, one of the points of comparison between Steinbeck and Hemingway in Lisca's 1969 "Steinbeck and Hemingway: Suggestions for a Comparative Study"[30] is that "both writers are notable for the depth of esthetic feeling touched by this Nature and their great ability to express it" (17). Here by implication, at least, one of the criteria by which art may be judged is the power of the "esthetic" to generate emotion and "feeling," to involve the mind and the heart so that they coalesce in that admiration similar to the Romantic concept of the sublime.

Interestingly, in his 1963 *John Steinbeck: An Introduction and Interpretation*,[31] Joseph Fontenrose concludes with a literal survey of events that takes up where *GW* ends, with Hitler's invasion of Poland and the resulting jobs or military roles for "Okies and Arkies . . . [who] found houses to live in, settled down, and remained employed when the war was over." He points out, however, that "Mexicans and Orientals once more harvested California's crops, and 'wetbacks' became a problem." Then Fontenrose moves from depicting the status quo to an emotional involvement with his report as he notes that "disquieting reports have been coming from the fields: more Americans are now employed in migratory farm labor than a few years ago, pay is low, and conditions are bad. Perhaps the story has not ended yet" (83). And the reader is again left dissatisfied and disquieted because of a novel that seems to have no end, that has mythic roots that burrow deeply into the very fiber of the national psyche--a curious, oxymoronic mixture of greed and fortitude, of prejudice and brotherhood/sisterhood, of hatred and redeeming love, liberty and oppression.

Such positive, heartfelt participation in *GW*, however, is not always the case even with the distancing of time. For some critics are still so passionate in their denial of the merits of *GW* that Lisca dubs their responses "hysterical" (Lisca/Hearle 557). William Fuller Taylor's 1959 "*The Grapes of Wrath* Reconsidered,"[32] for example, is particularly vitriolic in its dismissal not only of Steinbeck, whom he accuses of contributing to "interclass hatreds," but also of those critics who have written studies of Christian symbolism and "traditional American thought" in *GW* (144). Nonetheless, while he dismisses their ideas, he stops short of labeling the critics themselves.

Such is not the case with Harold Bloom's introduction to the 1988 *Modern Critical Interpretations: John Steinbeck's "The Grapes of Wrath."* Here Bloom disparages Steinbeck scholars as well as Steinbeck's work, labeling them "liberal middlebrows, both in this country and abroad."[33] Niggardly in his discussion of any merits that *GW* may have, he finds it "a very problematic work, and very difficult to judge." He does not hesitate to judge, however, and very harshly--maintaining that Steinbeck "aspired beyond his aesthetic means" and that "he fell into bathos in everything he wrote" (4).

Similarly, Leslie Fiedler's 1990 "Looking Back after Fifty Years" in *San Jose Studies*[34] echoes Bloom as he labels Steinbeck critics as "second-rank academics whose 'subject' is Steinbeck" and *GW* itself as "middlebrow," a term he reiterates and underscores in a conclusion that at once declares its ending as "blessedly out of control" and as an "archetypal scene":

"Mysterious" is . . . a confession on Steinbeck's part . . . that he does not understand where his story, here blessedly out of control, has taken him.
. . . But it is . . . this archetypal scene . . . which seems to me now to redeem at the last possible moment the inert stereotypes, the easy pathos, the *ersatz* transcendentalism, and the doctrinaire optimism which elsewhere flaw this problematical, middlebrow book. (60-61; 64)

Taylor, Bloom, and Fiedler all complain about the ethos of the Steinbeck persona or about the book's demand for reader participation, their final judgment of its artistic merits blurred by their own intuitive recognition of its empathic demands and their subsequent refusal to participate. Taylor bemoans "apparently calculated effects of shock and revulsion"; Bloom finds himself "uneasy" about his experience of re-reading *GW*; and Fiedler complains about Steinbeck's leaning "over our shoulders to explain exactly what he means." With Lisca, then, other critics may well dismiss these denunciatory, assertive, impressionistic views as more "hysterical" than revelatory.

In the preface to Agnes McNeill Donohue's 1968 *A Casebook on "The Grapes of Wrath*,"[35] she also acknowledges *GW*'s emotional pull: "Reactions to the novel at the time it was published (1939) and now are rarely temperate" (vii). Like Lisca, she recognizes its evocative power, to which critics and readers react, and the continuing "assertive" nature of the critical response to *GW*, especially in regards to its standing as art. Impressionistic "reactions," then, often govern the critical assessments of the novel's aesthetic and canonical standing. The question of how one must read Steinbeck, then, is especially important in approaching *GW* and arriving at a balanced analysis of its merits. What must a reader/critic bring to the experience of its art?

In the preface to the 1969 edition of *Steinbeck and His Critics: A Record of Twenty-five Years*,[36] E. W. Tedlock, Jr. wrestles with this question, finding himself left "with a feeling of pathos and, perhaps, one insight" (v). In both of these responses the cognitive, intellectual faculty is left on hold. In the "feeling of pathos," he draws on what has recently been discussed as "emotional intelligence": "Our times have no patience with good intentions or old-fashioned positions. The new perspectives being forced upon us may bring moral advances, but revolution is destructive of art, which requires a special love and tolerance." And for his "one insight," Tedlock takes an intuitive leap--going beyond existing evidence, or empirical verification, to an "aha" experience:

> There is at times in Steinbeck an experience that I think of as purely existential and native or basic to him, beyond cavil. It can be seen in a note of his on an early morning encounter with some farm laborers camped by the road. The note is of great objective purity, and is also most humanly attractive, . . . so beautifully natural and yet so vulnerable. (v)

John H. Timmerman's 1989 "The Squatter's Circle in *The Grapes of Wrath*"[37] (in this volume) exemplifies a close reading of a text that is at once analytical and participatory. Timmerman enters into the story, experiencing, feeling with the Joads in their distress. From him the reader learns how Pa Joad must have felt as he becomes more and more helpless, gradually relinquishing authority to Ma:

> In the California camp, the collection of men remains simply that: a collection. No cohesive unity cements their spirits together. The disruption in the Joad family is poignantly encapsulated in one sharp portrait where Ma fries potatoes over a hissing fire and "Pa sat nearby hugging his knees" (p. 371), almost as if Pa, in a degraded stance of the squatters' posture, clings futilely to a position now much diminished. (208)

Such a reading not only sharpens awareness of Steinbeck's underlying design in depicting changes in traditional male-female roles, it reveals as well quite "poignantly" and plaintively Pa's suffering and his increasing helplessness.

Studs Terkel's 1989 "We Still See Their Faces," the introduction to Viking's 1989 anniversary publication of *GW*[38] (reviewed in this volume), acknowledges Steinbeck's bardic, prophetic persona, pointing out that he was "driven" by "an almost messianic urgency" in telling this story of his "people." Terkel recognizes as well the two-fold nature of this persona: an authoritative, "messianic" figure who is at the same time a "constant companion"--attesting to a closeness, a presence, that occurs inside of the text and at the same time a close, authoritative voice that speaks through the text to the reader with a sense of "urgency" (xv).

Robert Murray Davis's 1990 "The World of John Steinbeck's Joads"[39] (in this volume) takes the reader on a leisurely tour of Joad country in and round Sallisaw, Oklahoma, in a documentary meditation on the verisimilitude of Steinbeck's portrayal of the land (pointing out that it was not even close) and the efficacy of a more poetic portrayal that builds "characters and their world from the inside out." He concludes with a humanistic reflection that lauds the empathic power of *GW*:

> Steinbeck understood and presented extraordinarily well certain kinds of process, from the way a good mechanic fixes a car to the way a people adapt physically and socially to new situations. That makes almost all of his novels unusually readable paragraph by paragraph. More important, he could show the kinetic satisfaction and the cultural and spiritual value inherent in process, building characters and their world from the inside out.

From the first, his novels also dealt with the necessity of human beings to
adapt in order to survive. Because *The Grapes of Wrath* does so most
thoroughly and tellingly, readers all over the world have **a clearer feeling**
[emphasis mine] not just for what it means to be an Oklahoman but for what
it means to be human. (404)

Note once more here a critic's view of what *GW* **does**--that is, it provides "a
clearer feeling . . . for what it means to be human"--rather than of what it **is**.

Stephen Railton's 1990 "Pilgrim's Politics: Steinbeck's Art of
Conversion"[40] compares *GW* to John Bunyan's *Pilgrim's Progress*--another
text in which "homelessness and suffering become the occasion of spiritual
growth" (32). Railton recognizes the Steinbeck persona's bardic role and
argues convincingly that "*The Grapes of Wrath* is a novel about conversion"
and that "thematically Route 66 and the various state highways in California
that the Joads travel along all run parallel to the road to Damascus that Saul
takes in Acts, or to the Way taken by Bunyan's Christian in *Pilgrim's
Progress*" (29). Steinbeck's method of achieving the affective impact
essential to the novel's "message," then, according to Railton, is to structure
it "as a series of inevitabilities. . . . Again and again what will happen next
is made narratively inescapable." As a result, "the narrative enacts its own
kind of oppression, and, by arousing in its readers a desire to fight this sense
of inevitability, it works strategically to arouse us toward action to change
the status quo" (32). Railton, then, goes beyond the discussion of what
Steinbeck does--that is, his empathic design "to rip a reader's nerves to
rags"--to show what the novel is and how he uses the classic rhetorical
concept of necessity to achieve his intentions.

Robert DeMott's 1996 "'This Book Is My Life': Creating *The Grapes of
Wrath*" in *Steinbeck's Typewriter: Essays on His Art* reveals the extent of
Steinbeck's involvement with the text and the reader and also the source of
his bardic, prophetic persona. DeMott suggests that the "creative, interior,
or *architextual* level of engagement is the elusive and heretofore
unacknowledged fifth layer of Steinbeck's novel" (183). Steinbeck's own
"internal bruise," DeMott maintains, "opened the floodgates of his affection,
created *The Grapes of Wrath*'s compelling justification, provided its
haunting spiritual urgency, and rooted it in the deepest wellsprings of
democratic fellow-feeling" (185). As a result of Steinbeck's own empathic
wounding, his suffering with the dispossessed and impoverished, he creates
a persona from this combination of the empathic, spiritual, and fraternal.
There is something that borders on the sacramental here, for as DeMott
suggests, the Steinbeck persona himself interacts and mediates between text

and reader--going beyond the usual relationship among author, text, and reader to enter into the text itself not only as its creator but also as a participant, not unlike the role of Christ at The Last Supper, or the first communion.

2

"He has gone farther than any other American writer towards being the poet of our dispossessed."
Harry Thornton Moore in his 1939
The Novels of John Steinbeck: A First Study

"Is *The Grapes of Wrath* a popular but inferior novel, or is it truly a work of art, a great book?"
Agnes McNeill Donohue in her 1968 *A Casebook on "The Grapes of Wrath"*

"The dance of an open mind when it engages another equally open one . . .occurs most naturally, most often in the reading/writing world we live in."
Toni Morrison in *The Dancing Mind*[41]

On 6 November 1996, in her acceptance speech for the National Book Foundation Medal for Distinguished Contribution to American Letters, Toni Morrison speaks of a "peace" that results from "the dance of an open mind when it engages another equally open one"--an activity that "occurs most naturally, most often in the reading/writing world we live in" (7). As Lisca attests, for the most part, in its "first fifteen years there appeared in literary journals fewer than half a dozen essays devoted to a critical analysis of *GW*" (Lisca/Hearle 548)--certainly a dearth of that dancing of open minds around the topic of *GW* and its artistic merit or lack thereof. Ironically, this dearth may result from the fulfillment of the author's intention to engage readers and critics empathically, an engagement that is essential to understanding but one that can backfire when a reader or critic does not want to be drawn into the story as a participant, wishing to remain coolly, aloofly objective. Since, as Lisca points out, "the current standing of a piece of literature is indicated to a large extent by its ability to sustain a dialogue among critics"--or to engage in what Morrison calls the "dance" of "open minds"--both the scantiness of early criticism of *GW* and the extent of negative criticism has served on occasion to bring into question its standing as a work of art, despite its continuing popular appeal (Lisca/Hearle 547; Morrison 7).[42]

This question of the aesthetic standing of *GW*, therefore, has become a critical commonplace. Donahue's 1968 *Casebook* on *GW*, for example, poses the question of its merit, issuing an invitation to students and readers to formulate their own "criteria for a great book" and to subject *GW* to their own "critical scrutiny" (vii). To an extent at least, those works that address this question of the novel's standing as a work of art do so by setting forth either a theory or a direct or implied definition of literary art by which to measure. When accompanied by a close and empathic reading, such theoretical approaches have served across time to elevate its reputation, if not Steinbeck's, among academicians and critics.

In chapter six of Joseph Fontenrose's 1963 *"The Grapes of Wrath"* in *John Steinbeck: An Introduction and Interpretation,* he studies the aesthetics of Steinbeck's style, by implication at least, in the light of the standard of decorum in classical rhetoric, that is, that the style be suited and fitted to the content, and declares that "some of these interchapters are masterpieces in themselves" (69). He notes the synaesthetic result of Steinbeck's skill in creating an occasion that at once serves to evoke imagery, tone, and ethos--all working together to draw the reader into the experience by participating in "a feeling tone": "As Lisca has pointed out, Steinbeck uses a variety of prose styles in these interchapters. In these short sketches he could experiment, endeavoring in each to evoke both a vivid picture of something that happened and a feeling tone" (60).

In addition to this classical measure of decorum, Fontenrose further discusses the Steinbeck style in the light of "the Psalms or Whitman or perhaps Sandburg," by such comparison placing him in the ranks of poets and mystics (71). Demonstrating as well a participation in that critical milieu that Lisca describes as a sustained "critical dialogue" and that Morrison, more poetically, calls the "dancing of open minds," Fontenrose cites and expands on previous discussions of "the mythical side" of *GW* and finds that "the biological and mythical strands fit. . . neatly together. . . . Each theme--organismic, ecological, mythical; and each phase of the mythical: Exodus, Messiah, Leviathan, ritual sequence--builds up to a single conclusion: the unity of all mankind" (82).

Collin G. Matton's 1970 "Water Imagery and the Conclusion to *The Grapes of Wrath* "[43] (in this volume) goes into the realm of archetype and myth, by implication placing Steinbeck among those writers who not only work in the realm of known myth but who also themselves become a part of the myth making. He examines "the water and flood archetype . . . to open a new interpretation to the conclusion of the novel": "No longer associated with destruction, the water image becomes a symbol of birth and regeneration. . . . Steinbeck extends the regenerative pattern from man's creations to God's creation, Nature" (44, 47).

Chapter 4, "The Fully Matured Art: *The Grapes of Wrath* " in Howard Levant's 1974 *The Novels of John Steinbeck: A Critical Study*[44] views *GW* as "an attempted prose epic, a summation of national experience at a given time" (93). Discussing "the relationship of the novel's structure to its materials," Levant states that Steinbeck's "central artistic problem is to present the universal and epical in terms of the individual and particular" (95, 98). On this basis he finds the first three quarters of the novel "masterful" (128), the last quarter less effective, primarily because he believes that Steinbeck finally reduces his materials to allegory. But Levant does not consider whether the last quarter of the novel descends into "the overwhelming artificiality that results from an extreme dependence on allegory" (129) or whether the "individual and particular" in the last quarter of the novel ascend into the mythic and universal, an appropriate ending for "an attempted prose epic."

In a return to what Lisca has called the assertive and hysterical in criticism, in his 1977 "Flat Wine from *The Grapes of Wrath*,"[45] Floyd C. Watkins takes verisimilitude as his artistic measure and histrionically searches through *GW* in search of factual inaccuracies, questioning the cultural veracity of the presentation of its characters and the accuracy of Steinbeck's depiction of everything from flora and fauna to the price of cotton. Not content to stop with treating a fictional work of art as though it were an encyclopedia or a dictionary, he maintains further that in *GW* Steinbeck "belittles" Christians and Christianity.

In contrast, Robert J. Griffin and William A. Freeman in their 1963 "Machines and Animals: Pervasive Motifs in *The Grapes of Wrath*"[46] study Steinbeck's use of the recurring and "crucially important motifs of machines and animals which contribute considerably to structure and thematic content." "This discussion can," they hope, "contribute to a fuller understanding of Steinbeck's novel as a consummate complex work of art" (569, 580). Evidently, as the Watkins, Griffin and Freeman studies illustrate, conclusions concerning *GW*'s aesthetic merit, or lack thereof, are to an extent dependent upon the critic's intentions and the efficacy of the chosen artistic measure.

Ray Lewis White regards his 1983 "*The Grapes of Wrath* and the Critics of 1939"[47] as "essential to all students of John Steinbeck, of American fiction, and of enumerative bibliography" (135). White has documented, annotated, and arranged in chronological order "108 American reviews . . . from 1939." These "annotations," he explains, "are actually quotations from the reviews--the seminal paragraphs of evaluation and judgment--here longer than most such excerpts because the debate about *The Grapes of Wrath* elicited extensive commentary" (134-35). This gathering of the diverse voices of the 1939 reviewers is a valuable addition to the scholarly paraphernalia of *GW*, providing a means by which to "find and measure the genesis, growth, and decline of authors' reputations amid the intellectual and social currents of their times" (134). Although White suggests here a "decline" in Steinbeck's reputation, Roy Simmonds, foresees a different outcome: "His work will date neither as rapidly nor with such finality as the work of some of his more stylistically daring and currently more highly regarded contemporaries."[48]

George Henderson's 1989 "John Steinbeck's Spatial Imagination in *The Grapes of Wrath*: A Critical Essay"[49] (in this volume) enters into that dance of minds wherein the criticism itself becomes an extension of as well as a response to the novelist's art. A graduate student in the doctoral program in geography at the University of California at Berkeley, Henderson writes an intriguing and persuasive cross-disciplinary discussion, acknowledging that *GW* "did fulfill a role as a regionalist and social realist interpretive text" but maintaining that "nonetheless, more can be asked of it" (212). This "more" as it is approached in this essay takes *GW* out of the realm of social documentation into the realm of art. Reading from the perspective of his discipline, he finds that Steinbeck sets up "a problem . . . of that recurrent human condition . . . that . . . is shaped by historical and social contingencies" in which these contingencies work together so that "it is from social and geographical relationships that meaning radiates, rather than from an individual character or action" (212). Along with his insightful view of "how meaning is produced, controlled, and disseminated with regard to social and workaday space," Henderson provides valuable interpretations of character couched in memorable prose. "Ma Joad," for example, "rose from the ashes of a burnt-out household, the vehicle for Steinbeck to expose the pitfalls of patriarchy" (221).

In their "Dialogic Structure and Levels of Discourse in Steinbeck's *The Grapes of Wrath*,"[50] (in this volume) Louis Owens and Hector Torres discuss "the . . . complex dialogic structure and levels of discourse in *The Grapes of Wrath*" (75). They conclude that "the narrative must both move within time and remain timeless, and there is no way to reconcile these two narrative impulses. . . .Thus the dialectical structure of *The Grapes of Wrath*, with its dialogic infrastructure and style (the various dialogic voices and syntax) effectively resists closure." They further indicate the extent to which such an ending involves actively responsive readers, requiring their participation. Readers must "approach the novel with the same ability to **resist** [emphasis mine] ideological closure, with no ultimate voice of authority, no transcendent teleology, no final scapegoat" (92-93).

While Barry Maine's study of "Steinbeck's Debt to Dos Passos"[51] (in this volume) reveals some commonalities between Steinbeck and Dos Passos—for example, Dos Passos's "Camera Eye" sections in *U.S.A.* and Steinbeck's interchapters in *GW*—differences in structure, characterization, tone, style, and vision (or lack thereof) bear the preponderance of the weight. He finds that *The Grapes of Wrath* is a testament to the power of the human spirit to endure and prevail over history, whereas *U.S.A.* is a testament to the power of history to triumph over Man. It was Marcel Proust who wrote that "style for the writer, no less than color for the painter, is a question not of technique but of vision." As much as it is form it is vision that separates and distinguishes these two writers of the Depression era" (26).

Critics such as Henderson, Owens, and Torres give evidence of at least a partial fulfillment of Tetsumaro Hayashi's hopes as stated in the preface to his 1990 *Steinbeck's "The Grapes of Wrath": Essays in Criticism*[52]: "May our new generation of Steinbeck students and scholars, blessed with more primary and secondary published sources, more critical and biographical materials, and more published research materials, find a greater enjoyment in reading, discussing, and writing about Steinbeck's enigmatic literature, appreciating and understanding his magic as an artist and craftsman" (viii-ix). The publication of such scholarly collections of essays together with the availability of biographical and bibliographical materials indicate that critics and scholars are now engaging in a sustained critical dialog--a dialog that, as Lisca has pointed out, is missing during *GW*'s first eighteen years while "its merits were debated as social documentation rather than fiction" (Lisca/Hearle 572). All of these advances bear evidence of Steinbeck's aesthetic achievement in *GW*.

In her 1992 "Poor Whites: Joads and Snopeses,"[53] (in this volume) Abby H. P. Werlock compares Steinbeck's depiction of the Joad family to Faulkner's portrayal of the Snopeses, maintaining that they "have come to signify different literary archetypes and divergent views of Christianity." In Jackson Benson's words, the Joads are an "idealized view of common man," but, Werlock states, "In *The Hamlet* . . . the narrator seems to approve the view of Snopeses not merely as inhuman, but as varmints, animals, reptiles" (64-65). She points out, however, that "both authors successfully employ their chosen "families" to make a similar point: Steinbeck and Faulkner articulate a resounding "No" to exploitation and totalitarianism and an emphatic "Yea" to the rights and dignity of the ordinary individual" (71).

Tetsumaro Hayashi and Beverly K. Simpson have edited and compiled the 1994 *John Steinbeck: Dissertation Abstracts and Research Opportunities*,[54] an attempt "to anthologize all known, American Steinbeck-related dissertation abstracts from 1946 to 1993" (vii). Timmerman's introduction points out the extent of this collection: "This volume includes 102 dissertation abstracts on Steinbeck and a variety of indexes--author, chronology, subject, title, university--that simplify the research process. . . . The collection itself reveals trends and new directions in Steinbeck scholarship." Even a brief perusal of the titles of a few of those dissertations dealing with *GW* affirms Timmerman's observation that "here one finds a fascinating history of both ideas and methodologies" (xiii).

The titles range from George Henry Spies, III's "John Steinbeck's *The Grapes of Wrath* and Frederick Manfred's *The Golden Bowl*: A Comparative Study," to Carl H. DeVasto's "The Poet of Demos: John Steinbeck's *The Grapes of Wrath* and Other Major Later Fiction," to David Alan Hecker's "John Steinbeck: America's Isaiah," to Leslie Thomas Pollard's "*The Grapes of Wrath* and *Native Son*: Literary Criticism as Social Definition." These comparisons between Steinbeck and other writers, connections among Steinbeck's works, and explorations of Steinbeck's relationship to America all promise engaging critical dialogues.

Immediately following the abstracts of dissertations, Christopher S. Busch's "Research Opportunities" provides a chronological overview of the dissertation research, "New Directions for Steinbeck Studies," and "Sources for Steinbeck Research." He suggests that

> profitable work might still be done . . . with regard to the respective influences of realism, naturalism, and romanticism on Steinbeck's unique aesthetic and with regard to Steinbeck's literary 'heritage,' that is, his thematic and stylistic relationships to writers who preceded and followed him." (154)

Busch thus extends an invitation to other scholars to participate in critical dialogue and, at the same time, offers a direction and beginning point for their study.[55]

Along with this survey of dissertations on *GW* and White's annotated bibliography of the 1939 reviews discussed above, the publication of other scholarly tools, such as Jackson J. Benson's monumental achievement in his definitive 1984 biography, *The True Adventures of John Steinbeck, Writer*;[56] Robert DeMott's 1984 *Steinbeck's Reading: A Catalogue of Books Owned and Borrowed*;[57] and Robert B. Harmon's 1990 "*The Grapes of Wrath*": *A*

Fifty Year Bibliographical Survey[58] further underscore an increasing interest in Steinbeck's art in *GW* and other works--the increase itself evidence of a continuing and sustained critical dialog and, hence, of its artistic merit.

Nicholas Visser's 1994 study, "Audience and Closure in *The Grapes of Wrath*,"[59] (in this volume) questions "just how politically radical *The Grapes of Wrath* ultimately is" even though its "generative context is the left-wing political culture of the 1930s, and Steinbeck's novel takes its place among the radical novels produced by that culture" (20). First, he explores the question of "what formal or discursive strategies" writers utilize in "radical novels . . . to gain access to an audience" (20). He finds Steinbeck particularly adept at establishing in *GW* "a tacit but also absolutely binding contract between author and reader that the reader can rely on the novel's general veracity"—without which, he maintains, "the novel would be almost entirely lacking in meaning" (27).

Second, he discusses "the other major formal challenge of the novel: how to end the narrative" (28). This aspect of effective closure he finds "somewhat less successfully handled" (28). Visser believes that successfully reaching an audience, here described as a "virtual public," and, at the same time, achieving a closure in line with radical politics may be mutually exclusive, that a writer may not be able to achieve both:

> At issue here is the very possibility of writing a novel that both reaches a wide audience and   remains politically radical. . . . One conclusion we can draw from Steinbeck's example is that the advice Engels gave Minna Kautsky about eschewing overtly "tendentious writing" in order to reach the "bourgeois circles" who are the only available audience may understate the consequences of the techniques novelists may have to use to accomplish that task. Reaching that audience might entail the simultaneous (and intimately related) dilution of the novel's politics and distortion of its form. (34)

In a note Visser cites "Stephen Railton's important 1990 study, 'Pilgrim's Politics: Steinbeck's Art of Conversion'" (discussed above), the conclusions of which are "strikingly different, indeed often directly opposed" to his own (35). As his title indicates, Railton sees *GW* as "a novel about conversion," whose readers are Steinbeck's proposed "converts" (29). He finds in Steinbeck's closure

> a strange but powerful tribute to Steinbeck's faith in selflessness as the one means by which men and women can transcend their circumstances in a world that is otherwise so harshly and unjustly determined. I think it

would be less powerful if it were any less strange. . . . Steinbeck wants to
save the nation from its sins. . . . Can the private, spiritual birth of a New
Man or a New Woman – the unrecorded "event" that the novel leaves at the
center of its narrative and its vision – affect that? (44; 46)

Still, Railton, like Visser, finally questions whether "social inequalities and
economic injustices" can be overcome and resolved by "the private, spiritual
birth of a New Man or a New Woman—the unrecorded 'event' that the novel
leaves at the center of its narrative and vision" (46).

Against the backdrop of *Travels with Charley in Search of America* and
America and Americans, my 1996 "Judge, Observer, Prophet: The American
Cain and Steinbeck's Shifting Perspective"[60] (in this volume) places *GW* in
connection with *East of Eden* and *The Winter of Our Discontent*, tracing the
development of an Every American in a greedy, materialistic, inhospitable
Cain figure who, nevertheless, across   time gains the self-knowledge,
strength, and enabling virtue essential to right choices. Steinbeck fervently
and optimistically (curiously, a trait that most annoys critics such as Bloom
and Fiedler) believes that this Every American is capable of making these
right choices:

> Steinbeck foresees this Every American as an active, effective participant
> in world affairs, but also as one who is at the same time a light-bearer,
> devoted to justice and compassion. Thus recording for posterity his own
> philosophical and mystical journey, he offers a panacea for the nation's
> ills. Grounded in the biblical story of the Fall, the battle between good and
> evil, and the hatred that leads to fratricide, Steinbeck depicts his own
> dreams and hopes for a future in which the ancient quarrel is resolved and
> The American Dream of virtue is finally actualized, combining with and
> increasing the nation's great strength and prowess. (240-41)

John Ditsky's 1976 "The Ending of The Grapes of Wrath: A Further
Commentary"[61] and Robert DeMott's 1996 "'This Book Is My Life': Creating
The Grapes of Wrath" in *Steinbeck's Typewriter* are necessary correctives
for Warren French's final evaluation of the aesthetic value of *GW* in his
1994 "Steinbeck 2000" in *John Steinbeck's Fiction Revisited.*[62] French's
opening paragraphs set the tone for his discussion and mark a return to the
assertive proclamations of some early reviewers and critics. There is, he
maintains, "an **unquestionable** decline in the artistic effectiveness of his
[i. e., Steinbeck's] fiction after World War II" [emphasis mine] (132). Such
an assertion is highly premature, for the issue of the artistic merit of
Steinbeck's work is far from decided, even for his later works.[63]

A highly respected Steinbeck scholar, French steps aside from positive involvement with those critics who have both evaluated and participated in Steinbeck's art and uses as a touchstone for his discussion of *GW* Harold Bloom's assessment that Steinbeck is "not one of the inescapable American novelists of our century." Following Bloom's lead, French reduces his appreciation of this novel to a contemplation of "why one is . . . compelled 'to be grateful' for *The Grapes of Wrath*" (133). (Again, note here in passing the compelling influence of *GW*, even over those reluctant to acknowledge its stature.) Unfortunately, French quotes from and agrees with Bloom's comment "that one thing that remains in Steinbeck's work is its 'fairly constant popularity with an immense number of liberal middlebrows, both in his own country and abroad.'"

No favorable outcome is possible following such an inauspicious acceptance of Bloom's assessment, and French finds *GW* "in one sense a magnificent failure" because of its attraction for "liberal middlebrows," evidence in itself, according to French and Bloom, of its failure to achieve Steinbeck's aesthetic intentions (135).[64] French raises once more the old spectre of "sentimentality":

> There is outrage, of course, in *The Grapes of Wrath*, but the author here wishes to leave readers with an enticing possibility of hope. . . . The line between sentimentality and compassion escapes clear distinction, but if compassion is not an aesthetic value, art petrifies, so that one must discriminate carefully in this area. (136)

And, still in lockstep with Bloom, and here also with his theory of writer influence,[65] French complains that Steinbeck does not acknowledge an indebtedness, or "kinship," to use French's term, with "the beat generation" (137).

Just two of these Bloom/French assertions need to be addressed here: the questions of the aesthetic merit of *GW* and of Steinbeck's supposed artistic "decline" after *GW*. First, only those who participate in the experience of this novel can appreciate it fully or judge it justly, and these reader/critics thus must bring with them to its reading an open heart as well as an open mind. Only then will the insights that signal understanding come, as if unbidden, so that the critic not only enters into the experience but the response becomes also an extension of its art. Although John Ditsky's 1976 "The Ending of *The Grapes of Wrath*: A Further Commentary" focuses on the ending, it fits these criteria and suggests the high overall aesthetic standing of *GW* as a part of the literary and mythic heritage of America. Like all truly good poetry, his conclusion speaks for itself:

> The narrative of the Joads has nowhere to go after Rose of Sharon draws the camera in to focus upon that mysterious smile, then holds the pose while the camera backs away . . . to make it clear that she has become the world's true center. . . . It is Woman picking up the pieces of the American dream and holding the man-caused shards together, the seams invisible. The power to work this miracle is implied in Rose of Sharon's smile. It is an Eastern smile, a smile of understanding, in this ultimate Western book. She has got it all now. All the lines of narrative come to focus in her; like light, they prism in her." (123)

Ditsky concludes with a quotation from the Magnificat of the Virgin Mary in Luke 1:48, 53: "For he hath regarded the low estate of his handmaiden: for, behold, from henceforth all generations shall call me blessed. . . . He hath filled the hungry with good things; and the rich he hath sent empty away." Nothing needs to follow the juxtaposition of these two achingly young women as the one folds to her bosom a child of God; and the other, the Son of Man. Here, Ditsky shows us, art and myth join hands--for those who have the eyes, and mind, and heart to see it.

Robert DeMott's 1996 "'This Book Is My Life': Creating *The Grapes of Wrath*" brings another poet's eye, ear, mind, and heart to bear on the evaluation of *GW* as art. Like Lisca and Fontenrose, he focuses on language and style: "It is not narrated from the first person point of view, yet the language has a consistently catchy eyewitness quality about it; and the vivid biblical, empirical, poetical, cinematic, and folk styles Steinbeck employs demonstrate the tonal and visual acuity of his ear and eye." DeMott finds that some "passages . . . come from a place far deeper than the intellect alone, come, rather, from the visceral center of the writer's being, where his whole body is brought to bear on his text." Quoting from a passage in an interchapter beginning, "There is a crime here that goes beyond denunciation," he points out that "the tempo . . . indicates the importance of musical and harmonic analogies to the text." DeMott himself takes this analogy and expands it resonantly, evocatively—like Ditsky's, his own critical and poetical art becoming an extension of Steinbeck's:

> Steinbeck's covenant was with his own radical sense of the fiction-making process, not with a well-made linear formula. Indeed his fusion of intimate narrative and panoramic editorial chapters enforces a dialogic concert. Chapters, styles, and voices all speak to each other, set up resonances, send echoes back and forth--point and counterpoint, strophe

and antistrophe--as in a huge symphony of language whose total tonal and spatial impression far surpasses the sum of its discrete and sometimes dissonant parts. (175)

A Steinbeck critic, then, need not follow Bloom's lead when there are other choices of partners in a dance of open minds, hearts, and voices—such as those of Ditsky, DeMott, and others of their ilk.

Chris Kocela's 1998 "A Postmodern Steinbeck, or Rose of Sharon Meets Oedipa Maas" (in this volume), reassesses "a few well-studied aspects of the novel in light of some recent influential theories of postmodernist fiction":

I will argue in the first section that Steinbeck's use of the interchapters exemplifies a postmodern strategy of "frame-breaking," whereby differences between history and fiction are established within the text only to be problematized, alerting the reader to the difficulties of historical and political representation. In the second section I will use Deborah Madsen's theorization of "postmodernist allegory" to examine how the problematic divide between history and fiction is further broken down by Steinbeck's superimposing of biblical and fictional worlds on the plane of the Joads' story. . . . Finally, . . because I think not enough attention has been paid to Steinbeck's influence on, and continuity with, a later generation of American writers, . . . I indulge in a brief comparison of *The Grapes of Wrath* and Pynchon's *The Crying of Lot 49*.

Kocela convincingly demonstrates that what Busch has called Steinbeck's "unique aesthetic" in *GW* is most amenable to postmodern theoretical approaches and that the interpretive insights gained from them enrich and expand the critical dialogue as it engages in that dance of open minds about which Morrison writes. Kocela's accompanying notes are likewise instructive, offering fresh perspectives--for instance, a suggestion that *GW* may have influenced the *Star Wars* trilogy, together with a brief discussion of points of comparison.[66]

3

"The Grapes of Wrath **will irritate the complacent,**
but excite the compassionate.
I hope every congressman reads it
and everybody in America
who loves his country and fellowmen."
Charles Lee in a 1939 review for *The Boston Herald*

> **"This essay . . . is inspired by curiosity, impatience, some anger,**
> **and a passionate love of America and the Americans."**
> **John Steinbeck in the 1966 Foreword to *America and Americans***

> **"*The Grapes of Wrath*'s appearance helped change**
> **the literary and cultural geography of the United States."**
> **Robert DeMott in his 1996 *Steinbeck's Typewriter***

On two occasions I have used *GW* as a text in freshman honors composition classes, teaching it alongside Jonathan Kozol's *Rachel and Her Children: Homeless Families in America* and Viktor Frankl's *Man's Search for Meaning*. With such an accompaniment, students have no difficulty in recognizing Steinbeck's almost consuming love for this country and its people. In *GW* the ethos and prophetic voice of the Steinbeck persona in the Merlin-like narrator and in characters such as Tom are so pervasive that students can readily imagine what Steinbeck would say about America today and can see the relevance of his mythic American story for their own times. And in their adolescent, Arthurian roles in relationship to the Merlin persona, they readily and fully participate in the America of Steinbeck's vision--bringing with them a curiously American combination of compassion and pragmatic Yankee know-how. I remember in particular the pensive conclusion of one highly privileged young man from a very conservative background: "God may not be a Republican after all." As Simmons, 1939 reviewer for the *Greensboro Daily News*, warns readers on the basis of his own experience with *GW*: "It gets you."

Critics across time have responded, as these students do, to Steinbeck in his authoritative role as an American Merlin in *GW*, as one who not only holds the mirror for Americans to see themselves as they are but also one who sees prophetically into the future of his country, bleakly hopeful and optimistic that its people are capable of change and worthy of redemption in spite of grievous faults and failures. In that this novel is uniquely American, it is also most universal; for that which is authentically true to the human condition in one culture translates well into another. In these responses, therefore, critics have expanded and broadened the reach of *GW* to include today and the millennium to come, as well as Americans and people of all cultures, so that this novel has joined the rank of those works of art that have become classics for all times. What, then, does Steinbeck have to say to America today? And where is Steinbeck criticism going from this point?

In order to address the first of these questions, it is necessary to consider *GW* in its relationship to two later novels: *East of Eden* and *The Winter of Our Discontent*.[67] Harry Thornton Moore's 1939 *The Novels of John*

Steinbeck: A First Study notes astutely that "*The Grapes of Wrath* is packed with meanings that may be partly understood in terms of his previous tendencies, though there are new beginnings which may lead to future developments (66)." These "new beginnings" and "future developments" are especially pertinent to this discussion of *GW* and its ties to *Eden* and *Winter*, and they are addressed in my "The American Cain and Steinbeck's Shifting Perspective" (in this volume).

In one of the journal entries accompanying *Eden*, Steinbeck informs Covici that this novel is to be "the story of my country and the story of me,"[68] revealing at once a purposeful epic sweep and an intense personal involvement. Extending this epic sweep and personal involvement from *Eden* to include *GW* and *Winter*, the "story" of Steinbeck's "country" broadens, in cumulative effect creating an epic structure to accompany this sweep and an implied Every American—a protagonist who is, more often than not, neither admirable nor heroic.[69] All three of these novels are played out against a sombre biblical backdrop—itself suggestive of epic import. *GW* is set against the backdrop of the children of Israel's exodus from Egypt; *Eden*, against the Genesis story of a lost Paradise and fratricide; and *Winter*, against the Easter story of Christ's crucifixion and resurrection.

GW, then, begins *en medias res* in this American story, with the Oklahoma Dustbowl, an image and a condition resulting from greed and excess. *Eden* continues with a movement back in time to the birth pangs of California as it is populated first by Indians, to be followed by "the hard, dry Spaniards, . . . greedy and realistic" and "the Americans—more greedy because there were more of them"—with each group opposing those following, pragmatically looking out for number one, holding the land for themselves, and viewing newcomers as supplanters.[70]

Winter concludes the epic sequence with the morally dwarfed figure of Ethan Hawley, a grocery store clerk living in the shadow of his Puritan grandfather, "Old Cap'n Hawley," or "Old Cap'n," who had been a man of high character and achievement. Steinbeck caricatures the Every American in the character of Hawley—the triviality of his life, words, and actions simultaneously heightened and made ridiculously small by the constant reminder of the biblical story of Easter and Good Friday in the background. Like T. S. Eliot's Prufrock writ large, Hawley measures out his life "with coffee spoons."

Steinbeck's depiction of greed and excess as defining characteristics of Every American reaches its culmination here in Ethan Hawley. In seeking financial gain and the accompanying prestige, Hawley betrays both his friend, Danny, and his employer--leading to the death of the one and the deportation of the other. Further, he makes complex plans to rob a bank across the street from the grocery store where he works and later--in a pique of self-hatred--contemplates and comes to the verge of suicide. In *Winter*, as in *GW*, Steinbeck has designs on readers, addressing them directly in a note preceding the title page: "Readers seeking to find the fictional people and places here described would do better to inspect their own communities and search their own hearts, for this book is about a large part of America today."

Sometimes with barely concealed anger, sometimes with a degree of objectivity, but always with hope, Steinbeck draws across and through these three novels this composite portrait and tells this "story" of his "country." Neither the portrait nor the story is complimentary, for they reveal a flawed national psyche with an oxymoronic mixture of strengths and weaknesses, a portrayal that looks nothing like the representative images of ourselves we hold dear--the staunch and starched Puritan forebears, the honest Quaker face gracing oatmeal boxes and oil cans, the spiffy image of Uncle Sam of World War II vintage, the harmonious mixture of culturally diverse faces in a Coke ad. Knowing us all too well because he is one of us, Steinbeck exposes a dark alter ego--greedy, inhospitable, materialistic, self-absorbed. Running parallel to and in relationship with this portrayal of an uncomplimentary side of an Every American runs an evolving, Merlin-like self-definition as Steinbeck finds his own identity in the role of national bard, or seer.

Intentionally taking this bardic role, he is compelled to tell this American story. And his reader in a sense is compelled to listen--both as much captives as are Samuel Taylor Coleridge's speaker in "The Rime of the Ancient Mariner" who must tell his warning tale and the guest on his way to a wedding, who, in turn, must linger behind the ceremonial procession to hear it. Steinbeck has thus constructed himself, built his own identity, as a member of a national community--America, a place with which his sense of self is so intertwined that he declares it to be "the macrocosm of microcosm me."[71]

Steinbeck defines himself, then, in and through these three novels especially. And like Whitman, Emerson, Thoreau, and others of his literary forebears, he becomes in the process a national bard who sometimes lovingly, sometimes sadly warns his fellow Americans not to succumb to their excesses but rather to learn to recognize the sacred in the grotesque among them, as in the final scene of *GW* in which a very young, somewhat shallow, and hitherto self-absorbed Rose of Sharon is transformed into a modern Madonna, with the starving, dispossessed man, one of God's little ones, at her breast.

Herein perhaps lies the source of some of the negative critical response to Steinbeck—the very closeness of this recognizable Every American, the affective power of the author's persona as bardic seer, and the grotesque "little ones"—a closeness insisting on awareness and proclaiming the possibility of transcendence. In discussing the question of "affect" in literature, Biddy Martin cites Helene Cixous's "astonishment" in finding that the "key" to understanding the works of "the Brazilian writer Clarice Lispector" is "love" and "attention": "And there, there is the treasure of events: we have only to love, to be on the lookout for love, and all the riches are entrusted to us. Attention is the key" (5).

Written from the vantage point of an intervener in the "radical feminisms of the late seventies,"[72] Cixous's assertion is as applicable to the works of Steinbeck as it is to those of Lispector. For in the broad sweep of these three novels, there is an epic theme at once as simple and as elegant as the wrath of Achilles in Homer's *Iliad* or the search for identity and home in the *Odyssey*: Every American—as Steinbeck insistently, persistently urges—has the capacity to transcend the national penchant for materialism and greed and to love God's "little ones," the grotesque and broken in the midst. Then, as a by-product of this "attention" and "love," the Every American will discover that Eden/Paradise has been there all along—in the here and now. From *GW*, then, to *Eden*, to *Winter*, simply and elegantly, runs this story of Every American played out against the backdrop of seemingly simplistic, seemingly sentimental and romantic themes of love and attention—universal themes that have nevertheless invited considerable critical aspersion among some academics.

An authorial persona, the reader, and a pervasive theme of avarice that must be overcome, therefore, become intrinsically, intricately, and purposefully woven into Steinbeck's artistic design, beginning with *GW* with its veritable catalogue of greed and fraud in action--vices later to be continued, sharpened, and refined but also faced, with the possibility of overcoming them, in the characters of Cal in *Eden* and Ethan Hawley in *Winter*. Although there is no evidence that Steinbeck himself thought of these three fictional works as all of one piece, considering them in relationship to one another is instructive and certainly no stranger than Toni Morrison's trilogy of *Beloved*, *Jazz*, and *Paradise* in which connections are more intriguing and suggestive than obvious. Also, this backdrop serves to place *GW* in a broader perspective of Steinbeck's fictional portrayal of

America and Americans--to borrow the title of a concern he addressed also in a documentary meditation on this topic.[73]

Considered together, then, these three novels address the whining self-absorption, materialism, and adolescent negativity that comprise the malaise of America in these times. But the Steinbeck view is always paradoxical, oxymoronic, so that the malaise is balanced by the hope, even optimism, that Americans will ultimately choose to grow up and to find in transcendence a corrective for this spiritual ailment. From the earliest reviews to the present time, critics have recognized Steinbeck's portrayal of this peculiarly American paradox.

A 1939 reviewer for the Portland *Evening Express*[74] writes: "*Grapes of Wrath* is the most moving story of human suffering and disillusionment this reviewer ever read. Its scope is larger than at first appears, because Steinbeck is actually trying to show America is no longer America if the plight of the migrant sharecroppers is permitted to continue." Quite perversely, in "But . . . Not . . . Ferdinand,"[75] *Newsweek's* 1939 reviewer, Rascoe Burton, understands quite clearly the same "message" to which the *Evening Express*'s anonymous reviewer responds feelingly. Burton, however, complains: "I can't quite see what the book is about, except that there are "no frontiers left and no place to go." What Burton refuses to see is the human tragedy incipient in having "no place to go." Flippantly, he puts aside the realities of the migrant situation as it is presented in the ending of *GW*. There is no food or appropriate human shelter. One of these migrants is on the verge of starvation. One is ill and exhausted from childbirth. There is no work, and winter is upon them. And one hears in Burton's complaint an echo of Cain's similarly flippant response when God asks him for the murdered Abel's whereabouts: "Am I my brother's keeper?"

Recognizing both this tendency to turn away from the suffering depicted in *GW* and to eschew Steinbeck's portrayal of an American problem, another of these early reviewers, Marjorie Lloyd, foresees a similar rejection on the part of some of Steinbeck's readers/critics: "Steinbeck will be criticized for so strongly presenting this message, but we feel that it is needed. It is no use shutting our eyes to conditions which surround us."[76] Edrie Ann Morse, too, finds the novel "an outraged indictment of the economic muddle America is passing through today,"[77] and W. W. Withington similarly finds it "an education on our migrant situation."[78]

In "*The Grapes of Wrath*," chapter six of Joseph Fontenrose's 1963 *John Steinbeck: An Introduction and Interpretation*, he recognizes that the final scene is "for Steinbeck . . . an oracular image, forecasting in a moment of defeat and despair the final triumph of the people--a contingent forecast, for only if the people nourish and sustain one another will they achieve their ends" (69). Here is that Merlin/bard/prophet persona that has troubled so many critics. And, as has been noted previously, Fontenrose brings this peculiarly American, unfinished story of *GW* up to date--the critic, like the author, leaving in the reader's hands the continuing problem of America's dispossessed: "Perhaps the story has not ended yet" (83).

As Fontenrose observes the mythic, continuing story of *GW*, so in the preface to her 1968 *Casebook*, Donahue discovers its continuing revelation of an American psyche:

> This novel has survived a 'rhetoric of praise and blame' and has come to be known as an American classic. To follow its turbulent history . . . is to make an excursion into American literature, history, myth, culture, and dream. It is a journey as perilous as that of the Joads to a shattered Eden known as American success. (vii)

On the edge of awareness of "unspeakable things unspoken," Donahue suggests that this particular literary "excursion" into *The Grapes of Wrath* is full of peril for the American reader--that the myopic national psyche finds something here too close for scrutiny--something that demands the attention of the most humane, something that tries the conscience of the most callous, something authoritative and knowing, difficult to put aside and ignore.

From the very beginning there have been those who recognize such a peril. Harry Schofield, one of the early 1939 reviewers,[79] bears witness to the effects of this "perilous" inner journey, particularly for the American reader:

> The tempo of the writing is suited to the character of the book miraculously. I found, however, the slow, ponderous deadweight of depression and suffering carried me beyond the point of vulnerability. . . . So much pain and wracking misery is heaped up before you that . . . you can feel it no more. (5)

Like Schofield, Rose Loveman Brewer, another of the early reviewers, observes that this novel is a portrayal of an economic problem that "makes each reader of the book one of the dispossessed, wandering, homeless, forlorn and hungered, seeking but an acre in the rich teeming land to wrest a living for his own, . . . and yet feeling . . . that as wags our world today, there is no way out."[80]

Less hopeful than Steinbeck, Schofield and Brewer suggest that their "world," that is, America in their day, may be incapable of change. Perhaps they have arrived at that perilous point that Donahue suggests—a point at which a reader/critic despairs and fears that the greedy, materialistic American psyche is irredeemable, incapable of change and that, as a result, those who are dispossessed—the wounded and grotesque in the midst—must perish. But this view is not Steinbeck's.

In "We Still See Their Faces," the 1989 introduction to Viking Press's deluxe anniversary edition of GW^{81} (review in this volume), Studs Terkel translates the America depicted in GW of 1939 into America as it might be depicted in a GW of 1989. On a 1989 trip he observes in Iowa and Minnesota "too many deserted streets that evoked too many images of too many rural hamlets of the Great Depression." Everywhere he goes, he cannot "escape the furrowed faces and stooped frames of John Steinbeck's people. . . . It was a flash forward fifty years" (vi). Drawing analogies among GW; the music of Tchaikovsky, Stravinsky, Mozart, and Fats Waller; and Frank Lloyd Wright's "organic" sense of architecture, Terkel underscores the novel's aesthetic merits and at the same time highlights "the aching relevance of Steinbeck's book." He notes that the "mean-spiritness" [sic] that characterizes so many Americans today "reveals itself even in our idiomatic language: Victims are defined as 'losers,' people for whom there is no place either at the top or the bottom, who fall into a Limbo-like 'dark recess'" (x).

In a vignette of Peggy Terry, who was schooled by The Great Depression and experienced in the life of the dispossessed, Terkel reminds us of the cherished American belief in the dignity and worth of each individual citizen, and of humankind as well: "She remembers the day somebody handed her a well-thumbed paperback. . . . 'And when I read *Grapes of Wrath*, that was like reliving my whole life. I was never so proud of poor people before as I was after I read this book.'" Terkel believes that "John Steinbeck would have valued that critique as much as the Nobel Prize for Literature he won in 1962" (xx). Functioning as an extension of Steinbeck's ageless story of dispossession that seems to have no end, Terkel's account, too, reminds Americans of their heritage and, by implication, their responsibility as well.

Railton's 1990 "Pilgrim's Politics: Steinbeck's Art of Conversion" goes beyond a vision of psychic perils to see clearly Steinbeck's intentions to stir and awaken the American conscience:

> The origins of the evils that the novel decries are . . . social and economic. . . . Can anything but a social revolution change that system? . . . Steinbeck wants to save the nation from its sins. Babies like Rose of Sharon's are dying because of social inequalities and economic injustices.

> Can the private, spiritual birth of a New Man or a New Woman--the
> unrecorded "event" that the novel leaves at the center of its narrative and
> its vision--affect that? (36)

Events in *GW* may be, as Railton describes them, "narratively inescapable,"
but Steinbeck's view of Americans and humanity is not. Like Rose of
Sharon, Steinbeck implies, they are capable of change, of growing up and
putting aside "childish things."

In her 1993 "California Answers *The Grapes of Wrath*,"[82] (in this
volume) Susan Shillinglaw examines "four of the most important
respondents" to Steinbeck's depiction of California landowners in *GW*:

> Two who defended California agriculture were highly respected
> professional writers: Ruth Comfort Mitchell, the author of *Of Human
> Kindness*, and Frank J. Taylor, a free-lance journalist who covered
> California business, farming, and recreation for the state and national press.
> And two were highly successful retired farmers, to use the word loosely:
> Marshall V. Hartranft, the Los Angeles fruit grower and real estate
> developer who wrote *Grapes of Gladness: California's Refreshing and
> Inspiriting Answer to John Steinbeck's "Grapes of Wrath,"* and Sue
> Sanders, touted as the "friend of the migrant," who wrote and published a
> tract called "The Real Cause of Our Migrant Problem." (146-47)

She concludes that, on the whole, these respondents' "faith in individual
initiative" and Steinbeck's "call for action" on behalf of America's
dispossessed—"rooted in group, not individual initiative"—are both
inherently American ideals. Unfortunately, however, these ideals are
irreconcilable. Nonetheless, in a concluding note Shillinglaw cites
Steinbeck's interview for the Voice of America on February 11, 1952, in
which he provides an ameliorating factor that bridges such divergent ideals:
"When the anger decreased these two sides, these two groups, were able to
get to know each other and they found they didn't dislike each other at all"
(186).

DeMott's 1996 "This Book Is My Life" in *Steinbeck's Typewriter*
reveals that *GW*, far from the sentimentality to which some critics would
reduce it, tends more towards the iconoclastic and prophetic and more
towards a reality that is so true to the American psyche that it moves into the
mythic. *GW* deprives Americans of their romantic vision of the cowboy's
forever riding off into the sunset towards some majestic mountains beyond
which there are ever new horizons. Instead, DeMott shows, this novel is "a
tale of dashed illusions, thwarted desires, unconscionable suffering, and

betrayed promises--all strung on a gossamer thread of hope" (194). And it is this "hope" that, to a large extent, makes *GW* such a uniquely American novel, for it points towards new horizons. But from henceforth those horizons must be inner and spiritual--there is no longer anywhere else to go.

Where does the criticism of *GW* go from this point? How should it be informed and educated? Essays in this volume offer at least a partial response to these questions. While earlier studies deal with verisimilitude and classification as in the early reviews and Ross and Whicher essays, more reflective views are represented by Fontenrose's observations on "the biological and mythical strands . . . in *The Grapes of Wrath*," by the Matton and Timmerman studies of imagery and theme, and by the Henderson and Railsback cross-disciplinary works, the one from the vantage point of cultural geography and the other from the perspective of Darwin and science. Evidence of abundant material on Steinbeck's personal, artistic, and public life, Meyer's "Steinbeck and the Critics: A Study in Artistic Self-Concept" explores the effect of negative criticism on Steinbeck's self-concept. Pointing towards a clearer vision of Steinbeck's aesthetic accomplishment, Kocela provides an explication demonstrating first, that the theoretical methodologies of the postmodernists bring fresh insights and second, that comparisons of "Steinbeck's influence on, and continuity with, a later generation of American writers" are worthy of critical attention. Meyers also provides a study of the influence of Eastern thought and philosophy, particularly that of Lao Tze, on Steinbeck's thought.

The studies of Werlock and Maine, like Lisca's earlier work on Steinbeck and Hemingway and Kocela's on Steinbeck and Pynchon, are comparative, one placing Steinbeck's Joads in perspective beside contemporary William Faulkner's Snopses and the other highlighting the likenesses and differences between Steinbeck's *GW* and Dos Passos's *U.S.A.* Davis and Shillinglaw look at *GW*'s reception, its verisimilitudes, and perspective—one from an Oklahoman and the other from a Californian point of view. Owens, Torres, and Visser explore rhetorical concerns, such as dialogic structure, levels of discourse, audience—including the relationship between author and reader and between reader and text. Swan shares views on the university student's response to the text. Also, both this introduction and the article on Steinbeck's shifting perspectives from *GW*, to *Eden*, to *Winter* show intriguing thematic and structural connections among these three novels that are worthy of further exploration.[83]

Mary Brown's 1998 "*The Grapes of Wrath* and the Literary Canon of American Universities in the Nineties" suggests that "it is highly possible that . . . the real position of *The Grapes of Wrath* in the American canon, indicated by how much it is read and how often it is assigned in the curriculum, may continue to decline in the 21st century." Brown attributes this neglect of *GW* among educators in the colleges and universities and the public schools alike to its length, its perceived out datedness, or its perceived lack of aesthetic merit. But, she maintains, "the stream of what is taught can change directions, as indicated by the current prevalence of books like Kate Chopin's *The Awakening* and Zora Neale Hurston's *Their Eyes Were Watching God* on college course syllabi" (18).

There are some current trends that may contribute to this reversal of the current tendency to neglect *The Grapes of Wrath* in academia. One of these trends is the current interest in the self, the individual's identity—which, paradoxically, is most often found in community, in relationships with an "other." Like Whitman in *Song of Myself*, Steinbeck has "sung" the story of himself, his country, and his fellow Americans, especially in *GW*, *Eden*, and *Winter* and in their nonfiction backdrops, *Travels with Charley in Search of America* and *American and Americans*. Those who want to discover an author's identity, a writer's aesthetic, or a philosopher's beliefs would find as ample evidence in Steinbeck's fiction, his journals, letters, and nonfiction as can be found for any other writer. Those who want to discover personal and national identity as Americans will find themselves in relationship to their country—including its grotesques—in these works.

Further, the current educational interest in emotional intelligence, or empathy, reveals a discovery of the obvious on the part of educators: that human beings are complex creatures who, as far as their ability to "know" and to learn is concerned, depend on heart and soul as well as intellect. That is, their empathic, emotional capacity must be engaged alongside the cognitive if they are to "know" anything other than discrete facts. For sadly, we have now learned that areas of knowledge as far apart as missiles or the human body may be misused or abused if human beings do not know what it means to be truly human and humane.

The critical response to *GW* has shown that Steinbeck knows all of this most passionately with his own bardic heart, mind, and soul. To borrow from Carpenter's depiction of the Steinbeck aesthetic, in *GW* he has shown a "moving picture" that begins a panoramic epic sweep that clearly suggests an "abstract idea of life" in America. And Steinbeck has spoken, sometimes thunderously, in a prophetic voice that not only offers "a criticism" of this life but also a panacea: love and attention--themes no more sentimental, no more simplistic than the Homeric themes in the *Iliad* and the *Odyssey* or the ancient biblical stories that depict what it means to be truly human or not. As French has pointed out, the story of the Joads is a story of an "education of the heart." The critical responses have shown us that Steinbeck has designs that draw in readers and critics also, involving them, insisting that they engage in a participation in the "actuality" that insists, in turn, on an engagement of mind and heart.

Perhaps the tardy recognition of the essentialness of "emotional intelligence" will remove some of the stigma from Steinbeck's insistence on empathic involvement with his text. Perhaps American critics, scholars, and professors may in time turn to Steinbeck's *GW*, suspending cool objectivity and with hearts as well as minds open to its "message" that celebrates an aesthetic that tells us who we are, or who we should be.

Or perhaps a new generation of scholars is already leaving the old behind and beginning this move towards involvement with Steinbeck and his text. In his 1995 *Parallel Expeditions: Charles Darwin and the Art of John Steinbeck*, Railsback analyzes, discusses, and dismisses the various arguments of "the novelist's literary executioners" as "slightly baffled" (1-3). There is even a note of humor in his depiction of Leslie Fiedler's 1989 "keynote address at an international conference, *'The Grapes of Wrath*, 1939-1989: An Interdisciplinary Forum.'" Railsback writes that

> Fiedler **blasted** the literary reputation of the novelist in the **vindictive** style used by a number of critics and reviewers since the 1930s. . . . He savored the result of his **assault**. . . . Fiedler's **damnation** of Steinbeck was **provoking** [emphases mine]." (1)

Railsback concludes, however, quite confidently and a bit pensively:

> Aside from his **odd** complaint that the novelist's characters are not mythic enough (comparing less favorably to such heroic figures as Scarlett O'Hara, Sherlock Holmes, and Superman), **the critic had little new to say** [emphases mine]. (1)

Like the child in the old fairy tale about the emperor's new clothes who proclaims—to the astonishment of his elders and all the wise people of the kingdom, who had suspected as much but did not dare speak—"But he has no clothes," Railsback has pointed out the obvious.

Note, however, that Railsback writes with more assurance and optimism than did E. W. Tedlock, Jr. in the 1969 preface on the occasion of the fourth printing and paperback edition of *Steinbeck and His Critics: A Record of Twenty-five Years*, that he had edited with then deceased C. V. Wicker:

> Now I find myself left with a feeling of pathos. . . . The pathos lies in the unequal public encounter between a writer inadequately trained for it in spite of the Stanford years, and the intellectuals who, from the vantage point of dialectically supported dogmas and morally assured activism, measured him against the correct responses to a whole series of contemporary crises. Our times have no patience with good intentions or old-fashioned positions. The new perspectives being forced upon us may bring moral advances, but revolution is destructive of art, which requires a special love and tolerance. (v)

At the completion of a truly memorable work of scholarship, Tedlock is saddened by the "fault-finding we had to include" (v). Although he does not know in what direction Steinbeck criticism is headed, he evidently fears and regrets what the future may hold.

But such "pathos" is not true of the present outlook for the continued critical and scholarly interest in *GW*. This is not to say that there are no problems with *The Grapes of Wrath* or that those who find such faults are necessarily "destructive of art." To illustrate, Visser argues persuasively that the theoretical and practical issues of audience and closure may be irreconcilable in such a novel. But Visser's study is nonetheless a paradigm for that "special love and tolerance" that Tedlock writes about, and he argues its necessary flaws within the acknowledged context of the novel's overall excellence and aesthetic merit. And this is the point to which criticism has taken us thus far. Critics during the first fifty years of *The Grapes of Wrath* have laid some solid groundwork, and critics in the nineties have shown how well the scholarly art of criticism has begun to build on this groundwork, optimistically preparing for Steinbeck studies in a new millennium.

Notes

1. Peter Lisca and Kevin Hearle, eds. *John Steinbeck, "The Grapes of Wrath": Text and Criticism* (New York: Penguin Books, 1997). Hereafter references to this work will be cited parenthetically within the text, identified as *GW* with pertinent page numbers. The original article by Lisca appeared in Viking's 1972 edition, reprinted from *PMLA* LXXII (March 1957), 269-309.

2. For example, see Harry Thornton Moore's *The Novels of John Steinbeck: A First Study* (Chicago: Normandie House, 1939). He complains that the conclusion is "too quiet," that there are "several things in the story . . . never rounded off satisfactorily" (69).

3. Steinbeck, Elaine and Robert Wallsten, *Steinbeck: A Life in Letters* (New York: Viking Penguin Inc., 1975). Hereafter quotations from this work will be cited parenthetically within the text, identified as *SLL* with pertinent page numbers.

4. In a January 1939 letter to Covici, Steinbeck writes, "Actually, if there has been one rigid rule in my books, it is that I as me had no right in them" (*SLL* 176). His assuming a bardic persona gives the reader some aesthetic distance from Steinbeck, the social critic, and, at the same time, bestows the authoritative voice of the omniscient narrator/commentator skilled in the affairs of human beings.

5. *Steinbeck's Typewriter: Essays on His Art* (Troy, New York: The Whitson Publishing Company, 1996). Hereafter references to this work appear parenthetically within the text. For the source of the reference within the quotation, see Robert DeMott, *John Steinbeck, Working Days: The Journals of "The Grapes of Wrath."* (New York: Penguin Books, 1990).

6. In Warren French's chapter nine, "The Education of the Heart" in *John Steinbeck* (New York: Twayne Publishers, Inc., 1961), he maintains that "at bottom, Steinbeck believes, like his great predecessor, Hawthorne, that the only lasting and meaningful reforms originate in the individual human heart" (112).

7. Steinbeck's concern for "balance" and "structure" is Aristotelian in its sense of a wholeness in which the parts of an action fit together so that "if one part is shifted or taken away the whole is deranged or disjoined." See *Aristotle, The Poetics* in *Literary Criticism: Plato to Dryden*, ed. Allan H. Gilbert (Detroit: Wayne State University Press, 1962), p. 81.

8. In postmodern terms the text is more "writerly," or "scriptible;" than it is "lisible," or "readerly." In a scriptible text a reader must participate in the making of meaning whereas in a more lisible text the reader discovers meaning. For example, in the conclusion of *Jazz*, Toni Morrison addresses and challenges the reader: "Say make me, remake me. You are free to do it and I am free to let you because look, look. Look where your hands are. Now" (229). Similarly, Steinbeck leaves his readers with a tableau, a frozen cinematic shot, with neither a resolution nor even a prescription for a resolution.

9. Thus, Studs Terkel's introduction to Viking's deluxe 1989 fiftieth anniversary edition of *GW* begins: "It is 1988. We could see the face on the Six O'clock News. It could be a Walker Evans or Dorothea Lange shot, but that's fifty years off. It is a face of despair, of an Iowa farmer, fourth generation, facing foreclosure" (v).

10. See note 7 above. It is not lisible, or readerly--that is, it is not a text in which readers discover meaning but is rather one in which they must participate in the making of meaning.

11. Other writers have also noted the evolution of an American psyche in *GW*. In "John Steinbeck: American Dreamer," *The Southwest Review* (July 1941), Frederic I. Carpenter, for instance, writes: "Jim Casy reinterprets the American dream, . . . transforms it, and (with Tom Joad) helps to realize it. . . . And if Tom Joad dies, . . . the dream will live. His soul will become the soul of America, struggling for freedom. . . . His soul goes marching on. The dream continues" (reprinted in Tedlock and Wicker).

12. On July 20, 1998, the "Today Show" featured the top one-hundred books of the century, a Modern Library project that takes into consideration both a book's popular appeal and also its critical acclaim. *GW* is number ten on the list. In a list compiled by students of the Radcliffe Publishing Course, *GW* ranks third--following *The Great Gatsby* and *The Catcher in the Rye*. Thanks to Roy Simmonds, who mailed a copy of the British "100 books that made a century" from *The Guardian*, January 20, 1997, that list is also available for comparison, as follows: "9. *The Grapes of Wrath*--John Steinbeck."

13. For a listing of early reviews and criticism, see the bibliography under that listing.

14. Hence, see Lisca's observation that this early period of criticism is noted primarily for "its assertive nature."

15. "Farm Tenancy Central Theme of Steinbeck."   16 July 1939, Sec. D, p. 6. Hereafter references to this work will be cited parenthetically within the text.

16. (MA), 22 April 1939, A, p. 7 and 17 June 1939, Sec. 1, p. 9. Hereafter references to this work will be cited parenthetically within the text.

17. Simmon's review retells a good part of the Joad story as well as sharing with readers its impact.

18. "Books." *Daytona Beach News-Journal* (FL), 14 April 1939, p. 10.

19. (CT), 14 April 1939, p. 4.

20. *Cleveland News* (OH), 15 April 1939, p. 12.

21. *New York Sun* (NY), 14 April 1939.

22. 13 (17 April 1939) and 13 (1 May 1939).

23. Chicago: Normandie House, 1939. Hereafter quotations from this work will be cited parenthetically within the text.

24. In the "Editors' Introduction: The Pattern of Criticism," Lisca and Hearle maintain that "the current standing of a piece of literature is educated to a large extent by its ability to sustain a dialogue among critics" (547). They observe that in its "first fifteen years there appeared in literary journals fewer than half a dozen essays devoted to a critical analysis" of *GW* (547).

25. *College English* II (January 1941), 315-25 (reprinted in Lisca/Hearle).

26. *The University of Kansas City Review*, XIX (Winter 1947), 149-54.

27. *College English* (May 1949), 432-38. Hereafter references to this work will be cited parenthetically in the text

28. (New York: Appleton-Century-Crofts, Inc.), 1951, 959-61. The search history for permission to publish Whicher's section on John Steinbeck in Quinn's *The Literature of the American People* is traced in "Copyright Acknowledgments," following the title page.

29. For example, see Harold Bloom, ed. *John Steinbeck's "The Grapes of Wrath."* Modern Critical Interpretations Series. (New York: Chelsea House Publishers, 1988). Bloom acknowledges that he remains "uneasy" about his experience in re-reading *GW* and reaches the grudging conclusion that this novel cannot be excluded "from a serious reader's esteem. . . . Wisdom compels one to be grateful for the novel's continuous existence" (5). In denigrating Steinbeck's aesthetic achievement in *GW*, Bloom provides an assertive but unconvincing and poorly substantiated comparison between the Steinbeck and Hemingway writing styles.

30. *Steinbeck Quarterly*, (Spring 1969), 9-17. Hereafter references to this work will be cited parenthetically within the text.

31. (New York: Barnes & Noble, Inc., 1963), 67-83. Hereafter references to this work will be cited parenthetically within the text.

32. *Mississippi Quarterly*, XII (Summer 1959), 136-44, reprinted in Donahue.

33. In specifying critics from abroad, Bloom goes far beyond the bounds of decorum. It should have been quite sufficient for his purposes to stop with labeling Steinbeck critics in general as "liberal middlebrows." As it is, American critics need to apologize to our colleagues from abroad for his rudeness.

34. *San Jose Studies*, XVI, Number 1 (Winter 1990), 54-64. In "Grasping for 'What Actually Is'" in his 1995 *Parallel Expeditions: Charles Darwin and the Art of John Steinbeck* (Moscow, Idaho: U. P., 1995), Brian Railsback has an opening epigraph taken from a 1961 *Newsweek* review of *The Winter of Our Discontent* : "Any critic knows it is no longer legal to praise John Steinbeck." This epigraph prefaces his discussion of Fiedler's lecture, which was first given as "the keynote address at an international conference, 'The Grapes of Wrath*, 1939-1989: An Interdisciplinary Forum,' held at San Jose State University

in California" (1). Finding critics such as Fiedler "slightly baffled," Railsback first sets the record straight concerning Steinbeck's critical reputation in order "to move beyond the legacy of critical misinterpretation." He then sets forth his own intriguing thesis, which his book addresses knowledgeably and persuasively: "Steinbeck was not only directly and indirectly influenced by Charles Darwin's work, but the author's quest for a true look at humanity leads him on an expedition in art that parallels in method and result the naturalist's expedition in biology" (9). It is instructive here to observe Fiedler and Railsback in this close proximity--the one as passionately negative as the other is passionately positive--the one refusing to participate in a dance of open minds, the other entering into it with alacrity. Hereafter references to both of these works will appear parenthetically within the text.

35. (New York: Thomas Y. Crowell Company, 1968). Hereafter references to this work will appear parenthetically in the text. For a listing of other collections of scholarly essays devoted specifically to *GW*, see the bibliography under that listing.

36. Albuquerque, New Mexico: University of New Mexico Press, 1969.

37. *Studies in American Fiction*, Autumn 1989, 203-11.

38. (New York: Viking Penguin Inc., 1989), v-xx, reviewed in this volume.

39. *World Literature Today: A Literary Quarterly of the University of Oklahoma*, 64:3 (Summer 1990), 401-04. Hereafter references to this work are cited parenthetically in the text.

40. *Studies in American Fiction*, 22:1 (Sprint 1994), 19-36.

41. (New York: Alfred A. Knopf), 7--from her speech of acceptance of the National Book Foundation Medal for Distinguished Contribution to American Letters, 6 November 1996.

42. See note 12 above for a brief discussion of the inclusion of *GW* in the top one hundred books of the century.

43. In *New Essays on "The Grapes of Wrath,"* ed. David Wyatt (New York: Cambridge University Press, 1990), 27-46.

44. Introduction by Warren French. (Columbia, Missouri: University of Missouri Press, 1974), 92-129. Hereafter references to this work are cited parenthetically within the text.

45. In *In Time and Place: Some Origins of American Fiction*. (Athens: University of Georgia Press), reprinted in Bloom.

46. *Journal of English and Germanic Philology*, LX (April 1963), 569-80, reprinted in Lisca/Hearle. Hereafter references to this work are cited parenthetically within the text.

47. *Resources for American Literary Study* 13 (Autumn 1983), 134-64. Hereafter references to this work are cited parenthetically within the text. See also McElrath, Joseph, Jessie Crissler, and Susan Shillinglaw, eds.. *John Steinbeck: The Contemporary Reviews*. Contemporary Reviews Series. (New York: Cambridge University Press, 1996).

48. See *Steinbeck's Literary Achievement*. Steinbeck Monograph Series, no. 6. Muncie, IN: John Steinbeck Society of America/Ball State University, 1976.

49. *California History*, 68:4 (Winter 1989/90), 211-23. Hereafter references to this work are cited parenthetically within the text.

50. *Arizona Quarterly*, 45:4 (Winter 1989), 17-27.

51. *Steinbeck Quarterly*, 23:1-2 (Winter/Spring 1990), 17-27.

52. *San Jose Studies*, 18:1 (Winter 1992), 61-71.

53. Introduction by John H. Timmerman. Steinbeck Essay Series, no. 3. Muncie, IN: Steinbeck Research Institute/Ball State University, 1990, vii-ix. Hayashi, editor of this series, describes this volume as "a collection of the finest seven essays on *The Grapes of Wrath* that have been published in the *Steinbeck Quarterly* in the 1970s and 1980s" (vii).

For other collections of essays on *GW*, as well as biographical and bibliographical materials, please see the bibliography.

54. Introduction by John H. Timmerman. (Metuchen, New Jersey: Scarecrow Press, 1994).

55. Perhaps even more promising than such "thematic and stylistic relationships" with writers in the American canon would be comparisons with his predecessors in the British canon, many of whom he admired and emulated. In *Travels with Charley in Search of America* (New York: Viking Penguin, 1962), for example, he writes: "Very early I conceived a love for Joseph Addison which I have never lost. He plays the instrument of language as Casals plays a cello. I do not know whether he influenced my prose style, but I could hope he did. . . . I remember so well loving Addison's use of capital letters for nouns" (38). And in an entry dated "Sunday, January 29, 1961," he imitates the Addison style:

> Yes, Joseph Addison I hear and I will obey within Reason, for it appears that the Curiosity you speak of has in no Way abated. . . . In regarding my Work, someReaders profess greater Feeling for what it makes than for what it says. Since a Suggestion from the Master is a Command not unlike Holy Writ, I shall digress and comply at the same Time. (39)

56. New York: Viking Press, 1984.

57. *Garland Reference Library of the Humanities*, vol. 246. (New York: Garland Publishing, 1984).

58. With John F. Early. Introduction by Susan Shillinglaw. (San Jose, CA: Steinbeck Research Center, 1990). For other biographies, bibliographies, and scholarly aids, please see the bibliography.

59. *Studies in American Fiction*, 22:1 (Spring 1994), 19-36. Hereafter references to this work are cited parenthetically within the text.

60. *South Dakota Review* , 34 (Summer 1996), 192-205, reprinted in this volume. Hereafter references to this work are cited parenthetically within the text.

61. *Agora* 2 (Fall 1973), 41-50, reprinted in *Critical Essays on John Steinbeck's "The Grapes of Wrath*," ed. John Ditsky (Boston, Massachusetts: G. K. Hall & Co., 1989), 116-123, reprinted in Lisca/Hearle. Hereafter references to this work are cited parenthetically within the text.

62. (New York: Twayne Publishers, 1994), 132-38. Hereafter references to this work are cited parenthetically within the text.

63. Although this study of critical responses focuses primarily on *GW*, it will also discuss this novel in relationship to two of Steinbeck's much maligned later works, *East of Eden* and *The Winter of Our Discontent*, and suggests that, taken together, *GW*, *Eden*, and *Winter* are the quintessential American epic. It will suggest further that, when approached with an appropriate theoretical measure and willing involvement with the texts, the weight of the three together may be found to be greater than the sum of their parts. For an insightful view of another of Steinbeck's works, one of those novels hitherto considered as evidence of Steinbeck's artistic "decline," see DeMott's discussion of *Sweet Thursday* in "Steinbeck's Typewriter: An Excursion in Suggestiveness," in *Steinbeck's Typewriter*, 287-317.

64. There is something inherently (and probably blindly) rude and arrogant in this poorly substantiated statement and its childish implication: "I am a highbrow. You are not."

65. Most unsuccessfully, Bloom applies this theory to his discussion of Steinbeck and Hemingway in his introduction to *Modern Critical Interpretations*. See note 29 above.

66. Michael Meyer's "Steinbeck, Stephen King, and Their Critics: A Study in Artistic Self-Concept" in this volume also addresses Kocela's concern that "not enough attention has been paid to Steinbeck's . . . continuity with a later generation of American writers.

67. Hereafter *East of Eden* is referred to as *Eden* and *The Winter of Our Discontent* as *Winter*.

68. *Journal of a Novel : The "East of Eden" Letters* (New York: The Viking Press, 1969), 3. Hereafter references to this work are included parenthetically within the text.

69. An exception occurs in *GW* where this figure is a dichotomy, with Ma Joad as a key heroic figure on one extreme and, on the other, a kind of alter ego, with the banks, large landholders, and those people in the "cars [that] whizzed viciously by on 66" as apathetic, inhospitable, self-absorbed people who, like Cain in the biblical Eden, refuse to take on the role of their "brother's keeper." In *Winter* these latter characters are telescoped into the characters of Ethan Allen Hawley, an Every American, and his fellow citizens.

70. (New York: Viking Penguin Books, Inc., 1952), 7-8. Hereafter references to this text are included parenthetically in the text.

71. *Travels with Charley in Search of America* (New York: Viking Penguin, Inc., 1962), 209. Hereafter references to this work will appear parenthetically in the text.

72. *PMLA* (January 97), p. 17.

73. See *America and Americans* (New York: Viking, 1966).

74. *Portland Evening Express* (ME), 15 April 1939, p. 6.

75. *Newsweek*, 13 (17 April 1939), 46.

76. "Off the Book Shelf." *Carmel Pine Cone* (CA,, 21 April 1939, p. 5.

77. Morse, Edrie Ann. "Book Review." *Altoona Tribune* (PA), 1 May 1939, p. 5.

78. Withington, Rev. W. W. "Books of the Times." *Santa Rosa Press-Democrat* (CA), 15 July 1939, p. 5.

79. "Today's Book." *Macon Telegraph* (GA), 23 April 1939, Sec. A, p. 4.

80. Brewer, Rose Loveman. "*The Grapes of Wrath*, An American Classic?" *Chattanooga News* (TN), 20 May 1939, p. 4.

81. (New York: Viking Penguin Inc., 1989). Hereafter references to this work will be cited parenthetically within the text.

82. In *John Steinbeck: The Years of Greatness, 1936-1939*. Ed. Tetsumaro Hayashi (Tuscaloosa: University of Alabama Press, 1993), 145-64; 181-86.

83. *Travels with Charley in Search of America* and *America and Americans*, along with Steinbeck's letters and journals, are also pertinent to any study of these novels.

PART I

1939–1989
LOOKING BACK ON THE
FIRST FIFTY YEARS

The Grapes of Wrath: The Tragedy of the American Sharecropper (Review)

Charles Lee

Steinbeck Eloquently Angry Over Fate of Little Farmer

When the great propagandists of literature are listed hereafter the name of John Steinbeck must stand with that of Stowe and Dickens. In "The Grapes of Wrath" (Viking $2.75), he has written as memorable an American novel as I have ever read. Long, superbly angry, lashing with sustained indignation, his story towers above the work of others who have essayed to translate the desperations and dreams of the sharecropper into words, above Wellington Roe's fine novel "The Tree Falls South," above Erskine Caldwell's "You Have Seen Their Faces," above Archibald MacLeish's poem "Land of the Free." That it so clearly surpasses in excellence such excellent works as these indicates something of its extraordinary potency; had he been a novelist Whitman might have told such a story as this.

Little Plot; Much Power

Of highly plotted story there is little. There is instead a long, fascinating series of episodes life-like in their content and color. And there are believable characters to act them out, so dimensional in their inner and outer composition they become real and visible as you hasten through the more than 600 pages of the volume: calm, unwavering Ma and Pa Joad; their ex-convict son Tom, one of a half a dozen children; Christ-like Casy; and a score of others who sink or struggle in the grim battle for survival. Helping to lend reality to the scene of men and the soil, marred occasionally for some perhaps by too earthy an epithet, but superb in its humor, speed, and honesty. There is, too, the high earnestness of the author: of his sincerity there can be no doubt. And there is, finally, the reader's reaction to the subject matter of the book. The ordinary reader, like myself, has no way of checking the veracity of the facts here offered, but he cannot help believing that things must be as Steinbeck has painted them. The fact that he does not want to believe and does demonstrates the emotional power of the book. Steinbeck has seen clearly, felt intensely, written passionately. As a result, the reader is absorbed, shaken, and convinced. "The Grapes of Wrath" is an ugly book as well as angry. It is ugly with immense distress, the plight of scores of thousands of destitute American families rooted out of their homes and lands, and wandering in frantic and fearful misery along the highways and byways of California. They are the American refugees, victims of dust storms, dwindling crops, dying livestock, greedy mortgage holders, and avaricious absentee landlords. Some of them can trace their American ancestry back for seven generations. The fathers and grandfathers of many of them had to stand against the Indian. For years no one has told them "where to put their feet" and escaped without a bullet in him or after him, or at least a bump under his eye. But now the tractors (and banks) have driven them off, and they are "a parade of hurts," sick and ragged in body, sick in soul, despised and feared and abused by those from whom all they ask is a roof and water and food to keep the hope from dying.

Ugliness and Anger

What is hope? The hope is everyman's hope--not just a dream. It means security, food to keep the body together, work to keep a man and his pride on speaking terms, money to clothe, school, and doctor his family. And what happens to the Joad family, whose story is made to symbolize that of the American sharecropper? The Joads lose their land and home. They trade in their possessions for an old "jalopy" (are swindled in fact, and, answering another swindle (handbills offering work on the fruit and cotton farms in California)), set off from Oklahoma on the 2000 mile trek to the land of oranges, peaches, and pick handles. Their journey is remarkably told. During the course of it Grampa and Granma die, Noah departs to lead the life of a hermit, and Connie, surrendering to his burdens, deserts his pregnant wife. Is this melodrama? So is eviction and flight. The story is melodramatic because the facts are. There is ugliness here, terrible ugliness as we follow the Joads in their successive disillusionments and despairs.

Hundreds are wanted to work, but thousands appear. Wages skid. Families break up, or rather are broken up. Children waste away for lack of food; grown-ups fight desperately to keep the final misery, starvation, from overwhelming them and theirs. Dirty, ragged, bruised in spirit almost to the breaking point, the "Okies" (as they are derisively called), are kept on the move, burned out of their tin-and-paper-Hoovervilles if necessary, so that they can't vote, obtain relief, or organize. Wealth and security attack this abject horde as "reds." When one young fellow asks an employer "What is these reds?" he gets this blunt answer, "A red is anyone that wants 30 cents an hour when we're payin' 25."

Eloquent Indignation

This, I have said, is also an angry book. The story speaks very well for itself, but Steinbeck has inserted eloquent narrative expositions (really little essays) between some of the chapters. You're not to miss the point. It is sledged home in these bursts of indignation, hymns almost, of hate against those "who own the things the people must have." How long before the bitterness of the dispossessed turns into "a dead terror" for the country? How long before brutalities finally create brutes? How long before this "problem" is seen for the atrocity which it is? "We've got a bad thing made by men," say the Joads and their comrades, and "some day the armies of bitterness will all be going the same way." Misery can lead to madness, and the "line between hunger and anger is a thin line." Need makes trouble. That is why Steinbeck addresses his plea to all those who have "access to history." It wasn't long ago, in fact, that Somerset Maugham said, "We live now on the eve of great revolutions."

Whether the facts bear it or not, here is magnificent resentment. It is doubtful whether this book could be such a tremendous experience were truth not at its core. At any rate Steinbeck has revealed a crime, which, even if only partly true, "goes beyond denunciation. . . . there is a failure here that topples all our success." "The Grapes of Wrath" will irritate the complacent, but excite the compassionate. I hope every congressman reads it and everybody in America who loves his country and fellowmen. Poverty may not be a disgrace, as someone once said, but that's the only nice thing you can say about it.

From *The Boston Herald* (22 April 1939), Sec. A, p. 7.

The Grapes of Wrath Tops Year's Tales in Heart and Art (Review)

Charles Lee

June is the month for roses, purges, girls to look forward, and book-reviewers to look backwards. In retrospect the year 1939 has been good to the passionate reader. It has offered more worthy books both in fictional and non-fictional fields than even the individual book-reviewer has been able to cover. And there is promise from the publishers that plenty of good things will roll off the presses before next Christmas. So in the coming summer months, with their long light and vacation days, no one, no matter how snobbish or modest his intellectuality, need be without something to read. There are excellence and variety enough for all.

Any one who has not yet raced through the tense, tragic, terrifying pages of John Steinbeck's novel of sharecropper life, "The Grapes of Wrath" (Viking: $2.75) has a literary and emotional thrill in store for himself that few books in our literature can provide. It is all the fine adjectives with which the critics have labeled it. It is great propaganda and great art, and will do honor to a Pulitzer award next May: this is not extravagance; Steinbeck's novel is one of the few perfectly articulated soarings of genius of which American literature can boast. One must go to Melville, Poe, and Whitman for comparisons. But there have been other fine novels, too. Of them all perhaps these four have appealed most to me: John Marquand's "Wickford Point" (Little Brown: $2.75), because it is so far the year's most scintillant satire; Pearl Buck's "The Patriot" (John Day: $2.50) because it so movingly describes in human terms the insanity of the Sino-Japanese war; C. S. Forster's trilogy, "Captain Horatio Hornblower" (Little Brown: $2.75), nautical adventuring in the grand manner; and T. H. White's "The Sword in the Stone" (Putnams: $2.50), as refreshing a fantasy as "Alice in Wonderland."

Novels and Short Stories

I have only room enough to mention other distinguished works of fiction: Nevil Shute's war study, "Ordeal" (Morrow: $2.50); Sholem Asch's picture of Jewish pioneer life, "Song of the Valley" (Putnams: $2.00); Elizabeth Page's epic of the revolution, "The Tree of Liberty" (Farrar and Rinehart: $3.00); Helen Hull's portrait of modern American family life, "Frost Flower" (Coward McCann: $2.50); Irving Fineman's "doctor" novel, "Dr. Addams" (Random House: $2.75); Dorothy Canfield's heartening message of New England idealism, "Seasoned Timber" (Harcourt, Brace: $2.50); Ben Ames Williams' romantic tale of Nantucket in 1812, "Thread of Scarlet" (Houghton, Mifflin: $2.50); Bess Streeter Aldrich's "Song of Years" (Appleton-Century: $2.75); Rupert Hughes' "Stately Timber" (Scribner's: $2.75); Elizabeth Bowen's "The Death of the Heart" (Knopf: $2.50); Cecil Robert's "They Wanted to Live" (Macmillan: $2.50), and John Jennings' "Next to Valour" (Macmillan: $2.75).

There have been some notable short stories. The best short story of the year is Kressman Taylor's heart rending and harrowing "Address Unknown" (Simon and Schuster: $1.00). Two excellent volumes of collected stories are Dorothy Parker's "Here Lies" (Viking: $3.00), and Jerome Weldman's "The Horse that Could Whistle Dixie" (Simon and Schuster: $2.50).

In non-fiction there have been several memorable contributions. Robert Frost (Hold: $5.00) and Robert P. Tristram Coffin (Macmillan: $3.00) have both collected their rich harvests of poems, and Edna St. Vincent Millay has written superb new sonnets and songs in "Huntsman, What Quarry?" (Harper's: $2.00).

Nineteen hundred and thirty-nine has been particularly generous in the autobiographical department--such fascinating life-stories as Edna Ferber's "A Particular Treasure" (Doubleday, Doran: $3.00), Pierre van Passen's "Days of Our Years" (Hillman, Curl: $3.50), William Lyon Phelps' "Auto-biography with Letters" (Oxford University Press: $3.75), Nora Waln's "Reaching for the Stars" (Little Brown: $3.00), and Mrs. Woodrow Wilson's "My Memoir" (Bobbs, Merrill: $3.50), all enjoying deserved recognition and popularity. The biographers have not been nearly so prolific; only Townsend Scudder's pleasant portrait of the Carlyles in "Jane Welsh Carlyle" (Mac-millan: $3.50) may be singled out.

Politics and Economics

In the field of politics and economics three books stand clear: the two translations of Adolf Hitler's "Mein Kampf" (Reynal & Hitchcock: $3.00; Stackpole: $3.00). Charles and Mary Beard's massive history of the United States in the last decade, "America in Mid-Passage" (Macmillan: $3.50), and John Gunther's indispensable volume on the Orient, "Inside Asia" (Harpers: $3.50). Deserving of mention in this category are Vera Michele Dean's analysis of Europe's crisis, "Europe in Retreat" (Knopf: $2.00); Lewis Mumford's fiery plea for Americanism, "Men Must Act" (Harcourt, Brace: $1.50), Mordecai Ezekiel's plan for balancing our production and consumption, "Jobs for All" (Knopf: $2.00); Quincy Howe's "Blood Is Cheaper Than Water" (Simon and Schuster: $2.00), and G.E.R. Gedye's "Betrayal in Central Europe" (Harpers: $3.50).

If your interest is race, Herbert Seligman's "Race Against Man" (Putnam: $2.75) is the book for you; if crime, read Earnest Hooton's "Crime and the Man" (Harvard University Press: $3.75); if essays, either Christopher Morley's engaging "Letters of Askance" (Lippincott: $2.50) or Rollo Walter Brown's shrewd comments on contemporary America, "I Travel by Train" (Appleton-Century: $3.00); if photographs, the Stephen Day Press pictorial of "Life Along the Connecticut River" ($3.75), and if pure unadulterated entertainment the clever concatenations of facts in Neal O'Hara's "Take It from Me" (Waverly House: $1.95).

And take it from me, there is a summer reading list varied enough in its suggestions to satisfy all tastes, moods, minds, conceits, and curiosities. Relax and read!

From *The Boston Herald* (June 1939), Sec. A, p. 7.

Farm Tenancy Central Theme of Steinbeck (Review)

Fritz Raley Simmons

A few months ago, many of us saw in the newsreels the great mounds of oranges that had been dumped in California. We looked at those hills of gleaming fruit and thought of the thousands of children suffering from malnutrition. Some of us talked about it. But that's all we did. One man sat down and wrote a book. It is such a powerful book that two printings were exhausted before the book was ever published. It is selling faster than any book on the American market. And it is said that a Hollywood moving picture company paid a fortune for the picture rights so they could shelve the book for good. They had good reason to see the story was never told again, in picture form.

"The Grapes of Wrath," by John Steinbeck, is not the kind of book that usually makes a best seller. It is terrific writing, but it is the kind of writing that makes one think and think hard. And it is especially disturbing to the kind of people who can afford to buy books.

In brief, "The Grapes of Wrath" is the story of the tenant farmers of Oklahoma. They lived a few years ago on the 20 and 40-acre plots that their great grandfathers had wrested from the wilderness. They had learned little since their grandfather's time. They planted the same old money crop over and over till the land was exhausted. When the rains came, and later the dry winds, the sickly vegetation was unable to hold the soil in place. Dust became master of the land. The farmers had to borrow enough money to tide them from one year to the next, from one crop expectancy to the next. The dust grew, and the farmers were swamped in debt. The banks demanded some return on their money. So they sent in tractors and plowed straight across field after field, doing with one steel monster what hundreds of men had not been able to do.

The little farmers were angry and bewildered. Over and over, they said that it was their father's land, and they wouldn't move. They blamed the tractors, saying that a tractor couldn't have a heart for the land. They tried to find a man to blame, but they were told it was the company that demanded return on its money. So by the hundreds of thousands they got into their second hand automobiles and migrated to California where they had heard one could work in the orchards.

In California they found huge farms that seemed as heartless as the tractors. Men who offered to pay 30 cents an hour for 800 men learned that they could pay 10 cents an hour because 5,000 men wanted work. The "Okies," as they were called, nearly starved. They were kicked from one camp to another, and hounded by police.

All the time, the Okies were kept from organizing. Because the planters knew that a hungry man is easily an angry man. And the Okies were finding that they suffered alone, but by helping one another and working together there was a kind of strength whose power they were just beginning to guess.

We will not attempt to tell the story of the Joad family, around whom the plot revolves. It is a vivid, living story. The people are crude in word and action. Yet they have a certain nobility of thought that justifies their being here. Ma Joad would have been a heroic character no matter what language she spoke. Tom Joad had the makings of a philosopher. Preacher Casy was a philosopher. He gave up preaching because he couldn't find a God to pray to. He went out in his version of the wilderness to think things over, and decided that all humanity had one soul, and that we were no good unless we functioned with that in mind.

There is no doubt left that John Steinbeck is one of the ablest, if not the ablest writer in the present scene. In this, his first full length novel, there is unity of form, and vividness of writing. His characterizations are superb. And there is majesty in the alternate chapters of the book.

When we started reading the book somebody was playing a piano sonata over the radio. We couldn't identify the music, but the soft, insistent notes kept falling into the pool of silence with a cumulative effect that built up into a climax that was as powerful as it was subdued. And that is the first chapter of "The Grapes of Wrath". It is a sonata in a minor key. It gets you.

From *Greensboro, N. C., Daily News* (July 1939), Sec. D, p.6.

John Steinbeck: Naturalism's Priest

Woodburn O. Ross

In a previous article on the work of Mr. John Steinbeck I tried to describe his basic ideas and mental processes and to interpret the "meaning" of his fiction, in a general way, in their light.[1] I wish now to approach his work from another point of view, trying to interpret not so much in terms of meanings as in those of values.

I

The triumph of naturalism as a popular philosophy has been so complete that many of us have perhaps forgotten the horror with which western Europe began to realize the implications of the new biology in the later nineteenth century. The very foundations of spiritual values seemed about to be swept away. A somewhat eminent Victorian, A.J. Balfour, writing in *The Foundations of Belief* (1894), puts the matter this way:

> According to the naturalistic philosophy. . .not only does there seem to be no ground, from the point of view of biology, for drawing a distinction in favor of any of the processes, physiological or psychological, by which the individual or the race is benefited; not only are we bound to consider the coarsest appetites, the most calculating selfishness, and the most devoted heroism, as all sprung from analogous causes and all evolved for similar objects, but we can hardly doubt that the august sentiments which

cling to the ideas of duty and sacrifice are nothing better than a device of Nature to trick us into the performance of altruistic actions.

But if, on the one hand, naturalism leveled values, on the other, by pointing to nature rather than to God as the source of value, it really deprived mankind of any suitable foundation for a moral code. Balfour says:

> I lay down two propositions. . . : (1) That, practically, human beings being what they are, no moral code can be effective which does not inspire, in those who are asked to obey it, emotions of reverence; and (2) that, practically, the capacity of any code to excite this or any other elevated emotion cannot be wholly independent of the origin from which those who accept that code suppose it to emanate.

Needless to say an impersonal nature inspires in him and, he thinks, in the rest of humanity none of these necessary emotions of reverence.

The development of the naturalistic point of view in the twentieth century has been accompanied by many of the results which Balfour feared. Western society now does experience difficulty in distinguishing between "the most calculating selfishness" and "the most devoted heroism," not simply because it is deceived by hypocrites, but because all ethics have tended to become purely relative and because permanent objective criteria by which acts can be measured are lacking. Theodore Dreiser states the case of the naturalist well in *The Titan*. Ethical principles, he explains, represent only a balance among the tensions to which the natural man is subject, and they certainly possess no transcendent validity. And in *Death in the Afternoon*, Ernest Hemingway, baffled by the difficulty of finding any adequate basis for morals, falls back upon the ultimate simplicity of "I know only that what is moral is what you feel good after."

On the other hand, persistent attempts have been made by some to resuscitate the sense of reverence, of a need for worship, and to use it, at least to some extent, to support principles of conduct. In literature such attitudes have been represented, for example, by the work of D.H. Lawrence, who completely rejected the rational sources of twentieth-century materialism and placed his trust in dark, subjective gods; and by that of Aldous Huxley, who has turned his face toward the East and has found in the ancient religions of India and China confirmation of the validity of the intuitive, mystical faith in which a small minority of his own people have always been willing to trust.

I suggest that much of the significance of the work of John Steinbeck lies in his partial affiliation with this movement. It is true, apparently, that to most readers he is a novelist interested in social reform. This interpretation of his work rests primarily upon certain obvious portions of *The Grapes of Wrath, Of Mice and Men, In Dubious Battle*, and, perhaps, upon the pamphlet *Their Blood is Strong*. But these works were products of the great depression, and he has written nothing like them since. Indeed, Steinbeck shows a distinct tendency to shift his apparent interests with the times. But beneath his frequent changes of subject, at which reviewers marvel, he has maintained relatively unchanged certain fundamental attitudes, which have controlled his treatment of his subjects. It is these attitudes which we shall now consider, and we shall find that they lead us far from any discussion of social reform.

II

Unlike D.H. Lawrence and the current Aldous Huxley, Steinbeck is, up to a certain point, the complete naturalist; he accepts the scientists' representation of life. *Sea of Cortez*, in fact, suggests that his interest in biology verges on the professional. He emphasizes in his stories and novels the value of human acts and attitudes which he considers in harmony with natural law. Junius Maltby in *The Pastures of Heaven* pays for his love of the natural life with the lives of his wife and two children and, to the scandal of the neighbors, raises a third child without regard to artificial, civilized values; and Steinbeck apparently sympathizes with Maltby throughout. He leads the reader to dislike the stiff, unnatural garden of Mary Teller in *The Long Valley*. His friendly description of "natural" conduct in *Tortilla Flat* and *Cannery Row* is, of course, familiar. To a great extent, though not completely, Steinbeck accepts the ethical implications which many have seen in natural science. One need only mention, for instance, the Lopez sisters in *The Pastures of Heaven* and refer again to "the boys" of *Cannery Row* and to the Joads to make this fact clear. His position, in so far as he is a naturalist, appears to be the common place one that, since humanity is a product of natural forces and since the profoundest biological urge is the urge for life, for survival and reproduction, then virtue consists in whatever furthers these ends. "There would seem," he writes in *Sea of Cortez*, "to be only one commandment for living things: Survive!"

Steinbeck's naturalistic ideas have clearly done much to determine the character of the fiction which he writes. Yet to describe him as a naturalist is in one sense false. The description is incomplete; for, while never repudiating the points of view which I have just described, he amalgamates them with others which many would consider contradictory; and the resulting body of thought is, I think, significant.

In trying to describe this other side of his work, I shall begin with a quality which is the result of an emotional bias rather than an intellectual conviction. Steinbeck's writing is outside the strict scientific, naturalistic tradition, in that it is not objective. Steinbeck loves whatever he considers "natural" and is keenly sensitive to its emotional values. In *Sea of Cortez* one of the reasons which he advances against teleological thinking is that thinking in terms of ends obscures spontaneous affection for whatever is, an affection which is the most important reaction that man should have to the world about him. He clearly loves human beings whom he considers to be living natural lives--the Joads, the *paisanos*, "the boys," and the characters of deficient mentality who appear often in his pages. A sensitiveness to the atmosphere of a piece of land, a recognition of a mysterious spirit of place, is a striking quality of his work. His love of the natural extends to naturalistic ethics; he loves natural behavior. He writes in *Sea of Cortez*:

> We sat on a crate of oranges and thought what good men most biologists are, the tenors of the scientific world--temperamental, moody, lecherous, loud-laughing, and healthy. . . . He must, so know the starfish and the student biologist who sits at the feet of living things, proliferate in all directions.
> . . . Your true biologist will sing you a song as loud and off-key as will a blacksmith, for he knows that morals are too often diagnostic of prostatitis and stomach ulcers.

The sympathetically drawn Grampa, in *The Grapes of Wrath*, is almost as virtuous as a biologist:

> He fought and argued, told dirty stories. He was as lecherous as always. Vicious and cruel and impatient, like a frantic child, and the whole structure overlaid with amusement. He drank too much when he could get it, ate too much when it was there, talked too much all the time.

Second, Steinbeck's ethical system, which, as we have thus far seen it, finds ultimate virtue only in obedience to the natural law which demands reproduction and survival, is in reality complicated by the introduction of a second major virtue, whose demands must be expected at times to be contrary to those of the former. It is altruism. Altruism is one basis of the satisfaction which the beaten-up radicals feel in "The Raid," a story in *The Long Valley*. It is certainly entangled among the inspiring emotions experienced by the narrator in "Breakfast." It is one of the forces motivating

Mac and Jim Nolan, the strike organizers in *In Dubious Battle*. It frequently controls the actions of the poor in *The Grapes of Wrath*--perhaps, indeed, too frequently for the novel to be wholly convincing. It is dramatically expressed by the final act of Rose of Sharon, as she feeds a starving man at her own breast. Indeed, I believe that throughout the entire body of Steinbeck's work he excites admiration for characters who in some fashion love their brothers as constantly as he does for those who prove that they can be natural. But he does not support his emphasis upon altruism by any scientific reasoning. The cause of his acceptance of this virtue seems to lie in his own affections, in his love of all nature, human included.

In the third place, Steinbeck has developed ideas about the unity of the cosmos which may fairly be called "mystical," ideas which, of course, ultimately go considerably beyond what his scientific naturalism would support but which are, I think, connected with his love of the natural. His notion of the unity of things is complicated, but in its simplest aspects, as might be expected, it is presented as a conclusion which goes but little beyond what is warranted by scientific observation. In reporting in *Sea of Cortez*, for example, the semiscientific expedition which he made to the Gulf of Lower California with Mr. E. F. Ricketts, he writes:

> There are colonies of pelagic tunicates which have taken a shape like the finger of a glove. Each member of the colony is an individual animal, but the colony is another individual animal, not at all like the sum of its individuals. Some of the colonists, girdling the open end, have developed the ability, one against the other, of making a pulsing movement very like muscular action. Others of the colonists collect the food and distribute it, and the outside of the glove is hardened and protected against contact. Here are two animals, and yet the same thing--something the early Church would have been forced to call a mystery.

Most of this passage could have been written by any conventional scientist, intent upon reporting his unusual observation of this experience in nature; but at the end there is a hint of Steinbeck's seeing hidden meanings, not quite understood.

Another passage, however, still from *Sea of Cortez*, will make more clear what he is thinking:

> . . . It seems that species are only commas in a sentence, that each species is at once the point and the base of a pyramid, that all life is relational to the point where an Einsteinian relativity seems to emerge. And then not only meaning but the feeling about species grows misty. One merges into another, groups melt into ecological groups until the time when what we

know as life meets and enters what we think of as non-life: barnacle and
rock, rock and earth, earth and tree, tree and rain and air. And the units
nestle into the whole and are inseparable from it. Then one can come back
to the microscope and the tide pool and the aquarium. But the little
animals are found to be changed, no longer set apart and alone. And it is
strange that most of the feeling we call religious, most of the mystical
outcrying which is one of the most prized and used and desired reactions
of our species, is really the understanding and the attempt to say that man
is related to the whole thing, related inextricably to all reality, known and
unknowable. This is a simple thing to say, but the profound feeling of it
made a Jesus, a St. Augustine, a St. Francis, a Roger Bacon, a Charles
Darwin, and an Einstein. Each of them in his own tempo and with his own
voice discovered and reaffirmed with astonishment the knowledge that all
things are one thing and that one thing is all things. . . .

Scientific interests lie behind all these passages; Steinbeck is concerned with
the organization and the interpretation of the observations which he and his
colleague made. But he cannot rest content with the naturalist's world of
sense experience. His grasping at mystical insight grows more evident as
one reads. The very list of names which he gives above is suggestive of the
ideological blend which he is trying to make: "Jesus. . . St. Francis. . .
Charles Darwin."

Finally, let me quote one more passage from *Sea of Cortez*, one which
goes still further in implying on the part of Steinbeck a mystical belief in the
oneness of creation:

Sometimes we asked of the Indians the local names of animals we had
taken, and then they consulted together. They seemed to live on
remembered things, to be so related to the seashore and the rocky hills and
the loneliness that they are these things. To ask about the country is like
asking about themselves. "How many toes do you have?" "What, toes?
Let's see--of course, ten. I have known them all my life, I never thought
to count them. Of course it will rain tonight. Of course, I am the whole
thing, now that I think about it. I ought to know when I will rain."

I have selected material demonstrating Steinbeck's mystical ideas of the
unity of things entirely from *Sea of Cortez*, because this work is expository
and the ideas are consequently presented here more directly than elsewhere
in his work. But to forestall a possible objection to the effect that this
attitude may have been transitory, let me point out that the conclusion of *To
a God Unknown*, one of his earliest novels, asserts the unity of the hero with
the universe--as a matter of fact, he is said to be the rain--and that *The Moon
is Down*, one of the latest of his novels, sees an invaded community as a

group strikingly like his schools of fish which "turn as a unit and dive as a unit."

Steinbeck never explains the nature of the unity of the cosmos which he perceives. How can his colonies of fish form a single creature? What is the nature of the consciousness of this larger being? In just what sense is a man the rain? Manifestly, he lacks data with which to answer; indeed, he is never able rationally to prove that the unity about which he speaks exists at all. But the fact that his notions about the unity of things are very incomplete and rest upon feeling, insight, intuition, rather than upon reason is neither here nor there. The fact is that as an artist he believes in these things. They represent a part of Steinbeck which is not controlled by scientific rationalism.

The fourth and last aspect of Steinbeck's thought which cannot be called naturalistic is yet harder to describe. We have already seen him referring to part of the organization of nature as "something the early Church would have been forced to call a mystery." A sense of mystery, of significance which is not quite open to rational understanding, appears at least occasionally in Steinbeck. It is more than a perception of a strange unity in the universe, though, as what we have just seen would indicate, the exact nature of the unity is indeed a part of the mystery. It is a feeling that there is a meaning in things which forever eludes explanation in terms of knowledge which is simply organized sense experience. Some words of Elizabeth, the wife of Joseph Wayne in *To a God Unknown*, help to show us how Steinbeck feels. She says at the close of the festival described in the book:

> It was such an odd day. There was such an awkwardness, the people coming and the man at the feasting and then the dance, and last of all the storm. Am I being silly, Joseph, or was there a meaning, right under the surface? It seems like those pictures of simple landscapes they sell in the cities. When you look closely, you see all kinds of figures hidden in the lines. Do you know the kind of pictures I mean? A rock becomes a sleeping wolf, a little cloud is a skull, and the line of trees marching soldiers when you look closely. Did the day seem like that to you, Joseph, full of hidden meaning, not quite understandable?

Steinbeck's perception of a mysterious significance in things is responsible for another episode in the book. Near the end of the story Joseph comes upon a strange man who lives at the end of a little peninsula jutting out into the Pacific Ocean. He lives there in order to be the last man on the continent to see the sun go down; and each evening as it sinks he kills some animal as a sacrifice. "You really want to know why I watch the sun--why I kill some little creature as it disappears?" he says. ". . .I don't know. . . . I have made up reasons, but they aren't true. I have said to myself, 'The sun is life. I give life to life. I make a symbol of the sun's death.' When I made up these reasons I knew they weren't true." Joseph broke in, "These were words to clothe a naked thing, and the thing is ridiculous in clothes."

III

Now much of Steinbeck's basic position is essentially religious, though not in any orthodox sense of the word. In his very love of nature he assumes an attitude characteristic of mystics. He is religious in that he contemplates man's relation to the cosmos and attempts, although perhaps fumblingly, to understand it. He is religious in that he seeks to transcend scientific explanations based upon sense experience. He is religious in that from time to time he explicitly attests the holiness of nature. Sometimes it is a mysterious plot of land which inspires him. In *To a God Unknown* Joseph Wayne, coming upon a curiously secretive glade, says to his brother: "Be still a moment, Tom. . . .There's something here. You are afraid of it, but I know it. Somewhere, perhaps in an old dream, I have seen this place, or perhaps felt the feeling of this place. . . . This is holy--and this is old. This is ancient--and holy." In *The Grapes of Wrath* Casy finds holiness in the unity of nature: ". . .There was the hills, an' there was me, an' we wasn't separate no more. We was one thing. An' that one thing was holy. . . ." And later he sees holiness in life itself: "All that lives," he says, "is holy." Steinbeck even finds holiness in "natural" conduct which, measured by conventional standards, would be found immoral. "Gonna lay in the grass, open an' honest with anybody that'll have me," says Casy. "Gonna cuss an' swear an' hear the poetry of folks talkin'. All that's holy, an' that's what I didn' understan'. All them things is good things."

Overtones of religious character are to be heard in Steinbeck's latest book, *The Wayward Bus*. It is, I think, significant that the phrase "El Gran Poder de Jesus" has been painted over on the bumper of the bus and the word "Sweetheart" put in its place. The bumper-palimpsest is, I take it, a symbol of the substitution by a wicked generation of a superficial interest in sex for a profound sense of the nature and reality of things. It is likewise worth noticing that Juan Chicoy, the hero, communes with an image of the Virgin as he drives. This is not to imply that Steinbeck represents him as an orthodox Christian. But to Juan the image is a kind of talisman, something in which he does not believe rationally but to which the depths of his mind do respond. A primitive part of his nature, uncomplicated by reason, finds in this image itself, in an animistic fashion, power, wisdom, and sympathy. Steinbeck seems to approve of these "natural," half-religious, half-superstitious gropings of Juan. They are of a piece with the rest of the unintellectual, instinctive conduct which makes him the hero of the book. Again, the command "Repent" printed on the cliff above the stalled bus can hardly be without symbolic significance. Steinbeck never says what is to be repented of. But, if one reads the book in the context of Steinbeck's previous work, one may be sure that the warning is directed not against any conventional sins but against failure to accept life and nature as they are and against failure to love life and man, to feel the mystery and unity of creation.

IV

Nineteenth-century fears that the development of naturalism meant the end of reverence, of worship, and of "august sentiments" are not warranted in the case of Steinbeck. He has succeeded in taking the materials which undermined the religious faith of the nineteenth century and fusing them with a religious attitude in the twentieth, though a religious attitude very different from what the orthodox in the nineteenth century would have thought possible. Nature as described by the scientist becomes not merely the foundation of a revolutionary ethic; it also supplies, as many in the nineteenth century thought it could not, the basis of a sense of reverence which affectively supports the new ethic, now surprisingly turned altruistic. Steinbeck is, I think, the first significant novelist to begin to build a mystical religion upon a naturalistic base. The important question, as yet, of course, unanswerable, is to what extent he, or the mystical movement with which he has affiliations, will prove influential in this century. Certainly, the Western world is gasping in the religious vacuum into which it has been plunged. It seeks an affective relationship with the universe. Steinbeck's answer is arresting for the reason that it does not require the West to forget or deny what it has learned about nature in the last hundred years, as, for instance, D.H. Lawrence's solution did. Steinbeck is in the current of positive scientific thought; in that respect he does not swim upstream. Yet he is both rational and irrational: he accepts all that reason can tell him and permits his intuition and affections to add what they will to the world created by reason and to determine his position toward the universe as it then appears.

This new religious attitude which Steinbeck, at least in some vague way, has been able to construct for himself out of unpromising materials bears on it the marks of its perilous birth. It is extremely primitive. It rejects more than two thousand years of theological thought. It abandons all attempts to discern the final purposes in life. It virtually reduces man again to animism; for, unlike Wordsworth, Steinbeck does not see through nature to a God beyond; he hears no intimations of immortality; for him there is no spirit which rolls through all things. There is only nature, ultimately mysterious, to which all things belong, bound together in a unity concerning whose stupendous grandeur he can barely hint. But such a nature Steinbeck loves, and before it, like primitive man, he is reverent.

In brief, the significance of Steinbeck's work may prove to lie in the curious compromise which it effects. It accepts the intuitive, nonrational method of dealing with man's relation to the universe--the method of the contemporary mystics. But, unlike them, it accepts as the universe to which man must relate himself the modern, scientifically described cosmos.

From *College English* (May 1949), 432-38.

Note

1. "John Steinbeck: Earth and Stars," Studies in Honor of A. H. R. Fairchild ("University of Missouri Studies," Vol. XXI, No. 1 [Columbia, Mo., 1946), pp. 177-91.

Proletarian Leanings

George F. Whicher

A sympathetic observer, by no means committed to the Communist party line, produced the most effective proletarian stories, one of the best strike novels, and a piece of documentary propaganda in fictional form which rivals *Uncle Tom's Cabin*. Because his interest was primarily in people rather than political measures, his work has never been considered quite satisfactory by left-wing leaders. Needless to say it has not found favor with conservative readers.

John Steinbeck (1902-   ) grew up in the Salinas Valley of California, where as a boy he worked enough in truck-gardens and fruit orchards to know the feel of the land and to establish first-hand acquaintance with migratory workers. Desultory schooling at Leland Stanford at various periods gave him a knowledge of the craft of writing. At twenty-seven he published a first novel dealing somewhat romantically with the career of the seventeenth-century buccaneer Sir Henry Morgan. In the short stories of ranch people collected as *The Pastures of Heaven* (1932) and in a second novel touched by agrarian mysticism, *To a God Unknown* (1933), he found his natural subject. Like Sherwood Anderson, he could project himself into the personalities of simple folk who lived primitively near the level of bare subsistence. He rapidly made literary capital of the section of California which he knew by heart.

Five successive books, all of them palpable hits, brought him to national prominence. *Tortilla Flat* (1935), a series of short stories presenting a happy-go-lucky group of *paisanos* near Monterey, mingles as many literary strains, from *Don Quixote* to the *Little Flowers of St. Francis*, as the assorted bloods which blend in the nondescript characters. The result is an amusing comic cycle, but of a somewhat factitious kind when compared, for instance, with Erskine Caldwell's tales of Southern crackers. Steinbeck's *paisanos* are never humanly vicious; they are everlastingly funny and cute.

It is difficult to strike the note of tragedy if the persons of the drama have no more dignity than chipmunks. For that reason Steinbeck's *Of Mice and Men* (1937), a streamlined novelette easily transformed into a play, possesses a superficial effectiveness but no lasting significance. Nominally the action of the ranch-hand George, who shoots his witless pal Lennie to save him from being lynched, is tragic, but the sympathies of the reader have been so powerfully alienated by the psychopathic weaknesses of Lennie that tragic emotion seems out of place. The ultimate effect is merely one of unpleasant shock.

Two short stories in the volume called *The Long Valley* (1938) successfully avoid the facility which is Steinbeck's greatest failing. "Chrysanthemums" is a fairly subtle character study of a middle-aged rancher's wife--a story that reveals a long advance in sureness of understanding on the author's part. "The Red Pony" is a poignant treatment of a boy's discovery of the heartless cruelty of natural law. In these stories Steinbeck's artistry in the depicting of human beings comes to full mastery.

His interest in social injustice, the second major theme of his work, first became evident in his novel describing a strike of migratory fruit pickers, *In Dubious Battle* (1936). The author's sympathies are decidedly with the oppressed laborers, whose wages have been reduced below a living standard, and with the Communist agitators who organize them to battle for a right to live. But his attitude, as reflected in the speeches of the Doctor, is experimental and philosophical. The book, despite its vivid justification of the workers, cannot be taken as revolutionary propaganda, and hence it was greeted with marked coolness by advocates of social overturn.

The chance of a lifetime for a novel of social significance came when the climax of the drought cycle in the nineteen-thirties forced thousands of tenant farmers in the Southwest to leave the "Dust Bowl" area in search of a land of promise. The majority of them swelled the ranks of itinerant labor in the lush but preempted valleys of California, creating extreme and sometimes insol-uble problems of adjustment for the local inhabitants. It would be too much to say that these problems were always squarely faced or wisely handled. There was undoubtedly much unscrupulous exploitation of the dispossessed farmers, some needless brutality and the usual inclination to deny the existence of the crisis as long as possible. Steinbeck with his highly developed and almost biological interest in proletarian behavior saw at once the rich possibilities which this folk-exodus offered. With a photographer he toured the line of march of the fleeing tenants, visiting roadside camps and "Hoovervilles," collecting information and compiling a pictorial record of the movement. He was then ready to put together the "propaganda novel" of the century, *The Grapes of Wrath* (1939).

The traditional techniques of fiction demanded that the situation should be dramatized in the story of a typical group of persons, and this Steinbeck achieved by the creation of the Joad family. He managed to include in the twelve members of the tribe, plus the supernumerary Casy who travels with them, practically the full gamut of types which the region offered, but only one of the group attained the status of a fully individualized personality. In Ma Joad we encounter one of the great authentic people of fiction. The rest are puppets with differentiating traits.

The figure of Casy, the one-time camp meeting exhorter, serves as a spokesman for the philosophic overtones of the book. He does not represent any dogmatic religious or political creed. He is observant, reflective, brooding, and puzzled, a kind of grass-roots Emerson clinging to a badly damaged optimism. In him we recognize the faith of the plain people, who know that they can be hurt but who refuse to believe that they can be permanently crushed.

The most original feature of the novel consists of the combination of the epic story of the Joads with "intercalary chapters" which sketch aspects of the historical background much after the fashion of the documentary film. Steinbeck had studied with profit such recent experiments in documentary pictures as Pare Lorentz's *The Plow that Broke the Plains* and *The River*, and the same creator's radio drama *Ecce Homo*. The lessons of these new techniques he successfully applied to the novel.

There is brilliant writing in *The Grapes of Wrath*, memorable description, episodes of moving power, forceful exposition of social injustice. Yet on reflection the final impression left by the novel is not of the author's indignation so much as of his cleverness as a contriver of effects. This is particularly true in relation to the final scene, in which Rosasharn offers the milk of her breast to keep life in a starving vagrant. Was it to indulge in such a moment of maudlin sentiment, cheaply derived from de Maupassant, that Steinbeck has carried us through the anabasis of the Okies? If so, the reader can hardly avoid feeling let down. That many experienced some such disappointment was evidenced by the reaction provoked by the book. The most insistent protest came from readers who were revolted by the bits of scatological realism and obscenity with which Steinbeck had salted his pages. For some, at least, the spectacle of human misery was less compulsive than the shock to their feelings of propriety.

In the ten years that have elapsed since *The Grapes of Wrath* was published, Steinbeck has done little to enhance his reputation. His next book was a study of marine biology, written in collaboration with a professional naturalist, and he has written during and since the war several pieces of competent special reporting. The three new ventures in fiction that he has produced represent a serious slackening of his grasp. His facile anti-Nazi novel, *The Moon is Down* (1942), is a slick and stagey performance--it was immediately dramatized--which suffers in comparison with a forthright, hard-hitting book like *The Cross and the Arrow* by Albert Maltz. *Cannery Row* (1945) and *The Wayward Bus* (1947) are relapses to the mixture of sordidness and whimsy of his earlier work. The sentimentality which deluges these books like cheap perfume is not a satisfactory substitute for a thorough emotional cleaning up.

In Arthur Hobson Quinn, ed. *The Literature of the American People: An Historical and Critical Survey* (New York: Appleton-Century-Crofts, 1951), 958-61

The Grapes of Wrath

Joseph Fontenrose

Shortly after the publication of *In Dubious Battle*, the novel in which he first gave attention to the plight of migrant farm laborers in California, John Steinbeck made a tour of "Hoovervilles," the itinerant workers' camps, in the Salinas and San Joaquin valleys. He picked fruit and cotton beside the field laborers and reported his observations of their living and working conditions to the *San Francisco News* in a series of articles called "The Harvest Gypsies" (October, 1936), later republished in pamphlet form as *"Their Blood is Strong"* (1938). Some of this material went into the interchapters of *The Grapes of Wrath*. The harvesters of California crops were no longer Mexicans and Orientals; now most of them were Okies and Arkies, families that had been evicted from their farms in Oklahoma, Arkansas, Kansas, Texas, and neighboring states. They had been tenant farmers or sharecroppers, burdened with heavy mortgages, and natural and economic forces had conspired to force them off the lands which they had called home. Dust storms and erosion exhausted the land and completed what economic depression had begun. The banks and the agricultural corporations (creatures of the banks) found it more profitable to foreclose mortgages and terminate tenancies, combine many farms into one plantation, and put it all to cotton. One man with a tractor could work an entire plantation for wages of three dollars a day. So the farmers and their families were evicted-- tractored off, their land plowed under and their houses pushed in, if they failed to leave promptly. Many went west to California, having heard or read that men were needed to pick the crops there.

In the fall of 1937, while returning from New York and Pennsylvania, where he had worked on the stage version of *Of Mice and Men*, Steinbeck drove through Oklahoma, joined migrants who were going west, and worked with them in the fields after they reached California. *The Grapes of Wrath* is thus a product of his own experience and direct observation; its realism is genuine. He was dissatisfied with his first attempt to deal with the displaced farmers' experiences in California, "L'Affaire Lettuceberg," completed in 1938, and would not allow its publication. Beginning anew, he produced *The Grapes of Wrath*, which was published in April, 1939.

It is the story of the Joad family's experiences from their eviction in Oklahoma to their first winter in California. There were twelve in the family, including Connie Rivers, Rose of Sharon's husband. Young Tom Joad was paroled from prison, where he had been serving a term for manslaughter, just in time to join them on their westward journey. With the Joads went Jim Casy, once a revivalist preacher. Starting off with little money and few possessions, having had to sell stock, implements, and furniture at outrageously low prices, they traveled in an old Hudson sedan converted into a truck. The trip took several days. Both Grampa and Granma died on the way, and Noah, Tom's retarded older brother, left them at the Colorado River. From the day of their entry into California at Needles they experienced the hostility of California policemen and residents. The second day, camping in a Hooverville near Bakersfield, they saw the misery and hunger of the migrant workers and the arrogance and cruelty of deputy sheriffs. Connie Rivers deserted them, and Jim Casy was arrested for striking an officer. Leaving the Hooverville just before vigilantes came to burn it, the Joads came to a federal government camp for farm workers where they stayed for a month, enjoying the friendliness, cleanliness, and self-government of this institution. But there was no work in that neighborhood at the time, aside from a short-term job that Tom found. When they no longer had money or food, they drove northwards and found work picking peaches on the Hooper ranch, which provided miserable lodgings and an overcharging company store. The Joads were unwitting strikebreakers, and Tom discovered that Casy, after a short time in jail, was now a strike leader. As Tom talked with Casy, vigilantes attacked the strike committee's tent. When a man killed Casy with a club, Tom seized the club and killed the attacker, receiving in turn a severe blow on his face from another vigilante. Keeping Tom under cover because of his swollen face, the Joads left the Hooper ranch and went to the cotton fields. While they worked, Tom remained hidden in the thickets nearby, until his young sister Ruth was heard boasting to other children that her big brother had killed a man and was then in hiding. Fearing discovery, Tom left his family, after telling his mother that he was going to carry on Casy's work for union of the farm laborers to demand justice. After the cotton picking there was no work for three months. The heavy winter rains came and swelled a creek's waters until the squatters' camp was flooded, just when Rose of Sharon bore a stillborn infant. The Joads took refuge in an old barn on higher ground, where they found a starving man whom Rose of Sharon fed from her breast.

There the story ends in *media res*. Some readers have objected to the closing scene, in which the young mother who lost her child suckles a grown man. The episode not only has folkloristic and literary antecedents, as Professor Celeste Wright has shown, but for Steinbeck it is an oracular image, forecasting in a moment of defeat and despair the final triumph of the people--a contingent forecast, for only if the people nourish and sustain one another will they achieve their ends. More than that, the episode represents the novel's most comprehensive thesis, that all life is one and holy, and that every man in Casy's words, "jus' got a little piece of a great big soul." The Joads' intense feelings of family loyalty have been transcended; they have expanded to embrace all men. Another image could have symbolized this universality, but, for Steinbeck, perhaps no other could have done it so effectively.

The novel has thirty chapters, fourteen of which carry the Joad story. The other sixteen chapters (called interchapters even though the first chapter is one of them) take little more than one sixth of the book and are either expository essays or sketches of typical situations in the great migration. They present the social, economic, and historical background, telling the story of all the migrants. With two exceptions the general experiences described in an interchapter are illustrated by the Joads' experiences in the following narrative chapter. Some of these interchapters are masterpieces in themselves. Chapter Seven is chiefly the monologue of a dealer in secondhand cars, who talks to customers, helpers, and himself in quick staccato sentences, revealing his coarse and inhuman avarice. Chapter five-- describing the bank, the tractor, and the tractor driver--presents a dramatic instance of the eviction of a family, and we see vividly what must have happened to the Joads; then, in Chapter Six as the narrative resumes, we see the completed act and its consequences. The roadside hamburger stand is as finally and definitively done in Chapter Fifteen as is the train ride in Wolfe's *Of Time and the River*.

As Lisca has pointed out, Steinbeck uses a variety of prose styles in these interchapters. In these short sketches he could experiment, endeavoring in each to evoke both a vivid picture of something that happened and a feeling tone. He employs paratactic Biblical language, go-getter talk, conversational narrative in Okie speech, the sound track of documentary films. Some interchapters are literally poetic. As Lisca shows, if we convert the ostensibly prose sentences into an arrangement of phrases, we get irregularly rhythmic verses that recall the Psalms or Whitman or perhaps Sandburg. An example of this metrical prose in folk-dance pattern may be seen in Chapter Twenty-Three, describing Saturday night dances in the government camps, where the sentences fall into the Chicken Reel rhythm:

> Look at that Texas boy, long legs loose,
> taps four times for ever' damn step.
> Never seen a boy swing aroun' like that.
> Look at him swing that Cherokee girl,
>
> red in her cheeks an' her toe points out.
> Look at her pant, look at her heave.
> Think she's tired? Think she's winded?
> Well, she ain't.
>
> Texas boy got his hair in his eyes,
> mouth's wide open, can't get air,
> but he pats four times for ever' darn step,
> an' he'll keep a-going with the Cherokee girl.

The Grapes of Wrath has little plot in the ordinary sense; there is no complex involvement of character with character, no mesh of events. The story of the Joads could be the true story of a real family. But there is character development, as Tom Joad, "jus' puttin' one foot in front a the other" at first, gradually reaches an understanding of Casy's message and takes up Casy's mission. And the Joads as a whole progress from an exclusive concern for family interests to a broader vision of cooperation with all oppressed people. Lisca has pointed out that the plot consists of two downward movements balanced by two upward movements. As the Joad family's fortunes decline, the family morale declines, too: the family loses members and is threatened with dissolution. We can put the process another way: the family unit, no longer viable, fades into the communal unit, which receives from it the family's strength and values.

Collective persons are important characters in this novel too, since the plot movement must be expressed in group terms. It can be read as a story of conflicts and interactions among several group organisms: the Joad family (representative of all Okie families), the Shawnee Land and California Farmer's Association (the organization of big California agricultural corporations, controlled by the Bank of the West), and the workers' union, still immature as the story ends. The Joad family is a democratic, cooperative organism; it is a cohesive group, and yet no member loses his individual character in the group. When the Joads act as a family, they act as a unit: "And without any signal the family gathered by the truck, and the congress, the family government, went into session." It met beside the truck, "the active thing, the living principle," for it was now "the new hearth, the living center of the family." The Oklahoma land company is another sort of organism entirely. It is one of the monsters of Chapter Five which "don't breathe air, don't eat side-meat." Such creatures "breathe profits; they eat the interest on money. It is a sad thing, but it is so." "The bank is something else than men. It happens that every man in a bank hates what the bank does, and yet the bank does it." As Doc Burton said in *In Dubious Battle*, a group's ends may be entirely different from the ends of its individual members. The monster is the sort of organism that absorbs its members, drains them of their individualities, and makes them into organization men. The tractor is the monster visible: "Snub-nosed monsters, raising the dust and sticking their snouts into it, straight down the country, across the country, through fences, through dooryards, in and out of gullies in straight lines." As the bank officer to the bank, so the driver to the tractor:

> The man sitting in the iron seat did not look like a man; gloved, goggled, rubber dust mask over nose and mouth, he was a part of the monster, a robot in the seat. . . . A twitch at the controls could swerve the cat', but the driver's hands could not twitch because the monster that built the tractor, the monster that sent the tractor out, had somehow got into the driver's hands, into his brain and muscle, had goggled him and muzzled him-- goggled his mind, muzzled his speech, goggled his perception, muzzled his protest.

He had no feeling for the land that he plowed and planted. It was nothing to him whether the sown seeds germinated or not. "He ate without relish" a lunch of "sandwiches wrapped in waxed paper, . . . [and] a piece of pie branded like an engine part."

The monster is in fact Leviathan. In discussing *In Dubious Battle* I alluded to the relation of the group organism to Thomas Hobbes's symbol for the state as collective person, "that great LEVIATHAN, or rather, to speak more reverently, . . .that *mortal god*, to which we owe under the *immortal God*, our peace and defense." Steinbeck's monster is as despotic as Hobbes's

Leviathan, but hardly as beneficial to man.   He is rather the original
Leviathan of Isaiah 27 and Psalm 74, enemy of the Lord.   When Casy saw
what the tractor had done to the Joad farm, he said, "If I was still a preacher
I'd say the arm of the Lord had struck.   But now I don't know what
happened." He soon discovered the true culprit: Here's me that used to give
all my fight against the devil 'cause I figured the devil was the enemy. But
they's somepin worse'n the devil got hold a the country, an' it ain't gonna let
go till it's chopped loose. Ever see one a them Gila monsters take hold,
mister?" If this monster is a mortal god, he is seemingly invulnerable:
"Maybe there's nobody to shoot." But we have seen him, a visible god, in the
tractor with its "shining disks, cutting the earth with blades--not plowing but
surgery . . . And pulled behind the disks, the harrows combing with iron
teeth . . ." Thus, as a participant in the action, the group organism, like the
individual characters, takes on a mythical role, derived from the Biblical
substructure of the novel.

The Joad family fled the Oklahoma Leviathan, only to run into his
brother, the California Leviathan--the Farmers' Association and its typical
member, the Hooper ranch, a veritable prison with its barbed-wire fences
and armed guards--much the same sort of creature, but even meaner. It is the
Growers' Association of *In Dubious Battle*, and its image is not the tractor,
but the fat-rumped deputy carrying a gun in holster on his hip. In legend and
folktale it makes little difference whether the hero faces a dragon or an ogre.

Leviathan made easy prey of the little fishes, the separate family units.
But these units became the gametes of a larger organism, a union of all
migrant workers. On the road one family met another:

> And in the night one family camps in a ditch and another family pulls in
> and the tents come out. The two men squat on their hams and the women
> and children listen. Here is the node, you who hate change and fear
> revolution. Keep these two squatting men apart; . . .Here is the anlage of
> the thing you fear. This is the zygote. For here "I lost my land" is
> changed; a cell is split and from its splitting grows the thing you hate--"We
> lost *our* land." . . . And from this first "we" there grows a still more
> dangerous thing: "I have a little food" plus "I have none." If from this
> problem the sum is "We have a little food," the thing is on its way, the
> movement has direction. Only a little multiplication now, and this land,
> this tractor are ours.

In just this way the Joads and Wilsons met on the road; the Joads shared
their little money and food with the Wilsons, repaired the Wilsons' car, and
joined forces with them for the journey westward.

Then several families came together in roadside camps. Perhaps twenty families would camp together at a suitable place. "In the evening a strange thing happened: the twenty families became one family, the children were children of all. The loss of home became one loss, and the golden time in the West was one dream." A world was created every evening and dissolved every morning, and was then recreated the next evening, complete with government and laws. And the members, being group-men in a new kind of group, were changed accordingly: "They were not farm men any more, but migrant men. . . . That man whose mind had been bound with acres lived with narrow concrete miles." In Archibald MacLeish's words he now had only "the narrow acre of the road."

The democracy, self-government, and fraternity of the roadside camps blossomed more perfectly in the government camps, where men were orderly and harmonious without police. And the government camps, in which a minority of the migrants lived, were the model for the future commune of all workers. When Tom went away, near the end of the book, he said to his mother,

> "I been thinkin' how it was in that gov'ment camp, how our folks took care a theirselves, an' if they was a fight they fixed it theirself; an' they wasn't no cops wagglin' their guns, but they was better order than them cops ever give. I been a-wonderin' why we can't do that all over. Throw out the cops that ain't our people. All work together for our own thing--all farm our own lan'."

Shortly after lamenting that the family was breaking up, Ma Joad, soul of the Joad family, attained the larger vision, agreeing with Mrs. Wainwright that the Joads would help the Wainwrights if they needed help: "Or anybody. Use' ta be the fambly was fust. It ain't so now. It's anybody. Worse off we get, the more we got to do." At the end of the book the new collective organism is still in its infancy. This is the child that has been born, not Rose of Sharon's that was conceived of the selfish Connie Rivers; and her final act symbolizes this truth. It is a ritual act: she who cannot be mother of a family adopts the newly born collective person as represented by one of "the people [who] sat huddled together" in the barns when winter storms came. It is the family unity and strength imparted to the larger unit. In primitive adoption rituals the adopting mother offers her breast to the adopted child.

The conflict of organisms is necessarily an ecological struggle, a disturbance of an ecological cycle. In *Sea of Cortez* Steinbeck describes a potentially perfect ecological cycle. At Cape San Lucas in Lower California the fishermen catch tuna and bring their catch to the cannery; the entrails and other waste are thrown back into the water; small fish come in to eat this refuse and are caught for bait; the bait is used to catch tuna. But the cormorants "are the flies in a perfect ecological ointment"; for they prey on the bait-fish and tend to keep them away from the cannery shore. So the natives hate the cormorants as subversives. Just such a cycle operated in California agriculture, and the migrants, driven from their homes, were absorbed into it. The agricultural corporations and big growers need pickers in great numbers to harvest their manifold crops. In the thirties they advertised everywhere for pickers with the object of bringing in more job-seekers than they needed; with too many men on hand they could lower wages and increase profits. When one crop was picked, the workers had to hurry on to another crop, if they were to make a bare subsistence. They never stayed long enough in one county to qualify for relief, and so the growers were saved higher taxes. When the time for the next harvest approached, the growers advertised again for pickers, sending handbills everywhere to bring workers back in great numbers. But there were flies in this ointment too: labor leaders, radical agitators, socialists, made the pickers dissatisfied with wages and working conditions, organized them in unions, promoted strikes, and were cordially hated by the growers.

Critics, of course, have noticed the biological features of *The Grapes of Wrath*, but without realizing how literally the monster, the family unit, and the workers' commune are meant to be real organisms. In fact, the biological and organismic side of the novel has been slighted, if not ignored. The mythical side, however, has been much more fortunate, in marked contrast to the neglect of mythical themes and structure in earlier novels. The title suggests a Biblical parallel, since Julia Ward Howe's "vintage where the grapes of wrath are stored" obviously alludes to Revelation 14:19, "the great winepress of the wrath of God." Peter Lisca has accurately pointed to the principal mythical model: the exodus of the Hebrews from Egypt to Canaan. He shows that the novel's three well-marked divisions---drought (Chapters 1-10), journey (11-18), and sojourn in California (19-30)--correspond to oppression in Egypt, exodus, and settlement in Canaan: the drought and erosion are the plagues of Egypt; the banks and land companies are Pharaoh and the Egyptian oppressors; California is Canaan, a land flowing with milk and honey; and the Californians, like the Canaanites, are hostile to the immigrants. Lisca also indicates several specific parallels: the symbolism of grapes to indicate either abundance (Numbers 13:23) or wrath and vengeance (Deuteronomy 32:32); the migrants are "the people," and Ma Joad's words, "we're the people--we go on," suggest a chosen people; in the roadside camps the migrants, like the Hebrews, formulated codes of laws to govern themselves; finally, among the willows by a stream John Joad set Rose of Sharon's stillborn child afloat in an apple box, as the infant Moses was placed in a basket among flags in the river.

There are other parallels that Lisca does not mention. The name *Joad*, I am sure, is meant to suggest *Judah*. The Joads had lived in Oklahoma peacefully since the first settlement, as the Hebrews had lived in Egypt, which knew not Joseph" (Exodus 1:8); and the monster, representing a changed economic order, and quite as hard-hearted as Pharaoh, knew not the Joads and their kin. In Oklahoma the dust filtered into every house and settled on everything, as in one of the Egyptian plagues the dust became lice which settled on man and beast (Exodus 8:17); plants were covered, as locusts devoured every green thing in Egypt (Exodus 10:15); the dust ruined the corn, as hail ruined the Egyptians' flax and barley (Exodus 9:31); and it made the night as black as the plague of darkness in Egypt (Exodus 10:22 f.). On the eve of departure the Joads slaughtered two pigs, more likely victims in Oklahoma than the lambs sacrificed by the Hebrews on Passover (Exodus 12). But whereas the Hebrews despoiled the Egyptians of jewels before leaving (Exodus 12:35 f.), the Joads and other Okies were despoiled of goods and money by sharp businessmen in the land that they left.

On the journey the Joads crossed the Colorado (Red) River (Steinbeck does not mention their crossing the North Fork of the Red River on Highway 66, although he refers several times to the red country of Oklahoma) and the desert. Grampa and Granma Joad, like the elder Israelites, died on the way. Connie Rivers complained about the conditions into which the Joads had led him, and finally deserted them: the Hebrews continually murmured against their leaders on the ground that they were worse off in the desert than in Egypt, and Korah rebelled (Numbers 16). The migrants' fried dough was the unleavened bread of the Israelites, and both peoples longed for meat. The laws of the roadside camp, like the Mosaic law, forbade murder, theft, adultery, rape, and seduction; and they too included rules of sanitation, privacy, and hospitality. In the camps "a man might have a willing girl if he stayed with her, if he fathered her children and protected them," as in Exodus 22:16, "And if a man entice a maid that is not betrothed, and lie with her, he shall surely endow her to be his wife." The migrant lawbreaker was banished from all camps; the Hebrew lawbreaker was either banished or stoned. Steinbeck's repeated "It is unlawful" echoes the "Thou shalt not" of the Decalogue.

On the road west the Joads met men who were going back to Oklahoma from California. These men reported that although California was a lovely and rich country the residents were hostile to the migrant workers, treated them badly, and paid them so poorly that many migrants starved to death in slack periods. In Numbers 13, scouts whom Moses sent ahead into Canaan came back with the report that "surely it floweth with milk and honey"; nevertheless they made "an evil report of the land which they had searched unto the children of Israel, saying, The land . . .is a land that eateth up the inhabitants thereof"; and the natives were giants who looked upon the Hebrews as locusts. Yet the Joads, like Joshua and Caleb, were determined to enter the land. The meanness of California officers at the border, the efforts to turn back indigent migrants, the refusal of the cities and towns to let migrant workers enter, except when their labor was needed--in all this we may see the efforts of the Edomites, Moabites, and Amorites to keep the Israelites from entering their countries.

In spite of the Canaanites' hostility the Israelites persisted and took over the promised land. The Book of Joshua ends with victory and conquest. But *The Grapes of Wrath* ends at a low point in the fortunes of the Joads, as if the Exodus story has ended with the Hebrews' defeat at Ai (Joshua 7), when the Canaanites routed an army of 3,000 Israelites and killed a number of them, "wherefore the hearts of the people melted, and became as water. And Joshua rent his clothes, and fell to the earth upon his face. . ." The defeat came upon Israel because Achan had "taken of the accursed thing," that is, from Canaanite spoils which belonged to the Lord he had taken silver, gold, and fine raiment. The migrant workers met defeat because they had not learned to give up selfish desires for money and possessions: still too many wanted to undercut the pay of fellow-workers and had no feeling of common cause. But they would accomplish nothing if they did not stand together. The issue is left there, and a happy ending depends on an "if": if the migrants should realize their strength in union. Casy, Tom, and Pa Joad predict a change that is coming, a better time for the people, when they will take matters into their own hands and set them right. And the author foresees doom for the oppressors: "Every little means, every violence, every raid on a Hooverville, every deputy swaggering through a ragged camp put off the day a little and cemented the inevitability of the day." Only future events will tell us how the story ends: it had not ended in 1939.

Perhaps the most striking episodic parallel to Exodus occurs near the end of the novel. When Tom killed the vigilante who struck Casy down and left the region when it looked as if he would be found out, he acted as Moses had done. For "when Moses was grown" he saw an Egyptian beating a Hebrew laborer, and he killed the Egyptian and hid the body in the sand. The next day when he reproved a Hebrew for striking another, the angry offender said, ". . . intendest thou to kill me, as thou killedst the Egyptian?" And Moses, seeing that his deed was known, "fled from the face of Pharaoh, and dwelt in the land of Midian." In the Pentateuch this happened in Egypt before the Exodus; in *The Grapes of Wrath* it happened in California after the migration. It is another Steinbeck myth inversion. The "house of bondage" is in the new land; in the old land the people had lived in patriarchal contentment until they were forced to leave. It was more like Israel's earlier migration from Palestine to Egypt. Just after they reached California, Tom said to Casy, ". . . this ain't no lan' of milk an' honey like the preachers say. They's a mean thing here." So Moses' task of delivering his people from bondage is just beginning, not ending; it is now that he strikes the first blow. The migrants have gained nothing by merely exchanging one land for another; they must still deal with the "mean thing."

Hence a stillborn child is set adrift upon a stream at the end of the story, rather than a living child at the beginning. It was a "blue shriveled little mummy." This time the first-born of the oppressed had died; yet it was a sign to the oppressors. John Joad said, "Go down an' tell 'em. Go down in the street an' rot an' tell 'em that way. That's the way you can talk." What message? It is given in Chapter Twenty-Five: oranges, corn, potatoes, pigs, are destroyed to keep prices up, though millions of people need them. "And children dying of pellagra must die because a profit cannot be taken from an orange."

Tom Joad becomes the new Moses who will lead the oppressed people, succeeding Jim Casy, who had found One Big Soul in the hills, as Moses had found the Lord on Mount Horeb. As a teacher of a social gospel Casy is more like Jesus than like Moses, and nearly as many echoes of the New Testament as of the Old are heard in *The Grapes of Wrath*. Peter Lisca and Martin Shockley have listed several parallels between the Joad story and the gospel story. Jim Casy's initials are JC, and he retired to the wilderness to find spiritual truth ("I been to the hills . . . like Jesus went into the wilderness . . . ") and came forth to teach a new doctrine of love and good works. One of the vigilantes who attacked him pointed him out with the words, "That's him. That shiny bastard"; and just before the mortal blow struck him Casy said, "You don' know what you're a-doin'." And Casy sacrificed himself for others when he surrendered himself as the man who had struck a deputy at Hooverville. Two Joads were named Thomas, and one became Casy's disciple, who would carry on his teaching. Tom told his mother, "I'm talkin' like Casy," after saying that he would be present everywhere, though unseen, "If Casy knowed," echoing Jesus' words, "Lo, I am with you always, . . ." Lisca and Shockley have also perceived the Eucharist in Rose of Sharon's final act, when she gave her nourishment (the body and blood) to save the life of a starving man.

The correspondences between the gospel story and Steinbeck's novel go still deeper than these critics have indicated. Thirteen persons started west, Casy and twelve Joads, who, as we have seen, also represent Judea (Judah) whom Jesus came to teach. Not only were two Joads named Thomas, but another was John; Casy's name was James, brother and disciple of Jesus. One of the twelve, Connie Rivers, was not really a Joad; he is Judas, for not only did he desert the Joads selfishly at a critical moment, but just before he did so he told his wife that he would have done better to stay at home "an' study 'bout tractors. Three dollars a day they get, an' pick up extra money, too." The tractor driver of Chapter Five got three dollars a day, and the extra money was a couple of dollars for "[caving] the house in a little." Three dollars are thirty pieces of silver--remember Sinclair Lewis' Elmer Gantry, who received thirty dimes after his betrayal of the old teacher of Greek and Hebrew at the seminary. We should notice too the crowing of roosters on the night when Casy was killed--the only passage, I believe, where this is mentioned--and this at a time when the Joads had to deny Tom.

Casy taught as one with authority: "the sperit" was strong in him. His gospel coincided in certain respects with Jesus' doctrine: love for all men, sympathy for the poor and oppressed, realization of the gospel in active ministry, subordination of formal observances to men's real needs and of property to humanity, and toleration of men's weaknesses and sensual desires. When Casy said, "An' I wouldn' pray for a ol' fella that's dead. He's awright," he was saying in Okie speech, "Let the dead bury their dead" (Luke 9:60).

Casy's doctrine, however, went beyond Christ's. He had rejected the Christianity which he once preached, much as Jesus, starting out as John the Baptist's disciple, abandoned and transformed John's teachings. In *The Grapes of Wrath* John Joad, Tom's uncle, represents John the Baptist, who had practiced asceticism and emphasized remission of sins. John Joad, of course, has almost no literal resemblance to John the Baptist; but he did live a lonely, comfortless life in a spiritual desert, and he was guilt-ridden, obsessed with sin. He was a pious man, a Baptist in denomination; and we hear about his baptism "over to Polk's place. Why he got to plungin' an' jumpin'. Jumped over a feeny bush as big as a piana. Over he'd jump, an' back he'd jump, howlin' like a dog-wolf in moon time." John, trying to atone for his "sins," was good to children, and they "thought he was Jesus Christ Awmighty." He was, however, the forerunner: for one greater than he had come. When Casy gave himself up to the officers to save Tom, then

John realized how unworthy he was beside Casy : "He done her so easy. Jus' stepped up there an' says, 'I done her.'"

It is John Joad's Christianity that Casy rejected. After worrying about his sexual backslidings, Casy came to the conclusion that

> "Maybe it ain't a sin. Maybe it's just the way folks is. . . . There ain't no sin and there ain't no virtue. There's just stuff people do. It's all part of the same thing. And some of the things folks do is nice, and some ain't nice, but that's as far as any man got a right to say."

His doctrine of sin led to his positive doctrine of love: ". . . 'maybe it's all men an' all women we love; maybe that's the Holy Sperit--the human sperit-- the whole shebang. Maybe all men got one big soul ever'body's a part of.'" And so he arrived at the doctrine of the Oversoul. "All that lives is holy," he said, and this meant that he should be with other men: "a wilderness ain't no good, 'cause his little piece of soul wasn't no good 'less it was with the rest, an' was whole." In a California jail his doctrine took complete shape as a social gospel, and Casy's ministry became the organizing of farm workers into unions.

In colloquial language Casy and Tom express the book's doctrine: that not only is each social unit--family, corporation, union, state--a single organism, but so is mankind as a whole, embracing all the rest. It is, in effect, a transcendental version of the social-organism theory: Comte's religion of humanity with an Emersonian content, as Woodburn Ross has pointed out. The wine of this new gospel is poured into the old bottle of Christian scripture. Through echoes of the evangelists the author wants to make clear that this is the evangel for our times. The passage quoted above, on the two squatting men who are the anlage and zygote of the new communal organism, recalls Matthew 18:20: "For where two or three are gathered together in my name, there am I in the midst of them." The "crime . . . that goes beyond denunciation," "a failure . . .that topples all our success"--want and hunger in the midst of plenty--that is the sin against the Holy Ghost. The large tracts of uncultivated land that landless farmers could work, and the prophecies that the absentee owners, grown soft, will lose those lands to the dispossessed, strong in adversity and in union, recall the parable of the vineyard: the wicked husbandmen will be destroyed and the vineyard let to other husbandmen who will produce as they should (Matthew 21:33-41). Such owners are like the Scribes and Pharisees, who do not go into the kingdom of heaven themselves, and refuse to let anyone else go in (Matthew 23:13); instead they bind heavy burdens on men's shoulders (Matthew 23:4). Finally, the concluding theme, that family interests must be subordinate to the common welfare, that all individual souls are part of one great soul, corresponds to Jesus' rejection of family ties for the kingdom of heaven's sake: "For whosoever shall do the will of my Father which is in heaven, the same is my brother, and sister, and mother" (Matthew 12:50).

Tom, Casy's disciple, is a Christ figure, too. He seems at first just another Okie, a man quick to wrath who had killed another man in a brawl at a dance, often rough of speech, and not always kind to others. But we gradually become aware that he is different from his kinsmen. His mother said to him, "I knowed from the time you was a little fella. . . . Ever' thing you do is more'n you. When they sent you up to prison I knowed it. You're spoke for." In prison he had received a Christmas card from his grandmother, and on it was the verse "Jesus meek and Jesus mild"; thereafter his cell-block mates called him Jesus Meek. The Messianic succession was complete when Tom said farewell to his mother, announcing his intention of taking up Casy's work and trying to induce "our people. . . [to] work together for our own thing," to take over all "the good rich lan' layin' fallow" ("he hath anointed me to preach the gospel to the poor, . . . to set at liberty them that are bruised": Luke 4:18, quoting Isaiah). Though he would vanish from his parents' sight and they would not know where he was, yet, if Casy was right, if a man has no soul of his own, but only a fragment of the one big soul,

> "Then it don' matter. Then I'll be all aroun' in the dark. I'll be ever'where--wherever you look. Wherever they's a fight so hungry people can eat, I'll be there. Wherever they's a cop beatin' up a guy, I'll be there. If Casy knowed, why, I'll be in the way guys yell when they're mad an'--I'll be in the way kids laugh when they're hungry an' they know supper's ready. An' when our folks eat the stuff they raise an' live in the houses they build--why, I'll be there."

It is not only "Lo, I am with you always" but also "where two or three are gathered together . . . there am I in the midst of them," and it is identity with the hungry, thirsty, sick, naked, and imprisoned, as expressed in Matthew 25:35-45. This means also no hate even for wrongdoers: "The other side is made of men" too, as Doc Burton said in *In Dubious Battle*. When Tom Joad reproved the one-eyed man who reviled his employer, he was in fact saying, "And why beholdest thou the mote that is in thy brother's eye, but considerest not the beam that is in thine own eye?" (Matthew 7:3).

Jesus is a dying god, and the dying god is the year spirit, the rituals of whose cult are entwined in this novel with rituals of migration and colony-founding. The sunset was red "and the earth was bloody in its setting light" on the eve of the Joads' departure for California in summer drought; then the family congress went into session, and just after that two pigs were slaughtered. The slaughter is described in detail, as was the slaughter of cows in *In Dubious Battle*. The migrants were leaving the graves of their ancestors behind them, personified in Mule Graves. He was stubborn, as his nickname indicates, and he refused to leave the country, although he had no house to live in: ". . . There ain't nobody can run a guy name of Graves outa this country," he said, and "I'm jus' wanderin' aroun' like a damn ol' graveyard ghos'." "Like a ol' graveyard ghos' goin' to neighbors' houses in the night." Then Grampa died before the Joads were out of Oklahoma, and he was buried in his own country's soil. Granma died in the night that followed their arrival in California. The new venture is not for the ancestors; but the pauper's grave that Granma received in California links the old country to the new and the Joad family to another land: this is now their home. Finally, Casy made the supreme sacrifice at a moment when the Joads were already down and out. It was already fall; the nights were now chilly (the Hooper ranch must have had a very late peach crop). The Joads moved to the cotton fields and settled in the camp where the winter rains overtook them. The storms were destructive and yet harbingers of the new year: "Tiny points of grass came through the earth, and in a few days the hills were pale green with the beginning year." The migration and the year are one thing.

In no Steinbeck novel do the biological and mythical strands fit so neatly together as in *The Grapes of Wrath*. The Oklahoma land company is at once monster, Leviathan, and Pharoah oppressing the tenant farmers, who are equally monster's prey and Israelites. The California land companies are Canaanites, Pharisees, Roman government, and the dominant organism of an ecological community. The family organisms are forced to join together into a larger collective organism; the Hebrews' migration and sufferings weld them into a united nation; the poor and oppressed receive a Messiah who teaches them unity in the Oversoul. The Joads are equally a family unit, the twelve tribes of Israel, and the twelve disciples. Casy and Tom are both Moses and Jesus as leaders of the people and guiding organs in the new collective organism. Each theme--organismic, ecological, mythical; and each phase of the mythical: Exodus, Messiah, Leviathan, ritual sequence-- builds up to a single conclusion: the unity of all mankind.

To liken the Okies to the Israelites--this too may seem incongruous. Yet the parallel is really close. The oppressed laborers in Egypt were as much despised by their masters as the migrant workers in California. Moses was certainly a labor agitator, and Jesus appealed to the poor and lowly and called rude fishermen and taxgatherers to his company. Again the mythical structure imparts a cosmic meaning to the tale. These contemporary events, says Steinbeck, are as portentous for the future as was the Hebrews' migration from Egypt, and for the same reasons.

The myth is accompanied by symbolic images. As the title would lead us to expect, the imagery of grapes, vineyards, and vintage is abundant. As Lisca has pointed out, the grapes mean abundance at first and then bitterness, which turns to wrath as abundant harvests are deliberately destroyed: "In the souls of the people the grapes of wrath are filling and growing heavy, growing heavy for the vintage." The turtle of the early chapters that persistently kept to his southwestward course has been noticed by nearly every reviewer and critic who has discussed *The Grapes of Wrath*. The snakes in this novel have received less attention. After their first view of the fertile California valley from Tehachapi, the Joads went down the road into it, and on the way down they ran over a rattlesnake (Tom was driving), which the wheel broke and left squirming in the road. This is an omen which betokens fulfillment of the behest spoken in the "Battle Hymn of the Republic": "Let the Hero, born of woman, crush the serpent with his heel." The snake represents the agricultural system of California, which the immigrants are destined to crush. Later Al Joad deliberately ran over a gopher snake; when Tom reproved him, Al gaily said, "I hate 'em . . . Hate all kinds." The Okies do not yet know who their friends are.

Steinbeck left the conclusion of his story to events. How did it turn out? On September 1, 1939, fewer than five months after *The Grapes of Wrath* was published, Hitler invaded Poland and began the war which interrupted the course of events that Steinbeck foresaw. In 1940 America began to prepare for war and was in it before the end of 1941. This meant an end of unemployment. The Okies and Arkies came to work in the shipyards of San Francisco and San Pedro bays; they replaced enlisted men in industries and businesses everywhere; and many, of course, were enlisted, too. They found houses to live in, settled down, and remained employed when the war was over. Mexicans and Orientals once more harvested California's crops, and "wet-backs" became a problem. So did *The Grapes of Wrath* never find a conclusion, cut off by the turn of events? Had the owners learned their lesson and improved conditions? Disquieting reports have been coming from the fields: more Americans are now employed in migratory farm labor than a few years ago, pay is low, and conditions are bad. Perhaps the story has not ended yet.

From *John Steinbeck* (New York: Barnes & Noble, 1963), 67-83.

Steinbeck and Hemingway: Suggestions for a Comparative Study

Peter Lisca

From many points of view it seems inevitable that John Steinbeck and Ernest Hemingway should be closely associated in any critical survey of American fiction from the late twenties to the present, especially as these two figures are the foremost heirs of our naturalistic literary tradition. Thus they share certain specialized as well as general studies of American literature. They are sometimes even examined in the same chapters of such books. But curiously they have very seldom been studied closely together with the purpose of yielding reciprocal illumination. The present essay assumes simply that such an interlocking examination of two writers with so broad a common base might lead to a sharper perception of each one's particular accomplishment, and proposes to suggest certain possible fruitful areas of inquiry.

To begin with the most obvious and least important, it is strange that two such thoroughly professional writers so much in the public eye should have left so little notice of each other. Of course all the facts are not known yet in either case; but if Hemingway, who felt so compelled to publicly attack the abilities and personalities of so many of his contemporaries, has left any judgment of Steinbeck, it has not yet been generally noticed. Although, on the other hand, Steinbeck did not much care to enter into criticism of his contemporaries, some remarks about Hemingway have come to light. The gist of all of them is a sincere admiration. To Covici of the Viking Press he wrote (ca. Feb., 1939), "I'm convinced that in many ways he is the finest writer of our time," and later, to his friend Ed Sheehan he confided, "I was afraid to read Hemingway until I was well along...I knew he would influence me." Responding to the present writer's suggestion (1956) that certain passages of *To a God Unknown* (1933) has been strongly influenced by the Hemingway style, Steinbeck replied that he "didn't read him until about 1940." This awareness of Hemingway as a fellow writer was accompanied by an interest in the personality. To Ed Sheehan, he wrote that when Hemingway was reported dead in Africa (1935), "I was stunned--held a sort of personal wake....Hemingway was terribly worried about immortality. It was a gnawing thing with him." And to the same correspondent he wrote that when Hemingway received the Nobel Prize in 1954 he was as pleased as if he had gotten it himself.

The literary careers of Steinbeck and Hemingway hold some basic differences, but also some interesting and perhaps more significant similarities. Hemingway started in journalism and began writing seriously in Europe under the tutelage and practical encouragement of such figures as Pound, Joyce, Stein, Fitzgerald, and others. But Steinbeck in California had no such help from the *déjà arrivé*. Thus Hemingway was better known in critical circles with the appearance of his first little book, *Three Stories and Ten Poems* (Paris, 1923), than Steinbeck was in 1936 after the publication of four novels and several excellent short stories, including two parts of *The Red Pony*. Ironically, Hemingway, who started his career in the capitals of Europe, led most of his creative life in such places as Key West, a *finca* in Cuba, and a ranch in Idaho. He professed to detest New York and never stayed there except for brief visits. Steinbeck, on the other hand, moved from rural and small town California to New York, where he lived the last twenty-four years of his life. Yet Steinbeck the New Yorker never stimulated the degree of public recognition as a personality of our time that did Hemingway the geographic recluse. Whereas in his early career Steinbeck did very little journalistic work, this was a form of writing on which he leaned heavily from World War II until the end of his life. And, except for a few pieces in the 1930's and some of his war dispatches, that journalism is of a very low caliber. But Hemingway did some distinguished work in this field throughout his career. Both writers won a Pulitzer Prize, Steinbeck for *The Grapes of Wrath* and Hemingway for *The Old Man and the Sea*. Both also received the Nobel Prize for literature, Hemingway in 1954, and Steinbeck in 1962.

When we turn from this angle on the two writers' personal careers to the progression of their work, certain important similarities appear. Both writers have published non-fiction books which are philosophically central to their major work: Hemingway, *Death in the Afternoon* (1932) and *Green Hills of Africa* (1935); Steinbeck, *Sea of Cortez* (1941). What bullfighting and big game hunting are to one writer, marine biology is to the other. Hemingway's love of Spain led him to propaganda and documentary work in *The Spanish Earth* (1937), and his personal efforts on behalf of the Loyalists. In *The Forgotten Village* (1941), Steinbeck turns to propaganda and documentary to help the Mexican villages come into the twentieth century. Within one year of each other were published *The Grapes of Wrath* (1939) and *For Whom the Bell Tolls* (1940), both again devoted to social causes, both large novels, in some important senses epics, and both perhaps their respective authors' peak artistic achievements. In *The Pearl*(1947), Steinbeck reached the end of a long line of development started with *To a God Unknown* (1933). In Kino's throwing the pearl back into the sea Steinbeck returns man completely to the bosom of Nature, very much as Santiago returns in *The Old Man and the Sea* (1952), blessing birds, marlins, and even some sharks. Both are short, poetic, highly symbolic works. Finally, in Colonel Cantwell of *Across the River and into the Trees* (1950) Hemingway returns to his earlier, younger embodiments as Nick Adams and Frederick Henry in order to destroy them--symbolically, with that gesture on the bank of the Basso Piave; and realistically in the death of Colonel Cantwell. With essentially the same purpose, Steinbeck in *Sweet Thursday* (1954) returns to Doc of *Cannery Row* and, symbolically at least, kills him off by cheapening his character and marrying him to the prostitute, Suzy. Neither writer returned again to those areas of their material.

Similarly, in what may be called, loosely, the "materials" of their fiction, Steinbeck and Hemingway, while contrasting obviously, are unexpectedly similar. Most obvious is the degree to which the two writers are auto-biographically present in their work. Hemingway's presence, from the early stories to *Across the River and into the Trees*, has been so pronounced as to seriously hamper an objective criticism and understanding of his work. Steinbeck, on the other hand, except for appearing quite directly in *East of Eden*, has very little autobiographical presence in his fiction--nothing approaching Nick Adams, Frederick Henry, Robert Jordan, and Colonel Cantwell.

If the period of their writing is divided into the nineteen-twenties, the thirties, the forties and the fifties, further interesting comparisons emerge. For example, Hemingway while only three years older than Steinbeck (and graduating from high school only two years earlier) seems a whole generation older by his participation in World War I and his involvement in the expatriate movement and the "lost generation." Although 1929 saw the appearance of Steinbeck's first novel (*Cup of Gold*) and only the second novel of Hemingway (*A Farewell to Arms*), the latter novel completed an already solid fictional world created by the two editions of *In Our Time* (1924, 1925), and *The Sun Also Rises* (1926). This is an important part of our literary and cultural heritage, a world to which Steinbeck, except in passing (*East of Eden*), has no reference.

It is also interesting to observe, and surprising in view of the strong tendency to identify Steinbeck's work with the proletarian movement of the thirties, that in fact not until 1936, with *In Dubious Battle*, did he publish any proletarian fiction. *The Pastures of Heaven, To a God Unknown, The Red Pony*, and *Tortilla Flat* have little reference to the current social scene. It was partly this lack of reference which made the latter novel so difficult to publish in 1935. While not as obviously proletarian as Steinbeck's strike novel, Hemingway's *To Have and Have Not* was published in book form only a year after the strike novel; and it was he, not Steinbeck, who in that year addressed the Second American Writers' Congress. Of the seven books of fiction Steinbeck published in the 1930's, only three are concerned with the depression; and only one of the stories in *The Long Valley* deals with it directly. If, in a strictly limited sense, Hemingway's personal interest in the Spanish Loyalist cause can be called a proletarian one, then with his film documentary, his reporting, his play *The Fifth Column*, and *For Whom the Bell Tolls*, his involvement in the political-social realities of the 1930's can be seen as comparable to Steinbeck's, although the latter's involvement was entirely American.

Although both writers served as journalists in World War II (Hemingway, of course, in a more flamboyant manner), neither produced a novel using the war as major material. Steinbeck's *The Moon Is Down* (1942) can be identified with that war only by inference, purposely so; and Hemingway deals with that war but briefly through the reveries of Colonel Cantwell in *Across the River and into the Trees* (1950). Of the two writers only Steinbeck, in *The Winter of Our Discontent* (1961), has produced a work of fiction dealing directly with post-World War II society, particularly in America.

But then another contrast between the two writers is that Hemingway has seldom written about America at all, except in some early stories and *To Have and Have Not*. Although his major protagonists (except Santiago) are Americans, they live or at least act in Europe. Steinbeck, on the other hand, excluding his first novel--a historical romance--has set none of his major fiction outside the United States, unless one excepts *The Pearl*. In this connection it is pertinent to remark that of the two authors it is Steinbeck who in his fiction almost always give us the sense of physical communities; and they may be as various as those in *The Pastures of Heaven, Tortilla Flat*, and *The Winter of our Discontent*. With few exceptions (in some early stories, *To Have and Have Not*) Hemingway presents us with a community which is not so much physical as it is spiritual--an "in" group, whither they be a lost generation, fellow army officers, *aficionados*, hunters, guerillas, etc. This difference is vitally related to the phenomenon that one tends to recall Stein-beck's fiction in terms of themes and Hemingway's in terms of characters.

Thus proportionately much more of the criticism has dealt with Hemingway's characters than with Steinbeck's. Certain comparisons, however, can be made. Both writers have been accused of creating animal-like characters on a very low level of morality and ratiocination. There is not adequate space to discuss these familiar arguments here; but it should be pointed out, first, that both writers have created characters of considerable moral and intellectual sophistication--Jake Barnes, Robert Jordan, Colonel Cantwell; and Dr. Burton, Ethan Hawley, Doc, Samuel Hamilton. Secondly, those characters not of this intellectual caliber are employed very skillfully by both writers to reveal with great force significant aspects of human life not so readily accessible in more sophisticated personalities. Another similarity in their respective characters is the extent to which both writers admire in them skillfulness and knowledge. In Steinbeck, the whole gamut of his admiration appears in *The Wayward Bus*, from auto mechanic to stripteaser. In Hemingway this is equally obvious in his good soldiers, fishermen, or even economics professors (*To Have and Have Not*). Related to this admiration in both writers is the frequent mentor-neophyte relationship between characters, as for example Colonel Cantwell-Renata and Bill Buck-Jody. The two writers are also similar in some ways in their treatment of women and the relationship between men and women. In Hemingway, perhaps only Brett and Pilar achieve real independence, and they seem to do so at the price of their femininity. And although Hemingway writs much more than Steinbeck about sexual love, it is the latter who most often presents married women sympathetically. Both writers frequently present a close male companionship such as that of Jake and Bill or George and Lennie. Apropos of Lennie, it is interesting that Steinbeck should, like Faulkner, so frequently use characters whom, as he describes Tularecito, "God has not quite finished." There is hardly a novel that does not contain a subnormal character. Hemingway, on the other hand, eschews this kind of character completely, but does create and effectively use homosexual characters with surprising frequency. They are totally lacking in Steinbeck. Related to this point is Steinbeck's long sustained interest in psychology, particularly the Jungian variety, which is most important in his work before 1950. Significantly, his interest in Freudian psychology is associated with his later, least successful novels.

Certainly a major difference between the figures moving through these two authors' works is that between their heroes. In Hemingway, even Robert Jordan the most committed and engaged of his heroes, is yet in an important sense an outsider, a loner pursuing essentially personal goals. The distinguishing personal mark of practically all Steinbeck heroes is their leadership and complete involvement in a communal action. There is another important difference which is almost a similarity. In Hemingway, the hero's action frequently demonstrates that a man may be destroyed but not defeated; in Steinbeck, that a man frequently survives, but does not succeed; dreams, but does not accomplish.

Style, of course, in all its aspects, is a major point of comparison, although it is the most difficult to discuss adequately here. Steinbeck uses a much greater variety of prose styles than does Hemingway, who really has variations on only one style. But in some short stories and such novels as *In Dubious Battle, Of Mice and Men,* and *The Pearl* there is much ground for comparison. Steinbeck's prose is hardly ever the iceberg seven-eights under the surface that Hemingway describes as his own ideal. Hemingway does make much more use of implication, the spaces made meaningful by the author's firm knowledge of what is left out. But both writers have reached a large popular audience in part because of a deceptively simple surface and their ability to write in terms of sensations, although here Steinbeck is more often abstract. It is no accident that both men have expressed a preference for the music of Bach. True, Steinbeck has his Wagnerian tempests, but in those works which are most successful the dimensionality is an effect of clean counterpoint and not of massed chords.

Symbolism is very important in both writers, also, and the differences in its nature and purpose revealing. Both make extensive use of natural objects as symbols, and of animals, such as mice, turtles, bulls, fish, ducks; also, both use landscape for this purpose, and climate--mountains, gulfstream, swamp, rain, snow, drought, valleys, tidepools, caves. An important difference, however, is that Steinbeck, in addition, moves much more frequently for his symbols into the worlds of literature, legend, and myth, some novels taking their basic structure therefrom--*Tortilla Flat, In*

Dubious Battle, The Grapes of Wrath, East of Eden, The Winter of Our Discontent, and others. He thus creates a "fourth dimension" of external reference not accomplished by Hemingway, whose own "fourth dimension" is achieved by "rituals or strategies," "rites and ceremonies," and remains within the work itself.

Another point of contrast in style between the two writers is their use of narrative point of view. This is closely related to the differences in the nature and role of their hero figures, as discussed above. With the exception of his last novel, Steinbeck employs only third person more or less objective point of narration. Hemingway, however, uses varieties of first person narration extensively and also experiments with mixing or merging points of view. There is a philosophical as well as formal significance here.

Finally, we come to those comparisons perhaps most important, but difficult to disengage entirely from those matters of style and materials discussed above. And here we return to these two writers' common base as heirs of literary naturalism. But while Hemingway has never abandoned, and consistently modified, this inheritance, Steinbeck has, since *The Wayward Bus*, moved steadily away from it toward a view and value system essentially suburban-Christian. Thus Hemingway in his last novel, *The Old Man and the Sea*, arrives at an almost mystic acceptance of man's consanguinity with all of Nature very similar to that out of which Steinbeck wrote, before 1947, such disparate works as *The Grapes of Wrath* and *To a God Unknown*. Santiago, in fact, is quite similar to Joseph Wayne of the latter novel (1933). Until this change in Steinbeck, however, and some remnants of the earlier view persist, fossilized, in later works, this common inheritance of the two writers led to another important similarity--that between Hemingway's stoic acceptance of a deterministic, indifference universe, and Steinbeck's non-teleological thinking, as it is defined in *Sea of Cortez*.

Other corollaries follow. Both writers often present man in situations of violence. But whereas the Hemingway hero frequently makes a career or avocation of such violence, whether hunting, bullfighting, boxing, running contraband, or soldiering, in Steinbeck's fiction (with the exception of the "Cain" figures in *East of Eden*) the characters engage in violence only for some communal goal, as an unavoidable contingency of their purpose. They are capable of great violence when necessary, but do not seek it out, as do Hemingway's characters sometimes, as the author has stated about his own adventures, to avoid doing violence to themselves. This contrast between the two writers is pointed up hilariously in that account of the hunt for bighorn sheep in *Sea of Cortez*.

But despite this difference about violence, both writers are notable for the depth of esthetic feeling touched by this Nature and their great ability to express it; and both also present man as incomplete without intimate contact with that world. Here Hemingway (except for Santiago) stops, with Nature as sensation and physical discipline. But Steinbeck goes on to scientific engagement with Nature as well, while at the same time speculating earnestly on pantheistic, quasi-religious relationship. This contrast is to be expected in two authors of whom one (*Green Hills of Africa*) rejects the "small, dried" minds of the nineteenth-century American transcendentalist, and the other accepts as one of the major sources of his thinking in his greatest novel--*The Grapes of Wrath*.

Admittedly, such an essay as above does not answer many important questions. And sometimes, perhaps, not enough evidence has been given to warranty *raising* them. Also some comparisons, though not many it is trusted, seem oversimplified, particularly as space severely limits discursive qualifications. But what is hoped emerges is the fact of the value of pursuing further such comparisons and others which may suggest themselves; and, in addition, the fact that those similarities between the two writers which may at first seem slight may be much more important than certain obvious differences, the reverse also being true.

From *Steinbeck Quarterly* (Spring 1969), 9-17.

Water Imagery and the Conclusion to *The Grapes of Wrath*

Collin G. Matton

A great deal has been written concerning John Steinbeck's use of Biblical motifs and allusions in *The Grapes of Wrath* (1939). However, one symbolic pattern from the Judaeo-Christian tradition has not been adequately traced as a revealing leitmotiv in Steinbeck's commentary on social conditions in the United States during the 1930's. Examination of the water and flood archetype as used by Steinbeck, particularly in Chapter 29 of the novel, seems to open a new interpretation to the conclusion of the novel.

At first, Steinbeck's use of water imagery furthers the tragic overtones of the novel. In showing water as a destroyer before developing the creative power of the symbol, Steinbeck seems to be using the motif structurally. This order of presentation carries the reader from the tragedy of the first part of the novel to the regenerative pattern of the conclusion.

The destructive features of the water archetype, in this chapter, follow a pattern of hierarchical importance. Water destroys nature, the nature, the works of man, and finally even attempts to destroy man himself. The destruction of nature reverses the Biblical account of creation. In the Biblical pattern of creation, the first three days are days of separation: light from darkness, the waters above from the waters below, and the dry lands from the water. The account in *The Grapes of Wrath*, however, mingles light and darkness in gray, the waters above and those below in a flood, and the land and water in mud.   The effect of this is to reverse a clearly organized creative account into an apocalyptic vision of chaos and destruction.

The references to gray (a combination of light and dark) are numerous in the chapter under consideration.

> Over the high coast mountains and over the valleys the gray clouds marched in from the ocean. The wind blew fiercely and silently, high in the air, and it swished in the brush, and it roared in the forests. The clouds came in brokenly, in puffs, in folds, in gray crags; and they piled in together and settled low over the west. And then the wind stopped and left the clouds deep and solid. The rain began with gusty showers, pauses and downpours; and then gradually it settled to a single tempo, small drops and a steady beat, rain that was gray to see through, rain that cut midday light to evening.[1]

The grayness of the landscape suggests a reversal of the clearly separated light and dark of the first day of creation. The cluster of images in this passage, which includes clouds, showers, downpours, and drops, contains further references to water, the main symbol of the chapter. At this point in the novel, the water symbol is still associated with destruction.

Destruction is suggested, moreover, by a reversal of the second day of creation. This day is associated with the separation of the waters above from the waters below. Steinbeck reverses this pattern of separation by combining the waters above (in the sky) with those below (the puddles and streams).

> For two days the earth drank the rain, until the earth was full. Then puddles formed, and in the low places little lakes formed in the fields. The muddy lakes rose higher, and the steady rain whipped the shining water. (386)

This passage is closely related to a reversal of the creation of the third day when the dry land was separated from the watery land. In Steinbeck's apocalyptic vision of destruction, the two--dry and wet--blend to form mud.

> The muddy water whirled along the bank sides and crept up the banks until at last it spilled over, into the fields, into the orchards, into the cotton patches where the black stems stood. . . . Then the water poured over the highways, and cars moved slowly, cutting the water ahead, and leaving a boiling muddy wake behind. (386)

The destructiveness of the rains affects both God's creation, Nature, and man's creations. The rains "brought down the trees," "bent the willows deep in the current." They also "poured over the highways," "wet the beds and blankets," "fouled the ignition wires and fouled the carburetors." Finally, after destroying both the creations of God and those of man, the rains begin to destroy man himself.

> Then from the tents, from the crowded barns, groups of sodden men went out, their clothes slopping rags, their shoes muddy pulp. They splashed out through the water, to the towns, to the country stores, to the relief offices, to beg for food, to beg for relief, to try to steal, to lie. (387)

The destruction of man presented here is both moral and physical. It is the previous destruction of the natural order that has made it possible for man's ethical system to become destroyed. Since the harmony of nature has been destroyed, the harmony among men may falter--hence, men may steal and lie.

The destruction suffered by man is not only ethical, but also physical. "Then the sickness came, pneumonia, and measles that went to the eyes and to the mastoids" (387). Aside from the obvious physical destruction caused by disease, Steinbeck uses a very subtle symbol in the destruction of the "eyes," a symbol that can again be traced to analogues in the creation account. It was, after all, in the Genesis account that God *saw* that His creation was good. In Steinbeck's novel, however, the objects of creation have been destroyed as well as the eyes with which to see.

After having focused on the negative, or destructive, features of the water symbol, Steinbeck uses the creative aspect of the symbol to end the tragedy of the first part of the novel and to hint at a regenerative pattern near the end of *The Grapes of Wrath*. The dual nature of the water archetype is suggested by Mircea Eliade's interpretation of the water symbol. "A flood destroys simply because the 'forms' are old and worn out, but it is always followed by a new humanity and a new history."[2] This new humanity is suggested by Steinbeck early in the interchapter.

> In the wet hay of leaking barns babies were born to women who panted with pneumonia. And old people curled up in corners and died that way, so that the coroners could not straighten them. (387)

This passage is to be contrasted with an earlier passage.

In the barns, the people sat huddled together; and the terror came over them, and their faces were gray with terror. The children cried with hunger, and there was no food. (387)

Although the setting remains the same in both instances, the direction of the imagery alters the import of the selections. In the first passage, the pattern of human life is cyclic.[3] It is the women "who panted with pneumonia," not the children. It is the "old people" who were "curled up in the corners." In spite of these destructive elements, the creative element is given birth-- "babies were born." Significantly enough, the babies were born "in the wet hay of the leaking barns."

In the later passage, the grayness of nature is carried to the faces of the people. The destructive element of hunger is brought even to children, usually a regenerative force. The pattern of human life is linear in that it points to final destruction of both young and old. What must be kept in mind is that the passage which is destructive in tone is placed before that which is optimistic. It is at this point that Steinbeck seems to shift the tone of the chapter, and that of the novel.

It is in this chapter that Steinbeck repeats the water archetype with different connotations. No longer associated with destruction, the water image becomes a symbol of birth and regeneration. Again, Steinbeck extends the regenerative pattern from man's creations to God's creation, Nature. "Tiny points of grass came through the earth, and in a few days the hills were pale green with the beginning year" (383). The rejuvenative pattern is quite clearly expressed through the "beginning" year and the color of green, always associated with fecundity and hope.

From *Northeast Modern Language Association Newsletter*, vol. 2 (1970), 44-47.

Notes

1. John Steinbeck. *The Grapes of Wrath* (New York, 1966), p. 385. All subsequent references to the novel are taken from this edition.

2. Micea Eliade, *Patterns in Comparative Religion* (Cleveland, 1963), p. 210.

3. As Eliade has pointed out, the deluge archetype is usually associated with a cyclic conception of the history of man.

John Steinbeck's Spatial Imagination in *The Grapes of Wrath*

George Henderson

Introduction: Representation as Social Action

The winter of 1937-38 was especially wet in the San Joaquin Valley. Steady and heavy rains saturated the San Joaquin flood plain, particularly in cotton-growing Madera County. In February of that winter John Steinbeck wrote to his agent Elizabeth Otis:

> I must go over into the interior valleys. There are about five thousand families starving to death over there, not just hungry but actually starving. The government is trying to feed them and get medical attention to them with the fascist group of utilities and banks and huge growers sabotaging the thing all along the line and yelling for a balanced budget. In one tent there are twenty people quarantined for smallpox and two of the women are to have babies in that tent this week. I've tied into the thing from the first and I must knock these murderers on the heads. Do you know what they're afraid of? They think that if these people are allowed to live in camps with proper sanitary facilities, they will organize and that is the bugbear of the large landowner and the corporation farmer. The states and counties will give them nothing because they are outsiders. But the crops of any part of this state could not be harvested without these outsiders. I'm pretty mad about it. No word of this outside because when I have finished my job the jolly old associated farmers will be after my scalp again (Steinbeck and Wallsten 158).

For several years Steinbeck had been eyeing the situation of migrant agricultural workers in the "interior valleys." In October 1936 *The San Francisco News* ran "Harvest Gypsies," a series of Steinbeck's articles, commissioned by the paper's chief editorial writer (see St. Pierre, 79-81 for excerpts). In those brief pieces a reader could find most of the major themes about California agriculture that Steinbeck would later chronicle in *The Grapes of Wrath* in 1939.

Shortly after "Harvest Gypsies" was printed, Steinbeck's *Of Mice and Men* and *In Dubious Battle* appeared in the bookstores. *In Dubious Battle* was selected by the Book of the Month Club, and within a month one hundred thousand copies had been purchased. Both novels concerned the social costs and unique social formations that Steinbeck attributed to the system of corporate agriculture in the valley (St. Pierre, 81). Thus, by the time Steinbeck began *The Grapes of Wrath*, his vision was keen and his hand well practiced.

The new novel began to take on a spectacular life of its own. Six months after publication, when two hundred thousand copies had been sold, *Commonwealth* magazine noted that "when a book sells like that, and when it causes the comment and controversy this book has, it becomes a cultural phenomenon of important dimensions. The literary and critical industry of the country is not really geared to handle it" (quoted in St. Pierre, 98-101). The critic lamented the lack of attention to the book's literary merit. Most readers only wanted to know whether or not California resembled Steinbeck's depiction (see Kappel, for example, on the novel's ban in Kern County). Too much criticism, both good and bad, had been geared to assessing the factual content and background of *The Grapes of Wrath*. Only in later years did the "pattern of criticism" turn to an assessment of the novel's relationship to themes, such as biblical allegory and the "Wagons West" idiom.

During the late thirties anyone who cared could have corroborated the general events, if not the details, provided by Steinbeck--the Hoovervilles and Resettlement Administration camps, grower-induced labor surplus, crop specialization by region, the migrant trek from the Dust Bowl states, the vigilantism and the relief work, and the importance of cotton as *the* new speculative crop.

The release of *The Grapes of Wrath* could not have been better timed in relation to the publication of Carey McWilliams' *Factories in the Field* (1939). In broadly supported and convincing prose, McWilliams wrote a mirror text for Steinbeck's novel, although the two writers did not collaborate. Although many contemporary readers apparently did, they did not need to refer to the novel in order to understand the historical reliance of much of California's agricultural production upon a migrant labor class. Yet *The Grapes of Wrath* did fulfill a role as a regionalist and social realist interpretive text. The novel stands as a document of social change. Nonetheless, more can be asked of it.

For example, it might be interesting to turn to a problem of the human condition that Steinbeck apparently set up in *The Grapes of Wrath*. One of Steinbeck's fundamental concerns was to represent the migration of white Midwestern families to California as part of that recurrent human condition, while arguing that the human condition itself is shaped by historical and social contingencies. He asked what relationship the laws of nature had to human-made situations: nature does not transcend or determine history, nor does history supersede nature. This idea, I think, accounts for the immortal qualities of some of Steinbeck's characters. At the same time, only the historical moment, the intervention of social relationships, could reveal what might be enduringly true: Ma Joad's heroic will to survive--to humanize the natural survival instinct--was only manifested by economic threat. Tom Joad's and Casy's ultimate belief in a transcendent human family was hammered out only by virtue of their ability to gauge just how far power relations had penetrated the local situation. Steinbeck's adeptness at elevating demoralized and beaten migrants to the epochal level of history makers, and inverting social relations by phrasing specifically local questions in terms of grandiose themes, fueled his detractors, who would not have dared to vest moral authority in a rootless, landless class. The point, then, is that Steinbeck registered the duality of history and nature in terms of a social inversion.

One of the devices by which Steinbeck infused his work with this thematic content was to saturate his readers' minds with an understanding of the genetic, formative *processes* that seemed to push the story along in such a way as to make every character and every action part of an enveloping process. This point seems to lie behind Peter Lisca's observation over thirty years ago:

> Kenneth Burke has pointed out that "most of the characters derive their role, which is to say their personality, purely from their relationship to the basic situation." But what he takes to be a serious weakness is actually one of the book's greatest accomplishments (Lisca, "*The Grapes of Wrath* as Fiction," 736).

The Grapes of Wrath was indeed relentlessly didactic, even formulaic, but by ensuring that the readers grasped the processes involved (or the "basic situation," as the above quote would have it) Steinbeck could then suggest how different orders of experience represented and contained others by virtue of the overarching causes; for example, attachment to land represented a wholesomeness of body and spirit. What is inherently geographical also turns out to be inherently social, both constituting, and constitutive of, the same processes. It is from social and geographical relationships that meaning radiates, rather than from an individual character or action.

In this way small details were charted with representing *and* bearing out larger processes. This seems like just the sort of thing befitting a philosophical argument of naturalism. But it should not be forgotten that it was the modernization of agricultural production and its attendant forms of consciousness that, Steinbeck argued, brought about this state of affairs; in particular that aspect of *modernization* whereby technological change loosens boundaries, brings into contact formerly discrete things and persons, and allows for a seemingly small event to be nested inside something more significant. The particular importance of the modernizing process as detailed by Steinbeck was that it foreshadowed representation (the power to grasp cognitively the rending and reshuffling of traditional social bonds) itself as a precursor to social action. A fundamental dilemma for the Joads was the inappropriateness of their own daily thought and practices to an interpretation of the new political and economic order. Nowhere was this contradiction more evident than in the endless bickering over the value of talking over their problems. Steinbeck himself took on the problem of representation insofar as the interchapters re-narrated the story as a form of documentation. Moreover, representation became by the end of the novel *both* a narrative strategy *and* a form of social action.

Taking these general points, I want to explore how they conferred a particular kind of imaginative process to Steinbeck's writing of *The Grapes of Wrath*. This imagination orchestrated the geographical sites and the *situation* of characters depicted in the novel, the particular social processes as they unfolded across space, which only people swept up in the modernizing process could have understood.

The Grapes of Wrath cannot be understood fully unless the characters are seen to develop in relationship to the places through which they moved-- places that they also reconstituted, if only momentarily. This approach is meant to be a general, illuminating one and not necessarily an argument to be sustained for each character. Rather, the interpretative approach addresses action in the novel as a totality. Since Tom Joad carries a large proportion of the thematic load of the novel from such a perspective, the bulk of my discussion will focus on him.

Steinbeck's primary thesis, in geographical terms, was that you cannot understand what is going on inside California unless you know what is occurring outside. The notion was borne out by the novel's overwhelming concern with mapping the Joads' migration across the western states. Given the family's goal of obtaining a family-size farm in California, it could be argued that the Joads never really got where they were going. The migration upon which they embarked has no conclusion in the novel other than an ironic symmetry between beginning and ending. The literary "map" charted in *The Grapes of Wrath* was finally not just a geographic product, but was laden with social meaning. It is important, then, to move the line of questioning away from how the Joads got from one place to the next, and by which routes, toward how meaning is produced, controlled, and disseminated with regard to social and workaday space. Also, we need to discover where Steinbeck sat in regard to a general theory of place formation in capitalist society. Specifically, I would like to show how Steinbeck demonstrated his awareness of social/geographic space as the medium and the outcome of certain process: the division of labor along class and gender lines; the territorial demands of capitalist agribusiness; and family and community needs to appropriate space for their own production, reproduction, and private fulfillment. These processes, conditioned by the modern era, were brought to bear on the Joads' travails as they encountered the wider social world and it, in turn, received or resisted their arrival.

In a sense my outlook may be criticized as too economistic. Let me state at the onset that I am familiar with some of the common cultural and ideological idioms of Steinbeck's work, including the myth of the garden, the family farm as *reformist* ideal, and the closeness of women to nature. While Steinbeck appeared to have left these myths intact, and indeed to have relied upon them, he dismantled others of a specific local and regional character: the innocence of California's agricultural bounty, the myth of an egalitarian frontier in the West, and the family farm as a basic unit of democracy. Instead of treating each of the above concepts explicitly, I will simply let them inform my thinking, drawing on them as necessary or appropriate.

Steinbeck, I think, *structured* the meanings of the places in which the book's characters were situated on two levels. First, each place took on meaning through its dynamic relationship with an opposite kind of place, either real or imagined. Second, the interaction of these polarities transformed or overturned social relations.

How can two places "interact"? Contradictions among the processes of the division of labor, capitalist agribusiness, and small social units arise as each asserts its territorial demands for space--critical to its very continuation

--and brings the novel's places and characters into a dialectical relationship. With the notion of dialectically interacting places in mind, I would, then, posit three sets of relationships among the primary settings in *The Grapes of Wrath*. These oppositions constitute major literary devices through which Steinbeck represented the processes of the creation of social/geographic space. The three sets of oppositions are:

1. The tension between places where power is centered--or represented --and places of socially marginal activity for peripheralized people;

2. The contradiction between California as a visible, knowable, Edenic landscape and the Joads' invisibility and ignorance within it;

3. The conflict between divergent modes of transforming nature and producing humane habitats.

Places of Centralized Power and Marginalized Activity

The geography of power and disenfranchisement is relatively straightforward in *The Grapes of Wrath*. A primary distinction is drawn between towns and banks, on the one hand, and Routes 66/99 and the migrant camps on the other hand. The implication, which comprised the fundamental antagonists in Steinbeck's book, was the finance capital, fixed in places (the banks), and the entrenched urban settlement pattern were both hostile to the "independent" and dispossessed rural smallholder and migrant worker. Oklahoma banks extended their domain to foreclose on small or mid-size farms, while California towns resisted the onslaught of the displaced migrants. Migrant families were thus pushed from two directions: away from their homelands and away from the small-town sanctuary of the farmers and merchants. Bankers, big farmers, and town-dwellers alike feared that the Joads would find a place in which to belong. Fixity translated into power, whereas uprootedness was the best assurance of continued disenfranchisement. From this point, Steinbeck wrote what might be called a drama of settlement.

The settlement drama has two dimensions in the novel. In one, Steinbeck imagined a reinvention of a natural, organic society formed by the exigencies of the highway life along the "Great American Roadside." This new, transitional society both challenged and rivaled the exclusive claims to authenticity held by the historically validated, pre-existing settlement pattern, in which moral authority and political power were vested in fixed centers, either towns or farms. Steinbeck reversed this notion and outlined a vision of moral purity and impending political power as they were taking shape on the road:

The cars of the migrant people crawled out of the side roads onto the great cross-country highway, and they took the migrants way to the West. In the daylight they scuttled like bugs to the westward: and as the dark caught them, they clustered like bugs near to shelter and to water . . . Thus it might be that one family camped near a spring, and another camped for the spring and for company, and a third because two families had pioneered the place and found it good. And when the sun went down, perhaps twenty families and twenty cars were there.

In the evening a strange thing happened: the twenty families became one family, the children were the children of all . . . .

Every night relationships that make a world, established; and every morning the world torn down like a circus . . . gradually the technique of building worlds became their technique. Then leaders emerged, then laws were made, then codes came into being . . . (p. 264-5).

Steinbeck wrote into the situation a sort of moral regeneration of American society, borne on the backs of its most beleaguered members. At first, the new society seemed a parody, a "circus," but it was simply that the basic social rules, forgotten by the dominant society, must be learned anew. This proposed change was resisted by those who were socially well-placed: the haves against the have-nots. A manifestation and medium for this struggle was the new spatial form of social relations overlaid on the landscape of the new, depression-era West:

The families, which had been units of which the boundaries were a house at night, a farm by day, changed their boundaries. In the long hot light, they were silent in the cars moving slowly westward; but at night they integrated with any group they found.

Thus they changed their social life--changed as in the whole universe only man can change. They were not farm men any more, but migrant men (p. 267-8).

The struggle to which Steinbeck implicitly alluded at this point in the novel, was one over legacy, over historical authenticity, over the notion of "free" land in the West. Migrant culture stretched out into a great protective net across the roads of the west. No longer was the land the democratizing element. Rather, geographical mobility was the great social leveler, because its laws had been revised to accommodate lives as lived on the road. In the new landscape, the trucker was the benefactor. Steinbeck was enamored of the new roadside culture--the diner, the truckstops--just as he ridiculed its transgressors--the fee campgrounds, the salesmen peddling used cars for ill-gotten profits.

The other dimension of the settlement fantasy is the raising of individualized forms of consciousness to the level of class. Steinbeck wrote that "one man, one family [is] driven from the land." The single migrant is "alone. . .and bewildered." But then something happens. Two men meet, "squat on their hams and the women and children listen. . . ." This meeting, Steinbeck pointed out, is the "mode" of revolution. "Here 'I lost my land' is changed. . . [to] 'We lost *our* land.'" (p. 206). Steinbeck continued the reasoning in the succeeding passages to foretell a day of revolution, unforeseen by large propertied interests because they were still in an "I" frame of mind, not yet liberated into communal consciousness.

The author presented a pattern of fragmentation of the rural freeholder class which moved toward a portentous regrouping on the road. The road in this role is transformed from nemesis to necessity, if history is to follow the contradictory logic of modernization. Yet the road maintained ambiguous status in the novel. It beckoned at the same time as it restrained.

Route 66 was essential for the formation of the migrants' new social consciousness, yet for all its symbolic and cultural weight, it led the Joads down a circular path in their search for house and garden. After the Joads' scrape with the law in the first California "Hooverville" they came to, they made a narrow pre-dawn escape *down* Route 99. It is tempting to think that Steinbeck was manipulating the route numbers themselves to reveal their symbolic content (p. 384). Turning south on "99" inverted the route number to "66." The Joads were far from home, but essentially on the same highway that used to lead to their old front door.

The Joads' Invisibility and Ignorance within a Visible, Edenic Landscape

A critical juncture in the book arrived as the Joads were astride the top of the Tehachapi Mountains, looking out over the Central Valley toward Bakersfield. They had just endured the disappointment of Needles ("Gateway to California"), a funeral procession through the Mojave Desert, and the agricultural inspection station at Daggett:

> Al jammed on the brake and stopped in the middle of the road, and, "Jesus Christ! Look!" he said. The vineyards, the orchards, the great flat valley, green and beautiful, the trees set in rows, and the farm houses. . . The distant cities, the little towns in the orchard land, and morning sun, golden on the valley . . . The grain fields golden in the morning and the willow lines, the eucalyptus trees in rows.
>
> Pa sighed, "I never knowed they was anything like her."

... Ruthie and Winfield scrambled down from the car, and then they stood, silent and awestruck, embarrassed before the great valley ... and Ruthie whispered, "It's California" (p. 309-10).

This moment, when they were faced with the spectacle of California, was foreshadowed in the novel when the Joads took a respite outside Needles. Tom Joad wondered then whether the image of California would pan out in reality: Pa said, "Wait till we get to California. You'll see nice country then." Tom admonished, "Jesus Christ, Pa! This here *is* California" (p. 278).

Moments later Tom talked with a man versed in the subtler aspects of the California landscape. He told Tom what to expect, and although he was leaving California, he encouraged Tom to go see for himself:

> "She's a nice country. But she was stole a long time ago. You git acrost the desert an' come into the country aroun' Bakersfield. An' you never seen such purty country--all orchards an' grapes, purtiest country you ever seen. An' you'll pass lan' flat an' fine with water thirty feet down, and that lan' layin' fallow. But you can't have none of that lan'. That's a Lan' and Cattle Company. An' if they don't want ta work her, she ain't gonna git worked. You go in there an' plant you a little corn, an' you'll go to jail!" (p. 279)

The migrants had seen pictures of California--a rural paradise draped with a snow capped background (p. 271). In the scenes depicted above the Joads are brought to confront and question that image. But even when the visible landscape seemed to fit the pictorial myth, the social and economic reality had brutal implications. The landscape, a spectacle, as presented to the observer from the crest of Tehachapis, concealed the enveloping contradiction between the subsistence potential of the soil and the monopolistic tendencies of the large landowning companies.

Still, however, the Joads asserted their blind, almost masochistic fortitude, (that evidence of the survival instinct bordering on animal drive-- bugs "crawl," the Joads "crawl") which flew in the face of everything they had heard along their migration. They were distrustful of "words" and "talk":

> [Uncle John by the riverbank outside of Needles] ". . . We're a-goin' there, ain't we? None of this here talk gonna keep us from goin' there. When we get there, we'll get there. When we get a job we'll work, an' when we don't get a job we'll set on our tail. This here talk ain't gonna do no good no way" (p. 283).

Indeed, Uncle John foresaw the truth of their experience in the great valley. Yet he could not have seen any of the particular features and would not have been able to map out the continuation of their journey from the vantage point at the pass in the Tehachapis. The crisis of representation here had two expressions. One was the inability of the Joads to convey to each other what they were getting themselves into. The other expression of the crisis was the very landscape that lay before them. The power of the landscape, to represent future events as they would be shaped by social/power relations and to lend predictability to the migrants' lives, rapidly diminished. The landscape ambiguously revealed *and* concealed its contents. All along, the Joads had been making the equation between the visible and the possible, between reality and representation. The notions of "there" and "here" as points on a map, or as elements of the field of vision that could be identified and reached, were continually obscured because the Joads were lured in the first place by the spectacle of California. Or, rather, California was revealed to them only *as* a spectacle. What they found, in fact, was a parallel, though peripheralized, world.

The apotheosis of the peripheral world was the Hooverville. A parody of the American small-town ideal and a continuation of Steinbeck's settlement myth, these squatter settlements could be found outside of every "real" town: "The rag town lay close to water; and the houses were tents, and weed-thatched enclosures, paper houses, a great junk pile" (p. 319-20). The "rag town" was really nothing but the discharge point of the effluvia of the social order: "a great junk pile." The description alluded to the flow of goods, but the Hooverville made a mockery of real economic exchange. The flow of goods was uni-directional. And the settlement was illusory--houses were merely tents and paper constructions.

Yet it was in Hooverville that the Joads comprehended the basic contradictions that drove the plot forward. The migrant camp on the outskirts followed the "mother of invention" dictum, but the camp was an essential geographical instrument for concentrating surplus labor in a region where one extensively planted crop ripened all at once over a broad area. In Hooverville, Tom Joad is lectured to by a world-wise, old hand about how the gathering of surplus workers enabled employers to pay miserable wages. "S'pose them men got kids . . . Jus' offer 'em a nickel--why they'll kill each other fightin' for that nickel." The men had been lured by handbills, and "You can print a hell of a lot of han'bills with what ya save payin' fifteen cents an hour for fiel' work," explained Tom's instructor. He continued:

"They's a big son-of-a-bitch of a peach orchard I worked in. Takes nine men all the year roun'." He paused impressively. "Takes three thousan' men for two weeks when them peaches is ripe . . . They send out han'bills all over hell. They need three thousand', an' they get six thousan' . . . Whole part a the country's peaches. All ripe together. When ya get 'em picked, ever' goddam one is picked. There ain't another damn thing in that part a the country to do. An' then them owners don' want you there no more. . . . So they kick you out, they move you along. That's how it is" (p. 334-5).

The California spectacle was revealed as a horrific production racket involving key combinations: a division of labor with a painfully seasonal and spatial underpinning, extensive mono-cropping, and the short term needs of migrant families and individuals to keep the diurnal body and soul together. Although any *one* Hooverville was a temporary arrangement in the migrant world, Hoovervilles were to be found on the edge of every town. Each was fragile over time. Over geographical space they were extensive and threatening. Thus, they had their hand in a dialectical turn of events: "every raid on a Hooverville, every deputy swaggering through a ragged camp put off the day a little and cemented the inevitability of the day [when the land will belong to the workers]" (p. 325).

Just as the Joads were awed and inspired (*embarrassed* too) by the view of the landscape from atop the Tehachapis--a vision of an ordered, productive, and beneficent world--the owners of property, the producers of that landscape and the image of California as a haven for the dispossessed, wished to keep the migrants moving. The landscape itself was to be a fixed, closed entity, and the idea of keeping the outcasts moving was to keep from thinking of them as part of the real picture. The point was to define the laborer merely as a means of production rather than as an agrarian tradition, one of which would be the very privilege of belonging to the landscape by being a landholder.

Steinbeck attached a particular form of consciousness--historical knowledge--to land ownership. Ironically, it is the great landowner who understands the lesson that when there are masses of dispossessed, revolution will surely follow. But workers need to grasp their role in the historical process. How does the worker in *The Grapes of Wrath* come into that consciousness? How do the Joads as peasants know that they have become "workers"?

The Joads were not ascribed any potential for social mobility. In addition, their spatial mobility was almost thoroughly restricted, if not prescribed. Thus, a plunge into the self brought about a realized relationship to history and society. In spatial terms, seclusion was required. Steinbeck carefully chose places that gave a character a renewed and empowering vantage point from which to see social relations as fraught with contradictions (p. 571-2). Characters must be placed in a position from which to view their world upside down, with the social order reversed. Invariably, these places mere marginal, both in the productivity of nature and in the hierarchy of human habits.

Divergent Modes of Transforming Nature and the Production of Humane Habitats

Steinbeck tried to capture the historical place and time in which putting land into production meant different things to different classes of people. The primary event that set *The Grapes of Wrath* in motion was the Joads' loss of their homestead to a bank that foreclosed on the property. Steinbeck drew a fundamental distinction between a spatial proximity of a people to their land and, conversely, a spatial disjunction:

> [Muley Graves] "Place where folks live is them folks. They ain't whole, out lonely on the road in a piled-up car. They ain't alive no more. Them sons-a-bitches killed 'em'" (p. 71).
> [Later, a fragment from an interchapter] The man who is . . . walking on the earth, turning his plow point for a stone, dropping his handles to slide over an outcropping, kneeling in the earth to eat his lunch; that man who is more than his elements knows the land that is more than its analysis. But the machine man, driving a dead tractor on land he does not know and love, understands only chemistry; and he is contemptuous of the land and of himself. When the corrugated iron doors are shut, he goes home, and his home is not the land (p. 158).

Steinbeck was very keen on establishing the notion that an emotional relationship to land depends on close physical contact with the soil. Because Muley Graves did not join the Joads, he failed to recognize the opportunity for renewal in the experience of migration. However, he *was* clever enough to recognize the ways and means of survival in a land wholly given over to an alien system of agricultural production. In an early scene on the old Joad homestead, Muley explained to Tom and Casey the fine art of hiding in a land where there was supposedly nowhere to hide (p. 77-8). Cotton had been planted so extensively at the old farm that it likened flushing out the fugitives to looking for a needle in a haystack. To a degree, their invisibility in the cotton field opposed the inability of the small farmer to pin the responsibility of foreclosure on a real *person.* Each side was a stranger to the other. The modern system divided them, as it brought them together.

Ultimately "tractor farming" became the small landholder's nemesis. The small farmer could no longer make the land support a crop. Under a system of modernized production, extensive monocropping of cotton engulfed the Joads' farm.

> The Reverend Casy and young Tom stood on the hill and looked down on the Joad place. The small unpainted house was mashed at one corner and had been pushed off its foundations so that it slumped at an angle, its blind front windows pointing at a spot of sky well above the horizon. The fences were gone and the cotton grew in the dooryard and up against the house, and the cotton grew close against it . . . They walked toward the concrete well-cap, walked through the cotton plants to get to it, and the bolls were forming on the cotton, and the land was cultivated (p. 54-5).

In a number of such passages Steinbeck brought together potent images of two rural orders in conflict. The new large cotton farm annihilated all former distinctions between the various microplaces of the Joad farm: no more fences, no dooryard, no clear path to shed, outhouse, or trough. There were no places even for "proper weeds that should grow under a trough." The phrase "proper weeds" seems like an oxymoron, yet gets the point across that the old rough and tumble homestead was part of a good and natural scheme.

It was such a scheme that the Joads and others dreamed of reproducing in their exile. The idea that land should be used and occupied, rather than left fallow, was stymied, however, by the power of the large landowner to let arable land remain idle:

> . . . And along the roads lay the temptations, the fields that could bear food.
> That's owned. That ain't our'n.
> Well, maybe we could get a little piece of her. Maybe--a little piece. Right down there--a patch. Jimson weed now. Christ' I could git enough potatoes off'n that little patch to feed my whole family!
> It ain't our'n. It got to have Jimson weeds (p. 320-1).

Any attempts to cultivate the "secret gardens" fail--unless the New Deal intervenes (p. 321). Outside of Bakersfield the federal government established the migrant labor camp, Weedpatch.

Weedpatch is reminiscent of both the "secret gardens" and the "rag town" Hoovervilles. The government camp provided momentary respite, even appeared idyllic. Yet in the final analysis it was little more than a glorified sanitary facility and could not support the desire for a permanent habitat:

> Tom walked down the street between the rows of tents . . . . He saw that the rows were straight and that there was no litter about the tents. The ground of the street had been swept and sprinkled . . . Tom walked slowly. He neared Number Four Sanitary Unit and he looked at it curiously, an unpainted building, low and rough (p. 393).

Weedpatch was the vector of several important themes in the novel. It drew on the idea of geometric orderliness and cleanliness as support for the moral authority of the American small town. Its setting resonated with a secure and bounded rural propriety. It was a point from which the power of the migrant "folk" could emanate amidst the enveloping enterprise of agribusiness. Most powerfully, Weedpatch was the over-lapping space of three "institutions": the short term needs of the migrant workers, federal relief policy, and large scale capitalist agriculture. For all its importance in bringing these systems together, however, Weedpatch remained a marginal place. It was a holding area for the worker in a place where employment was scarce after the harvest. Inside, the migrant community was strong and thwarted attempts of local vigilantes to incite a riot. Ultimately, though, it was agribusiness that set the rules. The Joads and others like them were forced to leave and look for work.

If the "secret garden" failed to sustain the myth of yeoman independence, Steinbeck experimented with the notion that it is in the seams, or cracks, in the agricultural landscape (the in-between places where *process,* rather than the final outcome, of the appropriation of nature can be viewed), where the self can retreat and become empowered through contact with nature, fragmentary though it may be. In *The Grapes of Wrath* this idea was expressed in the context of the agricultural production process. In this way Steinbeck located in a specific time and place what otherwise would be an historical notion. He took pains to explain that modern farming in Oklahoma and California entailed forms of subordination and social control (p. 50-1; 316-20). Steinbeck's whole point, of course, was to suggest how these consequences can be resisted.

In order to understand how these arguments work in the novel, we can examine certain events as they occur in irrigation ditches and hedgerows-- two types of seams, or cracks, in the agricultural landscape that represent gaps in apparently seamless power relations.

Tom Joad, the primary character in the novel, experienced two baptisms in irrigation ditches. The first was performed by Casy when Tom was a boy and Casy a revivalist preacher. His first baptism did not mean much to young Tom. Its meaning only became clear when Tom was *re*-baptized--this time by himself--after doing something out of conviction and a sense of social justice. In this scene, Tom's actions were less blind, more than merely the result of the things that he was always bumping into. Tom had just discovered Casy and a number of other labor organizers. In a scuffle with a group of vigilantes who were tailing them down a stream, Casy was killed. Tom fatally struck down the killer, was himself struck, and made his escape up the embankment:

> He bent low and ran over the cultivated earth; clods slipped and rolled under his feet. Ahead he saw the bushes that bounded the field, bushes along the edges of an irrigation ditch. He slipped through the fence, edged in among vines and blackberry bushes. And then he lay still, panting hoarsely. . . . He lay still on his stomach until his mind came back. And then he crawled slowly over the edge of the ditch. He bathed his face in the cool water . . . .
>   The black cloud had crossed the sky, a blob of dark against the stars. The night was quiet again (p. 527-8).

This second "baptism" was more figurative and secular than the first, but Steinbeck meant them to be parallel events. In each instance Tom and Casy were present. In each case Tom's baptism followed some form of violence. The first baptism occurred under conditions which were too naive to lend any meaning to Tom's life. The second, however, marked his passage into a period of solitary resolve and spiritual rekindling. For the moment he was emancipated--"The black cloud had crossed the sky. . . . The night was quiet again." That the baptisms occurred in irrigation ditches was simply consistent with the setting of the story. Yet their location has something to say about sites of spiritual renewal and resistance in a space of seemingly total social control.

The irrigation ditch is an essential feature and instrument of agriculture in a semi-arid environment. It is part and parcel of the transformation of nature, and hence, of the production and labor process (one of the few jobs Tom gets is digging an irrigation ditch). The ditch of the second baptism is at the field's edge, protected by water-seeking bushes. As much as it represents evidence of the dominant class's mastery over nature, it remains its own kind of environment, with water so elemental that its restorative properties are unsullied. The water, unlike the social and economic system that manipulates it, is not selective about to whom it gives life.

The second environment of solitary reflection, and precursor to resistance, is the hedgerow at the margins of the cotton fields. Like the irrigation ditches these micro-environments help build the novel's architectural symmetry. And similarly they see Tom's movement from a state of partial denial to affirmation of his role in social change. Twice the reader finds Tom Joad hiding at the edges of cotton fields. The first time is with Muley Graves at the Joads' old farm, when Tom and Casy follow Muley to a place where they can stay the night. It turns out to be a cave in the bank of a water-cut ". . . Joad settled himself on the clean sand. 'I ain't gonna sleep in no cave,' he said. 'I'm gonna sleep right here.' He rolled his coat and put it under his head" (p. 81-2).

Tom is hiding despite his pride and deliberations to the contrary, but he falls short of entering the cave as Muley does. The scene presages Tom's future exile in a similar situation in California: Muley warns Tom that he will be in hiding "from lots of stuff." Tom himself dug the cave at the edge of the field when he was a youth "Lookin' for gold"--what more appropriate place in which to end up than California at the edge of a cotton field.

After Tom escapes with this family from the peach orchard (where they were working at the time of Casy's death), Muley's prediction comes true:

> Al turned right on a graveled road, and the yellow lights shuddered over the ground. The fruit trees were gone now, and cotton plants took their place. They drove on for *twenty miles* [italics mine] through the cotton . . . The road paralleled a bushy creek and turned over a concrete bridge and followed the stream on the other side. And then, on the edge of the creek the lights showed a long line of red box-cars, wheelless; and a big sign on the edge of the road said, "Cotton Pickers Wanted." Al slowed down . . .
>
> ". . . Look," he [Tom] said. "It says they want cotton pickers. I seen the that sign. Now I been tryin' to figger how I'm gonna stay with you, an' not make no trouble. When my face gets well, maybe it'll be awright, but not now. Ya see them cars back there. Well, the pickers live in them. Now maybe they's work there. How about if you get work there an' live in one of them cars?"
>
> "How 'bout you?" Ma demanded.
>
> "Well, you see that crick, all full a brush. Well, I could hide in that brush an' keep outa sight. An' at night you could bring me out somepin to eat. I seen a culvert, a little ways back. I could maybe sleep in there" (p. 550-1).

While Tom was secure in the hedgerow above the creek by the cotton field, he could not only reflect on the recent events, but represent them to his mother in their full meaning. In his hiding place he found his kinship to a humanity beyond the family boundary, and came into a sense of overarching social purpose. Steinbeck intimated that Tom would follow in Casy's steps (p. 570).

By repeating the hiding pattern established earlier in the novel, Steinbeck foreshadowed the internal change in Tom's character. Steinbeck played seclusion and personal empowerment against the geographically extensive and demoralizing agricultural working conditions. The spatial reach of agri-business in the thirties, which seems to have leveled the distinction between one worker and another, is shown in *The Grapes of Wrath* to have enough cracks to allow certain people to individuate themselves. These cracks reflect on the contradictions of the production process, sustaining the idea of unexploited nature as a reserve for the human spirit during historically specific and dehumanizing conditions. Thus, Tom Joad had to be alone *in a particular kind of space*, in a special relationship with nature, before he could realize that, after all, he is part of a social group, of an historical moment--before he could grant authority to the representational and political value of language.

In *The Grapes of Wrath* Steinbeck appeared to praise the values and unswerving pragmatism of the migrant workers and families. Through Tom Joad, however, who finally discovered in his hideout that talking, thinking, and language are worthy tools for understanding practical predicaments, Steinbeck also criticized the shortcomings of the Joad family's "common sense," in which discussion and the very idea of representation--not learned in myth, but as relearned in the kinds of spaces where the individual can represent first to himself, then to others, a version of reality closer to the truth. In order for the human family to unite, the boundaries of the nuclear family had to be loosened. Ma Joad's "fambly" could not remain intact. She realized that, while her family had land, they were a bounded, cohesive entity. Without it they were falling apart (p. 536). However, only through their disintegration would they really think and act beyond themselves.

Finally, we are left to wonder how Steinbeck ultimately appraised the situation of the "Okie" migrant worker. To his credit Steinbeck did not see the migrant class as a monolith, but rather as differentiated. For example, toward the conclusion of the novel Ma and Pa Joad have taken divergent, gender-based viewpoints. Pa became preoccupied with looking backwards, so nos-talgic for a time when he was head of the household division of labor that he could not participate in the present. Ma was forward looking, acknowledging that the land in California was, after all, better than their Oklahoma farmland. She rose from the ashes of a burnt-out household, the vehicle for Steinbeck to expose the pitfalls of patriarchy. Pa remained stuck in the historical moment, if not in the past itself. Ma, as a woman, adapted readily to changing situations, accepting life as a "flow." However, the positions ascribed to Ma and Pa are not based on an historical sense of masculine and feminine. For both Pa's nostalgia and Ma's philosophy of "flow" were occasioned by their entrapment in an historical and geographical flux. It was Ma, while still in Oklahoma, who first experienced nostalgic attachments. The tragedy of the migrants' situation, therefore, seems not so much that they had to leave home, but that California did not yet offer the permanent place they thought it promised.

Steinbeck took the view that migrant workers were caught in a complex of relations modernizing the western states, that the particular features of their experience also depended on the forms of consciousness and practice that they brought to situations, and that rules and ideologies set by modern capitalism also relied in part on a laboring class such as the Joads represented. I have suggested that Steinbeck was keenly aware that the division of labor, agricultural production within capitalist agribusiness and the family farm, and the consciousness of individuals and social groups, all had requirements that grew out of and were projected onto contradicting geographical spaces. The particular oppositional motifs, a series of tensions, that I think Steinbeck used to convey his argument, were: the spaces of power and disenfranchisement, the ambiguity of the landscape as a depicting *and* concealing agent, and the conflicting modes of transforming nature.

These oppositional motifs were the means by which Steinbeck created a space for certain characters to resist the oppressing forces. The Joads were never completely marginalized; power was not *all* powerful. The attempts to make the Joads invisible in the landscape, a cog in the production process, contributed in some sense to their redemption. Nature was never entirely mastered nor subdued, and it was by virtue of its transformation by the class in power that restorative gaps were left.

From *California History*, Vol. 68 (Winter 1989/90), 211-23; 262.

References

Babcock, Barbara. (1978) *The Reversible World*. Ithaca: Cornell University Press.

Cosgrove, Denia. (1983) *Social Formation and Symbolic Landscape*. London: Croom, Helm.

Federal Writers' Project of the Works Progress Administration. (1984) [1939] *The WPA Guide to California*. New York: Pantheon Books.

French, Warren. (1966) *The Social Novel at the End of an Era*. Carbondale and Edwardsville, Illinois: Southern Illinois University Press.

Kappel, Tim. (1982) "Trampling Out the Vineyards--Kern County's Ban on *The Grapes of Wrath*." *California History*. 61.3: 210-21.

Lisca, Peter. (1977) [1957] *"The Grapes of Wrath* as Fiction." In *Steinbeck* (1977): 729-47.

Lutwack, Leonard. (1984) *The Role of Place in Literature*. Syracuse, New York: Syracuse University Press.

Martin, Stoddard. (1983) *California Writers*. New York: St. Martin's Press.

McWilliams, Carey. (1969) [1939] *Factories in the Field: The Story of Migratory Farm Labor in California*. Archon Books.

St. Pierre, Brian. (1983) *John Steinbeck: The California Years*. San Francisco: Chronicle Books.

Stallybrass, P., and White, A. (1986) *The Politics and Poetics of Transgression*. Ithaca: Cor-nell University Press.

Steinbeck, Elaire, and Robert Wallsten (1975) *Steinbeck: A Life in Letters*. New York: The Viking Press, Inc.

Steinbeck, John. (1977) [1939] *The Grapes of Wrath: Text and Criticism*. Peter Lisca, ed. (The Viking Critical Library) New York: Penguin Books.

Taylor, Frank J. (1977) [1939] "California's Grapes of Wrath," in *Steinbeck* (1977): 643-56.

Taylor, Walter Fuller. (1977) [1959] "The Grapes of Wrath Reconsidered," in *Steinbeck* (1977): 757-68.

Dialogic Structure and Levels of Discourse in Steinbeck's *The Grapes of Wrath*

Louis Owens and Hector Torres

The development of the novel is a function of the deepening of dialogic essence, its increased scope and greater precision. Fewer and fewer neutral, hard elements ("rock bottom truths") remain that are not drawn into dialogue.

--M. M. Bakhtin, *The Dialogic Imagination*

Much attention has been paid to the most basic level of narrative structure in *The Grapes of Wrath*, to the alternation of the story of the Joads with the story of the Dust Bowl exodus as a whole. Critics have discussed Steinbeck's rationale for such a structure and have closely examined devices the author uses to weld the two kinds of chapters into a unified novel.[1] In spite of long interest in the immediate dialectic of the alternating chapters, however, almost no attention has been devoted to the still more complex dialogic structure and levels of discourse in *The Grapes of Wrath*.

In attempting to write the story of a human tragedy on a national scale, Steinbeck was faced with a dilemma. The documentary, a form with which he was thoroughly familiar, tended to give the big picture, tended to focus on the suffering multitudes, with the effect of educating the viewer or reader but at the same time distancing him from the intimate suffering and pain of those caught up in the disaster. "It means very little to know that a million Chinese are starving unless you know one Chinese who is starving," Steinbeck wrote in 1941 in the preface to his script for the documentary, *The Forgotten Village*. In discussing the film, he added:

> A great many documentary films have used the generalized method, that is, the showing of a condition or an event as it affects a group of people. The audience can then have a personalized reaction from imagining one member of that group. I have felt that this was the more difficult observation from the audience's viewpoint. . . . In *The Forgotten Village* we reversed the usual process. Our story centered on one family in one small village. We wished our audience to know this family very well, and incidentally to like it, as we did. Then, from association with this little personalized group, the larger conclusion concerning the racial group could be drawn with something like participation.[2]

"Something like participation" is what Steinbeck wanted for *The Grapes of Wrath.* The reader must not only be shown the enormity of the widespread suffering, he must also identify with the migrants, and feel their loss, their hope, their frustration and futility, their enduring strength on a personal level. It is this participation in the lives of the Joads that captures the reader and propels him through the long book, and it is only through this participation that the full emotional impact Steinbeck desired can be achieved. The subject of the novel, however, was not the suffering of the single family. For the novel, as Steinbeck conceived it, to be successful, the reader must be aware that the Joads are only selected specimens, and that what Steinbeck is writing about is tragedy on an enormous, epic scale, tragedy for which no individual blame can be assigned.

Steinbeck's answer to this dilemma is the dialectical structure of *The Grapes of Wrath*, with chapters telling the story of the Joads' trek westward alternating with those that depict the larger exodus from the Dust Bowl. The result of Steinbeck's narrative experiment is a pattern of expansion (interchapters) and contraction (Joad chapters) that runs throughout the novel from beginning to end, creating a powerful dialectic between regional disaster and intimate pathos as we move between macro- and microcosm. Of the thirty chapters in *The Grapes of Wrath*, sixteen—less than twenty percent of the novel—are what Steinbeck called intercalery chapters, or interchapters. Beginning with the novel's first chapter, those narrative interludes allow the narrative eye to pan back, away from the intimate picture for a broad view of generalized experience. The Joads appear in none of the interchapters, which Steinbeck referred to as "repositories of all the external information" in the novel. They give us not only the broad picture of the migrants' suffering, but also provide necessary background information, such as the history of agriculture in California.

Although this narrative movement on its most basic levels has often been discussed by critics, with acknowledgment of the influence of Dos Passos, the complex dialogic structure has yet to be fully appreciated.[3] An examination of three key chapters—the first chapter, the "jeremiad" chapter, and the final chapter of *The Grapes of Wrath*—may demonstrate this point. Steinbeck consistently develops each interchapter from a general level of narrative time and space to a quite specific social context that contains and represents the dialogic nature of his story and discourse.[4] In the opening chapter we encounter not only the basic narrative patterns that Steinbeck uses to frame his story and discourse, but also the author's use of an epic, biblical voice of some immensity and scale. This voice recurs throughout the novel, evolving from the broad lyricism of Genesis at the beginning of the novel to the admonitory tone of the biblical jeremiad in chapter twenty-five. The Dust Bowl setting counter-balances this pure mythic voice and gigantic scale as the story and discourse locate themselves in a well-known historical period. At the same time, the narrative syntax bears clear markers that (i) claim mythic scale for the narrative but, (ii) paradoxically undermine any kind of absolute epic voice. In other words, Steinbeck uses the forms of epic discourse but takes away their implicit claims to absolute privilege. And in doing this, Steinbeck shows no interest in substituting one "monologic" voice for another. Instead, in keeping with the non-teleological narrative stance of his fiction, he creates a text in which no single voice speaks with final authority: the endings of neither the Joad chapters, nor the interchapters, nor the novel as a whole can be taken as final narrative closures. Rather, these endings foreground Steinbeck's complex view of the subject and subjects of his novel and the complex levels of discourse contained within it.

Scrutiny of narrative time in the following "temporal" sentences from chapter one illustrate this point:[5]

I. *Temporal Sentences/Movement of Narrative Time*
   A. *In the last part of May* the sky grew pale (1).
   B. *Then it was June*, and the sun shone more fiercely (1).
   C. *When June was half gone*, the big clouds moved out of Texas (2).
   D. *During a night* the wind raced faster and faster over the land (2).

    E. *The dawn came*, but no day . . . *and as that day advanced*, the
       dusk slipped back (2).
    F. *In the middle of that night* the wind passed on and left the land
       quiet (3).
    G. *In the morning* the dust hung like fog, and the sun was as red
       as ripe new blood (3).
    H. *As the day went forward* the sun became less red (4).

These phrases denote successively smaller segments of temporal reference. This progression exemplifies the temporal structure of the novel. In each chapter the narrative establishes the time of the season, and then focuses on a particular but not a specific day, thus connoting a narrative time that simultaneously (i) is tied to the seasons and the day but also, (ii) has no ultimate anchors. For this reason the grammatical past tense of each verb connotes a past time that can be any season of any year, any day or any time of any night. In sentence 1.D for instance, *night* is modified by the indefinite article *a*, and where a definite article or demonstrative appears before a similar noun, as in I.E, F, G, and H, the references still do not ground the narrative time to specific dates. This temporal unanchoredness contributes significantly to the mythic tone of Steinbeck's narrative. By the same token, however, this general past time passes in relation to the impending events of the Dust Bowl and in relation to the specific natural events that brought it on. In all the sentences above, for instance, the syntax pairs temporal adverbial constructions with references to nature, while I.B pairs the time of June with the sun's fierce shining. Together, the sentences denote a time that passes, in conjunction with the colors and moods of nature, over a barren and thirsty land inhabited by people who can no longer make their living from it. Through the dialectic suggested here, and with the resulting tension between specific, natural time, and mythic, unanchored time, Steinbeck subtly and very effectively mirrors the bipartite structure of the novel itself as it moves from the immediate, intimate story of the Joads to the timeless, mythic Exodus-like story of man.

    Next, let us look at the same phenomenon from the perspective of narrative space:

    II. Spatial Sentences/Description of Landscape Setting
    A. . . . the rains came gently, and they did not cut *the scarred earth*
       (1).
    B. *The surface of the earth crusted*, a thin hard crust, and as *the sky*
       became pale, so *the earth* became pale (1).

C. *The air* was thin and the *sky* more pale; and every day *the earth* paled (1).
D. *The finest dust* did not settle back to *the earth* now but disappeared into *the darkening sky* (2).
E. All day *the dust* sifted down from *the sky*. . . An even blanket covered *the earth* (3).
F. As the day went forward the sun became less red. It flared down on *the dust-blanketed land* (4).

Here Steinbeck denotes a narrative ground that begins with a scarred surface, becomes crusted, and ends with a blanket of dust that suffocates the productive soil. On the level of mythic discourse, these sentences evoke the ethereal quality that comes from a merging of earth and sky, the thin film of dust that hands in the aid mediating between these two elements. By the time the dust settles on a scorched earth to reveal an overpowering sun, the American Dust Bowl has become the scene for a new Exodus. But implicit in this scene is the suggestion that, for Steinbeck, humanity takes comfort in its will to survive as an intimate part of nature, never independent of it. Moreover, again the reader is distanced from the human suffering taking place amid the immense, mythic landscape that will serve to counter-balance the intimate suffering of the Joad chapters. Underscoring the dialectical structure of the novel, the narrative has panned back.

Dialogically, in those passages the reader is "overhearing" nothing less than Steinbeck "in conversation" with the language of biblical epic discourse and the broad, sweeping denotations, which so often characterizes it. In I.A-H, we see a narrative time that appears to stand still, unanchored. In II.A-F, we see a narrative space that hearkens back to the plague-stricken Egypt of biblical times. And yet, in neither the temporal nor the spatial narrative structures established by these sentences do people exercise any absolute will to power; instead, humanity is represented as an apparition that suffers along with the rest of nature. In effect, on this narrative ground there is no transcendent "outside." Implicit here, in the novel's opening pages, is the fact that the narrative time and space of *The Grapes of Wrath* can admit no apocalyptic vision, or "uncovering" of eternal truths, an implication that anticipates the novel's closing syntagmatic opposition between intercalary and Joad chapters. Here the earth is suffocated by water. What Steinbeck does, then, is make the authority of monologic biblical discourse descend to the level of human time, where it becomes subject to the dialogic forces of human language and discourse. In *The Grapes of Wrath*, it is the suffering of humanity that is eternal, and the suffering of one is the suffering of many.

To reinforce this nonteleological view of history, Steinbeck not only relies on the forms of biblical discourse, he also employs the speech of his characters and the discourse of his narrator to this end. As narrator, Steinbeck assumes a role in his own narrative (a strategy he later develops extensively in *East of Eden*), speaking with the voice of a participant, one who knows his characters from first-hand experience, and those characters, of course, have voices with which to tell their own stories. Author, narrator, and characters enter into dialogue with each other. An examination of the structure of the dialogic interaction in the last paragraph of chapter one illustrates this point:

> III.A. *Dialogue/Story & Discourse Voices*
> A. Men stood by their fences and looked at the ruined corn . . *they were silent and did not move often* (3).
> B. And the women came out of the houses to stand beside their men—*to feel whether this time the men would break* (3-4).
> C. *The women studied the men's faces secretly,* for the corn could go, as long as something else remained (4).
> D. The children stood near by . . . and sent exploring senses out to see whether men and women would break (4).
> E. After a while the faces of the watching men lost their bemused perplexity and *became hard and angry and resistant* (4).
> F. *Then the woman knew that they were safe* and that there was no break (4).
> G. Then they asked, *What'll we do?* and the men replied, *I don't know* (4)
> H. *But it was all right* (4).
> I. *Women and children knew deep in themselves* that no misfortune was too great to bear if their men were whole (4).

The generic references to women, children, and men show the narrative eye situated at some distance from the subjects it observes: the observations are of a people, not of individual persons. This spatial distance allows the narrator to complicate his presentation of the scene. The apparent impersonality afforded by a narrative eye distanced from the subject frames the characters within a spatial perimeter, inside of which the narrator notices the motionlessness of the men, the emergence of the women from their houses, and the children standing nearby. Here, the impersonal level of discourse connotes something like an objective narrator, an observer and chronicler of an immense human tragedy.

Other details in this passage bridge the spatial gap between narrator and characters and place the narrator squarely in the midst of the people. Moreover, with this close-up view comes a privileged access to the consciousness of the characters. For this reason, in III.B we see that the narrator can enter into the thoughts of the women about their men. Likewise, the use of the adverb "secretly" refers us to the invisible narrator's own secret perception of the women observing the men. III.C gives a glimpse of the narrator involved in a dialogic exchange with the women as he participates in secretly observing the men. The narrator speaks with the language of the women, using it to interact with both the male and female characters. Thus, the story voices heard in III.G contain their own internal dialogism, and also provide an occasion for the narrator to address his characters: *"But it was all right."* On this account, the dialogic exchange below with its simple question and response between the women (A) and their men (B), implies the story as a whole. This utterance pair in fact anticipates the thematic tension that arises at the end of both intercalery and Joad chapters. In those chapters Steinbeck chooses to depict humanity's sheer will to survive, creating a metaphor whose tenor refuses to be bound in its vehicle, a vehicle that is literally the *end* of the book. Steinbeck wants to tell a story that will not be easily ignored or quickly forgotten, and thus these voices tell their story with unflinching candor:

III.B. Character Speech/Story Voices
    1. (A) What'll we do?
       (B) I don't know (4).

Furthermore, what we see in the narrator's comment in III.H is, for all practical purposes, a direct response to the women and their men, and the optimism the narrator feels is the optimism of the women, as III.1 quickly affirms. Hence, the narrator can delve deeply into the uncertainties and eventual faith the women feel towards their men, and, in general terms, one sees here an interaction between impersonal and personal perspectives, the one framing the story and the other participating in it. As a type of participant-observer, the narrator, like the characters, is caught in the play of life's natural forces. Indeed, the lack of quotation marks also signifies the extent to which Steinbeck *requires* that his narrator enter into dialogue with the story's anonymous characters.

A fourth level to this complex dialectic is added in III.G and I as it becomes clear that Steinbeck is "dialogizing" with both his narrator and his characters. To begin with, Steinbeck avoids making his narrator omniscient, as is evident in the fact that at the end of this opening chapter, the narrator observes that the men are deep in thought but does not penetrate those thoughts. That Steinbeck's narrator is not allowed this privileged information demonstrates that, as author, he is in dialogue with his narrator. Furthermore, "But it was all right" contains not only the narrator's voice but also Steinbeck's. (Bakhtin calls this type of construction, one in which a single construction contains two speech styles, a hybrid construction.) Implicit in the narrator's evaluation is Steinbeck's own affirmation of the ontological resoluteness with which these anonymous and hence allegorical characters will fight to survive. Clearly, such survival need not be of the individual, but of the species.

In this complex passage, Steinbeck once again balances levels of discourse: on the one hand, the impulse towards impersonal and allegorical discourse, and on the other the immediacy of the dialogic voices of not simply a single speaker but of many. Narrator and characters alike are left not knowing what trajectory history will take. In effect, Steinbeck successfully infuses his narrative with the dual dialectical impulses of universality and particularity, the latter affirmed through the dialogic essence of language and the former through humanity's drive to survive in the face of misfortune and political and economic oppression, at times through sheer strength of will.

If chapter one introduces the primary dialectic and complex dialogism of the novel, chapter twenty-five—the jeremiad—reveals Steinbeck's careful stylization of dialogic voices. In this key chapter, in which we encounter a complex alternation of narrative voices, Steinbeck differentiates and stylizes the various voices by using specific syntactic markers, with each cluster of syntactic markers constituting a distinct topic in the discourse and story. In the following passage, for example, the cluster of syntactic markers constitutes a coherent, independent discourse:

IV.A Topic: *The Men of Knowledge*
      1. Syntactic Markers: (i) present tense, (ii) present perfect aspect
      2. Narrative Voice: Discourse-framing narrator

    a. Behind the fruitfulness *are* men of understanding and
       knowledge, and skill, men who experiment with seed
       (382).
    b. They *have transformed* the world with their knowledge.
       The short, lean wheat *has been made* big and productive.
       Little sour apples *have grown* large and sweet, and that
       old grape . . . *has mothered* a thousand varieties (383).
    c. And the men of knowledge *have worked, have considered*
       and the fruit is rotting on the ground, and the decaying
       mash in the wine vat is poisoning the air (384).
    d. Men who can graft the tree and make the seed fertile and
       big *can* find no way to let the hungry people eat their
       produce (384-85).
    e. Men who *have created* new fruits in the world *cannot*
       create a new system whereby their fruits may be eaten
       (385).
    f. The works of the roots of the vines, of the trees, must be
       destroyed to keep up the price, and this *is* the saddest,
       bitterest thing of all (385).

In this topical segment of text, Steinbeck's narrator establishes the broad
thematic concern that informs the various narrative voices, and in relying on
the present and present perfect tenses the narrator maintains his discourse at
a high level of generality. The present tense establishes the discourse as
factual, while the perfective marks it as relevant to the immediate present,
an on-going and persistent fact. This discourse is primarily concerned with
exposing the absurdity of not taking advantage of the fruits of agricultural
technology, and ultimately of letting agriculture become controlled solely be
economic interests. If we look at another topical segment of text, we can see
how Steinbeck carefully differentiates a second narrative voice through the
use of specific syntactic markers:

    IV.B Topic: An Impossible Harvest
        1. Syntactic Markers: (i) present tense, (ii) first person
          plural pronoun, (iii) imperative clauses, (iv) idiolectal
          speech
        2. Narrative Voices: Character speech/the little farmer

a. Cent and a half a pound. Hell, we can't pick 'em
   for that.
b. My God, we can't pick them and dry and sulphur
   them. We can't pay wages, no matter what wages.
c. Five dollars for forty fifty-pound boxes; trees pruned
   and sprayed, orchards cultivated—pick the fruit, put
   it in boxes, load the truck, deliver the fruit to the cannery——forty boxes for five dollars. We can't do it.
d. (A) We can't make good wine. People can't buy
   good wine. *Rip* the grapes from the vines, good
   grapes, wasp-stung grapes. *Press* stems, press dirt
   and rot.
   (B) But there's mildew and formic acid in the vats.
   (A) *Add* sulphur and tannic acid.
   (B) Oh, well, it has alcohol in it anyway. They can
   get drunk (384).

This topic emerges from the speech of the farmer telling his own story, talking about his own economic dilemma. The use of idiolectal speech gives the story a profound authority because the little farmer knows through and through the cold economics of what it takes to bring in a successful harvest, and that not even making wine will turn a profit since there is no market for good wine. His idiolectal speech carries with it all the despair of one who knows that the market is being artificially controlled and manipulated. Consequently, the only alternative for the little farmer is to make cheap wine. The order to make the wine even in vats with mildew and formic acid, as the voice of a third person reminds him, underscores the desperation and utter resignation that grips the little farmer in the face of powerful economic interests. Once again, the casting of these story voices in anonymity simultaneously connotes two levels of discourse. At one level, the grammatical present tense, the first personal plural pronoun, and the dialogic structure of IV.B.d lend the narrative authenticity and immediacy. At another level, the idiolectal speech of the little farmer carries a reference to all those farmers that were forced to accept the economic severities imposed on them by the powerful business interests that then ruled agricultural California. What we see in these story voices is an account, from within, of these business interests.

In contrast, we see in the topical segment below an account from without; that is, Steinbeck differentiates a third narrative voice that confirms what the farmers are saying:

IV.C. Topic: The debt of the little farmer
1. Syntactic Markers: (i) past tense, (ii) present tense, (iii) future perfect tense, (iv) address to a third person, (v) deictic forms
2. Narrative Voice: confirmatory narrator
   a. The little farmers *watched* debt creep up on them like the tide (384).
   b. They *sprayed* the trees and sold no crop, they *pruned* and *grafted* and could not pick the crop (384).
   c. And *taste the wine*—no grape flavor at all, just sulphur and tannic acid and alcohol (384).
   d. This little orchard *will be* part of a great holding next year, for the debt will have choked the owner (384).
   e. This vineyard *will* belong to the bank. Only the great owners *can* survive, for they own the canneries, too (384).
   f. Carloads of oranges *dumped* on the ground. The people came for miles to take the fruit, but this could not be (385).
   g. And the men with hoses *squirt* kerosene on the oranges, and they are angry at the crime, angry at the people who have come to take the fruit (385).
   h. A million hungry people, needing fruit—and kerosene sprayed over the golden mountains (385).

The narrative voice uses the past tense to recount actual, temporally defined events to someone else. Then, in IV.C.c, the switch to present tense as the narrator offers wine to his interlocutor functions as direct evidence of what he has recounted in IV.C.a and b. Also, the deictic forms of *this little orchard* and *this vineyard* signify respectively that the narrator is, in some way, in a place where he can point to the specific orchard and vineyard as he talks. In fact, it is because this narrator is so close to his subject, knows it so well, that he can make the predictions that he makes, and by implication can verify the story that the farmers have told about their impossible harvest. And in the same way that the farmers see their plight in relation to the poor, those unable to afford the fruits of their orchards, the grapes from their vineyards, perhaps even their cheap wine, so this narrator brings his point back around to the injustices caused by certain powerful, callous owners. As in IV.C.a-b and c, the narrator again alternates between past and present tenses in IV.C.f and g in order to create a sense of immediacy in his telling.

In particular, the irony of the angry owners considering it a crime that the hungry take what they need to survive calls into questions the authenticity of the American myth of boundless westward expansion and capitalistic enterprise.   The golden mountains of California oranges, soaked with kerosene and set alight, connote a shared suffering between disenfranchised humanity and impersonal nature. Steinbeck masterfully develops his critique of the American myth of prosperity in the discourse of a narrator who points to concrete social events and speaks with a direct and insightful irony.

It is in the biblical jeremiad, however, that Steinbeck unleashes the full force of his irony in this chapter, as the following topical segment illustrates:

IV.D. Topic: Prophetic political discourse on the grapes of wrath
    1. Syntactic Markers: (i) present tense, (ii) imperative
       clauses, (iii) *there*-clauses, (iv) present progressive aspect
    2. Narrative Voice: Biblical/jeremiad style
       a. The decay spread over the state, and the sweet smell is a great sorrow over the land (384).
       b. And the smell of rot fills the country (385).
       c. Burn coffee for fuel in the ships. Burn corn to keep warm, it makes a hot fire. Dump potatoes in the rivers and place guards along the banks to keep the hungry people from fishing them out (385).
       d. There is a crime here that goes beyond denunciation. There is a sorrow here that weeping cannot symbolize. There is a failure here that topples all our successes (385).
       e. . . . . and in the eyes of the hungry people there [is] a growing wrath. In the souls of the people the grapes of wrath are filling and growing heavy, growing heavy for the vintage (385).

In this segment, as in chapter one, we see Steinbeck overtly using the forms of biblical discourse, in particular the jeremiad so often employed in America to move the nation toward repentance. In Steinbeck's version, the complaint carries a strong political content, implying that whatever transcendence humanity may achieve is inevitably in humanity's own image. Thus, the imperative clauses of IV.D.c resound with the irony of challenge: any waste of the food the land produces is a blow to humanity.   The universality of this irony is reinforced in the syntax of the existential *there*-clauses of IV.D.d. The affirmation that a crime, a sorrow, and a failure exist that exceed denunciation, symbolization by any weeping, and the highest human achievement, demonstrates the lengths that Steinbeck would go in order to expose the fundamental failure and absurdity of the American Dream. In his view, neither human language and discourse, nor the suffering of America's hungry and disenfranchised could express the utter emptiness of American mythology. In suggesting that the forms of biblical discourse and the zeal for American mythology live in political complicity, Steinbeck denounces this complicity by showing that the claims of these two forces to transcendence and prosperity curiously leave out a whole mass of hungry people, while potatoes float down rivers, oranges are sprayed with kerosene, and pigs are slaughtered and covered with quick-lime. As a result, Steinbeck's brilliant jeremiad is above all a lamentation for the suffering of America's poor and hungry as well as a concrete political discourse against capitalistic duplicity and greed.

Given the complex interaction of such syntactic markers as tense and aspect, clausal forms, and personal pronouns, it is not surprising that Steinbeck's text exhibits a corresponding complex alternation of narrative voices. As we have seen, Steinbeck stylizes the speech of each narrator by marking it with distinctive syntactic phenomena, allowing the reader to identify the voices of a variety of narrators. One narrator, for instance, speaks in the technical vocabulary of one who understands modern developments in the science of agriculture. Another narrator speaks with an intimate knowledge of the economic plight that befell the California farmer at the hands of ruthless capitalism. And, in their own voices, the farmers tell their own story. And it is in the prophesying voice of the jeremiad that Steinbeck brings these other voices together to deliver a stinging denunciation of the injustices a whole mass of humanity needlessly suffers. The conjoined powers of the ironies of which these narrative voices speak effectively topples the pretensions of American capitalist ideology, and if these voices ultimately focus on the same thematic level of discourse, it is only because the dialogic forces of language make it difficult to gloss over the enormous suffering that America's hungry and poor have undergone. For Steinbeck, the dialogical interaction of narrative voices forms the ideological matrix in which his own authorial voice becomes paradoxically universal, transcendently allegorical and anagogical, while remaining necessarily existential, definitively temporal and political.

The penultimate chapter of *The Grapes of Wrath* provides a final example of Steinbeck's implicit reliance on dialogism. In this, the novel's final intercalary chapter, Steinbeck brings the reader back to the beginning of the novel. Nothing has changed because Steinbeck, from the beginning, has made no gestures toward inscribing into the narrative as a whole any kind of ultimate closure. Indeed, narrative closure is immaterial because Steinbeck, in myriad ways, indicates that survival of the species is what counts, not survival of the individual. From the beginning, this human survival, like the survival of the American nation, has not been in doubt. The manner in which Steinbeck requires his narrator to enter into dialogue with the characters of the story in the opening chapter certainly serves notice of this. In the hybrid syntax of statement III.H, *But it was all right*, Steinbeck joins with his narrator in affirming humanity's inevitable survival. This is why the last intercalary chapter, with its multiple voices anticipating a difficult future, is not, when read in terms of the novel's dialogic discourse, unremittingly tragic:

> V.A. Topic: Deluge, Joblessness, Survival
>> 1. Syntactic Markers: (i) present tense, (ii) idiolectal speech
>> 2. Narrative Voices: Characters' speech
>>> a. (A) It'll soon be over.
>>>   (B) How long's it likely to go on? (478)
>>> b. They's rules—you got to be here a year before you can git relief. They say the gov'ment is gonna help. They don' know when (478).
>>> c. They ain't gonna be no kinda work for three months (478).
>>> d. (A) No work till spring. No work.
>>>   (B) And if no work—no money, no food..
>>>   (C/A) Fella had a team of horses, had to use 'em to plow an' cultivate an' mow, wouldn' think a turnin' 'em out to starve when they wasn't workin'.
>>>   (E/B) Them's horses—we're men (480).

As these story voices speak their misery, they identify both the forces that oppress them as well as the philosophical outlook that will get them through periods of profound misery. Not only must these people weather the storms of nature but they must also contend with a faceless, inefficient government bureaucracy. The hardship these destitute folk experience is the result of a government heavy under the burden of its own ineptitude and the crude ease with which it wastes vast resources. Presented in the speech of one of the novel's nameless characters, the team of horses analogy, in typical hybrid style, makes clear Steinbeck's affinity with socialist political philosophy. And then, in a voice which could belong either to participant (A) again or to a brand-new character (E), we hear the humanity of these marginalized people. It is this affirmation of their humanity that denotes, *a fortiori*, the indubitable persistence of the displaced Okies. In other words, in one humble conversational exchange about their shared wretchedness, these story voices, licensed by Steinbeck, raise the discourse to a high level of ontological and political understanding.

To remove any ambiguity in the discourse of the story voices, Steinbeck relies once again on the semi-omniscient narrator of the opening chapter:

V.B. Topic: *Anger turns to wrath and wrath to survival*
  1. Syntactic Markers: (i) past tense, (ii) present perfect aspect, (iii) past tense modality
  2. Narrative Voice: semi-omniscient narrator
     a. The rain *stopped* . . . And the men *came* out of the barns, out of the shed. They *squatted* on their hams and *looked* out over the flooded land. And they *were* silent. And sometimes they *talked* very quietly (479).
     b. The women *watched* the men, watched to see whether the break *would* come at last. The women *stood* silently and *watched* (480).
     c. And where a number of men *gathered* together, the fear *went* from their faces, and anger *took* its place (480).
     d. And the women *sighed* with relief, for they *knew* it was all right—the break *had not come*; and the break *would never come* as long as fear *could turn* to wrath (480).
     e. Tiny points of grass *came* through the earth, and in a few days the hills *were* pale green with the beginning year (480).

Steinbeck's narrator again takes the perspective of the women and has access to their consciousness, and, as in the opening chapter, he is able to tell the reader what the women know about their men. As the women see that their men have not been broken, they also know that they all have undergone and survived the most extreme testing possible. The use of the modal verbs *could* and *would* show the close proximity of the narrator to the subjective modality through which the women perceive their men. The narrator, just like the women, understands that no condition under which the emigrants could break exists because, if they were going to break, what they have just gone through would have done it. In addition to the privilege of knowing this, the narrator also has the "authority" to turn the last sentence of his discourse (V.B.e) into a metaphor that signifies the possibility of new life for the subjects he observes. With this metaphor of hope, grounded as it is in nature and the seasons, Steinbeck once again places humanity squarely inside the narrative time and space of the first intercalary and Joad chapters. The juxtaposition of the closing intercalary chapter with its twin, the closing Joad chapter, represents a syntagmatic opposition that encodes the extent to which Steinbeck wants to leave his reader with the uneasy tension that comes of having just finished reading a work that resonantly captures the dialectics of hope and despair, of difference and indifference. Thus, Steinbeck suggests, people hope and will continue to hope in the face of any clear ground for existence, in the face of utter indifference. Humanity—he again suggests—can and oftentimes does exist on nothing but a brutal dialectic between a thin thread of hope and the ironic despair of being alive, so forcefully represented in the figure of the smiling Rose of Sharon. Her decision to feed the sick and starving man with the milk that should have nourished her dead child, signifies, for Steinbeck, the lengths to which humanity will go in order to insure its own survival in the face of seeming indifference.

It is perhaps in this last syntagmatic opposition between intercalary and Joad chapters that Steinbeck is at his ironic best. The last sentence of this discourse topic--*Tiny points of grass came through the earth, and in a few days the hills were pale green with the beginning year*--also a species of the hybrid construction, clearly rings with the tenor of Steinbeck's authorial voice. But in pairing the figure of the smiling Rose of Sharon with the metaphor of a green earth and a fresh year, Steinbeck signals his choice to not unify the various dialogical voices under a single narrative trajectory, thus indicating his lack of interest in presenting his readers with a novel that speaks with absolute authority. Rather, what we see in this opposition of metaphors is Steinbeck's awareness that discourse--the life of language--is an on-going dialectic between (and among) syntax and grammar, style and ideology, aesthetics and politics. In this hybrid construction--the final line of the last intercalary chapter of the novel--Steinbeck records two simultaneous dialogic voices that articulate his commitment to a dialectical view of reality, to the writing of a novel that refuses narrative and thematic unity. One voice, that of the semi-omniscient narrator, moves the reader along in narrative time to the very end of the story, since the conjunction of the two clauses grounds those clauses according to a strict temporal sequence. First, the earth sprouts its new shoots of green grass and then the hills--a few days later in narrative time--become green "with the beginning year." The narrator, inevitably subject to narrative time, can only represent the pure movement of nature and the seasons. At the same time, however, the careful parallelism of the clauses recalls the voice of biblical discourse, the mythic timeless voice of the novel. These two voices are in tension; the narrative must both move within time and remain timeless, and there is no way to reconcile these two narrative impulses. In effect, the narrator has moved past the time in which Rose of Sharon sits in the barn with her mysterious smile, but Steinbeck has clearly told his reader that the new earth and the new time will abide. Hence, the Rose of Sharon figure that will appear in the final chapter of the novel is not a sign of final human despair. By the same token, however, the mythic biblical voice cannot itself be a sign of ultimate regal authority. Thus the dialectical structure of *The Grapes of Wrath,* with its dialogic infrastructure and style (the various dialogic voices and syntax) effectively resists closure and requires that the reader approach the novel with the same ability to resist ideological closure, with no ultimate voice of authority, no transcendent teleology, no final scapegoat.

Notes

1. See for example, Peter Lisca, *The Wide World of John Steinbeck* (New Brunswick, N. J.: Rutgers University Press, 1958) 177-77; Louis Owens, *John Steinbeck's Re-Vision of America* (Athens: University of Georgia Press, 1985) 128-40; and Louis Owens, *The Grapes of Wrath: A New Eye in the West* (Boston: Twayne, 1989).

2. John Steinbeck, *The Forgotten Village* (New York: Viking Press, 1941), unpaginated preface.

3. In employing the notion of "dialogic structure," we are, as our epigraph suggests, following the systematic elaboration M. M. Bakhtin gives in *The Dialogic Imagination: Four Essays,* trans. Caryl Emerson and Michael Holquist, ed. Michael Holquist (Austin: University of Texas Press, 1981), relying specifically on essay four, "Discourse in the Novel." In that essay Bakhtin discusses what he takes as the distinctive feature of the novel, arguing that: "The fundamental condition of the novel, that which makes a novel a novel, that which is responsible for its stylistic uniqueness, is the *speaking person and his discourse*" (emphasis in the text, 332). On such a constitutive and regulative principle, the lexical and syntactic choices that go into the creation of discourse in the novel are subject to the same ideological forces that shape everyday speech. Bakhtin goes on to argue that, "The

novel, being a dialogized representation of an ideologically freighted discourse, . . . is of all verbal genres the one least susceptible to aestheticism as such, to a purely formalistic playing about with words"(333). Thus, in narrative discourse, the lexicon and the syntax of a language carry the semantic and discursive traces of everyday dialogue, which is constantly being charged with the exigencies of daily political life. In every respect then, the internal dialogic structure of discourse denotes the complex social life of language—its tie to the dynamic forces of authority and persuasion, question and response, and conversational give and take, with one's self and with others. For another succinct definition of Bakhtin's concept of dialogic structure, see also the glossary compiled by the editor and translators of *The Dialogic Imagination*.

4. With respect to the terms "story" and "discourse" we have in mind the traditional formalist definitions. Thus, in any narrative, the story represents the narrated events as they take place in strict temporal order, while the discourse represents the complex stylistic choices made by an author in order to reveal his or her attitude toward the story. Clearly, in the critical vocabulary of "dialogic," "story," and "discourse" upon which we rely, it is the first term that is the inclusive one. For an extended discussion of the notion of discourse in the novel from a linguistic perspective, see Geoffrey N. Leech and Michael H. Short, *Style in Fiction: A Linguistic Introduction to English Fictional Prose* (New York: Longman, 1981) 257-87. From the same perspective, see also Roger Fowler, *Linguistics and the Novel* (London: Methuen, 1977) 71-122, who also incorporates Wayne Booth's notion of narrative voice into a linguistic model of stylistic analysis, and offers a short and useful historical sketch of the story/discourse distinction.

5. For its ease and accessibility, all references are from John Steinbeck, *The Grapes of Wrath* (1939; New York: Bantam, 1969). For ease of exposition, we have adopted an outline method for presenting our analysis of the dialogic structures of Steinbeck's text. As the analysis proceeds it will facilitate reference to specific sentences and segments of text. We italicize to highlight the lexical and syntactic features of the text particularly relevant to our analysis.

The Squatter's Circle in
The Grapes of Wrath

John H. Timmerman

In John Steinbeck's *The Grapes of Wrath*, the indomitable Ma Joad emerges as a hero and the leader of, in her words, "the fambly of man." In so doing, however, she also displaces Pa Joad from his traditional position of authority in the family. While several critical studies have examined those qualities of Ma Joad that direct her leadership--qualities of humor, a steadfast vision, and a resilient ability to bend and adapt to new situations without breaking-- Pa Joad has disappeared from critical scrutiny as if of no account. In fact, Steinbeck very carefully directs the reversal of leadership roles through the use of the "squatter's circle" motif.

That the migrant family of the 1930s was strongly patriarchal has been demonstrated by Tom Collins' detailed reports on California migrant camps during the late 1930s. Collins was the manager of the Kern County Migrant Camp and was also Steinbeck's most profitable source of information about migrant traditions. He personally escorted Steinbeck through both the established government camps and the squatters' camps. More importantly, Steinbeck took back with him to Los Gatos hundreds of pages of Collins' reports and assessments of migrant families. These reports figured directly into Steinbeck's composition of his novel.[1]

Collins' weekly reports from Kern County's Arvin Camp, prototype for the Weedpatch Camp in *The Grapes of Wrath*, testify that these migrant families, while traditionally patriarchal, were experiencing a revolution of matriarchal uprising. As the men foundered in the bewildering tides of joblessness, indirection, and poverty, the women assumed dominant authority in the family.

One of the most revealing parts of Collins' reports in this matter of family authority appears in his weekly entry entitled "Bits of Migrant Wisdom." Here Collins diverges from his statistical information, his detailed accounts of camp activities, and his necessarily objective analysis to satisfy the governmental bureaucracy, to probe intimately the nature of migrant lives. Frequently such musings and probings focus upon marital relationships. After recounting at some length in his report for June 6, 1936, one protracted and often violent lover's quarrel, Collins observes: "We just let her cry. In fact we encouraged her to cry and bawl to her hearts [sic] content. That's what she wanted to do. Migrant women are that way."[2] But he does not leave the portrait with this traditional depiction of the weakly crying woman. There is tougher stuff in the camp women, and one has an idea that Collins appreciates the woman he quotes two paragraphs further in the story: "A woman neighbor summed the incident thusly: 'She aint ole nuf ter u'stand men folks. She'll larn sum day. What she shuld a-dun was ter kick him plenty in the fanny, only she wont.'" Collins observes, "we believe she will do that soon." While he portrays the migrant women in their customary matriarchal roles of canning, housekeeping, and sewing, he also senses a tide of revolution sweeping through them.

A second observation of Collins, appearing in his report for June 13, 1936, recounts a specific example of a woman revolting against the patriarchal system:

> Reversing the usual migrant system whereby the man is the master of the house, the bride in this instance rules the roost. She can be heard every evening after the boy's return from work, laying down the law. On one occasion we saw her sitting down giving him orders on proper dish washing and later, instructions regarding sweeping out the tent and doing the family wash. He grunted a lot but went about the task as "ordered."

Collins closes with a terse reflection: "Maybe a new day has dawned for the migrant woman, eh?" If it had, nowhere would it be more evident than in Ma Joad's reversal of the patriarchal role in the family.

In *The Grapes of Wrath*, Ma Joad rises as the force that unifies and directs the disintegrating family. In order to do so, however, on several occasions she stands up to and eventually displaces Pa from his family role. The first such incident occurs on the road to California, when Ma brandishes a jack handle and orders Pa to keep the family together. Tom Joad has offered to lay over with Al to repair the blown connecting rod on the Wilson car, while the others travel ahead. Ma's rebellion is forthright and undeniable:

> And now Ma's mouth set hard. She said softly, "On'y way you gonna get me to go is whup me." She moved the jack handle gently again. "An' I'll shame you, Pa. I won't take no whuppin', cryin' an' a-beggin'. I'll light into you. An' you ain't so sure you can whup me anyways."[3]

Repeatedly, she defies and threatens Pa, and he finds himself bewildered in the face of her assertion of authority. Tom Joad wonders, "Ma, what's eatin' on you? What ya wanna do this-a-way for? What's the matter'th you anyways? You gone johnrabbit on us?" (p. 230). To which Ma replies with the first annunciation of her vision of the primacy of the family: "Ma's face softened, but her eyes were still fierce. 'You done this 'thout thinkin' much,' Ma said. 'What we got lef' in the worl'? Nothin' but us. Nothin' but the folks'" (p. 230). The effect is undeniable: "The eyes of the whole family shifted back to Ma. She was the power. She had taken control" (p. 231).

Certainly there is steely resolve in this woman's spine. When the family camps along the Colorado River, and Granma lies hallucinating in the unbearable heat of the tent, Ma has her care of Granma interrupted by a pompous law officer who tries to threaten her. Ma stands up to him brandishing her skillet like a war club. When Ma recounts the scene to Tom, he responds, "Fust you stan' us off with a jack handle, and now you try to hit a cop.' He laughed softly, and he reached out and patted her bare foot tenderly. 'A ol' hell-cat,' he said" (p. 293). Truly Ma can be "a ol' hell-cat." Once before she lit into a tin peddler with a live chicken, beating the peddler until "they wasn't nothing but a pair a legs in her han" (p. 65). Ma's standing up to Pa Joad, however, is not a fit of pique, nor a momentary explosion of temper; rather, it is standing up for a vision and a dream of her family.

This struggle for the family becomes clear in the second major episode of Ma's assertion of authority. Having enjoyed the comforts of the Weedpatch Camp for some time, having been solaced in the compassion of its members so that in Ma's words, "I feel like people again" (p. 420), Ma nonetheless insists that the family move on. The family is disintegrating through lack of challenge and work; its dependency, in her view, breeds a slovenliness of spirit. Ma's order is terse and to the point: "We'll go in the mornin'." Pa remonstrates: "'Seems like times is changed,' he said sarcastically. 'Time was when a man said what we'd do. Seems like women is tellin' now. Seems like it's purty near time to get out a stick'" (p. 481).

But his comments are no more effective against Ma's steely will than they were earlier. When Pa and Uncle John wander off, Tom remains to question Ma: "You jus' a-treadin' him on?" Work, Ma believes, absolves worry. Pa has had too much time to ponder; insufficient opportunity to provide: "Take a man, he can get worried an' worried, an' it eats out his liver, an' purty soon he'll jus' lay down and die with his heart et out. But if you can take an' make 'im mad, why, he'll be awright" (p. 481).

A third time Ma Joad asserts her dominance over the family. After Tom strikes one of the landowners' goons and has to go into hiding, Ma again makes the decision to go. This time Pa readily accedes: "Come on now. Le's get out to her. Kids, you come he'p. Ma's right. We got to go outa here" (p. 535). He capitulates to her authority, but not until his own authority has been hopelessly battered. In fact, the Joad family has no reasonable place to go; all order seems destroyed.

Huddled in a boxcar, afflicted by the deluge of winter rains, Pa reflects: "Funny! Woman takin' over the fambly. Woman sayin' we'll do this here, an' we'll go there. An' I don' even care" (p. 577). Pa himself recognizes the transference of authority, and in response to this recognition Ma delivers her eloquent and compassionate eulogy to the power of the woman: "'Woman can change better'n a man,' Ma said soothingly. 'Woman got all her life in her arms. Man got it all in his head. Don' you mind. Maybe--well, maybe nex' year we can get a place'" (p. 577). She adds, "man, he lives in jerks-- baby born an' a man dies, an' that's a jerk--gets a farm an' loses his farm, an' that's a jerk. Woman, it's all one flow, like a stream, little eddies, little waterfalls, but the river, it goes right on. Woman looks at it like that" (p. 577). At this final, bleak scene, a thoroughly defeated Pa, like a bewildered child, seeks the restorative comfort of Ma Joad, whose spirit flows like a river.

That moving description of man and woman by Ma Joad, however, also underlies the displacement of authority in the novel from thinking man to spiritual woman, from a rational life jerked apart to a life led by the heart that bends and flows like the river. To demonstrate this, Steinbeck parallels Ma's rise to authority with Pa's displacement from, and the destruction of, the squatter's circle. In the novel Steinbeck depicts the traditional physical posture for decision-making among the male leaders of the family as squatting on the haunches in a circle. It represents a high formality among the migrant men and functions in the novel as a testament to rational order and male authority.

In his typical pattern of introducing an event or condition in its broadest scope in the intercalary chapters and then focusing upon the microcosmic unit of the Joad family in the narrative chapters, so too Steinbeck introduces the traditional posture of the squatter's circle in Chapter 5, an overview of the dispossession of the migrant families. As the landowner's spokesmen come to evict the tenant farmers, "the tenant men stood beside the cars for a while, and then squatted on their hams and found sticks with which to mark the dust" (p. 42). The farmers band together in the face of adversity, drawing upon each other's strength to plot a course of action. When the owners drive away, the men are left to consider matters on their own. Steinbeck provides the first carefully ordered description of the squatter's circle according to the male hierarchy in the tenant family:

> The tenant men squatted down on their hams again to mark the dust with a stick, to figure, to wonder. Their sun-burned faces were dark, and their sun-whipped eyes were light. The women moved cautiously out of the doorways toward their men, and the children crept behind the women, cautiously, ready to run. The bigger boys squatted beside their fathers, because that made them men. After a time the women asked, What did he want? (p. 46).

In this instance, all their pondering and figuring prove ineffective, as the monstrous roar of Joe Davis' son's tractor drones over the land, destroying the homes, despoiling the family's hope. From the start of the novel, the male authority structure is threatened.

While the intercalary chapters introduce the large, universal, macrocosmic scenes, the narrative chapters place the particular instance of the Joads within that pattern. A more detailed rendition of the squatter's circle is delivered in Chapter 10 as the Joad family prepares to leave Oklahoma. Here each male member assumes his hierarchical position in the squatter's circle, the women and children rimmed around its edges:

> Pa walked around the truck, looking at it, and then he squatted down in the dust and found a stick to draw with. One foot was flat to the ground, the other rested on the ball and slightly back, so that one knee was higher than the other. Left forearm rested on the lower, left, knee; the right elbow on the right knee, and the right fist cupped for the chin. Pa squatted there, looking at the truck, his chin in his cupped fist. And Uncle John moved toward him and squatted down beside him (p. 136).

Grampa Joad comes out of the house and, too old to bend physically in the squatter's circle, takes his seat of pre-eminent authority on the running board of the old truck. That, Steinbeck writes, "was the nucleus," the three male heads of the family. But Tom and Connie and Noah "strolled in and squatted, and the line was a half-circle with Grampa in the opening" (p. 136). After them, Ma, Granma, and the children come: "They took their places behind the squatting men; they stood up and put their hands on their hips" (p. 136). It is a careful order in a careful ritual, this pattern of dominance and male authority. As the only non-family member, Jim Casy has the good sense to stay off to the side; only after the decision is made to include him on the journey may he come over and squat on the sidelines, a member of the male ruling hierarchy but still an outsider.

The squatter's circle represents several things in *The Grapes of Wrath*. First, the circle represents the hierarchy of male authority in the family. The men are ranged from the ruling eldest to the youngest or newest members; women and children are excluded from it as bystanders who only await the decisions. Second, it represents order, both a physical order in which the combined strength of the males unifies against the world, and a rational order in which decisions affecting the family may be discussed and decided. Third, it represents a chain of human unity; the members, within the hierarchy of authority, are one body. Within the circle there may be discussion and dissension, but when a decision is made the body is of one mind.

The squatter's circle is an emblem of unity, a physical testament to the preservation of old ways and the freedom to make choices. In his journalistic reports on the migrants, written for the *San Francisco News*, Steinbeck assessed this unique spirit of the migrants: "They are men who have worked hard on their own farms and have felt the pride of possessing and living in close touch with the land. They are resourceful and intelligent Americans who have gone through the hell of the drought, have seen their lands wither and die and the top soil blow away; and this, to a man who has owned his land, is a curious and terrible pain."[4] Despite their travail and oppression, Steinbeck asserts that "they have weathered the thing, and they can weather much more for their blood is strong."[5] Elsewhere in his journalistic entries, Steinbeck discourses on the most devastating blow to the migrants: the loss of dignity. The disruption of the squatter's circle in *The Grapes of Wrath* is also a dissolving of the fragile fabric of human dignity; as the circle breaks down, so too do the independence, freedom, and dignity of the migrants.

All levels of significance for the squatter's circle are severely tested in the drama of the story. The dissolution of the Joad family's squatter's circle lies in direct correlation to Ma Joad's assumption of authority. When the Wilson car breaks down and Tom proposes his idea of laying over to repair it while the others go ahead, Pa and Uncle John automatically drop to their hams in a makeshift squatter's circle to discuss it. This time, however, Ma Joad makes her defiant gesture of threatening Pa with the jack handle, thereby disrupting the circle.

The raw conditions of the long journey and the rough introduction to California also serve to break up the circle. At the first California camp, Tom and Al help Floyd repair his car. About them men are squatting in small circles, driven to the solace of the unit as they try to figure out the woeful working conditions. When a man drives up to contract workers, all the squatting groups move up and gather around him. The squatter's circles disrupt under the authority of the landowner, but the men also coalesce as a larger unit than that of the family. Floyd tries to galvanize the separate units of men into one unit, encouraging them to stand with one circle against the contractor.

In the larger artistic pattern of the novel, Steinbeck has anticipated this scene in intercalary Chapter 14. Here, too, men squat around, lamenting their common loss, trying to determine what action to take. The scene parallels the action of the California camp:

> And in the night one family camps in a ditch and another family pulls in and the tents come out. The two men squat on their hams and the women and children listen. Here is the node, you who hate change and fear revolution. Keep these two squatting men apart; make them hate, fear, suspect each other. Here is the anlage of the thing you fear. This is the zygote. For here, "I lost my land" is changed; a cell is split and from its splitting brews the thing you hate--"We lost *our* land." The danger is here, for two men are not as lonely and perplexed as one (p. 206).

In the California camp, Floyd's voice is the echo of this. And indeed this is the thing the landowners hate. They fight back with the indictment "he's talkin' red, agitating trouble" (p. 359). Under this banner they are free to disperse any group of men, disrupt any unit, abort any zygote. In the California camp, the collection of men remains simply that: a collection. No cohesive unity cements their spirits together. The disruption in the Joad family is poignantly encapsulated in one sharp portrait where Ma fries potatoes over a hissing fire and "Pa sat nearby hugging his knees" (p. 371), almost as if Pa, in a degraded stance of the squatter's posture, clings futilely to a position now much diminished.

Just as the later stay at the Weedpatch Camp is restorative to the Joad family spirit, so too it restores the dignity of the menfolk, particularly when they do unify here against the threat of outside aggression. Not surprisingly, the squatter's circles appear frequently in the narration as old routines are restored for a time. Yet, none of the men can escape the reality of joblessness. As if to turn their shoulders in protection against the fear, the men huddle frequently in the squatter's circle. At one point, the men squat by the porch of the manager's office. Pa opens the speculation on work, and the frightening reality of no work to be had. The mood of the circle changes; these men are restive, nervous. The strength of the circle has dissipated. Steinbeck repeats a grim refrain: "The squatting men moved nervously" (p. 462); "The circle of men shifted their feet nervously" (p. 463). The squatter's circle is no longer a hierarchical arrangement of authority, vision, and unity; it is a nervous assembly of men huddling in fear.

On the evening of the Joads' departure, the men fall back into the routine of the circle: "The evening dark came down and Pa and Uncle John squatted with the heads of families out by the office. They studied the night and the future" (p. 486). The future they see is grim indeed: the squatter's circle is a communion in despair. Only Ma's steely will drives them on. She makes the decisions. She instills order. She possesses the hope for the future. The family moves once again.

As the cold rains inundate the California valley, Pa and a body of men, unnamed and disorganized now that the family order has been ruptured, band together in a battle against the floods. The people's spiritual enervation and the depletion of male authority have already been established in intercalary Chapter 29. There Steinbeck establishes an overview of the dismal rains scouring California's valleys and depicts the men, weak and dejected, before the onslaught: "On the fields the water stood, reflecting the gray sky, and the land whispered with moving water. And the men came out of the barns, out of the sheds. They squatted on their hams and looked out over the flooded land. And they were silent. And sometimes they talked very quietly" (p. 592). The silence of the men is profound; here there is no purpose, no decision to be made, no work to go to. Only the vast desolation of the rain speaks.

This overview focuses in Chapter 30 upon Pa and a ragged band of migrants in their individual battle against the flood. That final warfare of male strength is paralleled neatly by the turbulent events of Rose of Sharon's birth and ultimately paves the way for her ascendancy to a position of authority as she changes from a naive, egocentric young girl to one who mysteriously rises to share Ma Joad's vision of the family of man. That ascendancy happens only with the thorough dissolution of Pa's preeminence in the squatter's circle.

After slogging in the mud all night, bending his physical strength with a rag-tag band of warriors against the onslaught of the flood, Pa staggers into the boxcar where Rose of Sharon has just given birth. In one explosive passage, Steinbeck clenches the transference of authority: "Pa walked slowly to Rose of Sharon's mattress. He tried to squat down, but his legs were too tired. He knelt instead" (p. 604). Pa tries, terribly hard, to adopt the squatter's pose, his old position of authority and order, before Ma and Rose of Sharon, but he cannot. Weariness staggers him and he falls to his knees *before* them. From a position of authority he falls to a position of abnegation and supplication. He bends now before the authority of Ma. And Ma offers him the solace of her compassion: "Ma looked at him strangely. Her white lips smiled in a dreaming compassion. 'Don't take no blame. Hush! It'll be awright. They's changes--all over'" (pp. 604-05).

That transference also signals the victorious thematic closure to the novel, for Ma once more goads the family to action. She directs, gives orders. When the battered family enters the barn, Ma commands the men to get out. But there is no commanding Rose of Sharon; there is only the mystical passing of authority based upon human giving, the needy giving all they have to the needy. Ma and Rose of Sharon look deeply into each other, and Rose of Sharon murmurs, "Yes." It is more than assent to Ma's will and authority. She ascends to this new order, not of protecting the one family, as in the male-ordered squatter's circle, but of giving to others in the "fambly of man."

Rose of Sharon does not squat. Hers is not the posture of authority and order as in the squatter's circle. Bearing one of the names of Jesus from the Canticles (2:1), she enacts the Christ-like posture of laying down her life for another. The Rose of Sharon of the Canticles is described as having "breasts . . . like clusters of the vine," and here she gives the new wine, not the grapes of wrath, but the wine of human compassion and nurture to the starved father next to her. Once, perhaps, he too held his place of authority in the squatter's circle. And just as Pa Joad kneels before Ma's benediction of compassion, this man too is nurtured by the one who bends down beside him.

The pattern of displacement in *The Grapes of Wrath* is from the male-dominated squatter's circle of hierarchical authority to Ma Joad's vision of caring for the "fambly of man" and Rose of Sharon's physical enactment of it. That pattern also undergirds the thematic heart of the novel. In his reports for the *San Francisco News*, Steinbeck observed that "a man herded about, surrounded by armed guards, starved and forced to live in filth loses his dignity; that is, he loses his valid position in regard to society, and consequently his whole ethics toward society."[6] In *The Grapes of Wrath*, the migrant male does indeed lose his position, but not his ethics, for those ethics are nurtured by the ascension to authority of Ma Joad and her ethical vision of the family of man.

From *Studies in American Fiction* (Autumn 1989), 203-11.

Notes

1. Jackson J. Benson has examined the influence of Collins' reports upon the composition of *The Grapes of Wrath* in *The True Adventures of John Steinbeck, Writer* (New York: Viking Press, 1984), especially pp. 338-48, 361-71. In his "Background of *The Grapes of Wrath*," *JML*, 5 (1976), 194-216, Benson also provides a careful study of Steinbeck's personal relationship with Collins, including their labors together among the migrants. Steinbeck himself acknowledged his debt to Collins in several places, most notably in the epigraph to *The Grapes of Wrath*: "To TOM who lived it." During the writing of the novel, from June 1 to October 26, 1938, Steinbeck continued to receive correspondence and data from Collins. For example, in the journal he kept while writing the novel, recently published as *Working Days: The Journals of "The Grapes of Wrath," 1938-1941*, ed. Robert DeMott (New York: Viking Press, 1989), Steinbeck wrote: "Letter from Tom with vital information to be used later. He is so good. I need this stuff. It is exact and just the thing that will be used against me if I am wrong" (p. 33). Collins also visited Steinbeck at his Los Gatos home in early September, at which time Steinbeck was writing the Weedpatch chapters of the novel. Apparently the visit did not go well, very likely because of Steinbeck's acute exhaustion at this late state in the writing, and it was one of the last times the two men saw each other.

2. The Collins reports are held in the Farm Security Administration papers at the Bancroft Library, University of California, Berkeley, and the Federal Archives and Record Center at San Bruno, California. The sections quoted from in this study have been made available through the courtesy of the Steinbeck Research Center, San Jose State University. Quotations are cited by the date of the weekly reports.

3. John Steinbeck, *The Grapes of Wrath* (New York: Viking Press, 1939), p. 230. Further quotations will be cited parenthetically.

4. The *San Francisco News* reports, published from October 5-12, 1936, have recently been republished in one volume as *The Harvest Gypsies* (Berkeley: Heyday Books, 1988), p. 22. This edition reprints the striking photographs of Dorothea Lange that accompanied the original stories. In the articles, Steinbeck also points out the political disenfranchisement of the men that further robbed them of their sense of ruling authority: "They have come from the little farm districts where democracy was not only possible but inevitable, where popular government

. . . was the responsibility of every man. And they have come into the country where, because of the movement necessary to make a living, they are not allowed any vote whatever, but are rather considered a properly unprivileged class" (p. 23).

   5. *Gypsies,* p. 27.
   6. *Gypsies,* p. 39.

PART II

1990–1999
LOOKING FORWARD
TO A NEW MILLENNIUM

Steinbeck's Debt to Dos Passos

Barry G. Maine

A literary debt is something like the national debt: no one knows exactly how it is incurred, what it stands for, how it can be repaid, or if it means anything at all. Such is the nature of John Steinbeck's literary debt to John Dos Passos. Like all such debts, it is easier to describe a market influence than it is to pin down a specific borrowing. Dos Passos was at the center of the flowering of talent and experiment in American writing during the 1920s. His experiments with narrative form and technique, his ear for the American idiom, his mixing of fiction and non-fiction materials, and his wedding of private lives and public history have had a far-reaching impact upon American writing in the twentieth century. Jean-Paul Sartre has observed that it was Dos Passos and Hemingway who offered an alternative to analysis as a way of telling a story.[1] George Steiner, writing in the late 1960s, has suggested that because of his development of *montage* in narrative fiction, it is Dos Passos, not Hemingway, who "has been the principal American literary influence of the twentieth century."[2] Most recently Alfred Kazin, in his *American Procession*, claims that Dos Passos is a writer whom other American writers copy without realizing it.[3]

In the early 1930s Dos Passos was hailed in America and abroad as the most promising writer of his generation by such critics as Edmund Wilson, Malcolm Cowley, and Horace Gregory. The political left hailed Dos Passos as the leading voice among proletarian writers in America. In 1938, the year before the publication of Steinbeck's *The Grapes of Wrath*, Dos Passos's popularity reached its zenith with the publication of his complete *U.S.A.* trilogy. That same year, writing in France, Jean-Paul Sartre declared that Dos Passos was the greatest living writer in the western world.[4] Such a pronouncement probably reveals more about the direction of Sartre's development than the stature of Dos Passos's achievement, but I cite it as evidence of the fact that, though not much attention is paid to Dos Passos's work today, a great deal of attention was paid to it during the 1930s when Steinbeck was learning his craft.

We know from his correspondence that Steinbeck read and admired Dos Passos's work even though his own writing, at least before *In Dubious Battle* (1936), showed little inclination toward social realism or leftist politics.[5] And yet by 1941, Michael Gold, representing the political left before the Congress of American Writers, cited John Steinbeck as the writer who best demonstrated "the revolution of taste, morals, aspirations, and social consciousness" that has occurred in American writing during the 1930s.[6] Gold barely mentions Dos Passos, whose name had become anathema to the political left since the publication of *The Big Money* in 1936, a novel that confirmed what Gold and others saw as a defection from the left in Dos Passos's political statements in the mid-1930s and especially since the publication of *Adventures of a Young Man* in 1939 about Communist interference in the Spanish Civil War. Dos Passos was an early defector from the politics of Stalinist Russia. But having championed Dos Passos's work during the early thirties, Gold could only pretend to deny him a central role in the "revolution" he spoke of in American writing. The distance in political sensibility and literary art that Steinbeck traveled between *Cup of Gold* (1929) and *In Dubious Battle* (1936) is very great indeed, and his reading of Dos Passos certainly played some role in it. Malcolm Cowley is probably right that, although *The Grapes of Wrath* is not an imitative book, "it could not have been written without a whole series of experiments to guide him" among them Dos Passos's *U.S.A.*[7]

On the other hand, in both *U.S.A.* and *The Grapes of Wrath*, literary influences are clearly secondary to each writer's own emotional and artistic response to personal participation in contemporary events—Dos Passos's activities for the radical left during the 1920s, his participation in labor strikes such as the Passaic, New Jersey, Textile Strike, his efforts to free Sacco and Vanzetti in Boston, and Steinbeck's witness to the great western migration of farm workers and his involvement in the California migrant labor camps. If *The Grapes of Wrath* is indebted to *U.S.A.*, it is a debt that is more conceptual than thematic, probably more formal than organic, and more a matter of technique and narrative organization than political response. In seeking to define it more closely, my aim is not to measure it (for that is clearly not possible) but to explore some of the relationships between these two towering achievements in American literature written during the Great Depression.

In defining what *The Grapes of Wrath* owes conceptually and technically to *U.S.A.*, the so-called "interchapters," which Steinbeck acknowledged had been inspired by *U.S.A.*, seem as good a place as any to begin.[8] In *U. S. A.* Dos Passos interrupted his fictional narrative with three separate types of "interchapters": those he called "Newsreels," composed of actual headlines and excerpts from news stories and popular song lyrics, the fragments arranged in ironic juxtaposition, each item commenting on the other and the whole collage providing a larger social and historical context for the fiction; short biographies of public figures who in some way influenced historical events or symbolized historical forces at work in the lives of the fictional characters—figures like J. P. Morgan, Andrew Carnegie, Woodrow Wilson, Joe Hill, Eugene Debs, Bill Haywood, Randolph Hearst, Henry Ford, and others; and finally, a series of prose poems that Dos Passos labeled the "Camera Eye," installments in a kind of autobiography, tracing the author's participation in the life of his times in Joycean stream of consciousness. The total effect of these separate types of narration has often been compared to that of a cubist painting, a simultaneous rendering of many sides of the same truth, or in this work, the same historical picture.

The interchapters in *The Grapes of Wrath* also interrupt the flow of the fictional narrative to comment on and expose the social and economic conditions that the Joad family must face. Conceptually, the purpose of these chapters is, as in *U.S.A.*, to broaden the scope of the novel, to allegorize the Joad family saga by placing it in the larger context of American culture and economic conditions. In each interchapter the reader is pulled out of the Joad family troubles to view the larger picture, to encounter the social and economic forces that direct them and thousands like them to their unfortunate destinies in California.

The thematic emphases in both sets of interchapters are remarkably similar: the alienation of man from nature and the worker from his work by the profit motive that drives the capitalist system; the alluring and dehumanizing power of money; the challenges to human identity posed by advances in technology; the emergence of a mass culture, galvanized by the mobility made possible for the automobile; the price in human misery exacted by the cruel laws of supply and demand; and the resentment and distrust of the "haves" toward the "have-nots." With respect to method, although there is no systematic division of interchapters in *The Grapes of Wrath* by stylistic features, no systematic variation in the style or organization of narrative discourse from one interchapter to the next (nothing so clearly defined, in other words as a Newsreel section, a Biography, or an autobiographical Camera Eye section as in *U.S.A.*), Steinbeck does experiment with different kinds of narration within these interchapters, and the effects he appears to strive for are markedly similar to those of *U.S.A.* Consider, for example, the opening paragraphs of chapter seven:

> In the towns, on the edges of the towns, in fields, in vacant lots, the used-car yards, the wreckers' yards, the garages with blazoned signs—Used Cars, Good Used Cars. Cheap transportation, three trailers, '27 Ford, clean. Checked cars, guaranteed cars. Free radio. Car with 100 gallons of gas free. Come in and look. Used Cars. No overhead . . .
>
> Those sons of bitches ain't buying. Every yard gets 'em. They're lookers. Spend all their time looking. Don't give a damn for your time. Over there, them two people—no, with the kids. Get 'em in a car. Start 'em out at two hundred and work down. They look good for one and a quarter. Get 'em rolling. Get 'em in a jalopy. Sock it to 'em! They took our time.
>
> Owners with rolled-up sleeves. Salesmen, neat, deadly, small intent eyes watching for weaknesses.
>
> Watch the woman's face. If the woman likes it, we can screw the old man.[9]

The cataloguing of sights along the American roadside, the frequent ellipses in the narration, the colloquial diction, the colliding of anonymous, unidentified voices, the quick stereotyping through canned phrases and telling detail, all in the service of indicting the business of selling—such devices are very familiar to the readers of *U.S.A.* Is it only coincidental when, in *In Dubious Battle*, Steinbeck turns his attention to the labor struggle, that his people begin to speak like characters in a Dos Passos novel, or that when, in *The Grapes of Wrath*, Steinbeck tries to bring the actual dust and grit and junk and voices of the American roadside into his novel, he begins experimenting with narrative techniques that Dos Passos used for the same purposes in *U.S.A.*? Consider the following descriptions of weary travelers in *The Grapes of Wrath* and *U.S.A.* First from chapter fifteen in *The Grapes of Wrath*:

> Lines of weariness around the eyes, lines of discontent down from the mouth, breasts lying heavily in little hammocks, stomachs and thighs

straining against cases of rubber. And mouths panting, the eyes sullen, disliking sun and wind and earth, resenting food and weariness. (p. 211)

Now listen to Dos Passos's description of a weary traveler in the prologue to *U.S.A.*:

Feet are tired from hours of walking; eyes greedy for warm curve of faces, answering flicker of eyes, the set of a head, the lift of a shoulder, the way hands spread and clench; blood tingles with wants, mind is a beehive of hopes buzzing and stringing; muscles ache.[10]

The anonymity of the people described, the bodily metaphor for mental and spiritual privation, the clinical matter-of-fact tone, the staccato cadence— these could be passages written by the same author. Now consider the sudden intrusion of direct address in this conclusion to chapter fourteen of *The Grapes of Wrath*:

If you who own the things people must have could understand this, you might preserve yourself. If you could separate causes from results, if you could know that Paine, Marx, Jefferson, Lenin, were results, not causes, you might survive. But that you cannot know. For the quality of owning freezes you forever into "I," and cuts you off forever from the "we." (p. 206)

Although, like Dos Passos, Steinbeck experiments with modernist techniques in these interchapters, his analyses of economic determinism are more direct and explicit than in *U.S.A.* There is greater thematic clarity, for example, in Steinbeck's definition of a bank in chapter five than there is in Dos Passos's invective against J. P. Morgan in his biographical sketch entitled "The House of Morgan." Dos Passos strongly implies that war is "good growing weather" for banks and that America entered the Great War not to save democracy, but to save the Morgan loans. But the tone is bitterly ironic rather than straightforward, the rhetoric is inflammatory, and there is no direct statement—only innuendo.

Throughout the *U.S.A.* trilogy Dos Passos's method is to chronicle rather than to explain the events of the new century. The images rush by, as in a movie, the headlines flash on the screen, the lives of important historical figures parade through as examples of defeat or exploitation, and the author confesses his confusion and outrage in extremely fragmented, impressionistic autobiography. The reader makes history out of chronicle by attending to irony and motif in the editing. This is not to say that we are free to make whatever history we want out of this chronicle. Causality, as in the movies, is a hidden agenda. We are manipulated by the editing of materials to accept an essentially tragic view of American history that stresses the loss of democratic ideals. The scope and range and breadth of Dos Passos's documentary trilogy is ultimately as illusory as its objectivity, for the entire chronicle is infused with the author's disillusionment. Dos Passos sees the Great Depression as the tragic result of the nation's failure to live up to the ideals of its founders: freedom of speech (denied to striking workers), equal opportunity (mocked by monopoly capitalism), and equal justice under the law (corrupted by the power of money). Consequently, *U.S.A.* is more satire than it is documentary history.

Steinbeck's method is quite different because his vision of the country and its people is different. The illustrations for these novels, drawn by two of America's most talented painters of the 1930s, are reflective of this difference in vision. Reginald Marsh was commissioned by Dos Passos to do the illustrations for *U.S.A.* His drawings, in striking contrast to those by Thomas Hart Benton for *The Grapes of Wrath*, are plainly caricatures. The sharp, chiseled features of the character drawings are hammered into satiric stereotypes. They look like comic-strip characters with Dick Tracy profiles. The individualizing details are strong chins and flat stomachs or potbellies and distended gullets for the male characters, and hourglass curves or horn-rimmed glasses for the females. No sympathy or compassion is evoked by these character sketches, only revulsion. Benton's drawings of the Joads, on the other hand, display softly rounded features that are not so exaggerated for comic or satiric effect. They are humanized rather than hammered into stereotypes. The figures retain their human shape and dignity.

The sharp and vivid contrast in visual styles between artists mirrors the treatment of human characters by each author. Dos Passos maintains a satiric distance from his characters throughout the trilogy. The readers' emotions remain, for the most part, untouched by what happens to them, because they seem to march toward their fates like automatons. In both works we note, in the fictional chapters at least, the absence of authorial presence, the flat, objective tone of the narration, the emphasis on recording and reporting rather than explaining or analyzing. But we should also note that there are no Ma Joads in *U.S.A.*, and no Tom Joads either. All the Tom Joads are beaten in *U.S.A.*, or they have sold out. But there is more to it than that. The conception of human identity in *U.S.A.* is so heavily deterministic (unlike in Steinbeck's novel, where human dignity and feeling triumph over economic circumstances more crushingly adverse than in *U.S.A.*) that a fully human character such as a Tom Joad hardly seems possible. There is an air of unreality about Dos Passos's fiction. The characters never reflect upon the past. At some undefined but very early stage in their lives their fates are fixed by a weakness in character that plays directly into the hands of dehumanizing social and economic forces.

The point of view, in other words, is heavily expressionistic. Each character tells his or her own story in the third person, in the manner of Henry Adams in *The Education of Henry Adams*, only they tell it in words cut off from thought. "Everything is told as if by someone remembering," wrote Jean-Paul Sartre in the aforementioned essay, but the "someone remembering" has no memory.[11] Only the reader has, fed by Dos Passos's Newsreel of history. The characters roll along an assembly line without any understanding of where they have been or knowledge of where they are going. They tell their own stories in language that reflects their social backgrounds and sensibilities, but only in speech that emphasizes their shared cultural identity as Americans. The following is an excerpt from an early section in John Ward Moorehouse's narration set in the first decade of the twentieth century:

> He was twenty and didn't drink or smoke and was keeping himself clean for the lovely girl he was going to marry, a girl in pink organdy with golden curls and a sunshade. He'd sit in the musty little office of Hillyard and Miller, listing tenements for rent, furnished rooms, apartments, desirable lots for sale, and think of the Boer War and the Strenuous Life and prospecting for gold. (*The 42nd Parallel*, p. 160)

Later in the text we are introduced to another character, Eleanor Stoddard, in the following manner:

> When she was small she hated everything. She hated her father, a stout red-haired man smelling of whiskers and stale pipe tobacco. He worked in an office in the stockyards and came home with the stockyards stench on his clothes and told bloody jokes about butchering sheep and steers and hogs and men. . . . When she was sixteen in high school she and a girl named Isabelle swore together that if a boy ever touched them they'd kill themselves. (*The 42nd Parallel*, pp. 190-91)

Eleanor grows up to be an interior decorator, and Moorehouse finds a career in public relations. All of the characters in *U.S.A.* drift with the times and speak in cliches. They seem to sleepwalk through life. Each moment is succeeded by another without connection; each event slips into the past dead and forgotten. According to Sartre, the absence of reflection in these characters, their lack of depth, is as deliberate as it is stifling: in capitalist society, Dos Passos shows us that men do not have lives; they have only destinies. According to Sartre, Dos Passos writes this way so as to inspire us as readers to break the economic chains that bind us and these characters in servitude to the bourgeois success ethic.[12]

Judging the work by its effects in an ideological context, Sartre's phenomenological reading of narrative style in *U.S.A.* opens the door to a Marxist reading of Dos Passos that is more sophisticated and potentially more valuable than the simplistic response to content alone by American Marxist critics of the 1930s. But whether we accept Sartre's reading of Dos Passos's narrative style in *U.S.A.*, or the related but more commonly accepted view that the narrative style reflects a thesis about the cheapening and betrayal of words that Americans once lived by, only to see them defiled by the business of selling business to the American people, the difference in method between *U.S.A.* and *The Grapes of Wrath* should be clear enough: in the tradition of high modernism, *U.S.A.* is a language experiment, expressing—in its form, organization, and style—ideas about language, about how language limits us, defines us, turns our lives into cliches; *The Grapes of Wrath*, on the other hand, although it borrows from the tradition of modernism, especially in the interchapters, does not belong to it. It is not about language at all. *The Grapes of Wrath* is written in the realist tradition, and the language through which the Joad family is related to us is intended to be objective and transparent rather than expressionistic. Accordingly, their presence in the text is stronger, more immediate. We are moved by their troubles and by the tragedies they suffer. Even the religious allegory, as heavy-handed as it is, expands the meaning of the story without swallowing up the characters into its thesis. Steinbeck's characters seem more fully human. They experience a broader range of emotions. They have dreams of the future. They harbor regrets about the past. Their feelings for each other are genuine and rooted in firmer soil than desire or ambition or political loyalties. The world they inhabit, no matter how improbably or incredible it may seem to us in it most absurd moments, is unmistakably ours, or rather, *theirs*, whereas the America Dos Passos writes about is unmistakably, as Sartre tells us, "not real; it is a created object.[13] Perhaps this is why there are no truly memorable characters in *U.S.A.* Jose Ortega y Gasset, the Spanish philosopher and writer, has argued that all modernist writing and art, by virtue of its heavy stylization, is inherently dehumanizing.[14] Although this may betray a naive view of literature's relationship to reality, it is interesting to speculate that Dos Passos, who was a painter himself, displays the impressionist painter's characteristic lack of interest in human character. The interest is in atmosphere, not character. The following description of literary impressionism by Maria Kronegger

could easily pass for a description of Dos Passos's narrative method in
U.S.A.:

> As an impressionist painting, where there is no color peculiar to any
> particular object, the protagonists in impressionist literature lack a
> composed personality. It seems that human life is broken up into
> fragments at will, and that the person is reduced to a discontinuous series
> of states. . . . [The characters] see images which arise for an instant, then
> disappear. What remains is nothing but the sensation of contact with the
> object. Individuals seems to move, autonomous and enclosed, inside a
> system in which they attract, repel, and strike one another, without any
> fixed position. Their loss of a personal center and their consequent
> imperilment in a world of unconvincing vital relationships makes them
> passive victims.[15]

It is a fairly commonplace idea that if a writer does not care about his
characters, he cannot make us care about them. Dos Passos does not and
cannot; Steinbeck does and can. The characters in *U.S.A.* exist only for plot,
which is in turn only a metaphor, a formula for defeat and futility, a
blueprint for an ugly, nightmarish vision of American life and culture.
U.S.A. is like one of those trick mirrors at the amusement part that distort
human features all out of proportion. We do not recognize ourselves.
Neither do the characters of *U.S.A.*, who repeatedly study their mirror
reflections with growing bewilderment; they lose their human features in
molding themselves to a capitalist economy. Consequently, leaving aside the
impassioned rhetoric of the Camera Eye sections, which can stand alone, and
in a curious way do stand alone, not only because of their isolation from the
rest of the text but because of the recognizably human voice that speaks
through them, the trilogy as a whole is compelling only as long as, and to the
extent that, its metaphor for life under capitalism remains believable. Aside
from the Joycean figuration of autobiography in the Camera Eye sections, it
has all the human drama of a mathematical formula. It is impossible to
imagine a life for its characters outside the novel. On the contrary, in *The
Grapes of Wrath*, some of the characters can even project a life for
themselves beyond Steinbeck's telling, as in that famous speech of Tom
Joad's to his mother, and we believe in them, because we can sense their
presence beyond the text.[16]

That does not make the characters in *U.S.A.* necessarily less human; on
the contrary, it may be that, in their imprisonment, their incarceration in an
economic system and the material culture it has spawned, they are more like
ourselves than we care to admit. But if we are to understand and appreciate

Dos Passos's vision of America, we must first be willing to suspend or give up the notion that our humanity, our humanness, transcends history. It does *not* in *U.S.A.*, where Man is defined strictly in terms of his material culture, which determines his features and values and character. By contrast, there is something in the Joads that does transcend history and the circumstances of time and place in *The Grapes of Wrath*, which may account for its broader appeal. Its message is more comforting and a more inspiring one.

It is apparent to me that in setting out to write a novel about farm labor conditions in the American West, Steinbeck borrowed conceptually from U.S.A. in planning the structure of his novel, borrowed technical procedures from U.S.A. in developing the interchapters, and benefitted from whatever stock of American speech Dos Passos had floated into literary currency. That is the full extent of the debt. As a result of these borrowings, Steinbeck was able, in the interchapters, to enlarge the scope of his novel beyond the trials and tribulations of a single family, to comment more directly on the economic laws that pilloried his characters without violating the narrative conventions and transparency of the Joad story, and to suggest in brief dramatic monologues and quick anonymous exchanges the brittleness and anger in American voices on both sides, employed and unemployed, caught in the maelstrom of economic disaster.

In every other way the two novels are quite different because they are based on opposite conceptions of human experience. The tone, direction, thematic implications, politics, and vision of *The Grapes of Wrath* owe nothing to *U.S.A.* They are uniquely Steinbeck's. The tone is compassionate, the direction forward-looking, the politics collectivist, and the vision one of guarded hope in building a new community. In *U.S.A.* the tone is satiric, the direction backward-looking to a "storybook democracy," the politics disillusioned, and the vision of community bankrupt. *The Grapes of Wrath* is a testament to the power of the human spirit to endure and prevail over history, whereas *U.S.A.* is a testament to the power of history to triumph over Man. It was Marcel Proust who wrote that "style for the writer, no less than color for the painter, is a question not of technique but of vision."[17] As much as it is form it is vision that separates and distinguishes theses two writers of the Depression era.

From *The Steinbeck Quarterly 23:1-2* (Winter/Spring 1990).

Notes

1. Jean-Paul Sartre, "American Novelists in French Eyes," *Atlantic Monthly*, 201 (August 1946), pp. 114-18.
2. George Steiner, *Language and Silence* (New York: *Atheneum*, 1967), p. 116.
3. Alfred Kazin, *An American Procession* (New York: Knopf, 1984), p. 382.
4. Sartre, "Dos Passos and *1919*," *Literary and Philosophical Essays* (London: Rider, 1955), p. 96.
5. See Robert DeMott, *Steinbeck's Reading: A Catalogue of Books Owned and Borrowed* (New York: Garland, 1984), pp. 34-35; and Jackson J. Benson, *The True Adventures of John Steinbeck, Writer* (New York: Viking Press, 1984), pp. 201, 667.
6. Michael Folsom, ed., *Mike Gold: A Literary Anthology* (New York: International, 1971), p. 245.
7. Malcolm Cowley, *Think Back on Us: A Contemporary Chronicle of the 1930s* (Carbondale: Southern Illinois University Press, 1967), p. 350.
8. John Steinbeck to Joseph Henry Jackson, 1939. Bancroft Library, University of California, Berkeley.
9. Steinbeck. *The Grapes of Wrath* (New York: Viking Press, 1939), p. 83. All further page reference are to this edition.
10. John Dos Passos, *U.S.A.* (Boston: Houghton Mifflin, 1938), p. v. All further page references are to this edition.
11. Sartre, "Dos Passos and *1919*," p. 90.
12. *Ibid.*, p. 92.
13. *Ibid.*, p. 89.
14. Jose Ortega y Gasset, *The Dehumanization of Art* (Princeton, New Jersey: Princeton University Press, 1968), *passim*.
15. Maria Elizabeth Kronegger, *Literary Impressionism* (New Haven: College and University Press, 1973), p. 60.
16. One might argue that the film version of *The Grapes of Wrath* has something to do with this "presence" of Steinbeck's characters beyond the text, but I think it is just as likely that by restricting the reader's experience of his characters to their speech and actions, Steinbeck invites us to assume a life for them (of reflection, for example) beyond what he shows. By way of contrast, in *U.S.A.* the expressionistic point of view represents to the reader the "full consciousness" of each character (often with satiric effect) even as it exposes the limitations and cultural origins of that consciousness; consequently, there is no illusion created of any life beyond the text.
17. Marcel Proust, *Le Temps retrouve* (Paris: Livre de Poche, 1954), p. 256.

The World of
John Steinbeck's Joads

Robert Murray Davis

A hundred years ago as I write, people waited in covered wagons and on horses for the signal to begin the Oklahoma Land Run of 1889 and get a new start on free land. Fifty years ago John Steinbeck's *Grapes of Wrath* chronicled the beginning of the Joad family's trip west from Sallisaw, Oklahoma, out of an exhausted land, hoping for another new start in California. These images of Oklahoma dominate the popular imagination—and neither has much to do, geographically or historically, with eastern Oklahoma.

Steinbeck is so closely identified with Oklahoma that for years even scholars believed, apparently from internal evidence in the novel, that he had come to Oklahoma to travel west with the Okies. Jackson R. Benson, his first real biographer, actually traced his movements and discovered that he had driven across the state on U.S. 66, well north of the Joads' route until Oklahoma City, but did no special research. Steinbeck did travel with migrant Okies, but only in California.

Some Oklahomans were aware that Steinbeck knew absolutely nothing about the Sallisaw area, but even they concentrated on the general picture of the collapse of tenant and small farming and the destruction of a whole class of people and a way of life. Those who did notice seem, from Martin Shockley's account in "The Reception of *The Grapes of Wrath* in Oklahoma,"[1] to have used his errors in description as an excuse for rejecting the real point. In fact, the official position in Oklahoma was that big capital was benevolent, Oklahoma's agricultural workers were among the most fortunate in the country, there were no Joads, and all was for the best—considering.

Granted, my parents were not migrants, though they were certainly mobile during the Depression years; but I was born in the middle of the Dust Bowl. My family lived for a while in Coffeyville, Kansas, about sixty miles west of Galena, starting point for the Wilsons who accompany the Joads from Bethany, Oklahoma, to Needles, California. My grandparents and later my parents hid out from the Depression on hardscrabble farms in Morgan County, Missouri, back far enough in the woods that, like Winthrop and Ruthie Joad, I encountered my first flush toilet with deep suspicion. My father, moreover, had a good deal in common with Tom Joad, including his distrust of government and his attachment to family, besides their age.

Furthermore, although I am not, to Oklahomans, an Oklahoman, having lived here only twenty-two years, my roots are in the region, and to bicoastal types and Yankees of all descriptions, including my colleagues, I apparently sound, look, and act like their stylized conception of an Okie. So I had some idea how it feels—and an even clearer idea after my journey through the countryside and through the novel.

At the beginning of the trip, however, I was only interested in tracing the route of the Joads. In outline, the geography of the first part of the novel is fairly simple: the narrative begins with Tom Joad near the end of his journey from McAlester State Prison northeast to the farm where his family live as tenants. The land is so flat that a truck travels a mile to the first turn and the "distance, toward the horizon, was tan to invisibility."[2] The dirt and dust are red; the land is under intense cultivation except where it is "going back to sparse brush" (37).

Uncle John's farm is near a highway (U.S. 59?) roughly twenty miles west of the Arkansas border, less than a day's journey by horse-drawn wagon going "the back way, by Cowlington" (112). Thus the Joads live in northwest Le Flore County or northeast Haskell County, south of the Arkansas River, which forms the southern boundary of Sequoyah County, of which Sallisaw is the county seat.

In fact, though Steinbeck probably did not know and certainly, concerned with the plight of what he clearly thought of as real (i. e., white) Americans, did not care, the Arkansas was not only the boundary between the Choctaw and Cherokee Nations when this was Indian Territory, but it was one route for the Trail of Tears, which brought the Five Civilized Tribes to the region after an upheaval at least comparable to the Joads' displacement by dust and tractors. Eastern Oklahoma is no longer Indian Territory, and in fact some whites settled there by relatively peaceful means before the Territory was subsumed into Oklahoma; but a lot of Indians still live there, and they are very much present in the consciousness of Oklahomans. The only Indian the Joads are aware of is the one pictured on the pillow that Grampa Joad has appropriated. In the minds of the generic tenant farmers in an intercalary chapter, they have a right to the land because "Grampa took up the land, and he had to kill the Indians and drive them away" (45).

When the Joads themselves are driven off the land—Steinbeck has no sense of history repeating itself—they begin their journey on a red-dirt road until they reach Sallisaw, where they turn west on a concrete highway. From that point, and all the first day of the trip, Steinbeck gives precise mileage from town to town but almost no sense of the land on either side of the highway, because both he and the Joads focus intently on the road ahead.

The exact measurement illustrates in reverse Ernest Hemingway's theory that a writer can leave things out if he really knows them. Anyone who travels the Joad route can see that Steinbeck hadn't the vaguest idea what the country was like but took refuge in very sharp close-ups of individual figures and in tableaus of groups, counting on readers as well as characters to focus "panoramically, seeing no detail, but . . . the whole land, the whole texture of the country at once" (154). He was consistently wrong about what texture he gave. The land he purports to describe is in fact foothill country, the roads rising and falling, the horizons at most a mile or two away and always above eye level, the earth tan, the hills wooded, and the untended land soon choked with trees.

Of course, documentary precision has uncertain relationships to art, even to an art like Steinbeck's; and even had he been the most exact recorder of travels in the region, his novel would still be useless as a guide to the contemporary traveler. (Route 66, the Okie route to the Promised Land, has itself disappeared, subsumed into Interstate 44 east of Oklahoma City and into Interstate 40 westward.) Uncle John's farm would either be valuable lake-front property or at the bottom of Robert S. Kerr Lake. In fact, Oklahoma, its rivers dammed into lakes the shape of crab nebulae, now has more shoreline than Minnesota, and in eastern Oklahoma tourism and water sports are big business. As cause and by-product of all this water, modern Joads and landlords could ship their cotton via barge all the way to New Orleans on the Kerr-McClellan Arkansas River Navigation System. But there is no cotton to ship. The bottom land shows no signs of cultivation except for occasional huge cylinders of hay too big for any man to lift, products of mechanization that will be applauded by anyone who has bucked eighty-pound bales six high on a flatbed truck in July. The land is, as Muley Graves says it should have remained, grazing land.

Steinbeck's Jeffersonian ideal of "a little piece of land" is not dead, however. Just south of Sallisaw and just north of "We Never Sleep Bail Bonds" is a billboard for "Wild Horse Estates / Want a Small Farm? / We Got Them": two-and-a-half-acre tracts and running water, electricity, and telephone lines. As the various trailer parks and RV sales lots indicate, though, Oklahomans are still on the move—if Dan's Mobile Home Repo Center or the adjacent cemetery doesn't get them first.

Once under the bridge that carries I-40 across Oklahoma, franchised America gives way to the world—if not the country—of the Joads. In Sallisaw it becomes clear that Steinbeck did know something about the people of Oklahoma. A dark-haired man with an anxious look urges a battered yellow Japanese two-door along Cherokee Avenue, U.S. 64 and the main drag. A lean and ancient man—Grampa Joad buttoned up for Sunday—grasps a post supporting a metal sidewalk awning, his cane hooked over his free arm.

Scattered through town and all along the highway west are fossil records of the preinterstate era, when two-lane concrete U.S. highways were state of the art. The buildings (mission-style garages, Bonnie-and-Clyde tourist cabins, mom-and-pop frame grocery stores, tumbledown gas stations stripped of hand pumps become chic decor) stand because no one needs the space they occupy and because it is cheaper to board them up than to demolish them.

The highways—U.S. 64 to Warner, U.S. 266 to Henryetta (Steinbeck spells it Henrietta), U.S. 62 to Oklahoma City—exist in a time warp. They aren't quite the Joad route: the old Hudson Super Six traveled eighty-two miles from Sallisaw to Henryetta; today the trip is ten miles shorter. Essentially, though, the road is the same: two lanes, no shoulders, the hard edge of the slab visible and dangerous, expansion joints whupping at the tires and jolting up through the backside every ten feet or so even in a modern car.

At Henryetta the Joads' route disappears for nineteen miles into Interstate 40, and the modern traveler is forced to reenter the late twentieth century. Here life is an accelerated version of what Steinbeck described in his intercalary chapters. The trucks are bigger, faster, and scarier than ever, and the drivers can no longer casually turn aside for a cup of coffee, a piece of pie, and a solitary flirtation with a fading waitress in a roadside diner; now they gather in flocks at enormous truck stops that have everything a temporarily homeless man needs, including bunks, showers, electronic games, and sometimes assignations with hookers who conduct their business in mobile homes.

Some descendants of the Joads now travel the interstates. Ahead of me is a pickup truck bought, the little sign on the tailgate shows, in Blanchard, Oklahoma, loaded neatly, mattresses on edge, lengthwise in the center, smaller pieces to either side, all roped snugly down. The driver, lean, weathered, and glum, his right hand atop the steering wheel with a cigarette sticking up between the index and middle fingers, might be, fifty years later, the reality of what Al Joad dreamed of becoming.

The man from Blanchard is too well off and not anxious enough to be a Joad. In fact, very few modern Joads use the interstate, because their cars cannot maintain the pace. Occasionally you will overtake a rusting, quivering, oversize American car of uncertain color and vintage, battered outside and tattered within, driven by an unshaven man with both hands firmly on the wheel, a shapeless wife beside him, and a bevy of tousled children staring from every window—open, in the summer, because either the car never had air conditioning or it no longer works. If you think like a social scientist, you will agree with the Oklahoma sociologist, sympathetic in intention, who commented: "The farm migrant as described in Steinbeck's *The Grapes of Wrath* was the logical consequence of privation, insecurity, low income, inadequate standards of living, impoverishment in matters of education and cultural opportunities and a lack of spiritual satisfaction."[3]

If you are an ordinary person, you will feel a moment's empathy for anyone condemned to that pace in that feeble a machine before thinking, in truckers' parlance, "I couldn't live like that." If you are in heavy traffic, you will curse the car and its inhabitants for clogging the flow of vehicles and will check the side mirror to be sure that no one is going to cowboy through by changing lanes right in front of you; but you are not likely to think that the inhabitants of the truck are anything like you, because if you did, or did for very long, you would not be able to stand the thought of someone living by standards of food, shelter, clothing, hygiene, and general quality of life that you could not endure. One of Steinbeck's major accomplishments as a polemicist and as a novelist is that he presents us with a picture of a life we could not endure, lived by people we could not tolerate for a minute in everyday life, and not only gives us no alternative to seeing them as human but makes us turn against our own kind and ourselves for looking away in distaste from a sleazy roadside diner or for driving too fast in new cars to avoid a dog on the road.

We didn't see any Joads on Interstate 40, but we did overtake a Mercedes 300, driven well under the speed limit by a man dressed in camouflage fatigues and picking his nose. I assume that Steinbeck's waitress would label him a "shitheel." That is an interesting term, undefined by Steinbeck but apparently referring in a literal sense to someone so accustomed to indoor plumbing that, when forced to defecate in the woods, he or she is so unpracticed as to befoul the backs of the feet. Literally, if the fatigues were for use rather than for fashion, the man in the Mercedes may not have deserved the label. Most of us would, though, and we would most especially deserve it in the connotative sense for equating humanity with a particular stage of domestic technology—or a regional accent or set of customs. The Joads, and to some extent these heirs of their dispossession, seem alien to us because they live in the way that country people had done for centuries before the rivers were dammed and the high lines brought Rural Electrification Administration power to light the houses and run the motors on the wells so that hand pumps could be replaced by indoor plumbing and before tanks of liquified petroleum gas made wood gathering a recreation rather than a necessity.

That was not a comfortable life; it seemed, and was, a long way to the outhouse on a winter night, and even a chamber pot chills quickly after the fire dies. A coal-oil lamp doesn't give off much light or a wood stove much heat, and you have to keep about both in ways that even modern farmers cannot imagine. In fact, however, that life wasn't as hard to live as it is to imagine, because country people had always lived that way. It was the culture they knew, material and otherwise, and they knew how to use it.

We don't, which is what makes us shitheels in varying degress. But not very far beneath the surface, all of us Oklahomans—the sour man in the Chevy half-ton, the nose-picker in the Mercedes, and me in my stockpiled vita and '81 Honda—are Okies to somebody because of the way we talk or where we live or what we do and how we do it. To the sophisticated we are all quaint and irrelevant to what is really going on.

That morning I had left a motel whose marquee boasted, or pleaded, "AMERICAN OWNED." The man from Blanchard carried a bumper sticker with the legend "BUY AMERICAN GROWN, AMERICAN MADE—IT MATTERS." Perhaps I should get a bumper sticker reading "HUMANISM: LOVE IT OR LEAVE IT" in response to new and alien technologies.

Like Muley Graves and the nameless tenant farmers in the intercalary chapters of *The Grapes of Wrath*, someone we don't know is doing something we don't understand and have no control over that is going to affect our lives in ways we don't even want to think about. We are going to have to change what we do or at least the way we do it, and at the same time, to preserve continuity and dignity, we must preserve a sense that what we did was coherent and valuable. The difference between us Okies, geographic and spiritual, and the rest of humanity is that we know it and resent it, asking in our various ways the question of Steinbeck's baffled tenant farmer: "Who do I shoot?"

The next question, less satisfying but more constructive, is "What do I do now?" The first step is to understand that there is a process and then to discover how to adapt to it, and if you are lucky or clever, to adapt it to your tastes and abilities. The Joads begin by feeling the process and then discover the difficulty of adapting to a world in which their skills and values are irrelevant. That is what the first half of the novel is about, and Steinbeck understood and embodied this material very well. In the second half the Joads begin to understand the process and to perceive the necessity of shifting from "I" to "we" and from clan to class. This sounds like whistling in the dark, though it is difficult to suggest a better way of building a kinder and more caring society. The last part of the novel presents the excruciating possibility that nothing can be done. Steinbeck understood and presented extraordinarily well certain kinds of process, from the way a good mechanic fixes a car to the way a people adapt physically and socially to new situations. That makes almost all his novels unusually readable paragraph by paragraph. More important, he could show the kinetic satisfaction and the cultural and spiritual value inherent in process, building characters and their world from the inside out. From the first, his novels also dealt with the necessity for human beings to adapt in order to survive. Because *The Grapes of Wrath* does so most thoroughly and tellingly, readers all over the world have a clearer feeling not just for what it means to be an Oklahoman but for what it means to be human.

From *World Literature Today: A Literary Quarterly of the University of Oklahoma* 64:3 (Summer 1990), 401-04.

Notes

1.   Martin Schockley, "The Reception of *The Grapes of Wrath* in Oklahoma," *American Literature*, 14 (1944), pp. 351-61.

2.   John Steinbeck, *The Grapes of Wrath*, New York, Viking, Critical Library edition, Peter Lisca, ed., 1972, p. 37.   Subsequent page references are given parenthetically in the text.

3.   Shockley, as reprinted in the Viking Critical Library edition, p. 682.

Poor Whites: Joads and Snopeses

Abby H. P. Werlock

John Steinbeck and William Faulkner first met in 1955, for cocktails, at the Steinbeck's New York city apartment—with predictable results.[1] Faulkner was drunk, moody, and taciturn. To a woman guest who kept trying to elicit responses about his fiction, Faulkner finally retorted, "Madam, I write 'em, I don't read 'em," and abruptly left the party.[2] Mrs. Steinbeck later remarked to a friend that Faulkner was "a very strange man" (Blotner 1523). For Steinbeck the unpleasant evening clearly continued to rankle, for, when Faulkner later apologized for his behavior, saying he must have been terrible, Steinbeck replied, "Yes, you were" (Benson 770).

This lack of amicability between the two men might have been expected, considering the disparaging and faintly hostile statements each writer had been making about the other for a number of years. On occasion Steinbeck had privately referred to Faulkner as part of the "neurosis belt of the South" (Benson 773). On occasion Faulkner had privately criticized Steinbeck for his view that man and society could improve; such an approach, said Faulkner, "softened Steinbeck's view and made him a sentimental liberal" (Blotner 1470). Steinbeck complained to a friend that Faulkner was "a good writer... turning into a god damned phony" and that he "stole" Steinbeck's words from a recent *Saturday Review* article.[3] Knowing Faulkner's humorously infamous statement about the artist's inherent right to steal from anyone, even his own grandmother, one might be less apt to doubt Steinbeck's accusation. In any case, Steinbeck's bitterness focused particularly on Faulkner's receiving the Nobel Prize which, he said, if it ruined everyone the way it had Faulkner, then "thank God I have not been so honored" (Letters 529).

Somewhat ironically, perhaps, in 1962, just months after Faulkner's death, Steinbeck received word of his own Nobel award. Thus he joined the ranks of those who in Alfred Nobel's words wrote "work of an idealistic tendency."[4] At that point Steinbeck told interviewers that he admired nearly "everything" that Faulkner ever wrote (Benson 915). We should also recall that, just before receiving his Nobel Prize in 1949, Faulkner at least twice had ranked Steinbeck among the top five writers of the day (Blotner 1213, 1232).

Indeed, it was fitting for the Nobel Prize selection committee to honor the two men. In a number of their works, both authors not only feature but clearly admire the dignity and integrity of humankind, as seen particularly in their poor white characters. As their Nobel Prize acceptance speeches attest, both writers concern themselves with human tenacity and endurance, celebrating the assertion of traditional values in the face of seemingly impregnable evil. Moreover, both stress the importance of the relationship of a man to his land and detail the tragic results accruing when he is denied or deprived of that land. Steinbeck places a number of his writings, including *In Dubious Battle*, in the era of the Great Depression. Faulkner writes not only of those years but of the hungry ones leading up to them: the South in the mid- to late-20s, when he began to work on *The Hamlet*, was already in economic difficulty.[5] Poverty and loss of property afflict the characters in Faulkner's Civil War novels, *The Unvanquished* and *Absalom, Absalom!*; in these works, set in the 1860s, Faulkner's first Snopes appears to take advantage of the Civil War-induced privations of women, ex-slaves, and children.

Whereas Faulkner's Snopes family features in his trilogy—*The Hamlet, The Town, The Mansion*—and appear in several other novels and short stories, Steinbeck's Joad family appear in only one novel, *The Grapes of Wrath*. Still, the two impecunious but ubiquitous clans share similarities in their inception. Both, for example, have a genealogical history. Paul McCarthy notes that Ma Joad has instilled in her children a sense of their heredity, including both Civil War and Revolutionary War ancestors, and the results are evident in a clear sense of family identity: "We're Joads," the family typically announces when introducing themselves, "and we're proud to meet you."[6] This sense of family history and dignity makes painful the departure from Oklahoma for California. In an ironically similar way, Faulkner's various character-narrators chronicle the Snopes antecedents from their initial 19th century invasion of Frenchman's Bend, Mississippi, in the person of Ab Snopes, father of Flem and progenitor of them all, to their 20th century invasion of the social, economic, and political worlds of Jefferson, Mississippi.

Tribal Journey

In fact, the journeying of the tribe is a motif in both novels. Joads came west and established themselves on the Oklahoma land; later their descendents journey further west when they are dispossessed of that land. That second migration is initially led by the hereditary patriarch of the family, Pa Joad, whose own father dies before they reach the Oklahoma state border. Critics often note both the journey concept and the Biblical language, especially the similarity to Genesis 12, in which Father Abraham leads his tribe out of Ur to Canaan. Similarly, Faulkner's early experimentation with the Snopes tribe—begun in 1926 as "Father Abraham" and later abandoned—describes Abraham, the earliest Snopes ancestor to appear in Yoknapatawpha County, Mississippi (Blotner 526-29). In the rest of Faulkner's saga, however, the original Abraham is recast as Flem, the vicious, chillingly amoral Snopes who traces his ancestry only to his father, Ab—not Abraham—Snopes, who gains a reputation as a mercenary and a barn burner. James Watson suggests that Faulkner changed his mind about the tribe genealogy because the Biblical parallels were too sympathetic to depict the truly animalistic nature of the Snopses.[7] Far more effective than tracing genealogy is the technique Faulkner employs consistently in the published trilogy. Therein Snopes's relationships are frequently presented in vague and confused terms. "They none of them seemed to bear any specific kinship to one another; they were just Snopeses, like colonies of rats or termites are just rats and termites.[8]

Both *The Grapes of Wrath* and the trilogy begin with an established patriarchal society that comes into question and realigns, as poverty, oppression, and injustice increase. The Joads and the Snopeses are first presented as tenant farmers, share croppers barely eking out a living: Tom Joad describes his father's "forty acres. He's a cropper, but we been there for a long time."[9] And Mink Snopes describes himself and "all my tenant and cropper kind that have immolated youth and hope on thirty or forty or fifty acres of dirt that wouldn't nobody but our kind work."[10] Adumbrating trouble for both families, the dust chokes the Joads's land at the beginning of *The Grapes of Wrath*, the "small unpainted house . . . mashed at one corner" (54); and weeds choke the Snopeses's land at the beginning of *The*

Hamlet, the "sagging broken-backed cabin set in its inevitable treeless and grassless plot."[11]

The poverty and deprivation suggested here engender enormous survival difficulties and ensuing techniques for coping with hardship. Notably, while both Steinbeck and Faulkner were familiar with Darwin, each responded to Darwin's theories in different ways, which in fact marks a point where the books appear to part company. According to Warren Motley, Steinbeck hoped to reject Darwin's pessimistic theory of the survival of the fittest and, searching for an alternative, delved into such writers as Jan Smuts, Jan Elif Boodin, and especially anthropologist Robert Brifault, who advocated a return to an earlier matriarchal society.[12] Steinbeck's first wife Carol has affirmed that the portrait of Ma Joad is "pure Briffault" (quoted in Motley 398). On the other hand, Faulkner, according to Gail Mortimer, appears to have tacitly accepted and utilized Darwin's theories in his depiction of the adaptive and survival abilities of the Snopes clan.[13] Faulkner describes the Snopeses as a species covering the land, "the chain unbroken, every Snopes in Frenchman's Bend moving up one step, leaving that last slot at the bottom open for the next Snopes. . ." (*The Town* 8-9).

Although Joads and Snopeses are both regarded as inhuman or sub-human, Steinbeck appears to abhor the label, whereas Faulkner seems to approve of it. Throughout *The Grapes of Wrath*, the narrator's sympathy is implicit in his tone, as is his criticism of the speaker who observes, "Them goddamn Okies got no sense and no feeling. They ain't human. A human being wouldn't live like they do. A human being couldn't stand it to be so dirty and miserable. They ain't a hell of a lot better than gorillas" (*Grapes of Wrath* 301). This bigoted, insensitive view of the Okies is explicitly refuted throughout Steinbeck's novel. In *The Hamlet*, however, the narrator seems to approve the view of Snopeses not merely as inhuman, but as varmints, animals, reptiles. For example, Mink Snopes is "a different kind of Snopes like a cotton-mouth is a different kind of snake" (*Hamlet* 91). And an oft-stated goal of Faulkner's admirable characters—Gavin Stevens, V. K. Ratliff, Linda Snopes Kohl—is the defeat of Snopesism.

If Steinbeck does not actually sentimentalize his Joads and their ilk in government work camps, he certainly demonstrates through them, as Benson notes, an "idealized view of common man."[14] When they leave Oklahoma, the family are 12, as in the tribe of Israel—Ma and Pa, Grandma and Grandpa, Tom, Al, Noah, Ruthie, Winfield, Uncle John, Rose of Sharon, and Connie Rivers, joined by the preacher Jim Casy. Each is presented sympathetically, sometimes with humor, always with respect. Only Noah, the retarded brother, and Connie Rivers, Rose of Sharon's non-Joad husband, willfully desert the family. Compared to Faulkner's Snopeses, the Joads are absolute paragons. Faulkner, of course, portrays numerous poor white families who are similarly admirable, but, as Philip Cohen notes, they are Tulls, Armstids, Bookwrights, Littlejohns—rarely if ever Snopeses.[15] The goodness or nobility of Faulkner's poor whites is actually heightened because they compare so favorably with the Snopeses.

The non-aristocratic status of the Joads and the Snopeses is suggested by the very names of the two families. The Joads, according to Benson, actually did exist, at least in name, as an Arkansas clan ("To Tom" 166-67). The name seems humble and solid if not actually dull. Ma declares that no Joad ever refused food or shelter to anyone in need. "They's been mean Joads, but never that mean" (139). The name Snopes, though, connotes not merely commonness but meanness: as numerous critics point out, the name suggests all sorts of revolting creatures, including sneaks, snoops, and snakes—probably, as Frederick Burelback suggests, because of its "sn" phoneme.[16] Indeed, Snopeses are synonymous with the exploiters against whom the Joads vainly struggle. Snopeses metaphorically become the fruit growers and bankers who, lacking any humanity whatsoever, oppress the poor and force them off their land. Flem Snopes, of course, even before he succeeds to the bank presidency, is the star representative of this inhumanity, personifying, as Andrea Dimino observes, J. P. Morgan, Rockefeller, Hill, and other men who ruined the small farmers (Dimino 170). One of Flem's earliest coups is to cheat Henry Armstid of his mortgage, against which Armstid must then borrow from Flem and pay outrageous interest rates.

Ma mourns the break-up of the Joad family, but the Snopeses rarely exhibit that sort of loyalty. What makes the Snopeses worse is that they exploit not only the poor whites, but also each other. Each is more pernicious than the next. Montgomery Ward Snopes peddles soft-core pornography; Launcelot or Lump sells tickets to watch his own kinsman, the idiot Ike, make love to a cow; I. O. Snopes is a "blacksmith-cum-schoolmaster-cum-bigamist" (*Town* 36); Uncle Wesley Snopes, the revivalist song leader, is tarred and feathered for seducing a 14-year-old schoolgirl; and the list goes on: Virgil Snopes is known for his legendary sexual prowess—he can sexually satisfy more than two women in succession, and his cousin Clarence Eggleston Snopes, the entrepreneurial state senator, sells tickets to Virgil's performances. Ironically, however, one of the common Snopes traits, once they reach a certain rung of the Yoknapatawpha social ladder, is a hypocritical semblance of middle-class respectability: I. O. Snopes actually stops Lump from selling tickets to the Ike-and-cow spectacle because, he says, "A man can't have his good name drug in the alleys. The

Snopes name has done held its head up too long in this country to have no such reproaches against it like stock-diddling" (*Hamlet* 201).

Snopes Mutants

Within the Snopes themselves, however, exist contrasts and contradictions—mutants, perhaps, according to the Darwinian view. Such Snopeses are described as aberrations or illegitimate children: they cannot possibly be Snopeses if they do not behave badly. Eckrum, or Ick, Snopes literally breaks his neck saving the life of a Negro who works with him at the lumber mill; his son Wallstreet Panic, recognized as a non-Snopes by his second-grade teacher, marries a splendid young woman who, like other women in the novel who defy the Snopes principle, shouts aloud, "Them damn Snopes! God damn them! God damn them!" When the bemused Gavin Stevens asks why she does not simply change the name to something else, the decent Ratliff shrewdly explains, "She don't want to change it. She jest wants to live it down. . . . She's got to purify Snopes itself" (*Town* 148-49). Indeed, Snopesism is specifically equated to a type of person, not a name. And Faulkner makes clear that only men can be Snopeses. Because women are protected by their innate goodness, male Snopeses by and large continue to beget male Snopeses, "repeating that male principle and then vanishing" (*Town* 136). Faulkner's Flem personifies Steinbeck's impersonal "Bank," which is "a monster," a creature who does not breathe air or eat side meat, but constantly craves "profits," without which it dies (*Grapes* 43).

Although Faulkner conceived of the Snopes saga in 1926, nearly four decades elapsed before he completed the trilogy (Blotner 526-34). *The Grapes of Wrath* was published in 1939, a year before the first edition of *The Hamlet. The Hamlet* concludes with the defeat of even the shrewdest poor whites and an open declaration of the war against Snopesism with which the rest of the trilogy is concerned. Likewise *The Grapes of Wrath* concludes as Tom and Ma Joad articulate their conviction that people must act together to fight the banks, the fruit growers, the uncaring rich. Indeed, despite obvious differences between Joads and Snopeses, some curious parallels exist between *The Grapes of Wrath* and the final novel of Faulkner's trilogy, *The Mansion.*

Both novels contain imprisoned protagonists. As *The Grapes of Wrath* opens, Tom Joad, who has been jailed for killing Herb Turnbull in self-defense, has just been released from McAlaster Prison. Tom is journeying home, hitching rides, uninformed of the recent disasters at home and unaware that he is only at the beginning of his odyssey. Similarly Mink, imprisoned for murder in *The Hamlet*, is released from Parchman Prison. Although a Snopes, Mink is presented with increasing almost Joad-like sympathy: his victim Jack (Zack) Houston was a well-to-do landowner who demeaned the impoverished Mink with quasi-legal rulings and punishments, while every day Mink looked at Houston's warm house, his fat cattle, his mules and horses, until pride, hunger, and desperation drove him to murder. Everyone, including the sheriff, believed that Flem, the titular head of the clan, would hire a lawyer to free Mink. But Flem, a true Snopes, absented himself during the trial at which Mink was convicted and sent to the federal penitentiary for 20 years. Adding insult to injury, Flem sent another kinsman, Montgomery Ward Snopes, to jail and bribed him to persuade Mink to attempt an impossible prison break, thus ensuring Mink 20 more years at Parchman. Flem believed that during this time Mink would die.

But Flem is wrong; Mink does not die. Like Tom Joad, he is released from prison and hitches rides into a world so changed he does not recognize it. Both Tom and Mink indicate that their prison experiences had no reforming effect; both, significantly, leave prison ready to murder again. Tom says he would "squash Herb down with a shovel again" (*Grapes* 74), and Mink has nourished for 38 years his plan to kill Flem, his oppressor and the symbol of all the evil in the world.

On the way home from prison, both Tom and Mink link up with men of the church. Tom meets the former preacher Jim Casy, who resigned his ministerial duties when he realized he might have hurt a few people because of his insatiable desires for the women of his congregation. "I'd just get 'em frothin' with the Holy Sperit, an' then I'd take 'em out in the grass" (*Grapes* 30). He asks, "when a fella ought to be just about mule-ass proof against sin, an' all full up of Jesus, why is it that's the time a fella gets fingerin' his pants buttons" (30)? Mink's view of the hypocrisy of preachers is notably similar: churches are "places which a man with a hole in his gut and a rut in his britches that he couldn't satisfy at home, used, by calling himself a preacher of God, to get conveniently together the biggest possible number of women" (*Mansion* 5-6). And Mink doubtless knows that one of his relatives, Uncle Wesley, could simultaneously lead a "hymn with one hand and fumbl[e] the skirt of an eleven-year-old infant with the other" (*Town* 41). The Jim Casy that Tom Joad remembers, however, has changed, and in his new role he formulates a profoundly humanistic philosophy which deeply affects Tom. Journeying with the Joads to California, Casy now believes in the "Holy Sperit" embodied in all men and women, all the people. Depicted now as a Christ figure, he sacrifices himself twice for the Joads and for the workers. The second time he is murdered by the Snopesish law-enforcers, but not before he tells them, in effect, that they know not what they do (527).

Similar to Tom's, Mink's journey from prison takes him home by way of the religious camp of the Reverend Goodyhay, a preacher remarkably like Casy. An active supporter of the poor, the Reverend Goodyhay is an ex-Marine who survived Pearl Harbor, emerging with a Christian humanist vision. He prays with Mink, "Save us, Christ, the poor sons of bitches" (*Mansion* 271). His "congregation" consists of men, women, blacks, whites, "tenant farmers come up from the mortgaged bank- or syndicate-owned cotton plantation" (282). Like the Reverend Casy who understands that "we was holy when we was one thing, an' mankin' was holy when it was one thing" because there is "one big soul ever'body's a part of" (110; 33), the Reverend Goodyhay watches approvingly as "the white people on the bench mak[e] way for the Negro woman to sit down beside the young white woman and put her arms around her," then takes up a collection for Mink (282). With the money Mink buys the pistol which he later uses to kill his cousin Flem Snopes.

Retaliation Central

The question of angry, frustrated retaliation is central to both Steinbeck's and Faulkner's works. In *The Grapes of Wrath* a nameless tenant asks, "Who can we shoot? I don't aim to starve to death before I kill the man that's starving me" (52). Tom kills Casy's murderer and becomes a fugitive—but at least he has taken action and, in his own mind, avenges the wrongs that the working poor are so helpless to defy. Mink, too, suffers from pent-up rage at unjust treatment and, like Tom, acts decisively against the oppressor. Neither is able to eradicate the evil, but each strikes a symbolic blow against it. The difference is that although both kill twice, each murdering oppressors, Mink's second murder is within his own family.

In addition to their similar experiences with prison, men of the church, and impulses toward retribution, Tom and Mink are both aided by women relatives. These women, all of whom offer help to Tom and Mink when they most need it, even share physical similarities: Ma Joad is "heavy, but not fat, thick with childbearing and work" (99), Mink's wife Yettle is "big yet not fat" (259), and Mrs. Holcomb, the woman who helps Mink when he leaves prison, is "thick but not fat" (264).

Certainly both novels explicitly express awareness of female power and its effects on men. Tom recalls his mother beating "hell out of a tin peddler" who argued with her (64). Each man has been influenced by his mother---

Tom, powerfully by Ma Joad, who encourages him to be a man and to become an activist: "She seemed to know that if she swayed the family shook, and if she ever really deeply wavered or despaired, the family would fall, the family will to function would be gone" (100). Always his supporter, even after he kills Casy's murderer, she feeds him and gives him the money for his escape. In direct opposition to this feminine principle are Steinbeck's Snopes-like and inhuman men who drive the tractors: sitting on iron seats and operating iron pedals, they are incapable of seeing, smelling, or feeling "the warmth and power of the earth" (*Grapes* 48). Mink's awareness of the feminine principle is clear as he thinks, "the very moment you were born out of your mother's body, the power and drag of the earth was already at work on you; if there had not been other womenfolks in the family or neighbors or even a hired one to support you, hold you up . . . you would not live an hour. And you knew it, too" (*Mansion* 402). On his journey from prison, Mink, whose own mother died when he was small, recalls a scene with his stepmother—the only time he ever thinks of her. He recalls a golden fall day when without telling the father—who regularly beat them both—they kill a squirrel, then cook and eat it. Mink suddenly understands that "What a man [aches] to go back to "is not a place, but the "inviolable" and "splendid" memories of relishing together with his stepmother the food that the father-husband would have forbidden them (105-06).

Mink's mother, stepmother, and wife are long dead; it is Linda Snopes Kohl (not really a Snopes at all) who arranges for his early release. Mink cannot know that she has counted on his wanting to kill her "father," Flem Snopes. Just as Ma Joad defends her views on correct behavior by threatening violence with the jackhandle, Linda, an ambulance driver on the battlefields of Spain, where her husband died, and a ship riveter during World War II, has learned that one must "say No" to the evil represented by Hitler, Mussolini—and Flem Snopes. Formulating what amounts to military strategy, she masterminds the elimination of the worst Snopes of all, even, like Ma, arranging to give money to Mink so that he can escape after shooting Flem.[17] Thus, although Ma Joad and Linda are markedly different, each aids an embattled kinsman in his fight against oppression. As numerous critics persuasively argue, Ma is the strongest character in *The Grapes of Wrath*. But Linda, living a quarter-century later in *The Mansion*, is even better equipped to fight than Ma: younger and a well-educated combat veteran, Linda combines the tendencies of the men in *The Grapes of Wrath*, even, like some of the workers, joining the Communist Party while, like Jim Casy, she develops her humanistic philosophy to defeat those who victimize the weak—black, white, male, or female.

Both Steinbeck and Faulkner portray maternal figures to emphasize not only the mother-son relationship but also the mother-daughter bond. As Gladstein observes, both authors use the myth of Demeter and Persephone to suggest the "continuity" and "endless renewal of the female principle."[18] Ma, mother of Rose of Sharon, appears as a "goddess" (100), a mythical figure of maternal strength, and Eula Varner Snopes, mother of Linda, passes into local legend in numerous "goddess" images. However, whereas Ma, according to Gladstein, passes to Rose of Sharon the mantle of the nurturing female (104), Eula's relation to her daughter is somewhat more complex. Eula commits suicide in order to free her daughter from her stepfather Flem's influence, an act of self-sacrifice which ensures Linda's education and self-sufficiency, in turn leading to her compassionate activism in behalf of the downtrodden. By providing the means to eradicate Flem, Linda avenges in general all victimized humans and, in particular, her mother who suffered the bondage of marriage to Flem Snopes. In both novels, then, the daughters--Rose of Sharon Joad Rivers and Linda Snopes Kohl--effect powerfully symbolic acts: Rose of Sharon loses husband and baby but saves a life; Linda loses husband and mother and avenges both. Although their actions seem diametrically opposed, in fact each woman through symbolic gestures supports the rights of the poor, the victimized, the dispossessed. Their methods differ, but their effects are life-affirming. In both novels, with the decisive actions of women, the patriarchal structure diminishes.

Finally, both novels convey strong sympathy for victimized people everywhere. Jim Casy comments that "There ain't no sin and there ain't no virtue." and Pa Joad says, "We done the bes' we could" (32; 328). A quarter-century later Gavin Stevens says, "There aren't any morals. . . . People just do the best they can." And Ratliff replies, "The pore sons of bitches" (*Mansion* 428). Ma is the one who tells Tom, "We're the people. We go on" (383). Tom Joad and Mink Snopes, both described near the ends of their respective novels as preacher-like and both beneficiaries of aid and money from their women kinfolk, seem to transcend their puny and fallible frames (*Grapes* 572; *Mansion* 204/ 266). Tom tells Ma, "I'll be ever'where--wherever you look," for perhaps Casy was correct in his belief that each of us is only "a piece" of one big soul (572). Mink's last view of himself, as he gazes upward at exactly the "right stars," is inextricable from "all of them: the beautiful, the splendid, the proud and the brave, right on up to the very top itself among the shining phantoms and dreams which are the milestones of the long human recording" (435).

Although injustice claims its victims along the way, the fight against it continues at the ends of both novels. The communal effort advocated in both *The Grapes of Wrath* and *The Mansion* is mirrored in the collaborative work of Steinbeck and Faulkner as volunteers in President Eisenhower's People-to-People Program in the 1950s (Benson 709-801). Therein, old hostilities dismissed or ignored, the two writers discovered common ground in their mutual distaste for literary talk and in their disdain for oppression in any form. Steinbeck and Faulkner signed their names to a proposal to aid the Hungarian refugees, to disseminate American books in Eastern Europe, and to free America's "greatest poet," Ezra Pound (Benson 800-801). Although Steinbeck's Joads and Faulkner's Snopeses have come to signify different literary archetypes and divergent views of humanity, both authors successfully employ their chosen "families" to make a similar point: Steinbeck and Faulkner articulate a resounding "No" to exploitation and totalitarianism and an emphatic "Yea" to the rights and dignity of the ordinary individual.

From *San Jose Studies* 18:1 (Winter 1992), 61-71.

Notes

1. Jackson Benson, *The True Adventures of John Steinbeck, Writer* (New York: Viking Press, 1984), p. 770. Further references will be given parenthetically in the text.

2. Quoted by Joseph Blotner, *Faulkner: A Biography*, Vols. I and II (New York: Random House, 1974), p. 524. Further references will be given parenthetically in the text.

3. Elaine A. Steinbeck and Robert Wallsten, eds. *Steinbeck: A Life in Letters* (New York: Viking Press, 1975), p. 529. Further references will be given parenthetically in the text.

4. Mimi Gladstein, "Ma Joad and Pilar: Significantly Similar," *Steinbeck Quarterly*, 14, 1981, p. 93. Further references will be given parenthetically in the text.

5. Andrea Dimino, "Why Did the Snopeses Name Their Son 'Wallstreet Panic'? Depression Humor in Faulkner's *The Hamlet*," *Studies in American Humor* 3, Summer-Fall, 1984, p. 156. Further references will be given parenthetically in the text.

6. Paul Eugene McCarthy, "The Joads and Other Rural Families in Depression Fiction," *South Dakota Review* 19:3, 1981, p. 64.

7. James Gray Watson, *The Snopes Dilemma: Faulkner's Trilogy* (Coral Gables: University of Miami Press, 1968).

8. William Faulkner, *The Town* (New York: Random House, 1957; Vintage Edition, 1961), p. 40.

9. John Steinbeck, *The Grapes of Wrath* (New York: The Viking Press, 1939), p. 12. Further references will be given parenthetically in the text.

10. William Faulkner, *The Mansion* (New York: Random House, 1955; Vintage Edition, 1965), p. 90. Further references will be given parenthetically in the text.

11. William Faulkner, *The Hamlet* (New York: Random House, 1931; Vintage Edition, 1956), p. 18. Further references will be given parenthetically in the text.

12. Warren Motley, "From Patriarchy to Matriarchy: Ma Joad's Role in *The Grapes of Wrath*," *American Literature* 54:2, 3, October 1982, p. 398. Further references will be given parenthetically in the text.

13. Gail Mortimer, "Evolutionary Theory in Faulkner's Snopes Trilogy," *Rocky Mountain Review of Language and Literature* 40:4, 1986, p. 189.

14. Jackson Benson, "To Tom, Who Lived It: John Steinbeck and the Man from Weed-patch," *Journal of Modern Literature* 5, 1976, p. 190.

15. Philip Cohen, "Balzac and Faulkner: The Influence of *La Comedie Humaine* on *Flags in the Dust* and the Snopes Trilogy," *Mississippi Quarterly* 37:3, 1984, p. 350.

16. Frederick M. Burelbach, "The Name of the Snake: A Family of Snopes," *Literary Onomastics Studies* 8, 1981, pp. 125-26.

17. Abby H. P. Werlock, "Victims Unvanquished: Temple Drake and the Women in William Faulkner's Novels" in *Women and Violence in Literature: An Essay Collection*, ed. Katherine A. Ackley (New York: Garland Publishing, Inc., 1990), p. 38.

18. Gladstein, Mimi, The Indestructible Woman in Faulkner, Hemingway, and Steinbeck (Ann Arbor: UMI Research Press, 1986), p. 81.

California Answers
The Grapes of Wrath

Susan Shillinglaw

Four months after publication of *The Grapes of Wrath*, John Steinbeck responded sharply to mounting criticism of his book: "I know what I was talking about," he told a *Los Angeles Times* reporter. "I lived, off and on, with those Okies for the last three years. Anyone who tries to refute me will just become ridiculous."[1] His angry retort is largely on target—but the opposition was in earnest and had been even before his novel was published.

In 1938 corporate farmers in California responded forcefully to the consequences of continued migration: the twin threats of unions and a liberal migrant vote.[2] Beginning early that year a statewide publicity campaign to discredit the "migrant menace" had been mounted by the Associated Farmers and the newly formed CCA, or California Citizens Association, a group with the broad support of banks, oil companies, agricultural land companies, businesses, and public utilities.[3] Well-funded and well-placed, the CCA and the Associated Farmers produced scores of articles meant to discourage further migration, to encourage Dust Bowlers already in California to return to their home states, and to convince the federal government that California's migrant problem was a federal, not a state, responsibility. These articles vigorously defended farmers' wage scales and housing standards. They complained about the state's generous relief, which, at almost twice that of Oklahoma and Arkansas, had "encouraged" migration. And they often maligned the state's newest residents. "The whole design of modern life," noted an article in the *San*

Francisco Examiner entitled "The Truth About California," "has stimulated their hunger for change and adventure, fun and frippery. Give them a relief check and they'll head straight for a beauty shop and a movie."[4]   The publication of Steinbeck's novel in March 1939—followed shortly thereafter by Carey McWilliams's carefully documented *Factories in the Fields*— simply gave the outraged elite a new focus for their attack.

The campaign took on a new intensity. Editorials and pamphlets, many underwritten by the Associated Farmers, claimed to expose Steinbeck's "prejudice, exaggeration, and oversimplification," the thesis of one tract, or to discredit the "Termites Steinbeck and McWilliams," the title of another.[5] Of greater impact, however, were the more sustained efforts to counter what were perceived as Steinbeck's factual inaccuracies. I shall examine four of the most important respondents. Two who defended California agriculture were highly respected professional writers: Ruth Comfort Mitchell, the author of *Of Human Kindness*, and Frank J. Taylor, a free-lance journalist who covered California business, farming, and recreation for the state and national press. And two were highly successful retired farmers, to use the word loosely: Marshall V. Hartranft, the Los Angeles fruit grower and real estate developer who wrote *Grapes of Gladness: California's Refreshing and Inspiriting Answer to John Steinbeck's "Grapes of Wrath,"* and Sue Sanders, touted as the "friend of the migrant," who wrote and published a tract called "The Real Cause of Our Migrant Problem." Since each contributed to what can only be called a hysterical campaign against the migrant presence and Steinbeck himself, it is difficult not to cast them as villains. What must be recognized, however, is that each with great sincerity and, to a large extent, accuracy, described another California—a brawny, confident state that bustled with entrepreneurial zeal. Each defended California against Steinbeck's charges largely by ignoring much of the agony and cruelty he chronicled. Each sought an answer to the "migrant question" without fully comprehending—or perhaps, more significantly, empathizing with—the "problem," the migrants' plight. To understand each writer's perspective is to appreciate better the intensity of the political clashes of the 1930s, a period when, as liberal activist Richard Criley observed, "Social issues were so sharp and so clear . . . we were pulled to take a position because things were so acute, so terrifying in the need to change."[6] These interpreters of the California scene resisted change.

In the late 1930s, Los Gatos novelists Ruth Comfort Mitchell (1882-1954) and John Steinbeck shared a magnificent view of the Santa Clara Valley from their mountain homes six miles apart.[7] Similarities in perspective end there. The author of sixteen novels and several collections of poems, as well as short stories and articles published in *Woman's Home Companion, Century, Good Housekeeping*, and *McCall's*, Mitchell claimed as her fictional terrain the uncertain ground of young love. When she wrote a vaudeville sketch on the "great question of labor" in 1907, it was lauded as an "uplifting" piece that helped give the stage a more wholesome image. Mitchell's play, noted the review, "holds the human emotions paramount and introduces the labor and capital strike features as secondary."[8]

That comment holds true for much of her work. Mitchell always "liked to take the bright view," noted her obituary in the *New York Times*. Neither by temperament nor by class was she fitted to fully comprehend Steinbeck's Joads. She was one of California's elite, raised in comfort and married to wealth. "I know nothing about that stimulating lash of adversity that all of you people who have had to fight for your foothold talk about," she admitted to one reporter.[9] Her only contact with migrant labor was on her husband Sanborn Young's dairy farm south of Fresno, where the two lived for several years until Young became a state senator—and notorious strike buster—in 1925.[10] As early as 1918, when they built their Los Gatos summer home, she took to wearing only green, writing on only green stationery using green ink and stamps, and driving only green cars (a pose that Steinbeck almost certainly satirizes in the effete Joe Elegant of *Sweet Thursday*, whose manuscript is on "green paper typed with a green ribbon"). Mitchell's eccentricity was seen as part of her charm, and this prolific and witty author was much in demand as a public speaker for women's groups both locally and nationally. Often she discussed writing, read her poetry, or commented on her recent work. But just as often in the late 1930s Mitchell—state president of the National Association of Pro America, a Republican women's association—lectured on international politics.

The publication of *The Grapes of Wrath* gave her a fresh platform much closer to home. As novelist, popular lecturer, wife of Farmer/Senator Young, and efficient political organizer, she was the ideal candidate to help launch a campaign against Steinbeck's novel. In league with the Associated Farmers—in fact, she gave the keynote speech at their annual convention in December 1939—she threw her considerable resources into the superbly organized attack against the novel. On August 23, 1939, the day after *Grapes* was banned in Kern County, William B. Camp, president of the Associated Farmers, announced a statewide plan to recall the book.[11] In that same week, Mitchell was chair and key speaker at a meeting of Pro America in San Francisco, where "five hundred persons . . . heard speakers denounce recent books dealing with California's migrant problem, call for cessation of relief for transients, and praise efforts of individual farmers to better conditions for migratory workers."[12] This meeting may serve as a touchstone for all such gatherings and may demonstrate why Steinbeck could with truth call the "Ass Farmers"—his term—ridiculous. It was here that Mitchell contended that California farms were becoming smaller, and another speaker maintained that "farmworkers of California are better paid and better housed than agricultural workers anywhere else in the world."[13]

Even if such exaggerated claims characterized many attacks on the novel, it cannot be said that defenses of California agriculture rested on overstatement alone. The central thrust was not to ban Steinbeck's text statewide, although some in Kern County attempted to do so, or to discredit the man, although many tried. Rather, it was to replace one picture of California farm and migrant life with another. Mitchell set out to prove that California was a rural paradise, farmed by energetic, committed Americans. In June 1939 she began writing what became the longest and most highly publicized response to *Grapes*, her novel *Of Human Kindness*, published by D. Appleton-Century Company in 1940. As she was writing her book, she repeatedly declared to audiences and reporters that she told "the other side of the story," insisting that in doing so she did not intend to attack Steinbeck, merely to defend the rancher's position. Indeed, both she and her publisher took pains to dissociate her book from Steinbeck's. Her novel, she asserted, was fully outlined before Steinbeck's book was published. But this seems unlikely, since Mitchell's novel is crafted to dovetail with the Associated Farmers' own campaign.[14]

In their many tracts the farmer is invariably a heroic figure, a hard-working man protecting his home and minimal profits, enduring the uncertainties of weather and insects that affected his crops.   Prolific pamphleteer Philip Bancroft, farmer and Republican candidate for the state senate in 1938, described himself as enjoying the "out-of-doors life, simply and economically."[15]   Cut from the same cloth, Ed Banner, Mitchell's dairyman farmer, is as patriotic as his last name suggests—a point hammered home by his daughter's fiance, who calls her "Star Spangled." The Banners are "San Joaquin Valley pioneers, third generation in California; plain people, poor people, proud people; salt of the earth."[16] Their success, as Mitchell never tires of making clear, was achieved not through wealth, but by working "sixteen hours out of the twenty four." Indeed, the Banner matriarch "out-earth mothers" Ma Joad, thus proving the family's superior Americanism; she is supremely fair-minded, a "Dowager Empress in her authority, her calm, her composure, her wisdom. Old Buddha in a faded gingham dress" (*OHK*, p. 72). And she is altruistic to a fault: her own home is "less good than the cabins she had built for her men." Their farm community is similarly archetypal: poor but energetic, closely knit and supportive—the neighbors banding together to help the Banners clean their new house and to break up, rather gently, a strike.

In presenting the "other side," Mitchell takes pains to show that farm life, like migrant life, could be "hard and harsh and uncompromising" (*OHK*, p. 75). Only one farmer enjoys wealth and leisure, and he is compared to Simon Legree. This benighted farmer is "always undercutting the prevailing wage, charging them fifteen cents to ride out to the field, [and building] shacks a self-respecting pig wouldn't live it" (p. 221). But this "blood-sucker," "gorilla," and wife tormenter, Mitchell shows, is far from the norm.

This rural tycoon is as exaggerated a type as are the interlopers who threaten Arcadia. One Okie, Lute Willow, "okie-dokie Boy," intrudes and elopes with the Banner daughter. But the guitar-slinging Lute is hardly representative. His family owns a dairy farm in Oklahoma, and he came to California by choice, not because he was driven out of his home. Most significantly, under Ed Banner's tutelage he learns to work hard. And so Ed, initially rejecting the "dumb and shiftless" Okies, learns to accept this superior specimen. Mitchell's point is clear: a few migrants can be integrated into the valley communities if they are willing to work as diligently as have the farmers—precisely the Associated Farmers' announced position. In "The Truth about John Steinbeck and the Migrants," the laborers are said not to be the "beasts" Steinbeck portrays, but "honest, intelligent, and assimilable people."[17]

Neither Mitchell nor her supporters, however, were prepared to accept leftists who, they charged, entered the state only to inflame the workers. Most "replies" condemned the Communists. In Mitchell's text, the chief spokes-woman for what is clearly perceived as Steinbeck's position is a new history teacher who looks like a rabbit. Rude, flat-chested, sallow, and lesbian, Pinky Emory corrupts the valley children—the Banner son included—by arguing that migrants were "lured out to California by the farmers so oodles and oodles would come and they could get cheap labor and pay starvation wages!" (*OHK*, p. 81). This is, of course, Steinbeck's novel in a nutshell. There is also a union organizer, a "Carmen—and Delilah—Borgia" (p. 206), a "Black Widow" (perhaps modeled on labor organizer Caroline Decker)[18] who seduces the son, betrays the history teacher who adores her, and, after sending Pinky to her death, seizes her body and uses it to inspire the workers to action in a scene that echoes Mac's reaction to Joy's death in *In Dubious Battle*. The organizers are clearly a bad lot whose sexual deviance redundantly condemns their already perverse politics. As Philip Bancroft had earlier noted in an article characterizing the Communists: "Some of the most rabid and dangerous are attractive and educated women."[19] For Mitchell, the women's position is synonymous with Steinbeck's, and their siren songs are as fatal as his text. Indeed, what may have been most inflammatory about *Grapes* was its sympathy with collective action. In championing the "family of man" Steinbeck seemed perilously close to embracing a socialist ideal, and Mitchell, like all these interpreters, would not betray her faith in American individualism, its excesses notwithstanding.

What may be most remarkable about Mitchell's novel, however, is not her sublimely ridiculous characters—the noble farmers, sapphic leftist organizers, and uniquely respectable Okie—all of whom she judges against the Banner ethos and the rhetoric of the Associated Farmers. Rather, it is that, while waving the virtuous Banners—Ed and Mary—so vigorously before the reader, Mitchell nonetheless proclaims her objectivity. Clearly she wants the reader to believe that her novel is grounded, not in the self-interest of the landed class, but in fair-mindedness. Not merely a narrative stance, fair-mindedness is realized by her strong female characters: the Banner matriarch, Helga the public nurse, and the semiautobiographical, Mary Banner, whose perspective is the broadest in the book. Armed with an urban education and a rural practicality, Mary—like Mitchell herself— "bend[s] over backwards trying to be fair" (*OHK*, p. 221). (It was an acrobatic attitude many pamphleteers also assumed.) Thus, Mary articulates the book's (and, to a large extent, the Associated Farmers') central tenet: "I know just as well as you do that there's injustice and graft and greed here and everywhere, and ignorance and filth and suffering, but it's utterly false to say the world isn't better and going to be still better!" (pp. 178-79). And it is the farmers, not the staid city dwellers, who are most open to the meliorism she envisions, even though such change is gradual and often slow. When the students picket in support of their teacher, the politically chromatic Pinky, it is a farmer who tells the others that "most of us are too far to the right. We've got to do some fact-facing ourselves" (p. 190). Later the feisty Ed Banner, initially denouncing the Okies, learns to accept both his Okie son-in-law and his own political obligation to run for the state senate. For Mitchell, it is axiomatic that good farmers adapt. Hard and demanding rural life molds fair-mindedness. This seems to be Mitchell's central position, the objective "other side" she championed against the "prejudice, exaggeration, and over-simplification" seen in *Grapes*.

If Mitchell best articulated the Associated Farmers' position in fiction, Frank J. Taylor, free-lance journalist, was the farmers' most formidable advocate in nonfiction. Taylor (1894-1972) also attended the Pro America evening at the Palace Hotel in San Francisco late in the summer of 1939. For the previous ten years, he had covered the West Coast for national magazines, first writing articles on Yellowstone and the National Park Service, and then, as a self-styled "roving reporter" for the conservative *Country Gentleman*, covering California agriculture. Being a "scout for farming stories," he notes in an autobiographical piece, "quite naturally turned up some characters who were good material for the *Sat Eve Post*, *Colliers*, *Nation's Business*, and the *Reader's Digest*. These stories had to be slanted at people who lived in cities, rather than at farmers, who were the *Gent*'s readers."[20] Writing for these conservative national magazines and an urban audience, Taylor excelled in human interest stories about California entrepreneurs: beekeepers, vintners, and firework makers; the Burpees of seed company fame; UC Berkeley's Dr. Gericke, originator of "soil-less crops"; Walt Disney; and "Mr. Gump—of Gump's."[21] Taylor was a dyed-in-the-wool California booster. He admired the "shrewd individualists" who shaped the "Many Californias," men who wrested sizable fortunes from flowers, gold mines, and Oriental art, men who forged the state's cooperative farming and shipping interests. His perspective was, in fact, nearly identical to Mitchell's: positive, forward-looking, and pragmatic. Living and working in "the biggest and best" state, he looked around for what made it run smoothly.

Farmers did. As his 1938 article "The Merritt System" makes clear, Taylor champions the farmer's work ethic as vigorously as does Mitchell. The Merritts, father and son, owned the huge Tagus Ranch, probable site of Steinbeck's *In Dubious Battle*. But Taylor's ranch is most definitely not Steinbeck's. The benevolent Merritts "brought to farming the restless search for efficiency the elder Merritt had learned in the industrial world, and they have made Tagus Ranch a year-round producer." Furthermore, Taylor notes that they have created a utopian community for their workers, who live in "glistening white" houses they rent for two to four dollars a month, buy food from a company store at "chain store prices (where the "Merritts manage to lose a cent or two on every dollar of sales—purposely"), and send their children to the Tagus school, where they are given cod-liver oil if they appear malnourished despite the hot chocolate and graham crackers they are fed at recess.

The only flies in the ointment, reports Taylor, are the "radical labor organizers" who, seemingly without cause, "descended in force on Tagus Ranch" a few years earlier and "dragged fruit pickers from their ladders [and] threatened women and children." And, in a note at the end, he reports that the Merritts also have problems with Okies who are so accustomed to living in one-room shacks that they "chopped out partitions" in the cottages and "burned them when firewood was free for the cutting."[22] Clearly, Taylor admires the Merritts' industry and perceived goodwill toward workers. His detailed account of housing conditions is meant to counter frequent charges that farmers provided only substandard housing for workers. If Steinbeck looked for and found squalor, Taylor, like Mitchell, looked for and found the benevolent master.

He featured other farmer-entrepreneurs. In 1935, he published an equally glowing piece on "Teague of California," a wealthy man and "a farmer from the soil up . . . [who] wrested a sizable fortune from the California soil, starting with nothing in the way of assets but energy and ability and a willingness to work."[23] For Taylor, the Merritts and Teague were not capitalists but Jeffersonian gentlemen farmers, benevolent men, Horatio Algers of the soil. Yearly, they courageously faced uncertainties of weather or labor unrest; they were "beset even in times of industrial tranquillity by unusual hazards such as long-haul freight rates, danger of spoiling, cost of packing, and whimsies of the market."[24] But farmers endured, a point Taylor reiterates in several articles. As American icons, these energetic, courageous, and generous owners ("Mr. Teague has never received a red cent for the vast amount of time he has devoted to the citrus and walnut cooperatives") shaped California's destiny, and their produce helped make California farming vital to the nation's economy. To threaten their crops was to steal food from tables across America.

Communist organizers are thus, for Taylor as for Mitchell, serpents in the garden. Prior to 1939 Taylor wrote several articles on the labor situation in California. No reactionary, he does not denounce unions; indeed, he features businessmen who have learned to "play ball" with unions. Nor is he unsympathetic to workers, to the Okies' "natural urge" to "dig their toes into a patch of ground . . . and settle down."[25] What he, like so many Californians, could not tolerate was the organized threat to commerce— particularly agriculture. "Communists," he declared in a 1937 article on the Associated Farmers, "had singled out California agriculture for special attention because of the vulnerable nature of its perishable crops."[26] Thus, for Taylor, the farmers, who quite naturally rose to defend the land and their rights to market their produce, were the "minute men of California agriculture." In the Salinas lettuce strike of 1936, they "transformed themselves into bands of embattled farmers, armed and imbued with a Bunker Hill determination to fight it out."[27] Taylor's metaphors define his sympathies. For him, as for Mitchell, the Associated Farmers defended the homeland against aliens—and often the issue of unfair wages was simply ignored or dismissed.

After publication of *Grapes*, DeWitt Wallace, the editor of *Reader's Digest*, asked Taylor to "trace the travels of the Joad family" in order to "tell the rest of the world about California."[28] The resulting piece, published in both *Forum* and *Reader's Digest* in November 1939, is an impressively detailed defense, supported by statistics and by Taylor's own observations. He begins, "I made one inquiry during the winter of 1937-38, following the flood which Steinbeck describes; I made another at the height of the harvest this year."[29] What he sees on both trips—and in his fifteen-year residence in the Santa Clara Valley—are the migrants as field workers, "stoops," the lower class. During both trips, he is most impressed, not by the migrants' plight but by the state's relief efforts. And he is most interested in the health officials' responses to the migrants; at least one of them, Dr. Lee Stone of Madera County, was a virulent Okie hater. His reputation for scrupulous reporting notwithstanding, Taylor could not fully acknowledge the human misery that Steinbeck had seen in his two years of trips, nor could he bear witness to the tragic flooding in the spring of 1938. Undoubtedly well intentioned, Taylor, quite simply, shared Mitchell's elitest perspective. For these two, as for the majority of Californians, field workers were—and in fact still are—an invisible population. When the state was finally forced in 1938 to acknowledge the numbers of Dust Bowl migrants and, unlike the Mexican workers they replaced, their determination to settle in California, most Californians could hardly be expected to see the state's newest residents objectively.

To bolster his own observations, Taylor marshaled impressive statistics to show that the migrants' lot was not "the bitter fate described in *The Grapes of Wrath*." California wages, he notes, were higher than those in the southwestern states. Often true, but the cost of living was also higher. Relief payments in California, he continues, were almost twice as high as those in southwestern states, and thus migrants swarmed to California to claim this "comparative bonanza" ("CGOW," p. 233), which they were allowed after a year's residency. True, payments were higher, but, as Walter Stein observes, what many "neglected to admit was the critical role the Okie influx played in keeping wages so low that local residents actually lost money if they went off relief in order to pick the crops."[30] In addition, recent studies have shown that relief payments were not the key consideration in the migrant movement westward.[31]

To further demonstrate that migrants were well cared for, Taylor notes that during the first year, when ineligible for state relief funds, migrants could obtain emergency food and funds from the Farm Security Administration, "which maintains warehouses in eleven strategically located towns" ("CGOW," p. 233). That program, he fails to explain, had been approved only in 1938 and, more importantly, destitute migrants often could not travel, could not overcome their pride to ask for relief, could not help but fear unknown authorities. Finally, as he discusses at some length, hospitals and health facilities cared for the migrants. Like the above statistics, this was true, particularly in Kern and Madera counties. But concerned health officials could not eliminate all squalor and sickness, however impressive their efforts. Tom Collins's reports, Carey McWilliams's prose, and Dorothea Lange's portraits bear witness to the fact that outlying squatters' camps were as filthy as those in Steinbeck's novel. Both Taylor's observations and his facts demonstrate that the migrants were, for him, a group to be studied, classified. Striving for objectivity, he nonetheless accepted the Associated Farmers' absurd claims that "neither the Association nor the Bank [of America] concerns itself with wages. Rates of pay are worked out through the farmer cooperatives in each crop or through local groups" (p. 238). He recorded, as a subsequent letter to *Forum's* editor states, "only what is profitable to his state."[32] While the solidly middle-class Steinbeck, Collins, Lange, and McWilliams saw the poor as individuals, Taylor, like so many others, viewed them primarily as a social problem.

The central point of Mitchell's argument is the farmers' integrity, while Taylor's "defense" rests chiefly on the state and federal governments' benevolence to the migrants. Yet another emphasis is to be found in *Grapes of Gladness*, a book by the retired realtor and grower Marshall V. Hartranft, whose text underscores the migrants' potential for a self-sufficient existence. "Two men looked out from their prison bars," states the epigraph to the text. "One saw the mud, the other the stars."[33] Hartranft opts for stargazing and, cursing the mud-gazer "Steinbitch," invokes the spirit of Thoreau to prove that migrants can claim their own bit of land and become self-supporting.

Only Hartranft's enthusiasm for bountiful California qualified him as respondent to *Grapes*. As a fruit grower near Los Angeles he had been, in 1893, the first to sell at auction West Coast oranges to the East Coast market; subsequently, he settled in Los Angeles and founded horticultural trade dailies, the Los Angeles and the New York *Daily Fruit World*, which helped in "advertising the distinctive products of California and advancing the interests of the producers."[34] More significantly, as a Los Angeles real estate agent, he was "instrumental in the development of many of the state's large farming lands," primarily thorough the California Home Extension Association, which encouraged "group colonization" of desert lands. In his book, he sets out to prove Steinbeck wrong by enthusiastically summarizing his life's two projects—colonizing and cultivating California.

If the migrants' plight were taken out of the politicians' hands, he declares in the Foreword, and put into the hands of social engineers like himself, the Joads would settle as happily in California as do his own "authentic" family, the Hoags of Beaver, Oklahoma. Traveling west, the Hoags by some good fortune continue toward Los Angeles rather than swinging to the north. Highway 66 is their road to glory, papered with signs announcing the availability of "garden acres." "Population creates land values," these posters declare, as did Hartranft whenever founding one of his several land colonies. "We will loan an acre farm to any enterprising family of worthy American people," he writes. "Near Los Angeles industries, agricultural activities, and only one or two miles from the beach. You must dig a cess-pool for your first payment; carry the 6% interest of $4.00 a month—and taxes. We require no other money payment for five whole years. You must build at least a two room cottage within a year" (*GOG*, p. 17). The next one hundred pages tell how the Hoags' skepticism—most particularly Pa's—turns to partisanship as they do, indeed, find their fruitful acre.

What is most impressive about Hartranft's reply is its optimism, its wholehearted endorsement of the Edenic myth, which Ma reads about as they drive into Los Angeles. "Taking a living in California," preaches the literature they have picked up along the way, "is almost as easy as the natives have it in the South Sea Islands where they gather their living from the wild trees" (*GOG*, p. 58). Midway through the book, a Thoreauvean sage wanders into the Hoag camp, munching carob bean and "radiating" Thoreau's doctrines of simplicity and economy. Thus inspired, the optimistic Ma takes to reading Thoreau—"through its first chapter at least" (p. 61)—and to believing that they too can survive off the land. With another family, the Hoags find their garden plot on the outskirts of Los Angeles. And they learn "acre-culture," to live off what their gardens produce; to own pigs, not pups; to plant food-bearing trees that also have "foliage that would make a peacock stutter" (p. 105). Self-sufficiency is thus given highest priority—and government assistance is scorned.

Indeed, Hartranft's reply is as American a document as is Mitchell's— and Steinbeck's. What is particularly striking about these rebuttals is that the values endorsed are shared by Steinbeck's own migrants. The Joads, the Hoags, and the Banners all believe in hard work, in community loyalty, in family honor, in land ownership. What differs is not the values, but a belief in their ability to succeed. From the beginning of his career, Steinbeck rejected the axiom that any human, through individual efforts, is guaranteed happiness. Perhaps at some visceral level, what Mitchell and Hartranft found most subversive about Steinbeck's novel is that it radically questions the American faith in the efficacy of work. The wealthy Mitchell, the successful Taylor, and the enterprising Hartranft simply could not comprehend that worthy, energetic people could fail. Hartranft's book ends with a rather touching tribute to his faith; his Hoags, having recently read about their friends in a book (obviously *Grapes*), are heading toward Shafter to rescue them. The recent converts to the gospel of work have become its evangelists.

Sue Sanders was undoubtedly a Kern County phenomenon, the author of a small pamphlet of limited circulation, "The Real Causes of Our Migrant Problem."[35] Hers is a personal testimonial to her equally strong faith in the initiative of migrants. Neither her tract nor Hartranft's received the national attention given the others, but she deserves brief mention in order to clarify one other central tenet in the anti-Steinbeck campaign. What is intriguing about these defenses is their ambivalence toward the migrant. On the one hand, Okies were said to be far more "filthy and unenterprising" than Steinbeck had suggested. Prejudice against the southwesterners ran deep, particularly in the Central Valley. But defenses of the migrants were as common as denunciations, perhaps because, as Mitchell, Hartranft, and Sanders show, these white farm workers, unlike the Mexicans, were perceived as pioneers. They were farmers, only one generation removed from many Oklahomans who had migrated to California in the 1920s. And they exhibited early on that most admirable of American traits, the determination to make a go of it on the last frontier.

In short, Sue Sanders's tract is, like Hartranft's, a hymn to the pioneer spirit of the staunch American farmer. In mid-1939, she launched a one-woman campaign to solve California's migrant problem by proposing that the newcomers go back to Oklahoma to farm their home turf, or what was left of it. First, as she reports in her pamphlet, she toured the camps at Arvin and Shafter and confirmed the fact that these migrants were not, as she feared, shiftless. She writes: "I could be just as proud of these people as I had ever been" (RCMP, p. 12). So she traveled to more camps and lifted spirits by promising destitute migrants that she would, like the Wizard of Oz, help them return to the Midwest. She organized "Okie Farm Hours" at the camps and sponsored competitions with "cash prizes for the best talks on the Farm Hour on such subjects as 'How I Would Plant a Forty-Acre Farm in My Home State,' or 'My Methods of Canning Fruits and Vegetables,' or 'How I Would Make a Salad.'" With admirable naivete, she then went to

Oklahoma and asked farmers to give the migrants land. They refused. So she sadly returned to the camps and told her migrant friends that they couldn't go home again—but they could resist relief. "A country can go bankrupt in more ways than one," she concludes. "I'm not sure but that the most fatal way is by wasting the character resources of its citizens. That is exactly what is going on under the system of giving relief. We need a system of helping. Yes, by all means. But not a system that doles out charity and takes away initiative and self respect" (p. 70). Although her solution fizzled, her faith did not.

On the one hand, Sanders's and Hartranft's enthusiastic projects are ridiculous "defenses," just as Steinbeck declared. Hartranft's garden acres helped a tiny proportion of migrants who came to Los Angeles, while Sanders's vision of deportation improved spirits but temporarily. These "solutions" were Band-Aids, and the wound continued to fester. But in company with Mitchell's and Taylor's more searching analyses, these documents share an idealism that is far from ridiculous. It is staunchly American. Theirs is the faith in individual initiative. Theirs is the belief in land ownership, in the virtues of the yeoman farmer. All four demonstrated that any conscientious migrant could make it without clamoring for state aid or collective action. What Sanders discovered as she traveled among the migrants was that "They do so well with what they have. . . . They are clean and neat" and have "ingenuity in getting along with very little."[36] What was inimical to this way of thinking was the idealism of Tom Joad, a call for action as fully American as theirs, but one rooted in group, not individual, initiative. "The Battle Hymn of the Republic," which Steinbeck insisted be printed in full on the end papers of his text, calls for a collective march onward. And Steinbeck's novel marches to the same drummer. Californians attacked *The Grapes of Wrath* so viciously not only because of its language, but also because of its vision of poverty, and its attack on a system that, in fact, many agreed was flawed. These Westerners, proud and independent themselves, lambasted a book that flouted what seemed to them irrefutable American ideals.[37] The idealism of Mitchell, Taylor, Hartranft, and Sanders was, quite simply, irreconcilable with the idealism of Tom Joad.[38]

From *John Steinbeck: The Years of Greatness, 1936-1939*, 145-64; 181-86

Notes

1. Tom Cameron, "*The Grapes of Wrath* Author Guards Self from Threats at Moody Gulch," *Los Angeles Times*, July 9, 1939, pp. 1-2.

2. James N. Gregory, *American Exodus: The Dust Bowl Migration and Okie Culture in California* (New York: Oxford University Press, 1989), p. 88.

3. Walter J. Stein, *California and the Dust Bowl Migration* (Westport, Conn.: Greenwood Press, 1973), p. 97. Gregory calls this stage of reaction "the second anti-migrant campaign" (*American Exodus*, p. 88). Since the mid-1930s, valley residents had viewed the Southwestern migrants with increasing disdain, complaining of their poverty and strange ways and, more pointedly, of their need for schooling and health care, which had sent taxes soaring. The crisis in the migrant problem came in 1938, when the second Agricultural Adjustment Act set new controls for California cotton, resulting in fewer acres planted and fewer jobs for migrants.

4. Elsie Robinson , "The Truth About California: Red Ousters urged as State's Only Solution to End Migrant Evil," *San Francisco Examiner* ["March of Events" section], January 14, 1940, p. 1.

5. See George Thomas Miron, "The Truth About John Steinbeck and the Migrants" (Los Angeles, 1939), p. 4, Bancroft Library, University of California, Berkeley; and John E. Pickett, "Termites Steinbeck and McWilliams," *Pacific Rural Press*, July 29, 1939.

Interview with Richard Criley, June 21, 1990.

7. Similarities between the two are intriguing. Like Steinbeck, Ruth Comfort Mitchell loved dogs, the outdoors, and music, believing that of all the arts, "music is the only art that restores us to ourselves." While still a teenager, she, too, devoted her time to writing; her first poem, "To Los Gatos," was published in the local paper when she was thirteen, and at nineteen she had launched a successful career as a writer for vaudeville. Also like Steinbeck, she refused to see her most popular productions during their New York runs. When Mitchell and her husband built a house in Los Gatos in 1916, she, like Steinbeck, built a study "with the floor space of a postcard" where she wrote for four to twelve hours daily. See Stella Haverland, "Ruth Comfort Mitchell," pp. 122-26, Ruth Comfort Mitchell Papers, San Jose Public Library.

8. *Pittsburgh Dispatch*, August 29, 1909.

9. *Los Angeles Times Sun*, Ruth Comfort Mitchell Papers, San Jose Public Library.

10. Sanborn Young owned the two thousand-acre Riverdale Ranch, a dairy ranch near Fresno in the San Joaquin Valley; he was also part owner of the New Idria quicksilver mine in San Benito County. He took his new wife to his dairy farm after their marriage in 1914; it was during her few years on that farm and in subsequent visits that she gained her perspective on California's labor problems.

A senator from 1924 to 1928 and 1930 to 1932, Young became a prominent voice in state politics, largely through his support of narcotics control. In 1931 he and Mitchell attended an international conference on narcotics in Geneva

(May 27-July 13), and nine years later he remained a chief spokesman for this issue, claiming that "California has between 3000 and 6000 narcotics addicts, and addiction to marijuana—Indian hemp—is rapidly increasing" (*Los Gatos Times,* March 10, 1939, p. 3). Less highly publicized was his support for the Associated Farmers and, in all likelihood, for the CCA.

11. Tim Kappel, "Trampling Out the Vineyards—Kern County's Ban on *The Grapes of Wrath*," *California History* 61 (Fall 1982): 212.

12. "Pro America Gives 'Other Side' of Story to Migrant Problems,*"* *Los Gatos Times*, August 25, 1939, p. 1.

13. *Fresno Bee*, a report of a meeting on the status of California farm workers, August 12, 1939.

14. Mitchell repeatedly denied that her novel was written in response to Steinbeck's. In a letter to a friend, JHJ, she says: "Will you please PLEASE emphasize the fact—as you so kindly did once before—that it wasn't an 'answer' or 'challenge of GRAPES OF WRATH,' that it was planned, plotted, named before I read G-O-W, that I yield to no one in my admiration of the genius of John Steinbeck? . . . I sent JS a copy from a 'Los Gatos wild cat to a literary lion,' and he sent me IN DUBIOUS BATTLE, which is my favorite, altho' MICE AND MEN is a gorgeous pattern." (This was possible written May 8, 1940.) Mitchell Papers, Bancroft Library, University of California, Berkeley.

Mitchell's protests notwithstanding, her book played a part in the Associated Farmers' campaign. Mitchell was "preparing to give California's answer as principal speaker at the banquet on December 7 which opens the two-day convention of the Associated Farmers of California at Stockton" ("Ruth Comfort Mitchell to Address Meeting of Associated Farmers," *Los Gatos Times*, November 24, 1939, p. 5). She spoke on "her version of 'The Grapes of Wrath'" ("Noted Authoress Answers Charges of Novel, Defends Migrants," *Stockton Record*, December 8, 1939, pp. 1, 21). (See also "Writer to Discuss Steinbeck Book Before Farmers Meet," *Stockton Record*, December 5, 1939, p. 13.)

Furthermore, records indicate that she did indeed write in response to Steinbeck's text. The first notice of Mitchell's book in the Los Gatos paper is June 30, 1939—nearly three months after publication of *Grapes*. The contract for *Of Human Kindness* was not signed until October 19, 1939, and the book was not published until May 1940. (See also *New Republic* 103 [September 2, 1940], p. 305, where Carey McWilliams shows that Mitchell publicly responded to Steinbeck on many occasions.)

15. Philip Bancroft, "The Farmers and the Communists," [San Fancisco] *Daily Commercial News*, April 23, 30, 1935.

16. Ruth Comfort Mitchell, *Of Human Kindness* (New York: D. Appleton-Century Co., 1940), p. 5. Hereinafter identified as *OHK*.

17. Miron, "Truth about Steinbeck," p. 21.

18. Labor historian Anne Loftis pointed out this possible parallel to me. Stein, however, sees the "Black Widow" as Steinbeck himself.

19. Bancroft, "Farmer and Communists," p. 7.

20. Frank J. Taylor, "One Story Leads to Another," Frank Taylor Papers, Department of Special Collections, Stanford University Libraries.

21. See "The Flowers and the Bees," *Collier's* (September 9, 1939); "Color from California: More than Half the World's Supply of Flower Seeds Come from This State," *California—Magazine of Pacific Business* (November 1939); "Mr. Gump—of Gump's: A Romance of Treasure Trove in San Francisco," *California—Magazine of Pacific Business* (April 1937); "Soil-less Crops," *Country Home* (September 1936), pp. 18-19; "Mickey Mouse—Merchant: A Personality Sketch of a Native Son and California's No. 1 Merchandiser," *California—Magazine of Pacific Business* (March 1937); "What Has Disney Got that We Haven't," *Commentator* (October 1937). I wish to thank Frank J. Taylor's son, Robert Taylor, for generously showing me scrapbooks of articles written by his father.

22. Frank J. Taylor, "The Merritt System," *Commentator* (November 1938), pp. 84-87. (The article was reprinted in *Reader's Digest* 35 [February 1939], pp. 104-6. Frank Taylor Papers, Department of Special Collections, Stanford University Libraries.)

23. Frank J. Taylor, "Teague of California," *Country Home* (November 1935), p. 36.

24. Taylor, "The Right to Harvest," *Country Gentleman* (October 1937), p. 8.

25. Taylor, "Labor on Wheels," *Country Gentleman* (July 1938), p. 12.

26. Taylor, "The Right to Harvest," p. 8.

27. Taylor, "Green Gold and Tear Gas: What Really Happened in the Salinas Lettuce Strike," *California—Magazine of Pacific Business* (November 1936), p. 18.

28. Taylor, "The Story Behind 'The Many Californias—An Armchair Travelogue'—*R.D.*, January 1952." Frank Taylor Papers, Department of Special Collections, Stanford University Libraries.

29. Taylor, "California's *Grapes of Wrath*," *Forum* 102 (November 1939): p. 232. Hereinafter identified as "CGOW."

30. Stein, *California and Migration*, p. 41.

31. Gregory, *American Exodus*, pp. 19-35.

32. Maud O. Bartlett, "Wrath on Both Sides," *Forum* 103 (January 1940): p. 24.

33. Marshall V. Hartranft, *Grapes of Gladness: California's Refreshing and Inspiriting Answer to John Steinbeck's "Grapes of Wrath"* (Los Angeles: DeVorss and Co., 1939), p. 1. Hereinafter identified as *GOG*.

34. John Steven McGroarty, *History of Los Angeles County* (Chicago: American Historical Society, 1923), p. 767.

35. Sue Sanders, "The Real Cause of Our Migrant Problem" (1940). I wish to thank John Walden of the Kern County Library for his help with material relating to Sue Sanders and the film "The Plums of Plenty" (see below).

36. Mae Saunders, "Migrants Regard Sue Sanders as True Friend," *Bakersfield Californian*, October 21, 1939, pp. 12, 19.

37. One other response to *Grapes* should be mentioned, a short film, now lost, entitled "The Plums of Plenty." Perhaps because of its catchy title, this work is often referred to but seldom identified. In "Steinbeck and the Migrants: A Study of *The Grapes of Wrath*," an M. A. thesis written by John Schamberger at the University of Colorado in 1960, the film's history is summarized: "Emory Gay Hoffman, the manager of the Kern County Chamber of Commerce at the time of publication of *The Grapes of Wrath*, wrote a short story entitled 'Plums of Plenty' in answer to Steinbeck's novel. According to Hoffman, the six-thousand-word draft of 'Plums of Plenty' was lost which precluded its publication. However, a 'movie short' was published from the notes and . . . much of the colored motion picture was used by the old Kern County Chamber of Commerce and 'News of the Day,' a Movie Tone release. Hoffman stated that William B. Camp had sponsored the authorship of his book and the motion picture"""(pp. 64-65).

38. On February 11, 1952, Steinbeck gave an interview for the Voice of America, and he was asked if he saw "any changes in the conditions since the time that you were there [in the Dust Bowl] during the research for your novel?" Steinbeck's reply provides a fitting footnote to *Grapes* and to this article: "Oh yes. I found a great many changes. . . . When I wrote *The Grapes of Wrath* I was filled naturally with certain anger and certain anger at people who were doing injustices to other people, or so I thought. I realize now that everyone was caught in the same trap." In California, the migrants "met a people who were terrified, for number one, of the depression and were horrified at the idea that great numbers of indigent people were being poured on them, to be taken care of. They could only be taken care of by taxation, taxes were already high and there wasn't much money about. They reacted perfectly normally, they became angry. When you become angry you fight what you are angry at. They were angry at these newcomers. Gradually through government agency, through the work of private citizens, agencies were set up to take care of these situations and only then did the anger begin to decrease. So when the anger decreased these two sides, these two groups, were able to get to know each other and they found they didn't dislike each other at all."

Audience and Closure in
The Grapes of Wrath

Nicholas Visser

Although *The Grapes of Wrath* continues to be regarded as Steinbeck's major achievement, changing critical fashions have ensured that the novel's status remains uncertain. The novel's standing came under pressure as early as the decades immediately following its publication, as literary studies with the onset of the Cold War intensified a long-standing tendency in modern poetics to strip literary texts of social and political implications. It was not difficult to decontextualize most of the literature of earlier times, but because the thirties were part of living memory, and because so much of the decade's literature was politically left-wing, the need to depoliticize it was particularly urgent. Where critics could not manage that task, if only because social content was too firmly in the foreground to be obscured, they simply declared such literary works unworthy of serious attention. So strong were these pressures that one of the first critics to write a full-length study of Steinbeck, Harry T. Moore, later wrote an epilogue to the second edition of his book recanting his earlier approval.[1] Why he would have bothered to publish a second edition is unclear.

Recent criticism has done little to reverse the situation. Poststructuralist critics generally ignore, when they do not derogate, writers who presume to represent actual material conditions and social processes; accordingly a writer like Steinbeck, particularly the Steinbeck of *In Dubious Battle* or *The Grapes of Wrath*, has little to offer them. Even recent Marxist criticism has largely ignored Steinbeck.   Eager to demonstrate its intellectual respectability, which apparently requires that in order to distance itself sufficiently from the Stalinist penchant for socialist realism it repudiate representation altogether, recent Marxism criticism, particularly that current which has responded to the powerful gravitational tug of poststructuralist theory, has generally shunned politically explicit literature. What all this has meant is that *The Grapes of Wrath* has been either ignored or disparaged.

Since what follows seeks to examine the interplay of politics and form in the novel and as a consequence of that endeavor points to certain unresolved or incompletely resolved formal problems raised by *The Grapes of Wrath*, I am concerned that my comments will seem to grant attention to the novel at the cost of issuing in yet another negative assessment. There *are* problems with *The Grapes of Wrath*, even large problems, but no more so than in any number of more politically conservative novels of the same period that have enjoyed critical esteem. Furthermore, David Craig and Michael Egan are surely correct in their view that Steinbeck is "incomparable at presenting [working people's] way of life, with an attention to people's manual skills and their self expression which is signally missing from nearly all literature to date," and that the "bulk of [*The Grapes of Wrath*] is unrivaled in Western literature for describing, dramatizing, and *explaining* a large socio-historical process."[2] There are hardly insignificant achievements.

A substantial part of the novel's achievement lies in the way Steinbeck both renders such processes and simultaneously shields the novel from the abstraction and generalization such a description would seem to entail. Even in the interchapters, much of the purpose of which is to generalize the particular experiences of the Joads, the emphasis is on rendering a process rather than abstractly describing it. And for the Joad family, socio-historical process is not something consciously perceived as trends and circumstances prevailing in the society in which they live—the Depression, the dustbowl in the southwest of the United States and the mass migration to California, the increasingly rapid transformation of American farming into the highly mechanized, capital-intensive agribusiness of today, and the like. Rather, such broader processes are experienced as daily pressures in their lives. The farm which they once owned but on which they have been reduced to labor tenancy is lost through events and means that remain largely mysterious to them. They undertake their exodus to the false promised land of California through decisions both deliberately (and therefore apparently freely) taken by the family and utterly constrained by their material and social conditions. And when they arrive in California, the extreme exploitation to which they are subjected baffles them and destroys them as a family. Indeed, lacking analytical categories like "socio-historical process," the Joads and others in their situation feel an urgent need for some way of making these pressures more immediately present, more concrete and personal, so that they can attempt to gain some sort of purchase on them.

For all that it passionately castigates the social and political conditions under which the Joads live, there may be reasons for questioning just how politically radical *The Grapes of Wrath* ultimately is. At the same time, however, the generative context for the novel is the international left-wing political culture of the 1930s, and Steinbeck's novel takes its place among the radical novels produced by that culture. In rendering the efforts of the Joads to cope with the collapse of their world, *The Grapes of Wrath* brings to the surface two problems that arise repeatedly in politically radical novels. First is the obvious, but usually overlooked, question of how radical novels manage to gain access to an audience. What formal or discursive strategies do they adopt to that end? Second is the question of how radical novels conclude especially when, as in The Grapes of Wrath, the "large socio-historical process" of which Craig and Egan speak had not ended when the novel was published.

The problem of audience for politically radical fiction was succinctly identified by Engels in his famous letter to Minna Kautsky written in November 1885. After indicating that he is "not at all an opponent of tendentious writing as such," Engels nevertheless urges Kautsky to avoid revealing an overtly political stance in her novels on the entirely practical grounds that "the novel primarily finds readers in bourgeois circles, circles not directly related to our own." Accordingly, Engels suggests something quite different from the notion that radical literature should be directly insurrectionary. We may infer from what Engels says that in his view it is not properly the function of the "socialist tendentious novel" to mobilize the oppressed, since for practical reasons such as the lack of disposable leisure time, of the privacy and quiet needed to spend long periods reading, and in some cases even of the requisite levels of literacy, the oppressed are not realistically available as an audience. Instead, the project of the radical writer should be to act on the audience that is available for novels; more specifically, Engels writes, to shatter "the optimism of the bourgeois world," thereby "causing doubt about the eternal validity of the existing order."[3] The argument is persuasive, but there is one important consideration it does not address. Why, especially given the glut of novels which endorse bourgeois optimism, would bourgeois readers bother to read radical novels? How, then—to put the problem another way—does the radical novelist gain access to that actually available audience?

A good part of the answer to these questions lies in the contexts of a work's production and initial reception. In times of social and political crisis, for instance, the readership for politicized literature typically expands, if only for the duration of the crisis. At the same time, the awareness that authors gain of prevailing material and social forces and constraints can prompt them to develop formal strategies designed to win over readers, or at least to allay their suspicion and resistance. The strategies of *The Grapes of Wrath* derive from Steinbeck's understanding of what audience he was addressing and in what relation to it he wished to stand.

Much of the early debate over the novel hinged on the question of address, the opposing positions revealing how intimately address is understood to be bound up with the political position the novel stakes out. Peter Lisca examines expressions of the two standard views, one from an early attack entitled *The Truth about John Steinbeck and the Migrants* and one from an established critic, Stanley Edgar Hyman. The author of the first says that he "can think of no other novel which advances the idea of class war and promotes hatred of class against class . . . more than does *The Grapes of Wrath*." Hyman disagrees: "Actually . . . the central message of *The Grapes of Wrath* is an appeal to the owning class to behave, to become enlightened, rather than to the working class to change its own conditions."[4] Warren French sides with Hyman, arguing that Steinbeck does not advocate revolution; rather "he speaks as an observer, warning what may happen— what it regrettably appears will happen." He goes on to suggest that any apparently revolutionary passages in the novel

> are not rabble-rousing speeches inciting an outraged proletariat to rise against its oppressors; rather they are warnings to a comfortable and negligent propertied class to awaken it to what is happening around it. *The Grapes of Wrath* in its treatment of contemporary events is a cautionary tale.[5]

Both views misconstrue Steinbeck's handling of address in the novel. That the oppressed themselves are not the object of address—even accepting that Steinbeck could have made the mistake of assuming it was possible to address that audience directly—can be inferred from, among other things, the strongly "anthropological" mode of the novel, much of which is devoted to (re)presenting one social group to another. Hence the use of dialect and the explanations offered for details of daily life. Much of the novel's effect derives from giving the impression that it is engaged in revealing the hitherto unknown to an audience socially and culturally distant from the novel's characters.

The assertion that the "owning" or "propertied" class is the audience directly addressed is superficially more plausible but ultimately fails to account for much that goes on in the novel, especially the sustained and impassioned attack on "big business." Calling *The Grapes of Wrath* a "cautionary tale," as French does, links it with the long tradition of English-language reformist fiction in the manner of Dickens and Gaskell. Steinbeck shares much with the conventions of reformist or ameliorative fiction, but he differs sharply in one significant respect. Reformist fiction not only addresses the dominant class, it also depicts the dominated classes from a vantage point outside and above their own experience. That perspective is largely absent from *The Grapes of Wrath*. Instead, even though the anthropological mode of the narrative at times entails an exterior view, just as the occasional lapses into sentimentalism similarly establish a narrating position above the represented people, that discursive situation is never permitted to persist for long or to stray far from the textures of daily experience. For most of its course the novel, as Craig and Egan indicate, penetrates fully into the way of life, the everyday habits and skills and even the self-expression of the characters portrayed.[6]

If oppressed social groups are not the prospective audience for the novel, they may nevertheless assert their presence not as a directly addressed group but as what Sartre called a virtual public, made up of dominated groups who lack access to "high" or official culture. Since awareness of this virtual public typically exerts a certain pressure on progressive writers, Sartre's notion can tell us something about an author's alignment if not something directly about the actual or intended audience. They are the group an author would wish to address if that were practicable, or on whose behalf an author writes.[7] Responding to a virtual public would have been consonant with Steinbeck's developing feelings about the people he was depicting in his novel. His first effort to write *The Grapes of Wrath* resulted in a satire which he felt obliged to withdraw even though his publishers had already announced its impending release. He wrote to his publishers:

> I know that a great many people would think they liked this book. I, myself, have built up a hole-proof argument on how and why I liked it. I can't beat the argument, but I don't like the book. . . . My whole work drive has been aimed at making people understand each other and then I deliberately write this book, the aim of which is to cause hatred through partial understanding.[8]

Useful though the concept of virtual public is in grasping the puzzling modes of address in radical fiction, it is necessarily silent about the social bloc whose attention and interest Steinbeck did wish to engage. His conception of his audience stemmed from his awareness that in a time of acute social and economic crisis, the bourgeois audience of which Engels writes is unusually fractured, so that a much larger than usual segment of it is, temporarily at least, susceptible to the appeal of politically progressive ideas. As Sartre puts it: "If the real public is broken up into hostile factions, everything changes."[9] Steinbeck frames his novel neither, strictly speaking, for the oppressed groups, necessarily present only as a virtual public, nor for the owners. Instead he writes with a peculiarly modern notion of audience that comes into existence with the modern nation state and the forms of communication and cultural practice (including, centrally, the novel) that construct and sustain notions of national identity. He writes, in short, in the effort to influence "public opinion." The discursive situation Steinbeck imagines is not a bilateral relation between author and a readership but a triadic relation of author, audience, and owners. He seeks to influence public opinion to put pressure on a putatively beneficent national government to ameliorate the impossible conditions which big business and greedy landowners have imposed on the landless migrants in California. He is not, in other words, supposing that he is directly addressing the owners in the cautionary mode suggested by French, nor is he addressing the migrants: he may write *for* them as virtual public, but he does not, if only because he cannot, write *to* them.

The wish to influence public opinion makes it all the more urgent for Steinbeck to ensure that his project does not fail to reach its audience. Public opinion, after all, can equally be influenced to ignore or reject his message. One of the devices he employs to overcome the expected difficulties is attempting to gain control over the operative definitions of the words "Okies" and "reds." To reach his audience, Steinbeck had to find some way of bridging the social and cultural distance between them and his characters. An anthropological mode of discourse can create and even sustain interest in unknown social groups, but Steinbeck required more than interest. For his project to succeed he needed active sympathy: he needed his readers to wish so wholeheartedly for the amelioration of the conditions suffered by the migrants that public opinion would be swayed in their favor. One way of accomplishing that end was to neutralize the terms of contempt with which dominant groups label those they dominate.

The migrants are in one respect unusual as objects of prejudice: they lack a history of victimization. Because prejudice is not something they have grown up with, they actually have to be taught the meaning of the term used to vilify them.

> "You gonna see in people's face how they hate you. What the hell! You never been called 'Okie' yet."
> Tom said: "Okie? What's that?"
> Well, Okie use' ta mean you was from Oklahoma. Now it means you're a dirty son-of-a-bitch. Okie means you're scum. Don't mean nothing itself, it's the way they say it."[10]

For those who use the word, "Okies" functions to establish the greatest possible distance between themselves and those to whom it is applied, to constitute the latter as utterly different, absolutely other. Our privileged position as readers enables us to see the inadequacy of such labels and the descriptions which accompany them, to see how self-serving they are, how they end up blaming the victims for the oppression, how they seek to dehumanize the migrants and wind up instead desensitizing and dehumanizing those who use them. But situating us within the ambit of the migrants' experience, the novel decisively separates us from those who would use such words, from the landowners and their retainers.

If constituting readers as people who would not use a word like "Okie" shows canny insight into ways of managing social prejudice, Steinbeck, with equal canniness, recognizes that access to an audience as abstract, impermanent, and vacillating as "public opinion" requires anticipating and neutralizing anything likely to prompt rejection of his project. All it would take would be for one of the customary charges of the period—"radical" or "communist sympathizer," in short, "red"—to be convincingly leveled, and even the more open-minded members of his audience would shun the novel. The Joads begin to hear about troublemakers and agitators and reds even before they arrive in California. A campsite owner who regularly swindles the migrants retaliates when Tom Joad jokes bitterly about the owner's money-grubbing:

> The chair-legs hit the floor. "Don't you go a-sassin' me. I 'member you. You're one of these here trouble makers."
> "Damn right," said Tom. "I'm bolshevisky."
> "They's too damn many of you kinda guys aroun'."
> Tom laughed as they went out the gate (p. 205).

Laughter on the reader's part is exactly the desired effect. It comes partly from Tom's mangling of the word Bolshevik or Bolsheviksi: his ignorance is transparently his innocence. More important, the reader already knows Tom, and of course also knows the owner. The perspective of the narration ensures that accusations are subsumed under the valuings that have already been established for characters.

The same management of perspective shapes the reader's response to a later incident. The Joads leave a migrants' camp shortly before local vigilantes and hired goons violently destroy it. The newspaper story reporting the event reads:

> Citizens, angered at red agitators, burn squatters' camp. Last night a band of citizens, infuriated at the agitation going on in a local squatters' camp, burned the tents to the ground and warned agitators to get out of the country. (p. 312)

Because we have vicariously experienced the camp in the company of the Joads, we reject the report as an outrageous distortion. We might be inclined to assume from such passages that Steinbeck's point is that the Joads are not reds. But more is at issue. The crucial insight is provided by Tom immediately after he reads the newspaper account: "I watched it a long time. There's always red agitators just before a pay cut. Always" (p. 312). The accusation is a deliberate effort to discredit the migrants through a word so powerfully charged that once deployed it can usually be counted on to issue in stock responses. Such attempts to discredit the characters are equivalent to and anticipations of attempts to discredit the novel through using the same epithets. In devising strategies to deflect the one, Steinbeck seeks to deflect the other.

The discussion of the newspaper story continues until finally the migrants themselves are able to grasp what is going on in the accusation. When Tom asks, "What the hell is these reds anyway?" he is told a story about another man who had asked his boss the same question. The boss replied:

> "A red is any son-of-a-bitch that wants thirty cents an hour when we're payin' twenty-five!" Well, this young fella he thinks about her, an' he scratches his head, an' he says: "Well, Jesus, Mr. Hines. I ain't a son-of-a-bitch, but if that's what a red is—why, I want thirty cents an hour. Ever'body does. Hell, Mr. Hines, we're all reds."

After hearing this, "Tom laughed. 'Me too, I guess'" (pp. 315-16). Once again, then, laughter, our own as well as Tom's, is the response, but behind Tom's laughter and that of the other migrants is a growing political consciousness, an increasingly developed realization of how the owners and their hirelings deploy all the resources at their disposal, including discursive resources, to entrench and expand their domination of the migrants.

The interrogation of the word "reds" leads finally to a roundabout but unmistakable association of the words with Christ. As Tom tells Ma of Casy's murder, he relates Casy's last words, which, in keeping with the Biblical parallels established in the novel, closely echo Christ's last words on the cross:

> "Casy said: 'You got no right to starve people.' An' then this heavy fella called him a red son-of-a-bitch. An' Casy says: 'You don't know what you're a-doin'.' An' then this guy smashed 'im."
>   Ma looked down. She twisted her hands together.
>   "That's what he said—'You don't know what you're doin'?" (p. 415; Casy's words are first narrated on pp. 408-09).

In probing and contesting the meanings attached to "Okies" and "reds" Steinbeck seeks to disarm the discursive authority of the holders of social power, whose control over meanings is a powerful tool in maintaining social hegemony. To undermine the discursive practices of the dominant group is to steal their ideological magic, as it were. By prizing words out of their customary associations and valuings and laying bare the interests served by certain usages, thereby hampering efforts by the powerful to maintain control over meanings, Steinbeck makes it more difficult for public opinion to be turned against his project. It will not be enough to count on the social distance between audience and represented, nor will it be enough to dismiss the book as "red." Without those two weapons, the owners and those who labor for them in the management of public opinion are reduced to having to claim not that "Okies" are unworthy of sympathy—a tactic as likely to backfire as to succeed—or that Steinbeck is a "red," but that he gets his facts wrong, that he misrepresents the experience of the migrants in California. They are forced, in other words, to shift the terrain of dispute from a straightforward ideological plane to an empirical plane. And in the event empirical claims were easily dismissed.[11]

Efforts to resolve disputes over a novel by attempting to verify or falsify what it depicts may seem odd—even, in light of the way notions of reference are called into question by current literary theory, frivolous. Yet such efforts not only makes sense in relation to *The Grapes of Wrath*, they disclose a significant dimension of the novel's relation to its audience. Central to the reading experience of *The Grapes of Wrath* is the acceptance that what the narrative relates actually occurs in the life-world. In the absence of a tacit but absolutely binding contract between author and reader that the reader can rely on the novel's general veracity, the novel would be almost entirely lacking in meaning. Moreover, if it could be established that Steinbeck *had* distorted the truth, the novel would be felt to lose a substantial component of its value, and not just its value as social documentation (a function I would not wish to disparage) but its value as a novel, for who would read it today, when its documentary value alone could not count for much, if it had been successfully exposed as a fraud? At stake here, then, is not a question of the putative lifelikeness or verisimilitude of the realistic. We may not ordinarily feel compelled to ask of novelists if the events they depict can be matched to events of the real world; in the case of *The Grapes of Wrath*, however, the relationship between reader and text depends on the reader's conviction that people in the dustbowl actually lost their land when banks foreclosed on their loans, migrant camps really were raided and burned out, goons and vigilantes really were used to harass migrants and stymie efforts to organize labor unions, owners and their organizations genuinely colluded to drive down wages, and so on. Steinbeck revealed his sensitivity to the demands of the tacit contract with his readers in a letter: "There's one other difficulty too. I'm trying to write history while it is happening and I don't want to be wrong."[12] Being discovered to be wrong, especially deliberately wrong, would have proved fatal to the success of the book.

Even leaving aside whether it is theoretically possible for a novel (or any other discursive form) to give the reader access to the real, it is at least a challenge to the adequacy of such theorizing about reference to note that certain literary works, for all their fictiveness, depend for their import as well as their impact on successfully securing the reader's acceptance that reference is being actively accomplished. There should not be anything particularly surprising about such a conclusion. To cite just one example, Solzhenitsyn's *One Day in the Life of Ivan Denisovich* absolutely requires that its readers grant a referential axis of meaning, for in the absence of certain belief about Stalinist labor camps, not to mention the belief that the author experienced those camps at first hand, the novel could have no meaning. Similarly, the relationship which *The Grapes of Wrath* continues to establish with its audience, even long after the circumstances it depicts have been transformed, depends on readers accepting that those circumstances once actually existed.

Steinbeck's handling of his relation with his audience is one of the most interesting and successful features of *The Grapes of Wrath*. Somewhat less successfully handled is the other major formal challenge of the novel: how to end the narrative. Radical novels regularly encounter difficulties with closure. Although it is obviously not part of the project of radical novels to promote defeatism, they nevertheless repeatedly end either inconclusively or in failure. To cite just a few representative cases from among the many radical novels written in the same period as *The Grapes of Wrath*, Richard Wright's *Native Son* ends with the death of Bigger Thomas, while the insurrectionary movements of Andre Malraux's *Man's Fate* and Ignazio Silone's *Fontamara* end in crushing defeat. The list could be expanded to cover practically the entirety of radical fiction. Part of the problem stems from the customary attachment of radical fiction to the external world, to history. Since in most cases the material conditions and social iniquities portrayed in radical novels have not been resolved in the external world, or where they have been resolved they have issued in the defeat of progressive forces rather than in their victory, and since the success of the political project undertaken in a political novel hinges on persuading the reader that these conditions and iniquities actually exist or have existed, closure becomes a significant problem at a juncture where the formal properties of the novel and the political project undertaken in radical fiction converse.

Many things could be said about Steinbeck's ending, and it has probably as many defenders as detractors. But whether we find the moment when Rose of Sharon offers her breast to the starving stranger genuinely moving in the way it enacts the compassion the novel has promoted throughout, or painfully mawkish in the way it entraps the reader in a position tantamount to voyeurism,[13] it remains the case that closure is operating on an entirely personal level. The intensely intimate moment is obviously not generalizable in any literal sense, and even if it is given a more abstract form, the form, say, of "Do unto others," it shifts the arena of values from the social and economic and political to the personal and private and ethical, and does so without indicating how the one may be actively linked to the other. In short, the final moments end up telling the oppressed and exploited the old story: social justice can emerge only when there is a universal change of heart, only when people decide to be kinder to each other—a message which has always consoled those who gain advantage from the *status quo* more than it has to those who bear the costs of social inequity.

Why does a novel which has required the destruction of the bonds of family and neighborliness so that a broader collectivity can take their place suddenly, at the very last moment, provide resolution only at the most intimate, most personal level? Even Ma, the normative center of familial values in the novel, comes finally to comprehend that the family must give way to broader affiliations if the conditions confronted by the migrants are ever to be overcome: "Use' ta be the fambly was fust. It ain't so now. It's anybody. Worse off we get, the more we got to do." (p. 470). Rose of Sharon's moment of exemplary humanity in feeding the stranger, especially since it is the first generous action of a hitherto utterly self-absorbed person, may at first appear to enact that "more"; however, up to this point the novel has intimated that the social lesson being proffered is not the parable of the good Samaritan but the Aesopean fable of the bundle of sticks or the three-fold cord of Ecclesiastes (mentioned on p. 443), exempla rarely invoked by those in positions of religious or secular authority as models for social conduct precisely because, unlike the more frequently cited "golden rule," they disclose the potential strength of the group acting in concert and on its own behalf.

The move towards collective political action promises, ultimately falsely, to be the central trajectory of the novel's meanings. The destruction of the family, the developing political consciousness, the beginnings of an organized labor movement, the instilling of cooperative values in the Joad children during their stay at the government camp—all these and more in the novel ascribe preeminent value to collective social action. Such action would seem the logical culmination of the prophetic threats and warnings strewn throughout the novel. Whether they are "rabble-rousing speeches inciting an outraged proletariat to rise against its oppressors," the prophetic passages are explicit, pointed, and sustained. Not just obscurely phrased dire warnings to the powerful that if they do not act promptly to regain legitimacy something terrible may happen (terrible in the narrator's view as well in the view of the owners), the passages declare apocalyptically that, unless there is rapid, radical social change, this is what is coming. That at least seems to be the force of passages like the following:

> Here is the node, you who hate change and fear revolution. Keep these two squatting men apart; make them hate, fear, suspect each other. Here is the anlage of the thing you fear. This is the zygote. For here "I lost my land" is changed; a cell is split and from the splitting grows the thing you hate—"we lost *our* land." The danger is here, for two men are not as lonely and perplexed as one. And from this first "we" there grows a still more dangerous thing: "I have a little food" plus "I have none." If from this problem the sum is "We have a little food," the thing is on its way, the movement has direction. Only a little multiplication now, and this land, this tractor are ours. . . . This is the thing to bomb. This is the beginning—from "I" to "we" (p. 161).

A later passage in a similar vein adds, "if they ever know themselves, the land will be theirs" (p. 254).

Eventually the warnings of what will eventuate when isolated individuals and families join together in mass political action connect with the novel's title, a device which endows them with immense centrality, particularly since the title derives from a patriotic song ("Battle Hymn of the Republic") which in turn draws on the Bible. As the migrants approach the limit of what can be humanly endured, we read: "In the souls of the people the grapes of wrath are filling and growing heavy, growing heavy for the vintage" (p. 369).

These rumblings of ancestral voices prophesy revolution repeatedly in the novel (though much more in the interchapters than in the main narrative), but pointed and sustained as they are, they do not converge in or project any particular insurrectionary endeavor. They are prophecies without outcomes (even outcomes projected into the future)—portentous, apocalyptic, stirring, but finally never more than rhetorical. The gap they leave between prophecy and praxis is particularly clear in one feature of the narrative language of the passages: throughout, the reference is to what "they" will do; the threatened course of action is never unambiguously endorsed, never transformed into a "we" that includes the narrating voice. Of course, the anthropological mode of the novel presumes that Steinbeck's social locus is closer to his audience than to the social group he depicts. Nevertheless, not even optatively does the novel ever fully identify itself with any revolutionary action that might be undertaken by the oppressed; there is always a sense of holding back at the last moment, of taking fright at the very possibilities for widespread uprising which the novel discloses. What is promised in the interchapters is withdrawn in the main narrative, and particularly at its conclusion. What prevents Steinbeck from carrying prophecy through to action is not only that "history"—the material social circumstances both within which and about which he writes—had not yet provided a solution to the problems he investigates. He is incapable of imagining a resolution. He is confident enough at a purely oratorical level, but the level of actual social initiative is another matter. The source of his difficulty is the analysis he provides of existing American society and the vision he projects of an alternative to it.

From both the novel itself and statements he made at the time concerning his growing compassion for the migrants in California, we might reasonably infer that Steinbeck saw his role in writing *The Grapes of Wrath* as contributing to an effort to change their immediate conditions rather than providing in addition a critique of the social and economic structures and relations that create and maintain such conditions.[14] At the same time, the novel has to account for the situation in which the migrants find themselves.

The prolonged drought in the southwest accounts in part for why the migrants undertake their exodus, but it cannot on its own explain how they lose their land or make sense of what they experience once they arrive in California. For their suffering to be more than adventitious, the narrative has to provide some sort of explanation. The furthest Steinbeck is able to go to satisfy this narrative demand is to place blame on impersonal business and financial institutions and greedy landowners.

What he is unable to account for is how such institutions and individuals are able not only to act the way they do, but to persist in their actions. Where are the laws that constrain them? How are they able to use the police to assist their efforts? Why is there no speedy *political* solution to the growing conflict? Steinbeck makes it all but impossible to confront such issues once he carefully dissociates the state from the injustices he depicts. Throughout the novel, the state is assumed to be outside and above the causes of the migrants' suffering. Responsibility for all injustices falls to business corporations and avaricious individuals. The state is not only deemed separate from capitalism, the defining and enabling context of these institutions and individuals; it is seen (in a distinctively American strain of political populism) as positively antithetical to capitalism and the social relations it produces. Nowhere is this made clearer than in the government camp in which the Joads find temporary refuge. Discussing the actions of the owners and the police, one inhabitant of the camp says: "An' that's why they hate this here camp. No cops can get in. This here's United States, not California" (p. 353).

This view of the state is entirely consistent with, and might even be entailed in, the way Steinbeck defined his project. Only a neutral state, available for the role of impartial social arbiter, or a benevolent state, eager to remedy social ills once they are identified (Steinbeck hovers between the two views), can be envisaged as open to the influence of an awakened public opinion. Conceiving the state in these terms, however, thoroughly mystifies the deeply complicit relation between the state and capital, which in turn means that the narrative can provide no coherent account for the oppression and exploitation depicted. At no point does Steinbeck raise obvious questions: if the federal government is as well disposed towards the migrants as the government camps would suggest, why has it not already intervened to end oppression and relieve the migrants of their suffering? Such a government would not require a novel designed to outrage public opinion to be written before it responded. Paradoxically, then, the very act of writing *The Grapes of Wrath* refutes the analysis of American society on which the novel is based.

From the opening moments of the novel, when the issue of how Tom could have been so unjustly imprisoned is almost but never quite made explicit, to the conclusion, when the inaction of the state permits the wholesale destruction of migrant families, questions like these continually threaten to rise to the surface of the narrative, only to be pushed back out of sight. So consistently does Steinbeck decline to engage with the questions his narrative provokes that the question of bad faith eventually arises, for it is difficult to imagine any other way of accounting for how the novel ultimately issues in the familiar message: "The fundamental institutions of society are not bad, just certain individuals and isolated practices. Once these are corrected, things will be just fine." A novelist who gives every appearance of writing from a social and political perspective somewhere on an axis of left-liberal to radical socialist nevertheless produces a narrative which ultimately endorses the existing scheme of things (barring a few unfortunate anomalies) and declines to contemplate the possibility that the scheme itself needs overthrowing.[15] Instead of seeing the novel as an expression of bad faith, however, we might more fruitfully think of it, with its radical impulses and less than radical projections, as a "fellow-traveling" novel, bearing in mind Trotsky's important insight:

> As regards a "fellow-traveler," the question always comes up—how far will he go? This question cannot be answered in advance, not even approximately. The solution of it depends not so much on the personal qualities of this or that "fellow-traveler," but mainly on the objective trends of things.[16]

Steinbeck's inability to confront the most profound implications of his own narrative leaves him no way to end the novel, since the social horrors he has been depicting with such compassion require at the very least giving serious thought to a form of redress he is incapable of imagining except, as in the prophetic passages, in the most abstract and oratorical way. Unable to resolve the novel at the level of the social, economic, and political iniquities he renders in such compelling detail, he withdraws at the conclusion of the narrative to the merely interpersonal.

So reluctant is Steinbeck to confront the depredations of capitalism analytically rather than emotionally that he undermines still another dimension of his project. Implicitly or explicitly, the kind of novel Steinbeck has written, for which Craig and Egan have proposed the suggestive term "social tragedy," projects an alternative to the depicted social order, a social and political "possible other case."[17] That projection is a vital part of the utopian impulse of social tragedy as it gestures towards a realm beyond necessity. Deducing Steinbeck's projected alternative, at least in its broad features, seems at first glance a simple task. Most of the novel would seem to imply that a new social order would have to be built on collective principles and would have to exclude economic practices which depend on exploitation. Property would no longer be presumed as an absolute right, since accumulation would have to be regulated to ensure that land did not again fall into the hands of a few. Profit would have to give way to or at least be modified by notions of social benefit, so that people would no longer have their homes confiscated. No one would be permitted to have wealth beyond a certain level, and the gap between the richest and poorest in society would be kept fairly narrow. The rights of the workers to a living wage, to organize in labor unions, and to strike would be placed above the claims of owners. Or so the novel implies.

Yet surprisingly, whatever the society ultimately prefigured in the novel, it is certainly not any form of socialist or even social-welfare society. Tom's farewell to his mother—one of the few times the portentous tone of the prophetic passages, for the most part restricted to the interchapters, enters the main narrative—reveals in its closing sentence the boundaries of Steinbeck's vision of an alternative America: "An' when our folks eat the stuff they raise an' live in the houses they build—why, I'll be there" (p. 444). This is Steinbeck's alternative social order, a reiteration of Jefferson's vision of a society made up of independent small farmers eating the food they grow and living in the houses they build. Where in this is collective social life? How, if it was necessary for the family to be destroyed in order for people to discover their collective destiny, do the nuclear families return who will presumably inhabit these houses and grow the food? Where in the reconstituted household economy of small farms will be the space for what is ostensibly projected as a new status for women, achieved at such cost? All such considerations are overwhelmed by the "ache of ownership" which, far from rejecting in favor of collective ownership, Steinbeck gladly ratifies (p. 300).

A second strand to Steinbeck's vision of an alternative order emerges earlier in the same conversation, at the point where Tom remembers something Casy had once related to him: "Says one time he went out in the wilderness to find his own soul, an' he foun' he didn't have no soul that was his'n. Says he foun' he jus' got a little piece of a great big soul" (p. 442). Here, as collectivity gets absorbed into the ideas of yet another seminal American thinker with the barely veiled reference to Emerson's conception of the oversoul, Tom's memory takes on a regressive quality, for at this point the novel doubles back on its own development in character and action.

Tom recalls not Casy the labor organizer, who late in the novel, just before he becomes the victim of violent reaction, speaks eloquently and lucidly of revolution and counter-revolution (p. 407), but the Casy of their first encounter, who at the outset of the action was the prophet of the oversoul.

Tom's final conversation with Ma reveals the strains and confusions of the proffered resolutions of the novel's conflicts as the concluding chapters work to contain and defuse the revolutionary implications of the depiction of mounting class conflict. For all that Steinbeck may be linking his narrative to notions deeply embedded in American hegemonic cultural traditions, Jeffersonian and Emersonian ideas are inadequate to the weight placed upon them. The oversoul suggests something entirely different from revolutionary action; indeed it suggests no action at all, only some state of being exempt from the immediacies of the social and historical. Similarly, collective life is negated by the Jeffersonian ideal, a negation which can be felt in the contradictory quality of statements like "All work together for our own thing—all farm our own lan'" (p. 443). To further complicate matters, by the time of the conversation between Tom and Ma near the end of the novel, the appeal of the Jeffersonian ideas has long since been diminished by repeated suggestions of the guilty secret behind the land the farmers till— the violent dispossession of the Indians whose land it once was.[18]

The difficulties Steinbeck had with closure in *The Grapes of Wrath* may stem in part from the very success he had in gaining access to his audience. Appealing to public opinion entails granting a measure of legitimacy to the social order the presumptive audience inhabits. Appealing to specifically *American* cultural tradition further confirms legitimacy. Once legitimacy is granted, any revolutionary implications arising from the narrative must be curtailed, even if that means skirting some of the narrative's most profound insights into how the social order is actually constructed and in whose benefit it operates. What is involved here is not a question merely of an author's intention, even broadening that notion to include how authors of radical novels define for themselves the political projects in which they are engaged. At issue here is the very possibility of writing a novel that both reaches a wide audience and remains politically radical. Victor Serge's *Birth of Our Power*, a major radical novel of the 1930s, is remarkable among other things for the way it succeeded in keeping its leftist politics intact, but it did so perhaps at the cost of remaining all but unknown for many years. From its original publication to today it has probably not sold as many copies as *The Grapes of Wrath* sells in an average year. One conclusion we can draw from Steinbeck's example is that the advice Engels gave Minna Kautsky about eschewing overtly "tendentious writing" in order to reach the "bourgeois circles" who are the only available audience may understate the consequences of the techniques novelists may have to use to accomplish that task. Reaching that audience might entail the simultaneous (and intimately related) dilution of the novel's politics and distortion of its form.

From *Studies in American Fiction* (Spring 1994), 22:1, pp. 19-36.

Notes

1. Harry Thornton Moore, *The Novels of John Steinbeck: A First Critical Study* (1939; 2nd ed. New York: Kennikat, 1968).

2. David Craig and Michael Egan, *Extreme Situations: Literature and Crisis from the Great Way to the Atom Bomb* (London: Macmillan, 1979), pp. 162-63.

3. Frederick Engels, "Letter to Minna Kautsky, November 16, 1885," in *Marx and Engels on Literature and Art*, ed. Lee Baxandall and Stephan Morawski (St. Louis: Telos, 1973), p. 113.

4. Quoted by Peter Lisca, *The Wide World of John Steinbeck* (New Brunswick: Rutgers Univ. Press, 1958), p. 148.

5. Warren French, *The Social Novel at the End of an Era* (Carbondale: Southern Illinois Univ. Press, 1966), p. 47.

6. Craig and Egan, p. 162.

7. Jean-Paul Sartre, *What is Literature*, trans. Bernard Frechtman (London: Methuen, 1955), especially the chapter entitled "For Whom Does One Write," pp. 49-122. The notion of a virtual public raises a contentious issue, since theorists have recently been calling into question the practice of speaking "on behalf of" others, asserting that to do so is presumptuous and patronizing. While such reservations usefully lay bare what are often unfounded claims to be able to "represent" the oppressed in both the artistic and political senses of the word— something too readily assumed in much would-be radical literature—at the same time the position itself too easily absolves writers of any broader social role whatever and licenses them to confine their efforts to untrammeled textuality. For a succinct statement of the complex meanings of "represent," see W. J. T. Mitchell, "Representation," in *Critical Terms for Literary Study*, ed. Frank Lentricchia and Thomas McLaughlin (Chicago: Univ. of Chicago Press, 1990), pp. 11-22.

8. Quoted by Lisca, p. 146.

9. Sartre, p. 72.

10. John Steinbeck, *The Grapes of Wrath* (London: Pan, 1975), p. 218. Further references will be given parenthetically in the text.

11. See Benson, pp. 420-23 and Lisca, pp. 144-50.

12. Quoted by Benson, p. 375.

13. It is not usually noted that the awkwardness of the scene stems in part from the fact that while Ma shoos the family from the barn, learning Rose of Sharon

alone with the dying man, the reader is left watching the scene. Hence, we are left with the paradox that the intensely private scene, which derives much of its power from its intimacy, is nonetheless witnessed by strangers, that is, ourselves.

14. See Benson, pp. 293-352 and Lisca, pp. 145-47.

15. I had completed this essay before I had the opportunity to read Stephen Railton's important study, "Pilgrims' Politics: Steinbeck's Art of Conversion," in *New Essays on The Grapes of Wrath*, ed. David Wyatt (Cambridge: Cambridge Univ. Press, 1990), pp. 27-46. Though we begin from much the same political standpoint and focus on many of the same issues in the novel, we come to strikingly different, indeed often directly opposed, conclusions. The question of overthrowing a political order is just one of many issues on which we disagree.

16. Leon Trotsky, *Literature and Revolution*, trans. Rose Strunsky (Ann Arbor: Univ. of Michigan Press, 1960), p. 58. Benson describes Steinbeck's political ambivalence at the time, as well as his hasty retreat from political engagement after the publication of *The Grapes of Wrath* (pp. 386-87).

17. Craig and Egan, pp. 153-86.

18. The repeated references to Indians, often in direct reference to how land was obtained, qualify, if they do not utterly negate, the "blood and soil" claims to the land made by the Joads and others. See pp. 38, 219, 244, 345, 359.

The Darwinian
Grapes of Wrath

Brian E. Railsback

"I often bless all novelists. "
--Charles Darwin, The Autobiography of Charles Darwin, *1892*

A study of Charles Darwin and the art of John Steinbeck must, like any expedition through the novelist's life work, finally arrive at his masterpiece, *The Grapes of Wrath*. In no other book is Steinbeck's dramatization of Darwin's theory more clear; the novel resonates with the naturalist's ideas. Through Steinbeck's narrative technique, from the parts (i.e., the characters in the Joad chapters) to the whole (the intercalary chapters), we are presented with a holistic view of the migrant worker developed through Steinbeck's own inductive method. This epic novel demonstrates the range of Darwin's theory, including the essential aspects of evolution: the struggle for existence and the process of natural selection. The migrant workers move across the land as a species, uprooted from one niche and forced to gain a foothold in another. Their struggle is intensified by capitalism's perversion of natural competition, but this only makes the survivors that much tougher. Because of their inability to see the whole picture, the bankers and members of the Farmers Association diminish themselves by their oppressive tactics while the surviving migrant workers become increasingly tougher, more resourceful, and more sympathetic. Ultimately, seeing Darwin's ideas in *The Grapes of Wrath* enables us to perceive some hope for the Joads and others like them--here is Steinbeck's manifesto of progress, based on biological laws rather than political ideology. Despite the dismal scene that concludes the book, we come to a better understanding of what Ma Joad already knows, that "the people" will keep on coming.

Steinbeck embarked on an expedition of his own from 1934 to 1938 to gather information that would ultimately lead to his great novel. Jackson L. Benson's biography of Steinbeck provides a very complete and accurate account of the novelist's research, and, in direct reference to *The Grapes of Wrath* itself, Robert DeMott's introduction and notes for *Working Days* provide further illumination and detail.

Benson writes that Steinbeck, who "seems to have remembered in detail nearly everything he saw or heard," entered the world of migrant labor in California when he interviewed two starving, fugitive strike organizers in Seaside in early 1934 (*True Adventures* 291). Steinbeck gathered more information from James Harkins, an organizer who helped in the Imperial Valley strike (1934) and the Salinas lettuce strike (1936). Eventually strike organizers began to frequent the Steinbeck's cottage in Pacific Grove and discuss their "holy mission": "Since you were either for them or against them--there was no compromise--[Steinbeck] did more listening than talking" (294). Steinbeck also met the famous social reformer and muckraker, Lincoln Steffens, who was spending his last years in a house in nearby Carmel. Benson writes that Steffens and Steinbeck agreed on "the importance and value of observing and discovering" (295). Steinbeck, as early as the summer of 1934, had himself gone out to see the migrant labor camps in the Salinas area. All of the information he gathered, along with very detailed information from a union leader, Cicil McKiddy, eventually became a part of *In Dubious Battle*. Significantly, the book does not follow anyone's party line but rather works out many of Steinbeck's and Ed Ricketts's biological views.

Serious research for *The Grapes of Wrath* began with Steinbeck's assignment for *The San Francisco News* to write a series of articles about migrant farm labor in California, which necessitated observing conditions at various labor camps. He saw firsthand the destitution of migrant families in these government camps and spontaneous Hoovervilles. As Benson and DeMott show, a tremendous influence on Steinbeck as he prepared to write *The Grapes of Wrath* was Tom Collins, the manager of "Weedpatch," the government Sanitary Camp at Arvin (he is the "Tom" that the book is partly dedicated to). Collins was something of a social scientist who made meticulous reports and gathered statistics about the migrant's life which Steinbeck used extensively in *The Grapes of Wrath* (Benson, *True Adventures* 343-44). Even at home near Salinas, Steinbeck found more information to gather, as incidents of vigilantism were occurring as a result of the strike of 1936 (346). In 1937 Steinbeck took another, longer tour of migrant camps with Collins, and in February of 1938, Steinbeck went to the flooded areas of Visalia where, as he wrote to his agent, "Four thousand families, drowned out of their tents are really starving to death" (368). As DeMott writes, "What he witnessed there became the backdrop for the final scenes of *The Grapes of Wrath*" (*Working Days* 134).

When the author began to write up his observations into a novel, his first bitterly satirical attempt, "L'Affaire Lettuceberg," failed because he was too close to the subject. Like Darwin's *Origin, The Grapes of Wrath* is a gathering of observations fused by a hypothesis, in this case a biological consideration of cycles in land ownership. Of course, unlike *Origin*, it is fictionalized, and, above all else, a work of art. Still Steinbeck's method in putting together the novel resembles an inductive, scientific one. Anything less, in the hands of some other writer, might have been another political satire like the "L'Affaire Lettuceberg."

From the first pages of *The Grapes of Wrath*, Steinbeck's biological, holistic view is evident. The novel presents a large picture in which humans are only a small part; in the great natural scheme of sky and land, of rain, wind, and dust, they suffer with the teams of horses and the dying corn—all life forms are helpless in this huge canvas of natural machinations. And there are beasts at the door; not more than a night after the people leave Oklahoma enter new occupants who were always waiting outside: weasels, cats, bats, and mice (*Grapes* 126-127).

People are further associated with the natural world by being rendered in animal metaphors, either by their own language or the narrator's. In chapter 8, we meet the Joad family and hear that Ma fears Tom will be like Pretty Boy Floyd ("They shot at him like a varmint . . .man' then they run him like a coyote, an' him a-snappin' an' a-snarlin', mean as a lobo"); that Grampa once tortured Granma "as children torture bugs"; that Grampa had hoped the "jailbird" Tom would "come a-bustin' outa jail like a bull through a corral fence"; and that somewhere Al is "a-billygoatin' aroun' the country. Tom cattin' hisself to death" (82-89).

The narrator's famous image of the land turtle is the most extensive metaphor for the migrant worker. In chapter 3, the tough, wizened turtle navigates the road, pushing ahead with "hands" rather than front claws. Tom picks up the turtle and Casy observes, "Nobody can't keep a turtle though.. . . at least one day they get out and away they go off somewheres. It's like me." (21). When Tom releases it, a cat attacks it to no avail, and the turtle goes in the same direction that the Joads will: southwest. The connection is made even stronger when, in chapter 16, a description of the flight of the Joads and the Wilsons across the Panhandle is juxtaposed with the image of the land turtles which crawled through the dust" (178). Steinbeck's extensive use of personification and anthropomorphism underscores his view of *Homo sapiens* as just another species.

This recognition leads to the same collision with traditional religion that Darwin's theory encountered in Victorian England, by directly challenging the idea that the human is above the animals, a being made in God's own image. In an eerie scene, Steinbeck powerfully demonstrates the self-delusion of a group of "Jehovites" who pray in a tent for Granma. Aspiring to be superior to the natural world, they are more beastlike than those they call sinners: "One woman's voice went up and up in a wailing cry, wild and fierce, like the cry of a beast; and a deeper woman's voice rose up beside it, a baying voice, and a man's voice traveled up the scale in the howl of a wolf. The exhortation stopped, and only the feral howling came from the tent" (233). Like meetings Casy devised as a preacher, in which excited men and women went from the meeting place to the bushes to make love, traditional religion is only another veneer over animal nature.

Certainly the world Steinbeck portrays in *The Grapes of Wrath* demonstrates what Darwin, Ricketts, and he believed: humans are subject to the laws of ecology. That the Darwinian principles of competition and selection are an essential part of the novel is no surprise. The Joads and Wilsons are part of a movement of migrants, acting as a species turned out of a niche by natural and unnatural forces. The migrants go to a richer niche that would appear to have plenty of room for them, but many of them die, overwhelmed by competition and repression. Yet the survivors display an astounding ability to adapt. They come to California, a vigorous new species quite terrifying to the natives who, despite the crushing power of a brutal economic system which they control, act from a growing sense of insecurity. "They weathered the thing," Steinbeck writes of the migrant workers, "and they can weather much more for their blood is strong. [T]his new race is here to stay and heed must be taken of it" (*Gypsies* 22).

The process of evolution that leads to the creation of "this new race" is patently Darwinian. With drought upon the land and the dissolution of the tenant system, the farmer can no longer live in the region--forcing the migration west. In *The Origin of Species*, Darwin observes that if an open country undergoes some great change, "new forms would certainly immigrate, and this would likewise seriously disturb the relations of some of the former inhabitants" (Appleman 55; see also 97). From the first day of the Joads' migration, a process of selection begins; those who can adapt to the new way of life survive. Although a tough man, Grampa proves too rooted in the old land to adapt to the new, and his death, as Casy knows, is inevitable: "Grampa didn' die tonight. He died the minute you took 'im off the place" (*Grapes* 160). Muley cannot leave either, and his future is doubtful; ironically, Noah, who himself will wander off alone into oblivion, tells Muley, "You gonna die out in the fiel' some day" (121). Granma cannot recover from the death of Grampa and loses touch with reality and eventually life. The Wilsons also fail, despite help from the Joads; Ivy lacks the essential mechanical knowledge of cars to succeed, and Sairy is too physically weak to survive.

Because of the migrants' relentless trek, during which they are driven by the harshness of the weather, by poverty, and by cruelty, the ones who arrive in California already are transformed. As intercalary chapter 17 shows, the group has adapted to the new way of life on the road: "They were not farm men anymore, but migrant men" (215). The new breed pours into California "restless as ants, scurrying to find work to do." But "the owners hated them because the owners had heard from their grandfathers how easy it is to steal land from a soft man if you are fierce and hungry and armed" (256-57). Ma Joad typifies the strong blood that Steinbeck refers to, for she adapts to each new situation, meeting difficulties with whatever ferocity or compassion is needed, constantly working to keep the family together and push them forward. Toward the end of the novel, Ma gives her famous speech about the people, and certainly she has come to understand what survival of the fittest means: "We ain't gonna die out. People is goin' on--changin' a little, maybe, but goin' right on . . . some die, but the rest is tougher" (467-68).

A Darwinian interpretation of *The Grapes of Wrath* reveals the novel's most terrible irony: the owners' perversion of the natural process only hastens their own destruction. In states such as Oklahoma, the bank--the "monster"--must be fed at the expense of the tenant system, thus losing something precious: "The man who is more than his chemistry . . . that man who is more than his elements knows the land that is more than its analysis" (126). And the tenacity of these people, their potential, is drawn to another land. The Farmers Association of California sends out handbills to attract a surplus of labor, intensifying the competition for jobs so that the migrant laborers will work for almost nothing. But the owners are unconscious of the other part of the equation, that increased competition only toughens the survivors, as Darwin notes: "In the survival of favored individuals and races, during the constantly recurrent Struggle for Existence, we see a powerful and everacting form of Selection" (Appleman, *Origin* 115). The novel's omniscient narrator recalls "the little screaming fact' evident throughout history, of which the owners remain ignorant: "repression works only to strengthen and knit the repressed" (*Grapes* 262).

Steinbeck recognizes the untenable position of the owners in California. "Having built the repressive attitude toward the labor they need to survive, the directors were terrified of the things they have created" (*Gypsies* 36). As the economic system blindly pushes people out of the plains states and just as blindly entices them to California with the intention of inhumane exploitation, it proves a system of men who fail to see the whole. Often the owners win, and some workers are hungry enough to betray their own kind, such as the migrants hired to move in and break up the dance at Weedpatch. But at the end of chapter 19, the omniscient voice describes how in their suffering people come together, as the migrants gather coins to bury a dead infant; soon they will see beyond themselves and the illusion of their religion. "And the association of owners knew that some day the praying would stop. And there's the end" (*Grapes* 263).

The narrator describes the sense of coming change in more ominous tones at the end of chapter 25: "[I]n the eyes of the hungry there is a growing wrath. In the souls of the people the grapes of wrath are filling and growing heavy, growing heavy for the vintage" (385). The narrator presents the whole view, which characters like Casy and Tom eventually see but the owners remain blind to as they continue to create a breed that will be their undoing. "For while California has been successful in its use of migrant labor," Steinbeck writes, "it is gradually building a human structure which will certainly change the State, and may, if handled with the inhumanity and stupidity that have characterized the past, destroy the present system of agricultural economics" (*Gypsies* 25). This is the dynamic that Steinbeck describes in *The Log* after visiting Espiritu Santo Island, where in certain areas only one or two species dominate an ecosystem. He parallels the territorial habits of these animals with humans. While the "dominant human" grows weak from too much security, "[t]he lean and hungry grow strong. . . . Having nothing to lose and all to gain, these selected hungry and rapacious ones develop attack rather than defense techniques . . . so that one day the dominant man is eliminated and the strong and hungry wanderer takes his place" (97).

In the thinking of Darwin and Steinbeck, the California landowners' "inhumanity" is their keen lack of sympathy and their "stupidity" is the reason for that lack, the inability to see the whole. As Casy tells his assassin just before the death blow, "You don't know what you're a-doin" (*Grapes* 426). His last words appropriately echo Christ's, for in killing the leader of a cause, one leaves tougher disciples, such as Tom Joad.

From his knowledge of the whole, of past and present, and of humanity's true place in the scheme of nature, Charles Darwin nears the end of *The Descent of Man* with the interesting realization that he would rather be a "heroic little monkey" than the human "savage who delights to torture his enemies . . . knows no decency, and is haunted by the grossest superstitions" (Appleman 208). It is not the kind of statement that anyone with illusions about the inherent superiority of human beings would wish to hear. Darwin's view is certainly played out in *The Grapes of Wrath,* as we encounter a group of the most civilized people practicing many of the atrocities that delight Darwin's savage. They lack sympathy and therefore will lose their humanity and probably their existence as a group. In contrast, the migrant workers show a sense of compassion for their fellows that binds them together and can eventually insure their existence in a hostile environment, for the co-operation that grows out of sympathy is the greatest threat to the owner, as Steinbeck foresees: "And from this first 'we' there grows a still more dangerous thing: 'I have a little food' plus 'I have none.' If from this problem the sum is 'We have a little food,' the thing is on its way, the movement has direction. . . . If you who own the things people must have could understand this, you might preserve yourself" (*Grapes* 165-66). Steinbeck goes on to warn that "the quality of owning freezes you forever into 'I', and cuts you off forever for the 'we'" (166). Clearly, the owners do not understand this reality.

The other great irony of the novel is that, through a Darwinian process of adaptation and evolution, the dehumanizing conditions created by the owners only make the migrant workers more human. This process can be seen in nearly every chapter, as migrants share money, food, transportation, work, and ultimately their anger, as they briefly unite in a strike that is defeated by an influx of hungry workers who do not yet see the big picture. But as the suffering continues and more Casys are martyred and more Toms are created, the people will eventually move forward. As Casy tells Tom, "ever' time they's a little step fo'ward, she may slip back a little, but she never slips clear back" (425). Casy's words resonate with the narrator's definition of what man is in chapter 14: "This you may say of man . . . man stumbles forward, painfully, mistakenly sometimes. Having stepped forward, he may slip back, but only a half step, never the full step back" (164). owners, comfortable and rich, are frozen in their "I" mentality, the surviving migrants move forward; they are vigorous and continue to evolve into their "we" mentality. This process is the essence of Steinbeck's scientific, Darwinian belief in a progression for humankind based on biological principles generally and struggle in particular. This is why, by the time he wrote

America and Americans in 1966, he worries most of all that the country has lost its survival drive.

This particular kind of evolution is best illustrated through the development of Tom Joad, perhaps Steinbeck's most complete hero. Although Ma, too, shows a tremendous capacity for adaptation and sympathy, her sense of "we" does not extend much beyond the family unit, and while Casy certainly comes to see the whole picture and extends his sympathy to all oppressed laborers, the greatest change occurs in Tom, whose near-animal introversion becomes an almost spiritual extroversion during his family's struggle to survive. This change in character has been noted by several critics. Lisca calls Tom's conversion one from the personal/material to the ethical/spiritual ("Grapes" 98). Charles Shively believes that Tom's widening horizon reflects the influence on Steinbeck of American holistic philosopher Josiah Royce (there is no evidence the novelist had heard of Royce before 1948, however [see DeMott's *Steinbeck's Reading* 96, 169]). And Leonard Lutwack sees Tom's conversion through Biblical imagery, from his "baptism" when be kills Casy's assailant by a stream to his "resurrection from the tomb" while he speaks to his mother in the cave (70-71).

Tom has received so much attention from critics probably because he is Steinbeck's most dynamic character. At the beginning of the novel, Tom--like Grampa, Al, Ruthie, and Winfield--is preoccupied with his own needs. Sitting with Casy and Muley in his parents' wrecked house, Tom has only food on his mind while Casy talks about their pathetic existence: "Joad turned the meat, and his eyes were inward" (*Grapes* 54). Once the meat is done, Torn seizes it, "scowling like an animal" (57). Casy suddenly is inspired to go with the people on the road, but Joad merely rolls a cigarette and ignores the preacher's speech. Later, Tom rails at a gas station attendant who worries about what is happening to the country, then pauses, noticing for the first time that the attendant's station is near bankruptcy. Tom corrects himself, "I didn't mean to sound off at ya, mister" (139). When Casy questions Tom about the larger picture, about the fact that their group is only a small part of a mass migration, Tom begins to feel the inadequacy of his narrow vision: "I'm jus' puttin' one foot in front a the other. I done it at Mac for four years. . . . I thought it'd be somepin different when I come out! Couldn't think a nothin' in there, else you go stir happy, an' now can't think a nothin" (190). Like Ma, keeping the family together becomes a project for Tom; he finds his drunken Uncle John and feels pity for him, and later he sacrifices his natural anger for the good of the family (306, 309).

After Tom sees Casy killed, the change that has been gradually occurring in him becomes complete. He understands the entire structure, for he has been both in the camp with the laborers and outside with the strike leaders. His immediate concern is to flee to protect his family, but to appease Ma he hides in a cave of vines near the Joads' new camp. After Ruthie spills the news that Tom killed Casy's assassin, Ma goes to him in the cave for a final talk. Although he has been reduced to living like an animal, in the darkness of his cave Tom has been thinking about Casy: "He talked a lot. Used ta bother me. But now I been thinkin' what he said, an I can remember--all of it" (462). He has come to realize the truth of the "Preacher," a code of survival based on cooperation: "And if one prevail against him, two shall withstand him, and a three-fold cord is not quickly broken" (462). He gives a speech in which he becomes the ultimate expression of sympathy, for he is now less an individual and more the essence of the whole: "I'll be ever'where--wherever you look" (463). He has determined a truth goes beyond even Ma's comprehension, for she says at the end of his speech, "I don' un'erstan" (463). Because of his fierceness, inherited from Ma, he will pose a greater threat to the owners than Casy, who "didn' duck quick enough" (463).

In a work so full of apparently hopeless suffering, the Darwinian view of *The Grapes of Wrath* explains why characters such as Ma or Tom have a sense of victory. The processes of competition and natural selection, artificially heightened by narrow-minded landowners, create a new race with strong blood--a race that can adapt and fight in a way the old one could not. Endowed with a closeness to the land and an increasing sympathy, this new race represents a human being far superior to the old "I" savage. Because of the struggle, people like the Joads become better human beings, cooperating with each other in every crisis. "There is a gradual improvement in the treatment of man by man," Steinbeck wrote in a letter for the *Monthly Record* (a magazine for the Connecticut state prison system) during the period in which *The Grapes of Wrath* was being written. "There are little spots of kindness that burn up like fire and light the whole thing up. But I guess the reason they are so bright is that there are so few of them. However, the ones that do burn up seem to push us ahead a little" (3). Thus, even when famished and facing death herself, Rose of Sharon begins to see past her own selfishness and offers her breast to a starving man. She has reason to smile mysteriously, understanding something larger and greater than her oppressors will ever know.

On the morning of May 15, 1992 , Professor Stanley Brodwin of Hofstra University stood in the historic Admiral Coffin School hall on Nantucket

Island and gave a lecture titled "The Example of Darwin's Voyage of the Beagle in *The Log from the Sea of Cortez*." His talk was that rare recognition of Darwin's influence upon a book by Steinbeck. Brodwin discussed *The Log* as part of the larger genre of journals of expeditions by such naturalists as Darwin, Alexander von Humboldt, and Edward Forbes. He examined Steinbeck's book on another level among the four Steinbeck professed to be in it: "*The Log* remains a fully romantic work, its theological explorations maintaining a meaningful tension with its search for hard scientific information. . . . ."

It was a good day for Steinbeck studies, devoted to the truly deep element in his many-layered vision of humanity. His biological perspective came up again and again. When the conference moved to the Nantucket Marine Laboratory, where participants could examine experiments conducted by Dr. Joseph Grochowski and his associates, they peered into the bubbling tanks of marine life or looked out toward sun-dappled ripples in the harbor and talked of marine biology and the novelist's art. Had he been there, John Steinbeck would have been pleased.

From *Parallel Expeditions: Charles Darwin and the Art of John Steinbeck* (University of Iowa Press, 1995)

References

Benson, Jackson J. *The True Adventures of John Steinbeck, Writer.* New York: Viking, 1984.

Bloom, Harold, ed. *John Steinbeck.* New York: Chelsea House, 1987.

Brodwin, Stanley. "The Example of Darwin's Voyage of the Beagle in *The Log from the Sea of Cortez*." Steinbeck and the Environment Conference. Nantucket, 15 May 1992 (unpublished).

Darwin, Charles. *The Autobiography of Charles Darwin and Selected Letters.* Ed. Francis Darwin, 1892. New York: Dover Publications, 1958.

_____. *The Origin of Species and The Descent of Man.* Darwin. Ed. Phillip Appleman, New York: Norton, 1979.

DeMott, Robert. *Steinbeck's Reading: A Catalogue of Books Owned and Borrowed.* New York: Garland, 1984.

French, Warren. "How Green Was John Steinbeck?" Steinbeck and the Environment Conference. Nantucket, 16 May 1992 (unpublished).

Lutwack, Leonard. "*The Grapes of Wrath* as Heroic Fiction." *The Grapes of Wrath: A Collection of Critical Essays.* Ed. Robert Con Davis. Englewood Cliffs, NJ: Prentice-Hall, 1982, 63-75.

Steinbeck, John. "About Ed Ricketts." *The Log from the Sea of Cortez*, 1951. New York: Penguin, 1975. vii-lxiv.

_____. *America and Americans.* New York: Viking, 1966.

_____. *The Grapes of Wrath.* 1939. New York: Penguin, 1976.

_____. *The Harvest Gypsies.* 1936. Berkeley: Heyday Books, 1988.

_____. *In Dubious Battle.* 1936. New York: Penguin, 1979.
_____. *The Log from the Sea of Cortez.* 1951. New York: Penguin, 1975.
_____. *Sweet Thursday.* 1954. New York: Penguin, 1986.
_____. *Working Days: The Journals of The Grapes of Wrath.* Ed. Robert DeMott.
   New York: Viking Penguin, 1989.

Judge, Observer, Prophet: The American Cain and Steinbeck's Shifting Perspective

Barbara A. Heavilin

Concerned with how he writes as well as with what he writes, John Steinbeck often recorded his methods of obtaining materials for his books and his process in writing them. His observations reveal not only methods of invention but also an authorial point of view that modifies and shifts over time. For example, in gathering materials to write *Travels with Charley in Search of America*, he uses an inductive method to obtain feelings, facts, and exper-iences in order to have "the means to think." Traveling across America in his truck, Rocinante, he seeks first to discover "the small diagnostic truths which are the foundations of the larger truth," then to answer the question "What are Americans like today?" and finally to describe the "American image."[1] These "small diagnostic truths" of necessity provide a subjective, myopic view, an accumulation gathered bit by bit of the individual facets which make up his picture of "Americans." Later, from a distance, from a more contemplative and objective perspective, he draws a more composite picture in *America and Americans*, providing the reader with a sense of wholeness, of unity in diversity.

Aware of the effect of perspective and distance on the human viewpoint, Steinbeck muses, "Man has to have feelings and then words before he can come close to thought," a process which takes "a long time" (*Travels* 33). His observation here is reminiscent of the Romantic writers Jean-Jacques Rousseau and William Wordsworth.   In his *Confessions* Rousseau proclaims, "I felt before I thought: this is the common lot of humanity."[2] Similarly, in *Preface to Lyrical Ballads*, Wordsworth defines poetry as "the spontaneous overflow of powerful feeling: it takes its origin from emotion recollected in tranquillity."[3] All three writers thus suggest a progression from the subjective to the objective in the translation of human emotions, or "feelings," into words and thoughts--requiring observation of the self and its experiences from a distance. Thus given an ever widening focus, "powerful feelings"   become modified and diffused as time and reflection alter perspective.

Such an altering perspective occurs in Steinbeck's treatment of good and evil--the "one story in the world"--especially in his study of the biblical Cain figure as it represents the human capacity for hatred and fratricide.[4] Against the backdrop of his non-fiction discourse, *Travels* and *America and Americans*, the fictional works, *The Grapes of Wrath*, *East of Eden*, and *The Winter of Our Discontent* reveal an ameliorating shift in perspective. First, from a close, subjective vantage point, in *Travels* and *Grapes of Wrath*, good and evil are sharply dichotomized, and an unredeemable Cain figure, the dark side of the American psyche, is a monster. Later, from a modified perspective in *America and Americans* and *East of Eden*, good comes from evil, and Cain (in the persons of "the American" and Cal) gains self-knowledge at the expense of a sister or brother's life. Finally, in a prophetic voice, in *America and Americans* and *The Winter of Our Discontent*, good and evil intermingle, the strength of Cain combining with the goodness of his brother, Abel, to become Every American, an amalgamation of the traits of the feuding brothers.

Preparing for his journey in Rocinante to gather materials for *Travels*, Steinbeck remembers a similar journey before writing *The Grapes of Wrath*:

> Once I traveled about in an old broken wagon, double-doored rattler with a mattress on its floor. I stopped where people stopped or gathered, I listened and looked and felt, and in the process had a picture of my country the accuracy of which was impaired only by my own shortcomings. (*Travels* 6-7)

Since the tendency in such a fact-gathering procedure is to see things as discrete, separate, and distinct, *Travels* and *Grapes of Wrath* are dualistic.

The title itself of *The Grapes of Wrath* implies a strong sense of intense evil, with the potential to call down God's wrath. Lacking the modification of reflection, then, in both *Travels* and *Grapes of Wrath* there is a dichotomy between good and evil, and the resulting Cain figure is monstrous.

Presented as materialist and bigot, the Cain figure either overtly or through neglect destroys those who get in the way of a personal profit and those who differ from himself. At times the motivations of materialist and bigot overlap, but their distinctive attributes remain: one destroys the land, which Steinbeck holds in reverence; and the other destroys the people, whom he regards with charity in its biblical sense.

Abel's reverence and Cain's irreverent carelessness are implicit in the Genesis story, leading to God's respect for Abel's offering and His rejection of Cain's. Unlike Abel's considerate, reverent, respectful offering of "the firstlings of his flock and the fat thereof," Cain, the first materialist, carelessly and hastily brings God a nondescript offering "of the fruit of the ground"--quite evidently not the best that he has to give (Genesis 4:3-4).[5] As a caretaker he thus displays a woeful lack of discernment of that which is good and fitting. In *Travels* Steinbeck describes such a careless materialist, "a newcomer, a stranger," in Monterey near his home:

> His senses must have been blunted and atrophied with money and the getting of it. He bought a grove of sempervirens in a deep valley near the coast, and then, as was his right by ownership, he cut them down and sold the lumber, and left on the ground the wreckage of his slaughter. . . . This was not only murder but sacrilege. We looked on that man with loathing, and he was marked to the day of his death. (*Travels* 189)

Like Cain, the murderer of these "holy" redwood trees carries a "mark" to the end of his days, setting him apart as evil, to be viewed with "loathing." As a result of desecrating the land, the "newcomer" bears the separating, alienating mark of Cain.

Similarly, a careless disregard for the land underlies the opening scene of *The Grapes of Wrath*, as Steinbeck portrays an inhospitable desert created by exploitation--the Oklahoma dust bowl. Negligence and destruction of the land, its produce, and any human being who gets in the way of a profit serve as defining characteristics of the materialist throughout the novel. Exaltation of the wisdom and scientific expertise invested in the fruitfulness and beauty of California shift to bitter denunciation of loss and wastefulness. While people starve, luscious ripeness gives way to decay and putrefaction as cherries, prunes, pears, and grapes fall and rot, and oranges are "dumped on the ground" and sprayed with kerosene in order to regulate prices and keep them at a high level. Bitterly the narrator comments, "And children dying of pellagra must die because a profit cannot be taken from an orange. And coroners must fill in the certificates died of malnutrition because the food must rot--be forced to rot."[6] While the agentless passive voice strives for objectivity and casts no overt blame, nonetheless the figure of a materialistic Cain, who sacrifices a child to make a profit, lurks in the background.

Whether the Cain figure is a materialist or a bigot, each results in a similar fratricide--the slaying of fellow human beings either overtly or by negligence. In both *Travels* and *Grapes of Wrath*, Steinbeck's view of bigotry is in part delineated, defined, and contrasted by its opposite--openhearted hospitality that overcomes obstacles and transcends barriers between human beings.

Defining by contrast as well as by example, in *Travels* Steinbeck's experiences with the French Canadian Canucks who have come to Maine for the potato harvest and with a mechanic "in Oregon, on a rainy Sunday" show Abel-like magnanimity and hospitality at its best while underscoring the niggardliness of the materialist and the bigot (*Travels* 184).   Sharing "a bottle of very old and reverend brandy" with the Canucks, Steinbeck experiences "the Brotherhood of Man growing until it filled Rocinante full-- and the sisterhood also":

> There came into Rocinante a triumphant human magic that can bless a house, or a truck for that matter--nine people gathered in complete silence and the nine parts making a whole as surely as my arms and legs are part of me, separate and inseparable. Rocinante took on a glow it never quite lost. (*Travels* 68-69)

On the opposite end from bigotry in the spectrum of human relationships, hospitality thus stands in contrast to intolerance and enmity.

Another such instance occurs on a rainy Sunday in Oregon when Rocinante blows out a rear tire, and a "mostly silent" mechanic with "a scarred face and an evil white eye" makes six telephone calls to locate new tires, persuades his brother-in-law to drive to two different places to get them, and has the truck ready to go again in "less than four hours." Viewing this mechanic oxymoronically as "my evil saint," Steinbeck asserts: "And if ever my faith in the essential saintliness of humans becomes tattered, I shall think of that evil-looking man" (*Travels* 185-86).   Once again, Steinbeck's *Travels* portrays Abel-like goodness as residing in a hospitable spirit and contrasts this "essential saintliness" with its opposite--bigotry and prejudice.

In *The Grapes of Wrath* bigotry is also defined in contrast to hospitality, at least in part.[7]   A key theme in this novel, hospitality is prominent throughout--from Tom Joad's depiction of "a good guy" as he persuades a trucker to give him a lift (*GW* 11); to Ma Joad's declaration that she "never heerd tell of no Joads or no Hazletts, neither, ever refusin' food an' shelter or a lift on the road to anybody that asked" (*GW* 139); to the ending where two strangers, a starving man and his son, provide "a dirty comfort" for Rose of Sharon who is weak from childbirth and feverish from exposure, and Rose of Sharon in turn nurses the starving father, providing the only food she has to offer (*GW* 617-19).

Similarly, in Chapter 15, midpoint in the novel structurally and thematically, at a cafe on route 66 the cook, the waitress, and truck driver customers share their bounty with an impoverished man and his children by giving them a fifteen-cent loaf of bread for a dime and two nickel candy bars for "two for a penny" (*GW* 218-219). In this chapter also inhospitable bigots are epitomized by the cars that whiz "viciously by on 66," carrying the self-centered and self-satisfied, oblivious to the needs of those who travel alongside (*GW* 221). Assaults on the Joads serve as an immediate prelude to and foreshadowing of their experiences in California, which they see as the land of promise and opportunity. As they enter Arizona, a border guard warns them to "keep movin'" (*GW* 274). Later, two men leaving California after a futile quest for work, warn Tom that in California he will be called "Okie," which no longer means "from Oklahoma. Now it means you're a dirty son-of-a-bitch. Okie means you're scum. Don't means nothing itself, it's the way they say it" (*GW* 280).

Finally, Steinbeck's experience with the South and "the Cheerleaders" in *Travels* shows the destruction of innocence and joy, the irrevocable damage of a child's psyche. A small African-American girl's childhood is crushed under the weight of prejudice and hatred as she goes up the long walkway to school, surrounded by United States marshals and jeering crowds. As she makes "a curious hop," Steinbeck observes:

> I think in her whole life she had not gone ten steps without skipping, but now in the middle of her first skip the weight bore her down and her little round feet took measured, reluctant steps between the tall guards. (*Travels* 257)

As she walks this gauntlet--terrified, bearing the weight of undeserved enmity--the child falls victim to "the vomitings of demoniac humans, . . . insensate beastliness" (*Travels* 258). This experience leaves Steinbeck wondering where the "thoughtful, gentle people" are, those "with a tradition of kindness and courtesy, . . . whose arms would ache to gather up the small, scared black mite" (*Travels* 259). Again good and evil are discrete and the Cain figure a destroyer of innocence.

Steinbeck's Cain further destroys by deprivation of human dignity and personhood, trapping his victims in that ominous aura of silence and fear that accompanies "playing nigger." The person trapped manifests an exaggerated humility and obeisance--seeming childish, even stupid. In *Travels* Steinbeck offers a ride to "an old Negro" thus trapped by a lifetime of servitude and humiliation. Addressing Steinbeck as "captain, sir," this man makes himself as inconspicuous as he possibly can:

> He clasped his hands in his lap, knotted and lumpy as cherry twigs, and all of him seemed to shrink in the seat as he sucked in his outline to make it smaller. (*Travels* 266)

Like the crowd and the Cheerleaders who destroy the small child's joy and innocence, in a silencing as effective as murder, this man's sense of worth and personhood has been diminished. Not daring to speak as human being to human being, he shrinks towards anonymity, his manhood effectually annihilated.

Cain figures in *The Grapes of Wrath* likewise attack the psyche. As the Joads spend the night in a roadside camp, "a brown-faced man" with a gun and a marshal's badge threatens to arrest them if they are not gone by morning: "Well, you ain't in your country now. You're in California, an' we don't want you goddamn Okies settlin' down" (*GW* 291). Instead of golden opportunity and hope, in California the Joads find desperation as they face the open hostility of those who would deprive them of human worth.

These California foes, however, destroy primarily by negligence. In a rich, fertile land which is either lying fallow or used for profit, hundreds of thousands of dispossessed people go hungry. "The great owners," as Steinbeck depicts them, are the Cains who pit themselves against "people" who are starving and whose children are dying from "black-tongue . . . from not gettin' good things to eat" (*GW* 324-26). By portrayal of their ignoring the ancient laws of hospitality to strangers as set forth in Greek myth and in the Hebraic-Christian tradition, Steinbeck implicates these "great owners," these unredeemable Cains who commit multiple murders. The dichotomy between good and evil, then, stands in sharp relief--the hospitable Joads set against the hatred of the greedy, negligent Cain figures which have run throughout the novel.

Modified by time and distance in *America and Americans* and *East of Eden*, Steinbeck sees good coming out of evil, in spite of evil. No longer unredeemable, the Cain figures gain both self-knowledge and redemption, but the lesson is learned at the expense of a brother's life.

Roy S. Simmonds describes *America and Americans* as "a genealogical and psychological portrait of the American people."[8] The tone of this "portrait" differs vastly from the barely concealed fury of *Grapes of Wrath* and passages in *Travels*. Although he finds the same faults of enmity and thirst for fratricide that he finds in the earlier works, here Steinbeck is not the condemning judge. Rather, he is "a gentle, genial sage, given to bursts of irascibility now and then, at times salting his deliberations with extended asides or searching condemnation, uttered more in sorrow than in anger."[9] Exchanging the voice of the judge for the voice of the observer, the storyteller, and the prophet, Steinbeck does not depict a sharp dividing line between the dark and light in the American psyche.[10] Cain, therefore, transcends his fratricide and ultimately chooses good over evil.

In the voice of the observer, Steinbeck views the dark side of the American psyche objectively--bemoaning "the youthful gangs in our cities," portraying the general national character of a people "who fight our way in, and try to buy our way out, . . . a nation of public puritans and private profligates."[11] He finds the human tendency to be predatory and "aggressively individual" intensified in Americans by a loss of rules, an atrophy of the sense of responsibility, and the poison of an obsession with things (*America* 137-39).

Like the Cain figures in *Travels* and *The Grapes of Wrath*, the typical American is a materialist and a bigot. Entrusted with the land, Americans treat it offhandedly and carelessly. They ravage, pollute, and destroy-- primarily to maintain their "power sources" (*America* 130). If they were to bring an offering to God, it would be like Cain's--sullied and inferior.

As Cain's enmity and jealousy lead to the callous murder of his brother, so bigoted, materialistic Americans irresponsibly continue to ask the question, "Am I my brother's keeper?" as they nurture strife and "withdrawn separateness" between the races (*America* 59). Steinbeck observes too that American Cains continue to destroy the land with which they have been entrusted and that their hatred leads to fratricide--either physically or psychically. But deeper retrospection has changed Steinbeck's view of the American Cain. From a narrow perspective in *Travels*, he remembered with anger and loathing "the stranger" who "slaughtered" the redwoods growing in a valley in his hometown. From a broader viewpoint in *America and Americans*, he remembers the same stranger with "sadness." Nor does he now see Americans as engaged in wanton destruction:

> No longer do we Americans want to destroy wantonly, but our new-found sources of power . . . spew pollution on our country, so that the rivers and steams are becoming poisonous and lifeless. The birds die for the lack of food; a noxious cloud hangs over our cities that burns our lungs and reddens our eyes. Our ability to conserve has not grown with our power to create, but this slow and sullen poisoning is no longer ignored or justified. Almost daily, the pressure of outrage among Americans grows. We are no longer content to destroy our beloved country. We are slow to learn; but we learn. . . . And we no longer believe that a man, by owning a piece of America, is free to outrage it. (*America* 130)

From their misdeeds and destruction Americans have gained self-knowledge and recognition of their capacity to poison the land. Like Cain, they have learned a lesson from a brother's murder. And Steinbeck implies that from such self-knowledge and awareness will come new rules and a renewed sense of responsibility for the preservation of the earth.

As an observer also, Steinbeck notes the beginnings of the American people's awareness of their own propensity for enmity, strife, and fratricide:

> Revolt against what is in the air--in the violence of the long, hot summer; in the resentment against injustice and inequality, and against imperceptible or cynical cruelty. There is blind anger against delay, against the long preparation for the long journey--perhaps the longest, darkest journey of all, with the greatest light at the end of it. (*America* 143)

Again, self-awareness and self-knowledge bring recognition of the problems brought about by enmity, preparing Americans for this "journey" towards the "light."

Like exiled Cain who founded a city for his progeny, this self-knowledge and awareness may enable Americans to create a more just and equable, a more kindly and hospitable nation, with room for all to grow and prosper.[12] Thus Steinbeck's Cain figure is no longer simply the monstrous, unredeemable dark side of the American psyche. Now a figure capable of redemption through self-knowledge and contrition, the American Cain may someday acknowledge responsibility for being a brother's "keeper."

Like *America and Americans*, in *East of Eden* there is no evil from which good does not come, but there is also no good unstained by evil. Like unredeemable Cain, Adam Trask's father, brother, and wife are all dark characters from whose lives, nevertheless, some good comes. Adam's brother, Charles, and his wife, Cathy/Kate, however, have the most prominent attributes of monster Cain. Both try to kill Adam, and both are in a sense exiles and outcasts who bear distinctive scars on their forehead.

Evil as they are, both Charles and Cathy/Kate have at least a glimmer of a redeeming human quality. After Charles's death even as Adam remembers "He tried to kill me once," he muses, "Sometimes I thought he loved me" (*EOE* 494). And Cathy-Kate, in the midst of plotting a murder, realizes that she does not want her son, Aron, "to know about her" (*EOE* 664). Daydreaming, she imagines his visiting her in New York:

> He would think that she had always lived in an elegant little house on the East Side. She would take him to the theatre, to the opera, and people would see them together and wonder at their loveliness (*EOE* 664).

Before committing suicide, she writes a note: "I leave everything I have to my son Aron Trask" (*EOE* 714). In these moments she glimpses what might have been, the affection she might have shared with her sons.

Adam's son, Cal, is a much more complex Cain figure than Cyrus, Charles, or Cathy/Kate. Although he bears no mark on his forehead, he too dwells in darkness--alienated, friendless, lonely:

> Always there was the darkness about him. . . . Associates he had, and authority and some admiration, but friends he did not have. He lived alone and walked alone." (*EOE* 576-78)

And typical of the materialistic American Cain, Cal tries to buy his father's love with an unclean gift--$10,000 earned by war profiteering (*EOE* 702).

Like his uncle and his mother, Cal is also capable of fratricide. His cruel revelation that their mother is the madam of a brothel leads directly to the death of his twin brother, the innocent and unsuspecting Aron. For in shock and confused desperation, Aron joins the army, shortly thereafter to be killed in battle.

But this dark side of Cal does not tell his whole story. Like "the American," awareness of his wickedness grieves him. When he learns that his mother is a prostitute, he fervently prays: "I don't want to be mean. I don't want to be lonely" (*EOE* 497). In contrast with his attempt to buy his father's love, he shows his love for Abra by bringing an acceptable, carefully chosen gift--sharing with her a picnic and the beauty of the first bloom of wild azaleas.

Further, after crushing Aron with the revelation of their mother's identity, he hates himself, feeling "like a broken bug": "His guilt assaulted him and he had no weapon to fight it off" (*EOE* 733). Fearful for Aron, Cal wants "to find him and build him back the way he had been," even though such a restoration involves sacrificing himself (*EOE* 733). Like Steinbeck's evolving American of the future, he no longer asks, "Am I my brother's keeper?"   With the contrition which is a necessary preliminary to redemption, he knows that he is Aron's keeper. Although he shares with Charles and Cathy/Kate some of the characteristics of monster Cain, like "the American" he is capable of redemption. At the expense of his brother's life, he learns that he has power to choose between good and evil.

In the prophetic passages in *America and Americans* and in *The Winter of Our Discontent*, Steinbeck's view of good and evil evolves further, intermingling them as the strength of Cain combines with the goodness of his brother, Abel, to become Every American. Having objectively portrayed the dark side of the United States, he characteristically looks beyond the immediate into a future of possibilities. A discussion of national dreams and "the American Way of Life" concludes:

> These dreams describe our vague yearnings toward what we wish [we] were and hope we may be: wise, just, compassionate, and noble. The fact that we have this dream at all is perhaps an indication of its possibility. (*America* 34)

This tone of optimism and refusal to believe that the darker side of the American psyche, the materialism and bigotry of monster Cain, may eventually triumph and destroy even the dream itself, pervades the entire book, culminating in the final chapter, "Americans and the Future," in which he looks into the future of his "people, a young people," with "some fear, more hope, and great confidence" (*America* 142).

Steinbeck is confident in the future of the American people because they yearn for goodness as well as for strength, highly valuing wisdom, justice, compassion, and nobility. They are not complacent or satisfied with themselves as they are or with the world as it is.   Their restless dissatisfaction prepares them for "the longest, darkest journey of all, with the greatest light at the end of it" (*America* 143). Like exiled Cain who founds a city for his progeny, thereby combining his brother, Abel's, potential for goodness with his own great strength, Americans have "places to go and new things to find," surrounded by "the fascinating unknown." Through their yearning for goodness, they have the capacity and strength to formulate "new rules" for new circumstances, to adapt to "the change that is coming" (*America* 143).

The "Afterword" ends on a similar note: "We have failed sometimes, taken wrong paths, paused for renewal, filled our bellies and licked our wounds; but we have never slipped back--never" (*America* 205). And the implication is that "we *shall* never slip back--never." Based on history, observations, personal experience, and a faith that is never shaken, the prophet's voice thus speaks with great optimism about the future of America and of the Americans. Combining the strength of Cain with the goodness of Abel, Americans shall overcome all of their obstacles, developing beyond their propensity for materialism, bigotry, and fratricide.

Similarly, in *The Winter of Our Discontent*, Steinbeck depicts Ethan Allen Hawley's greed and materialism as leading to fratricide, but, as a representative Every American, he overcomes evil to become a light bearer, passing to his daughter a familial heritage of goodness. The objective observer's voice portrays in Ethan (whom Michael J. Meyer calls "the American Everyman"), the ingrained greed, materialism, and fratricide that Steinbeck sees in the American people" (261). But the prophetic voice depicts in this same Ethan an Every American, embodying the hope for a better future--one in which the light does not go out but is rekindled by a formulation of new rules, a reinvigorated sense of responsibility, and a devotion to that which is just, compassionate, and kindly.

Basically an honest man and a loving husband and father, Ethan succumbs to the typically American Keep-up-with-the-Joneses and Everybody-does-it syndromes. A materialist like Cain, he denies responsibility for others or to others in his greedy play for money, power, and prestige. He devises, practices, and almost carries out an ingenious plan for robbing a bank; he turns his employer over to immigration authorities as an illegal alien, leading to his deportation and in effect to his destruction; by duplicity, he destroys his soul brother and friend, Danny Taylor; and he craftily outwits the devious banker, Mr. Baker. Like Cain, he can ruthlessly overcome his opponents and his brother and friend as well.

A bigot as well as a materialist, Ethan despises his employer, a foreigner who has taken over his family business. He looks down on his friend, Danny, as a drunk who does not count for much. And he disdains the banker because his grandfather set fire to his own grandfather's ship as it lay in anchor, thus diminishing the family fortune. Ethan's greed and bigotry lead to the physical or psychical destruction of anyone who might interfere with his bid for fortune and recognition.

When Ethan learns that his son has plagiarized an award-winning essay in the national "I Love America" contest, however, he realizes that the legacy of family goodness--the light-- is going out. In a reversal of Othello's "Put out the light" speech before he kills Desdemona, Ethan moves from the temptation of suicide--to put out his own light permanently--to the revelation that he is still himself a "light-bearer"[13] who must pass on a moral and humane heritage. In the midst of a paean for those whose light still burns-- Marullo, "old Cap'n," and Aunt Deborah--Ethan laments that his own "light," his moral and humane sensitivity, is "out, . . . blacker than a wick" (*Winter* 357). In a wish that is at once a prayer and a suicidal desire, he first wants "to go home" and then "to the other side of home where the lights are given" (*Winter* 357).   Ironically, or providentially, he discovers that his daughter, Ellen, whom he realizes is "the light-bearer," has already given him light by placing in his pocket the family talisman, a luminous and translucent stone that gathers "every bit of light" in the rapidly flooding cave where Ethan has intended to die. Struggling against the tide, he fights his way out of the cave to return the talisman, the light, to Ellen, its new owner. For now they are both light-bearers.

     The rest follows by implication. With his newly won influence in the world of business, which he has gained at the expense of Marullo's deportation, Danny's life, and Baker's trust, he has the overcoming strength of Cain. With his newly won insights on "light," essential human goodness, he has the enabling virtue of Abel. The qualities of strength and virtue are both essential for the American whom Steinbeck has envisioned in *America and Americans* and whom he has embodied in Ethan Allen Hawley, Every American. Symbolically, then, the talisman Ethan takes to his daughter is the only acceptable gift, the best that he has to offer: a heritage of strength, virtue, light, and hope in the future.

     From a perspective which has developed over time, which has modified and ameliorated as the author himself reflects, changes, and matures, Steinbeck has based his works on close, personal involvement with his topic, writing about the nation and the people he knows and loves. He has concerned himself with the "one story in the world, . . . good and evil"-- epitomized in the enmity which leads to fratricide in the biblical story of Cain and Abel (*EOE* 541). He finds American Cains to be materialists and bigots, who are willing to sacrifice kinfolk for a profit, willing to murder those different from themselves.

     Based on close and relatively recent observation, Steinbeck speaks from the perspective of judge in *The Grapes of Wrath* and *Travels*, in which the unredeemable Cain figure, self-centered and unconcerned, either overtly or by neglect destroys both the land and anyone who gets in the way of a profit. Retrospectively, in *America and Americans* and *East of Eden*, he depicts good as irrepressible, coming from evil, in spite of evil; and he portrays the Cains as capable of learning from their sins and mistakes, capable of redemption. In these latter works, therefore, both "the American" and Cal gain self-knowledge, awareness, and redemption from their propensity for destruction and murder.

From the vantage point of a seer, in the prophetic sections of *America and Americans* and in *The Winter of Our Discontent*, Steinbeck portrays the redemption of the American Cains. Even though they are still materialists and bigots, they finally overcome evil by combining the strength of Cain, won at the expense of a brother's life, with the virtue of Abel. Steinbeck foresees this Every American as an active, effective participant in world affairs, but also as one who is at the same time a light-bearer, devoted to justice and compassion. Thus recording for posterity his own philosophical and mystical journey, he offers a panacea for the nation's ills. Grounded in the biblical story of The Fall, the battle between good and evil, and the hatred that leads to fratricide, Steinbeck depicts his own dreams and hopes for a future in which the ancient quarrel is resolved and The American Dream of virtue is finally actualized, combining with and increasing the nation's great strength and prowess.

From *South Dakota Review* (Summer 1996) Vol. 34, No. 2, 192-206

Notes

1. Steinbeck, John. *Travels with Charley in Search of America.* (New York: Penguin Books, 1986), pp. 33; 6; 243-44. After the initial reference, this work will be identified as *Travels* with pertinent page numbers.

2.Rousseau, Jean Jacques. *Confessions. The Continental Edition of World Masterpieces.* Ed. Maynard Mack, et al. Vol. 2. (New York: W. W. Norton and Company, 1966), p. 268.

3.Wordsworth, William. *Preface to Lyrical Ballads. The Norton Anthology of English Literature.* Ed. M. H. Abrams, et al. Vol. 2. (New York: W. W. Norton and Company, 1979), p. 173.

4. John Steinbeck, *East of Eden* (New York: Penguin Books, 1986), p. 545. After the initial reference, this work will be identified as *EOE* with pertinent page numbers.

5. Genesis 4:3-4, *Holy Bible, New International Version, The.* Colorado Springs, Colorado: International Bible Society, 1984.

6. John Steinbeck. *The Grapes of Wrath. Text and Criticism.* Ed. Peter Lisca (New York: Penguin Books, 1977), pp. 476-77. After the initial reference, this work will be identified as *GW* with pertinent page numbers.

7. See Barbara A. Heavilin's "Hospitality, the Joads, and the Stranger Motif: Structural Symmetry in John Steinbeck's *The Grapes of Wrath*" in the Summer 1991 issue of *South Dakota Review* for a fuller discussion of the hospitality theme.

8. Roy S. Simmonds. "'Our land . . . incredibly dear and beautiful': Steinbeck's *America and Americans*," in *Steinbeck's Travel Literature*, ed. Tetsumaro Hayashi *(Steinbeck Monograph Series*, No. 10). (Muncie, Indiana: Steinbeck Society of America, Ball State University, 1980), pp. 23-24.

9. See Heavilin's 1993 discussion of *America and Americans* in *A New Study Guide to Steinbeck's Major Works, with Critical Explications*, edited by Tetsumaro Hayashi and published by Scarecrow Press, for a fuller discussion of voice.

10. John Steinbeck. *America and Americans* (New York: Viking Press, 1966), pp. 29-34. After the initial reference, this work will be identified as *America* with pertinent page numbers.

11. For the initial idea underlying this study, I am indebted to Ricardo J. Quinones's *The Changes of Cain: Violence and the Lost Brother in Cain and Abel Literature*, published by Princeton University Press in 1991. In particular, see Chapter Seven, "The New American Cain: *East of Eden* and Other Works of Post-World War II America," in which he discusses Caleb as "another kind of Sacred Executioner involved in a foundation myth that requires a fraternal sacrifice" (136-152).

12. Michael J. Meyer. "*The Winter of our Discontent* (1961)." *A New Study Guide to Steinbeck's Major Works, with Critical Explications*. Ed. Tetsumaro Hayashi. (Metuchen, N.J.: The Scarecrow Press, 1993), p. 261.

13. John Steinbeck. *The Winter of Our Discontent* (New York: Penguin Books, 1986), p. 357. After the initial reference, this work will be identified as *Winter* with pertinent page numbers.

A Postmodern Steinbeck, or Rose of Sharon Meets Oedipa Maas

Chris Kocela

John Steinbeck has made his feelings clear with regard to the critical classification of his work. In his response to two mid-fifties articles on *The Grapes of Wrath*, he writes: "I don't think the *Grapes of Wrath* is obscure in what it tries to say. As to its classification and pickling, I have neither opinion nor interest. . . . Just read it, don't count it!" (1955, 53). If this injunction did little to slow the work of critics forty years ago, however, it will be heeded even less by those of us who have grown up alongside the nebulous cultural/theoretical phenomenon called "postmodernism." Postmodernist fiction has been defined in part by its fostering of reading strategies which deliberately subvert those institutionalized by modernist literature.[1] Even if one were now inclined to follow Steinbeck's advice, it is almost impossible to separate "reading" from "counting" in an age which must have the work of Steinbeck's generation bottled and labelled before it can "read" its own. From this postmodern vantage any reassessment of *The Grapes of Wrath* is doubly "pickled." Yet as I hope to demonstrate, a return to Steinbeck's best-known novel from the perspective of contemporary fiction theory vindicates aspects of its structure and characterization often criticized in the context of a strictly modernist canon.

If it seems presumptuous to talk about a "postmodern Steinbeck" before his modernist orientation has been established, it should be noted that Steinbeck's modernism has always been portrayed as part "post-." In his two 1976 articles on the subject, Warren French simultaneously opens and closes the door on the issue of Steinbeck's modernity.[2] He argues that, although Steinbeck's early novels (especially *In Dubious Battle* and *Of Mice and Men*) are virtual paradigms of a modernist ironic sensibility, Steinbeck had already abandoned this viewpoint as early on as 1938. Instead of depicting alienation from society, his major novel, *The Grapes of Wrath*, marks a crucial shift in tone and becomes a "fiction of consciousness-raising" (1976b, 160) making Steinbeck "one of the significant prophets of Post-Modernism" (1976b, 161). This notion is echoed in Robert Con Davis' introduction to *Twentieth Century Interpretations: The Grapes of Wrath*, where he too argues the break between Steinbeck's "big novel" and the modernist school: "Central for understanding *The Grapes of Wrath* is the recognition that it runs counter to one of the main developments in twentieth century American literature--modernist fiction" (2) Finally, Robert DeMott's introduction to the Penguin Twentieth-Century Classics edition of *The Grapes of Wrath* describes Steinbeck as a "prophetic postmodernist" by virtue of his thematizing the "creative process itself" in the works following *Sea of Cortez* (xlii). While the later tradition that Steinbeck may be seen to prophesy remains obscure in these critics, French and DeMott both mark *The Grapes of Wrath* as a turning point in Steinbeck's aesthetic sensibilities.[3] I shall seek to develop this idea of *The Grapes of Wrath* as transitional between modernism and something "other"--postmodernism--while keeping alive these critics' implicit questioning of such terms.

My paper, therefore, will attempt a reassessment of a few well-studied aspects of the novel in light of some recent influential theories of post-modernist fiction. Specifically, I will argue in the first section that Steinbeck's use of the interchapters exemplifies a postmodern strategy of "frame-breaking," whereby differences between history and fiction are established within the text only to be problematized, alerting the reader to the difficulties of historical and political representation. In the second section I will use Deborah Madsen's theorization of "postmodernist allegory" to examine how the problematic divide between history and fiction is further broken down by Steinbeck's superimposing of biblical and fictional worlds on the plane of the Joads' story. There the frameworks whereby history grounds fiction, and myth grounds history, are broken down entirely by collapsing all of these realms into two highly charged, ontologically explosive scenes. Finally, it will become apparent that much of the theory to which I refer has arisen specifically out of critical attempts to deal with the work of Thomas Pynchon. For this reason, and because I think not enough attention has been paid to Steinbeck's influence on, and continuity with, a later generation of American writers, I take a step toward remedying this situation in my conclusion. As my title suggests, I indulge in a brief comparison of *The Grapes of Wrath* and Pynchon's *The Crying of Lot 49.*

Let me say up front, however, that I do not intend to argue for Steinbeck's wholesale inclusion among any "school" of postmodernist writers. Rather, because Steinbeck's fit with the modernist conventions of his contemporaries has long been considered problematic, I see Steinbeck as a figure who problematizes any notion of a radical break between the modern and the postmodern. It is my opinion that, in certain ways (not the least of which is its tremendous "complicity"[4] with the popular market) *The Grapes of Wrath* was a postmodern novel long before it was fashionable to be so. Yet the characteristics I will call postmodern have often been perceived as shortcomings or flaws that reduce the importance of Steinbeck's achievement. Such detractions usually take place in the shadow of the institutionalized American modernism represented by Steinbeck's contemporaries--in particular Faulkner, Dos Passos, and Hemingway.[5] And Stanley Fish suggests an alternative to this mode of examination when he attacks Brad Leithauser's review of the fiftieth anniversary edition of *The Grapes of Wrath.* Criticizing any assumption that literature is a normative category necessarily embodying transcendental myths (252), Fish challenges what he sees as Leithauser's standards of evaluation, whereby "a work rises to the stature of serious literature only if it transcends the local concerns that inspire its author" (Fish 242-43). The significance of this move is apparent. If, as Leithauser suggests, Steinbeck's failure to live up to our (I would say, modernist) expectations leaves us regretful "at how much better a writer he might have been" (93), we may find surcease of sorrow by rethinking those expectations. In what follows, then, I shall bracket what I take to be certain modernist critical ambitions for *The Grapes of Wrath* in order to pursue traces of a "prophetic" postmodernity at the heart of this great, transitional novel.

There is nothing very new or radical in stating that Steinbeck's novel about the dustbowl crisis of 1930's midAmerica is intimately bound up with the problems of historical representation. As his letters at the time demonstrate, Steinbeck was intensely conscious of the need to report accurately on the plight of California's migrant workers: "I'm trying to write history while it is happening and I don't want to be wrong."[6] But for Steinbeck the responsibility to document never took precedence over his controlling powers as an artist. The best example of this is his rather blunt rejection of Horace Bristol's photographic contributions once he had decided on the novel form (Howarth 77). Rather than using photographs as a historical ground for his fiction, Steinbeck opted for a series of narrative interventions that would "hit the reader below the belt" through the "rhythms and symbols of poetry."[7] The results are the interchapters of *The Grapes of Wrath*, which, as John Timmerman has noted, throw the fictional story of the Joads into "historical relief" (107).

Steinbeck's strategic use of the interchapters as a historical framing device is one of the most studied aspects of the novel (see Dircks 89-90). In the wide-brushed intercalary chapters, which describe the "last rains"[8] over Oklahoma (3), the "armies of bitterness" (119) in their move west, and the "western land, nervous under the beginning change" (204), evidence of broad social and environmental transformation provides historical context for the finely-drawn trials of the Joad family. Yet if the interchapters of *The Grapes of Wrath* owe a certain debt to the modernism of Dos Passos (Owens 1989, 28), in Steinbeck's hands the relationship between fiction and history-as-it-happens may also be seen to express the central *postmodern* problem of a vanishing ontological divide between history and fiction. The more contemporary history is posited as the "horizon" of the fictional adventures of the Joads, the more it is mythologized as a reenactment of biblical/symbolic, timeless, and hence *ahistorical* forms. And this in turns threatens the distinction between history and fiction on which the structure of the novel is based.

This process, labelled in some theories of postmodernist fiction as "frame-breaking,"[9] is evident in Steinbeck's novel as early on as the opening paragraph. There the historical event of the drying up of Oklahoma's farmland is depicted in both objective prose and heightened, biblical rhetoric: "In the last part of May the sky grew pale and the clouds that had hung in high puffs for so long in the spring were dissipated. . . . The surface of the earth crusted, a thin hard crust, and as the sky became pale, so the earth became pale, pink in the red country and white in the gray country" (3). In this description, a conflict occurs when historical specificity ("the last part of May") is placed in a context of timeless process or significance ("as the sky. . . so the earth"). This conflict between discourses has been given detailed analysis by Louis Owens and Hector Torres in their discussion of the dialogic structure of Steinbeck's interchapters. After isolating two competing voices--those of a semi-omniscient narrator and biblical discourse--running throughout the text of several interchapters, Owens and Torres reach the conclusion that "[t]hese two voices are in tension; the narrative must both move within time and remain timeless, and there is no way to reconcile these two narrative impulses" (1989, 92).   But backgrounded in their account is the ontological disorientation experienced by the reader as a result of this competition of discourses--a disorientation that weakens the historical framework of the interchapter structure itself. By diluting an objective *factual* history with biblical references, history is made to partake of some of the symbolic properties of the fictional text it is intended to "ground," threatening the ontological difference that separates them. The more that history is made to appear timeless and symbolic, the more purely textual it becomes, and the less secure are its ties to a reality beyond the fictional story of the Joads.

Moreover, what such rhetorical conflicts may be seen to signify is a brief collision of worlds--one biblical, and one objectively historical--in the superimposing of both on the same narrative plane. Owens and Torres only hint at this effect when they write of one biblical passage, "we see a narrative space that hearkens back to the plague-stricken Egypt of biblical times" (79).[10]   In such a highly charged passage, the reader sees both "plague-stricken Egypt" and drought-stricken Oklahoma in rapid alternation, such that one is briefly erased as the other appears. This oscillation not only weakens the historical frame, but emphasizes and problematizes the ontological boundaries between history and biblical analogue by forcing them into direct confrontation.   The perception of rapidly created and annihilated narrative spaces alerts the reader to the textuality of both fictional and historical worlds--an idea central to several definitions of postmodernist fiction.

One such definition is that of Brian McHale, who distinguishes between modernist and postmodernist fiction on the basis of a shift of "dominant" governing modes of critical interrogation. Modernist fiction, according to McHale, is characterized by an epistemological dominant, in that it foregrounds questions of *how* knowledge about a stable world can be established. Postmodernist fiction, on the other hand, backgrounds epistemological concerns to propose an ontological line of inquiry, asking *which* of many possible realities one inhabits at a given time (see 1987, 6-11). Postmodern "historical" novels like Pynchon's *Gravity's Rainbow* or E. L. Doctorow's *Ragtime* deliberately emphasize the "ontological seams" evident when historical and fictional worlds meet (1987, 17). The effect is a simultaneous heightening and blurring of the difference between them.

Linda Hutcheon devotes even more attention to this blurring of fiction and history in her study of postmodernist fiction. She goes so far as to reserve the title "postmodern" only for those texts which, in addition to their metafictional properties, render explicit the problems of historical representation.   Her "historiographic metafiction" is "self-reflexively metafictional and parodic, but also makes a claim to some kind of (newly problematized) historical reference" (1988, 40). In so doing, it reveals that the referents of both history and fiction are only more texts (1988, 119), and it therefore poses ontological *and* epistemological questions (1988, 50).

Of course *The Grapes of Wrath* is not formally parodic as are Hutcheon's examples of historiographic metafiction; nor is it ontologically pluralized to the extent of McHale's postmodernist texts. But in its deliberate weakening of its own historical frame, it embodies aspects of what McHale calls "limit modernism" (1987, 13), a border territory which *hesitates* in privileging either an epistemological or ontological mode of questioning. This hesitation is seen in the way in which "world-building" enters Steinbeck's text at both a structural and thematic level, and is made to serve both ontological and epistemological ends as a spur to reader consciousness.

The interchapters, with their simultaneous representation and prob-lematizing of a broader historical reality, provide a perfect vehicle for introducing on a structural level one of the central themes of *The Grapes of Wrath*: the impermanence of social worlds. The theme recurs throughout the interchapters themselves, from descriptions of the vacant and decaying tenant houses in chapter 11, to the original settling of California in chapter 19, to the "jeremiad" of chapter 25, where the scientists who have "transformed the world with their knowledge" (474) must watch it burn to protect profit margins. Most prominently, the idea of world-building takes center-stage in chapter 17, which depicts the routinization of migrant life *en route* to California. Here, the origin of world-building is framed in undeniable biblical allusion: "Thus it might be that one family camped near a spring, and another camped for the spring and for the company, and a third because two families had pioneered the place and found it good" (264). But if the migrant people seem to play God's role in a reenactment of Genesis, Steinbeck quickly emphasizes the need for *de*construction of established worlds in the name of collective progress. Hence:

> Every night a world created, complete with furniture--friends made and enemies established; a world complete with braggarts and with cowards, with quiet men, with humble men, with kindly men. Every night relationships that make a world, established; and every morning the world torn down like a circus.
> At first the families were timid in the building and tumbling worlds, but gradually the technique of building worlds became their technique. Then leaders emerged, then laws were made, then codes came into being. And

as the worlds moved westward they were more complete and better
furnished, for their builders were more experienced in building them.
(265)

Clearly, the laws which will preserve the migrants against social dissolution
will be fashioned only through this process of perpetual building and
destruction. The routinization of perpetual *change* exhibited by the migrant
people exhibits the same conflation of historicity and timelessness suggested
by Steinbeck's transposing of biblical and historical worlds. Therein lies the
hesitation that marks *The Grapes of Wrath* as borderline between a
modernist and postmodernist aesthetic. Steinbeck's novel does not
irretrievably *break* the framework in which fiction is grounded by history,
and history by mythical reference. What it does do is crack that framework
at critical points in order to emphasize the radical realignment of world-
views required by the reader in order to understand the magnitude of the
social problems the novel describes. As Steinbeck writes at another point:
"There is a crime here that goes beyond denunciation. There is a sorrow here
that weeping cannot symbolize" (477). In the end, the epistemological
problem of *how* to bring about understanding still underlies the need to cross
ontological borders, just as the migrant farmers must accept constant
destruction of their individual, lived worlds in order to arrive at the set of
social codes that will enable them to survive as a "people" in California.

In a sense, then, this "technique of building worlds" becomes
Steinbeck's own as he shapes the historical, mythical, and fictional materials
of his novel. The fissures which sometimes appear in the construction may
be seen as stress points at which the need to arouse the reader to some kind
of empathetic awareness takes precedence over the maintenance of
consistent narrative frames. At these points, the disorientation experienced
by the reader in the crossing of ontological boundaries becomes the
structural equivalent of that experienced by the migrant farmers as they cross
state borders toward the strange world of California.

Such moments of disorientation are experienced not only in reaction to
superimposed biblical and historical worlds. Ontological and discursive
fault lines also show up in another kind of world-collision within the text--
that experienced when intercalary material is conspicuously inserted into the
Joads' narrative. This method of ontological frame-breaking works to
dismantle the barriers erected around the interchapters as interpretive
commentaries on the more obviously fictional chapters. A simple example
of this occurs in the transition between chapters 3 and 4. In chapter 3, the
reader is shown the trials of a land turtle as it attempts to cross a highway,
inadvertently planting three wild oat seeds in the process. Here the narrative

scope rules out any reading of the chapter as a representation of broad historical reality; instead, it is marked as different from the Joads' narrative by the degree to which it stands as a prefiguration of their story. That this turtle enjoys an emblematic relationship with the soon-to-be-travelling Joad family has been observed before, and this relationship places its travels on a separate ontological plane. Yet this ontological distinction is questioned when, in the very next chapter, Tom comes across a land turtle on his way to his parents' farm. The resonance set up between this turtle and its emblematic forebear suggests that, in crossing the allegorical highway of chapter 3, the turtle may also have traversed an ontological boundary between narrative levels. Suddenly the distinction between inter- and fictional chapters appears to be based on nothing more than different rhetorical strategies for treating the same textual elements. In this case, the ability of the interchapters to offer authoritative commentary on the Joad world is threatened by their potential incorporation *into* that world.

This framebreaking technique has implications for the political and philosophical pronouncements central to some of the historical interchapters. One such statement occurs in chapter 14:

> This you may say of man--when theories change and crash, when schools, philosophies, when narrow dark alleys of thought, national, religious, economic, grow and disintegrate, man reaches, stumbles forward, painfully, mistakenly sometimes. Having stepped forward, he may slip back, but only half a step, never the full step back. This you may say and know it. (205)

There is perhaps no better way to undermine such an explicit truth claim than by giving it directly, as Steinbeck does, to a fictional character: "'the on'y thing you got to look at is that ever' time they's a little step fo'ward, she may slip back a little, but she never slips clear back'" (525). These are the words of Jim Casy's cellmate as recounted by Casy to Tom, and the number of narrative removes in his retelling is significant. In contrast to the commanding rhetoric of the interchapter, Casy's paraphrase is a reproduction in dialect of his cellmate's message, raising the question of how meaning might be altered through its forms of transmission. It therefore demonstrates particularly well how Steinbeck's novel situates itself on the line between a modernist and postmodernist aesthetic, for the descent of authorial commentary into the fictional frame opens up two distinct paths for critical interrogation.

Using McHale's distinction, a modernist reading would focus on the issue of transmission in order to examine how we arrive at conclusions about the world in which we live, and how they can be verified. Assuming the ontological integrity of a barrier between the authoritative historical sections of the text, and the fictional world of Tom and Casy, the mode of interrogation is essentially epistemological. It asks the question: how are Casy and Tom to learn the important truths of which the interchapters speak? This approach, or a variation on it, has been by far the more common critical approach to the novel. As I hope to have made clear, however, the boundary drawn between history and fiction on the basis of the interchapters is not necessarily impermeable. There exists the possibility that Casy's unnamed cellmate is Steinbeck himself, or at least the author of the intercalary statement Casy calls to mind. In this event the ontological distinctions between history and fiction, or "authoritative interchapter" and "interpreted fiction" can no longer be relied upon, since the author of the text would have at least one foot in the world of his characters. The critical question then becomes: in which world is the message of the interchapters to be interpreted as authoritative?

Following this line of questioning, the fact that Casy's paraphrase occurs immediately after the most direct political interchapter in the novel (the "jeremiad" of chapter 25) throws doubt on even that chapter's prophecy about the growing wrath of the migrant workers. Admittedly, to over-emphasize this doubt is to risk neutralizing much of the political urgency of the novel. But consider again what is being said at the very heart of the jeremiad chapter: "There is a crime here that goes beyond denunciation. There is a sorrow here that weeping cannot symbolize. There is a failure here that topples all our success" (477). To argue that these lines may not be an authoritative reading of events is simply to underline what their author is confessing: such magnitude of crime, of sorrow, is not to be contained in any political or symbolic representation. In a characteristic postmodern gesture, Steinbeck decodes the text in language that seems to bear all the responsibility of authoritative interpretation (the parallel structure of "There is . . . There is . . . There is . . ."), while admitting that no deep decoding is possible. Authority is offered and denied with the same gesture, leaving disorientation as a signal to the reader of the vast uprooting of a nation which the passage attempts to capture.

Where *The Grapes of Wrath* equivocates about the difference between history and fiction, it does so in part by emphasizing the timeless, mythical structures underlying its presentation of a historical context for the Joads' story. Yet these mythical references are not confined to the interchapters; indeed, biblical allusions within the Joad narrative itself have spawned a great deal of critical discussion about the allegorical intonations of the novel (see Timmerman 286, n. 1). Where the historical authority of the interchapters is rendered questionable by their revealed textuality, it is tempting to look to allegorical structures for an authoritative interpretive *text*. After all, the use of mythical allusion to give structure to an otherwise fragmented form is an important aesthetic trait of some modernist works. But allegory does not work so conveniently in *The Grapes of Wrath*. Steinbeck's allusion to biblical pretexts in the Joad story fail to act as authoritative "keys" to the text because they too, like the historical interventions, are forced to descend into the textual fray. Far from revealing any final truth about the fictional or historical events of the novel, biblical analogues are revised and reinterpreted as fictions themselves. This circumscribing of what Deborah Madsen calls a "hermeneutic circle" (15) is another important marker of the postmodernism of Steinbeck's text.

Madsen's study of postmodernist allegory locates its difference from traditional allegorical modes in part through its ontological footing. According to Madsen, all allegory is involved to some extent in the ontology of figuralism, an "historical mode of interpretation" which posits that temporal signs are never complete in their historical manifestations, but only fulfilled in God's eternal providential design (11). Traditional allegory is grounded in a figural hermeneutic that is ontologically stable because it is self-validating: "Spiritual truths are reserved for those who interpret spiritually. So figuralism encapsulates a basic epistemological dilemma: is the perceived figural pattern projected by the mind or does it reside in reality and, in either case, how can we know this with certainty?" (10). On this model, the figural order is validated by the authority believed to reside in the biblical pretext as a culturally important work (12). Postmodernist allegory, by contrast, does not have the luxury of this fixed ontological structure because in it, the authority of the pretext is questioned. Here a hermeneutic circle results from the fact that the pretext is portrayed as having the same fictive structure as that of allegory itself: it becomes both text *and* commentary (13). Hence "[t]he traditional exploration of metaphoric 'depth' becomes an investigation of the ontology of verbal surface" (12).

Steinbeck's use of biblical allusion to reinforce distinctly unChristian ideas (Railton 40) suggests that he viewed the Bible as a pretext not to be accepted without revision. In *The Grapes of Wrath*, some of that revision can be seen in the critique of allegorical structures dramatized by two of the novel's most poignant--and most controversial--scenes. I am thinking here of the final tableau and the scene in which the reverend Casy is killed by strike-busting vigilantes. At these moments, ontological disruptions occur when allegorical interpretation, normally the province of the reader, appears to be taken up by the characters themselves. This phenomenon is clearly marked by textual clues alerting the reader to an overlapping of fictional and biblical worlds; but beyond the sense of frame-breaking invoked, the effect is heightened by the possibility that the characters themselves are deliberately *acting out* allegorical roles, and revising their own relations to pretextual authority. In these two important scenes, the model by which certain characters and events are made to represent biblical analogues--establishing a metaphoric link between allegorical text and pretext--threatens to collapse into the pure verbal ontology of which Madsen speaks.

In Casy's death scene, this effect is so conspicuous as to tear the fabric of realistic narrative:

> A sharp call, "There they are!" Two flashlight beams fell on the men, caught them, blinded them. "Stand where you are." The voices came out of the darkness. "That's him. That shiny bastard. That's him."
> Casy stared blindly at the light. He breathed heavily. "Listen," he said. "You fellas don' know what you're doin'. . ." (527)

By this point in the novel the reader accepts Jim Casy's fairly obvious allegorical relation to Christ, suggested by their common initials and several comparisons made by Casy himself. Even the rhetorical signalling of Casy's role as a sacrificial figure has an earlier precedent.[11] But in this passage the anomalous description of him as "shiny," combined with his last words, which he repeats in the instant before his death, are so strongly suggestive that the metaphoric distance between Casy and Christ seems to vanish altogether. As in some of the interchapters, two worlds come shimmering into view: that fictional one in which Casy is killed, and that of the biblical analogues, in which Golgotha appears telescoped onto Gethsemane. The "revelation" that Casy dies as Christ is strangely hollow--even beside the point--in this scene, despite the fact that much of Casy's characterization has been to prepare the way for such a moment. This is because the central aesthetic effect of the passage, I believe, is a "flattening out" of revelation itself as a deep metaphorical structure. The effect of witnessing text and pretext in direct competition is a profound sense of decoding rendered *immanent*, so that no outside authority remains to establish a figural order whereby one set of symbols serves to interpret the other. Suddenly revelation goes in two directions, or nowhere at all. Moreover, Casy's repetition of Christ's words, and his (deliberate?) ducking down into the blow that kills him, suggest that he *knows* he has become a Christ figure. The reader, in turn, is stunned to find that his or her allegorical interpretation of the scene is rendered irrelevant by having already been done.[12]

In the pages that follow, it is debatable whether Steinbeck ever completely restores the metaphoric relationship between text and pretext which exists prior to Casy's death. In many ways the very attempt to restore this order is played out and then aborted at the level of the narrative by Tom, Ma, and Rose of Sharon, whose symbolic characterizations in the last hundred pages of the novel have often been criticized. Howard Levant, for example, complains that in the final quarter of the novel, "[c]haracters are fitted or forced into allegorical roles, heightened beyond the limits of credibility, to the point that they thin out or become frankly unbelievable. Scenes are developed almost solely as links in an allegorical pattern" (128). Yet this symbolic role-playing may be interpreted as the text's self-reflexive foregrounding of its own interrogation of allegorical structures. Clearly, Ma's repeated questioning of Tom about Casy's last words betrays her desire to reconstruct symbolic meaning from his death; but her refusal to articulate the meaning she finds, and her statement, "I wisht Granma could a heard" (535) finally relegates that reconstruction to a past generation. Even by the time of the government camp, Ma is able to reflect with wonder on the manner in which she and Pa were once able to interpret events on the stable world of the farm:

> "Remember what we'd always say at home? 'Winter's a-comin' early,' we said, when the ducks flew. Always said that, an' winter come when it was ready to come. But we always said, 'She's a-comin' early.' I wonder what we meant." (441-42)

With Grandma's death as toll for the passage into California comes the end of the old way of thinking, where signs can be read with regard to stable referents. The self-evident role-playing engaged in by the Joad family as the novel draws to its end exemplifies a world-building, as opposed to world-interpreting, aesthetic. Tom's retreat to the cave, Rose of Sharon's lying in the thicket, Tom and Ma's final meeting, and Uncle John's setting afloat of the stillborn baby dramatize a process of *constructing* meaning, rather than interpreting that which befalls them. This blossoming into self-made symbolic figures reflects a recognition that no pretext exists any longer to guide individual action: they must now create collectively both the text and commentary necessary for meaning.

This process of allegorical world-building reaches its thematic and structural climax in the final scene, the ontological resonances of which are captured in John Ditsky's influential summation: "The very theatricality of this final scene is . . . the end result of Steinbeck's careful structuring pattern. By it, the world of Joad and the greater family-of-man continuity of the interchapters are brought into an identical focus. . ." (219). The "theatricality" of Rose of Sharon's baring her breast to feed the starving man is the logical crest of ontological waves set in motion by the death of Casy. Ma Joad's deliberate orchestration of the whole tableau, from her knowing look at her daughter, to her ushering out of the rest of the family, is a self-reflexive commentary on Steinbeck's own artistic ordering of the scene. This is Ma's scene as much as it is Rose of Sharon's, as much as it Steinbeck's, for in it she proves worthy of her first, goddess-like characterization. In her sudden alignment with Steinbeck's authorial hand, she exemplifies the "superhuman understanding" that enables her to build, out of "inadequate materials" (*GW* 100), a new world with new hope for survival. In the process, Rose of Sharon is not so much "revealed" as the Madonna, or an Earth Mother, as by her "mysterious smile" she betrays her knowledge of *acting out* such roles, implicitly mocking their attempts to decode her triumphant act. The allegorical framework is exploded utterly by this smile, in which the relationship between text and pretext is consummated and obliterated.

   To argue that Steinbeck is in some way a "prophetic postmodernist" is, presumably, to have in mind a postmodern author or text he might be taken to have "prophesied." Some of the texts I have referred to in my reading of *The Grapes of Wrath* have been pointing at Thomas Pynchon to fill that role, either because they were written as explications of his work, or because his novels exemplify particularly well many of the key characteristics of postmodernist fiction. Even apart from this, however, there are good reasons for comparing Steinbeck and Pynchon, despite the fact that they are often presented on opposite ends of the spectrum of twentieth century American literature.[13] Both writers show a near-obsessive concern for the plight of the dispossessed and disinherited; both portray, and have a particular interest in, scientific discourse as a gloss on fiction-writing (marine biology in Stein-beck's case; thermal dynamics, rocketry, and just about everything else in Pynchon); and both engage in denunciations of California as a promised land (in Pynchon's *The Crying of Lot 49* and *Vineland*). Furthermore, Pynchon may be seen to invoke the famous Rose of Sharon tableau in *The Crying of Lot 49* as a reference point for his novel's postmodern portrayal of "revelation."

   By the time the reader of *The Crying of Lot 49* nears the end of that novel, the Tristero conspiracy pursued by Oedipa Maas, if it exists at all, has grown large enough to cast a shadow over the entire historical/geographical evolution of America since the civil war. What began for Oedipa as elementary detective work tracking down the assets of deceased California real estate mogul, Pierce Inverarity, has become a web of clues pointing to the existence of an underground postal system uniting a legion of disinherited Americans. Yet as the novel's end draws near (at which point-- so the first-time reader believes--the truth about these clues will finally be revealed), Oedipa begins to rethink many assumptions about her home state and country in light of her suspicions about the Tristero. The California to which she returns in her memories takes a shape familiar to readers of *The Grapes of Wrath*:

> She remembered now old Pullman cars, left where the money'd run out or the customers vanished, amid green farm flatnesses where clothes hung, smoke lazed out of jointed pipes. . . . She thought of other, immobilized freight cars, where the kids sat on the floor planking and sang back, happy as fat, whatever came over the mother's pocket radio; of other squatters who stretched canvas for lean-to's behind smiling billboards along all the highways, or slept in junkyards in the stripped shells of wrecked Plymouths. . . . She remembered drifters she had listened to, Americans speaking their language carefully, scholarly, as if they were in exile from somewhere else invisible yet congruent with the cheered land she lived in. . . .[14] (179-80)

Read as an oblique allusion to the final home of the Joads, this passage shows a "congruency" with the world of Steinbeck's novel that is not unique in *The Crying of Lot 49*.[15] But that suburban Oedipa should traverse--if only in memory--the same terrain as the Joads is particularly significant, given the sense of impending revelation that permeates this late stage of Pynchon's text. The central question to be answered as the novel draws to a close is whether, in nurturing her own suspicions, Oedipa's search throughout urban California has led her to conceive nothing more than a complex paranoid plot, or whether it has nurtured, instead, her awareness of a secret community of the disinherited. In the latter case, it is only fitting that such an act of communal mothering should establish for her a symbolic sisterhood with Rose of Sharon.

Indeed, Oedipa's problem of verification has already been cast in maternal metaphors. Just prior to this vision, the physical symptoms produced by her growing anxiety are portrayed as a strange form of morning sickness: "Her toothaches got worse, she dreamed of disembodied voices from whose malignance there was no appeal. . . .Your gynecologist has no test for what she was pregnant with" (175). And more significant is an earlier scene that recalls directly Rose of Sharon's communal gesture. Distressed by the ubiquity of the Tristero symbol in San Narciso, Oedipa journeys north to San Francisco, hoping that there her suspicions will "disintegrate quietly" (109). After a night of wandering alone through the city, however, Oedipa finds San Francisco to be just as infested with the muted post-horn as Inverarity's hometown. At last, unable to abort the growing "foetus" inside her, the next morning finds her comforting an old, dying sailor who bears a tattoo of the Tristero symbol on his hand:

> She was overcome all at once by a need to touch him, as if she could not believe in him, or would not remember him, without it. Exhausted, hardly knowing what she was doing, she came the last three steps and sat, took the man in her arms, actually held him, gazing out of her smudged eyes down the stairs, back into the morning. She felt wetness against her breast and saw that he was crying again. He hardly cried but tears came as if being pumped. "I can't help," she whispered, rocking him, "I can't help." (126)

This is certainly the most touching scene in Pynchon's novel, and the similarities to Steinbeck's tableau are unmistakeable. But where Rose of Sharon's "tired body" is still capable of nourishing the old man, Oedipa's breast is dampened only by his tears, symbolic of her inability to save him. For Oedipa, obsessed with reading everything in relation to the Tristero, her personal act of compassion does not make the transition into symbolic nurturing because she has not been able to break the "barrier of pregnancy" (GW 129) overcome by Rose of Sharon. In Rose of Sharon's case, it is the stillbirth of her baby that allows her milk to become the symbolic nourishment of her community. When, in letting go of the sailor, Oedipa feels "reluctant as if he were her own child" (127), it is her maternal *affection* (more for the Tristero tattoo on his hand than for him) that ironically prevents her from helping him. As Mark Conroy observes about this scene, Oedipa's failure is her refusal to recognize in the sailor's fate the "loss of reassuring, fixed and rational meaning itself" (66). Pynchon's evocation of Steinbeck's tableau serves to foreshadow the fact that, even in the end, Oedipa will *not* escape the confines of the tower she envisioned herself trapped within at the beginning of the novel (21). She is ultimately unwilling to respond to the man outside the structure of her "pregnancy," in which lies--or so she believes--all possible configurations of meaning.

Those configurations are crystallized in the "symmetrical four" alternatives she faces just prior to her vision of the abandoned freight cars. Either Oedipa has stumbled upon a real underground communication system, or she has hallucinated such a system, or an elaborate plot has been devised to deceive her, or she has imagined such a plot (170-71). The reader, however, senses that this polarization of choices has *not* been inevitable; instead, it has arisen, as the sailor-scene suggests, through Oedipa's fear "that her revelation not expand beyond a certain point" (166). Oedipa is fearful of the birth itself, afraid of its revealing any of the explanations she posits. This inability to bring her baby to term is the only revelation at the end of *The Crying of Lot 49*, which, in its use of tableau as self-reflexive commentary, again recalls Steinbeck's novel.

Like *The Grapes of Wrath*, Pynchon's novel ends famously without resolving its central plot. It presents instead a theatrical tableau which comments self-reflexively on that plot, challenging the very process of decoding. Oedipa, having learned that a possible member of the Tristero community is interested in purchasing Inverarity's stamp collection, decides to make one last attempt at discovering the truth. She attends the auction at which the collection is to be sold, hoping to find in the mysterious bidder the answer she has been seeking. But where Steinbeck's final scene explodes the allegorical frameworks of his novel by emphasizing the constructedness of meaning in self-conscious role-play, Pynchon's tableau emphasizes its own textuality. In it meaning remains frozen forever in its descent:

> Oedipa sat alone, toward the back of the room, looking at the napes of necks, trying to guess which one was her target, her enemy, perhaps her proof. An assistant closed the heavy door on the lobby windows and the sun. She heard a lock snap shut; the sound echoed a moment. Passerine spread his arms in a gesture that seemed to belong to the priesthood of some remote culture; perhaps to a descending angel. Oedipa settled back, to await the crying of lot 49. (183)

Here "revelation" is simply a reiteration of the novel's title—a reversion to the essential textuality of Oedipa's whole problem, which is not to be dissolved in the incarnation of any transcendant Word. Where Rose of Sharon plays the Madonna, Oedipa waits for a Gabriel who never arrives.

Thus both tableaus work toward a "flattening out" of revelation itself. As we have seen, Ma's closing of the barn door on Rose of Sharon is a self-reflexive commentary on Steinbeck's artistic structuring of the novel, in which the reader's synthesis of the historical/allegorical frameworks and the story of the Joads is finally preempted by the Joads themselves. Pynchon calls that process to mind through the nameless assistant who locks Oedipa into the auction room, but the terms are reversed. Oedipa, always the seeker after meaning, is finally unable to reach it. It is the reader who, though limited to Oedipa's interpretation of events throughout most of the novel, is alone able to see the textual "revelation" in the final line. Where interpretive reading gets the equivalent of a wink from Rose of Sharon, it becomes both means and end in *The Crying of Lot 49*. Ultimately, in Pynchon's novel, it reveals only more text, more reading, and a return to its own beginning.

This essay is an original contribution to this text.

Notes

1. Charles Newman argues that the "postmodern mentality" is a reaction against not only the "First Revolution" of modernist art, but also--and more importantly--against the "Second Revolution" of its critical transmission (27-35). To the extent that these Revolutions have become indistinguishable, "[t]he very act of fiction now implies an act of criticism, insofar as fiction is seen as a series of transformations in modes of thinking" (116). Brian McHale echoes this notion in his discussion of Pynchon's *Gravity's Rainbow*, which "holds the mirror up not so much to Nature as to Reading" (1992, 87).

2. The second of these, "John Steinbeck and Modernism," has been reprinted in Ditsky, *Critical Essays*, and I refer to that version, unable to obtain the original. This essay has also been revised in French's more recent book (1994). Notably absent in the latest revision are a number of speculations about the "postmodern sensibility" which was not, in 1976, buttressed by any group of representative works (1989, 161).

3. For French, it marks Steinbeck's attempt to go beyond modernism, which his later work shies away from in returning to a less successful premodernist mode (1989, 162). For DeMott, the novel effects Steinbeck's shift from social realism to metafiction through its "repugnant posterity," provoking in him an artistic "backlash" against its popular success (xliii).

4. For speculation about the politically subversive potential of best-selling postmodern novels, see Hutcheon 1988, 202-03.

5. One of the more blatant examples of this is Harold Bloom's assertion that "Steinbeck suffers from too close a comparison with Hemingway" (1). For a detailed refutation of this criticism, see Heavilin 1990.

6. This quote is presented in a summary of an undated letter from Steinbeck to Elizabeth Otis, in Steinbeck and Wallsten 162. DeMott places the date of the letter at March 23, 1938 (xxvii).

7. These lines are taken from a letter written by Steinbeck to Columbia undergraduate Herbert Sturz in February, 1953. The entire text of the letter can be found in Dircks 91-92. As she notes, it is Steinbeck's only explicit statement on the purpose of the interchapters (86).

8. All page references to Steinbeck's novel are to the 1992 Penguin edition, and will be prefaced GW where necessary.

9. Brian McHale describes this process as a relativizing of historical reality through exactly the techniques or methods used to establish it (1987, 197). For Linda Hutcheon, "[f]iction and history are narratives distinguished by their frames, frames which historiographic metafiction first establishes and then crosses..." (1988, 109).

10. John Timmerman further supports the ontological implications of this conflict: "Biblical allusion in a literary work evokes a secondary and anagogic imaginative sphere that is whole in its own right..." (34).

11. This rhetorical signalling occurs back at the Hooverville, when Casy intervenes to allow Floyd, a group agitator, to escape the police: "The deputy, sitting on the ground, raised his gun again and then, suddenly, from the group of men, the Reverend Casy stepped" (361).

12. Having said that, and given that this *is* an essay on Steinbeck and postmodernism, I feel less ashamed than I perhaps should to present another analogue for this scene. I confess I have never been able to dissociate the description of Casy ducking *into* the vigilante's pick-handle from Alec Guinness's similar act of self-sacrifice as Obi-Wan Kenobi in George Lucas' *Star Wars*. There, in a duel with Darth Vader, Kenobi deliberately puts up his lightsaber so that his apprentice, Luke Skywalker, can see him cut down. There has, not surprisingly, been little work done to establish the influence of *The Grapes of Wrath* on the *Star Wars* trilogy, but the comparison is not that ridiculous. Consider: the saga begins with Luke's unexpected discovery of an old hermit--a figure from Luke's childhood--not far from his aunt and uncle's farm. This hermit, Ben Kenobi, subsequently instructs the young Luke as they travel (with their interstellar "family") in a rickety spaceship toward a planet threatened by overwhelming evil. When they arrive, they find the world of their hopes already destroyed by that evil. Not long after, trapped in Vader's Death Star, Ben decides to leave the "family" to conduct a private mission that will allow them to escape, and when Luke finally meets up with him again, it is only to watch him die. Luke then picks up where Ben left off, and two sequels later we discover that hope for the future lies not only in Luke, but in his sister, Carrie Fisher/Princess Leia, who even wears her hair in a braided crown like Rose of Sharon. A deflation of Steinbeck's epic? As the evil Emperor would say: "So be it!"

13. Brad Leithauser describes *The Grapes of Wrath* as a "middle-brow" attempt at the Great American Novel, antithetical in style and political commitment to more contemporary, "Pynchonesque" examples (90). Robert Con Davis speculates that students accustomed to writers like Pynchon or Hunter S. Thompson are not prepared to understand Steinbeck (1).

14. All page references to Pynchon's novel are to the 1990 Perennial edition, and will be prefaced CL where necessary.

15. Another example would be Mucho Maas's traumatization as a used car dealer in light of Steinbeck's intercalary chapter:

The sight of sawdust, even pencil shavings, made him [Mucho] wince, his own kind being known to use it for hushing sick transmissions, and though he dieted he could still not as Oedipa did use honey to sweeten his coffee for like all things viscous it distressed him, recalling too poignantly what is often mixed with oil to ooze dishonest into gaps between piston and cylinder wall...

Yet at least he had believed in the cars. Maybe to excess: how could he not, seeing people poorer than him come in, Negro, Mexican, cracker, a parade seven days a week, bringing the most godawful of trade-ins: motorized, metal extensions of themselves, of their families and what their whole lives must be like, out there so naked for anybody, a stranger like himself, to look at... and when the cars were swept out you had to look at the actual residue of these lives, and there was no way of telling what things had been truly refused . . . and what had simply (perhaps tragically) been lost. . . . (4-5)

References

Bloom, Harold. 1988. Introduction. *Modern Critical Interpretations: John Steinbeck's The Grapes of Wrath.* New York: Chelsea, 1988.

Conroy, Mark. 1989. "The American Way and Its Double in *The Crying of Lot 49.*" *Pynchon Notes* 24-25: 45-70.

Davis, Robert Con, ed. 1982. Introduction. *Twentieth Century Interpretations* of *"The Grapes of Wrath."* Englewood Cliffs: Prentice Hall. 1-11.

DeMott, Robert. 1992. Introduction. *The Grapes of Wrath.* By John Steinbeck. New York: Penguin. vii-xliv.

Dircks, Phyllis T. 1991. "Steinbeck's Statement on the Inner Chapters of *The Grapes of Wrath.*" *Steinbeck Quarterly* 24.3-4: 86-94.

Ditsky, John. 1979. "*The Grapes of Wrath*: A Reconsideration." *Southern Humanities Review* 13: 215-20.

Fish, Stanley. 1992. "The Common Touch, or, One Size Fits All." *The Politics of Liberal Education.* Ed. Darryl J. Gless and Barbara Herrnstein Smith. Durham and London: Duke UP. 241-66.

French, Warren. 1976a. "Presidential Message: Steinbeck and Modernism." *Steinbeck Quarterly* 9.3-4: 69-71.

-----. 1976b. "John Steinbeck and Modernism (A Speculation on His Contribution to the Development of the Twentieth-Century American Sensibility)." *Critical Essays on Steinbeck's The Grapes of Wrath.* Ed. John Ditsky. Boston: G. K. Hall, 1989. 152-62.

-----. 1994. *John Steinbeck's Fiction Revisited.* New York: Twain.

Heavilin, Barbara A. 1990. Rev. of *Modern Critical Interpretations: John Steinbeck's The Grapes of Wrath,* ed. Harold Bloom. *Steinbeck Quarterly* 23.3-4: 96-102. Howarth, William. 1990. "The Mother of Literature:

Journalism and *The Grapes of Wrath*." *New Essays on The Grapes of Wrath.* Ed. David Wyatt. Cambridge: Cambridge UP. 71-99.

Hutcheon, Linda. 1988. *A Poetics of Postmodernism: History, Theory, Fiction.* New York and London: Routledge.

Leithauser, Brad. Aug. 21, 1989. "The Flare of Want." Rev. of *The Grapes of Wrath*, by John Steinbeck, and *Working Days: The Journals of the Grapes of Wrath 1938-1941*, ed. Robert DeMott. *New Yorker* 90-93.

Levant, Howard. 1974. *The Novels of John Steinbeck: A Critical Study.* Columbia: U of Missouri P.

Madsen, Deborah. 1991. *The Postmodernist Allegories of Thomas Pynchon.* New York: St. Martin's.

McHale, Brian. 1987. *Postmodernist Fiction.* New York and London: Methuen.

-----. 1992. *Constructing Postmodernism.* London and New York: Routledge.

Newman, Charles. 1985. *The Post-Modern Aura: The Act of Fiction in an Age of Inflation.* Evanston: Northwestern UP.

Owens, Louis. 1989. *The Grapes of Wrath: Trouble in the Promised Land.* Boston: Twayne.

Owens, Louis and Torres, Hector. 1989. "Dialogic Structure and Levels of Discourse in Steinbeck's *The Grapes of Wrath*." *Arizona Quarterly* 45: 75-94.

Pynchon, Thomas. 1966. *The Crying of Lot 49.* New York: Harper, 1990.

Railton, Stephen. 1990. "Pilgrim's Politics: Steinbeck's Art of Conversion." *New Essays on The Grapes of Wrath.* Ed. David Wyatt. Cambridge: Cambridge UP. 27-46.

Steinbeck, Elaine and Wallsten, Robert. 1975. *Steinbeck: A Life in Letters.* New York: Viking.

Steinbeck, John. 1939. *The Grapes of Wrath.* Introd. Robert DeMott. New York: Penguin, 1992.

-----. 1955. "A Letter on Criticism." *Steinbeck and His Critics: A Record of Twenty-five Years.* Ed. E. W. Tedlock and C. V. Wickers. Albuquerque: U of New Mexico P, 1957. 52-53.

Timmerman, John H. 1986. *John Steinbeck's Fiction: The Aesthetics of the Road Taken.* Norman: U of Oklahoma P.

Steinbeck and the Critics:
A Study in Artistic Self-Concept

Michael Meyer

John Steinbeck and Stephen King do not seem to have a lot in common. The first is known for classic fiction, novels, and short stories that are required reading in America's middle and secondary schools and as the winner of the Nobel Prize in 1962. The second is a cult hero, a prolific composer of mystery and horror stories, and an icon of contemporary pop culture. His newest works are seemingly guaranteed to be instant best sellers, but they are seldom assigned as classroom reading or material for serious study. Yet these authors share one specific character trait: an unstable artistic self image, causing them to take negative critical reception of their respective works as personal attacks. For example, both authors aspired to greatness, yet both made it clear that in their opinion it was their writing that mattered, not the fame or fortune that accompanied it. At one time, both were criticized as mere hacks, authors who churned out inferior prose for inferior minds; in addition, both were writers with a following who, after attaining initial recognition by a reading public, were able to produce best sellers time and time again, regardless of the topic. In fact, their books seemed to sell on the basis of reputation rather than on any intrinsic excellence of their own.

Finally, it was said of both that success corrupted them and that the quality of their writing deteriorated as they began to work for cash rewards rather than out of artistic desire for excellence. Of course, both denied such motives. In *Nightmares and Dreamscapes*, King stated: "But it *isn't* about money, no matter what the glossy tabloids may say, and it's not about selling out, as the more arrogant critics really seem to believe" (6). Similarly, Steinbeck refused to acknowledge that such petty concerns motivated him, asserting that fame is "a pain in the ass" and that he was "scared to death of popularity. It has ruined nearly everyone I know"[1] (Benson 318). Steinbeck also denied that monetary wealth was his goal, stating in his "Rationale," written for E. W. Tedlock, Jr. and C. V. Wicker's 1957 *Steinbeck and His Critics: A Record of Twenty-five Years*:[2]

> My basic rationale might be that I like to write. I feel good when I am doing it. . . . I find joy in the texture and tone and rhythms of words and sentences. . . . Writing may be simply a method or technique for communication with other individuals; and its stimulus, the loneliness we are born to. In writing, perhaps we hope to achieve companionship. What some people find in religion, a writer may find in his craft or whatever it is--absorption of the small and frightened and lonely into the whole and complete, a kind of breaking through to glory. (309)

King and Steinbeck further shared a belief that the best writers have a moral goal. And both felt that they did not deserve the hostility of reviewers and were incredulous at the negative reactions and comments by an elitist few in the literary community, who attempted to evaluate and quantify their success. Not surprisingly, their reactions to this kind of criticism are almost identical. In *Nightmares and Dreamscapes*, for example, King states:

> In reviews of every long novel I have written, . . . I have been accused of overwriting. In some cases the criticisms have merit; in others they are just the ill-tempered yappings of men and women who have accepted the literary anorexia of the last thirty years with a puzzling (to me, at least) lack of discussion and dissent. (5)

No doubt Steinbeck would have agreed with King's labeling critics the "self-appointed deacons of the Church of Latter Day American Literature" and his complaining about their individual tendencies "to regard generosity with suspicion, texture with dislike, and any broad literary stroke with outright hate" (*Nightmares and Dreamscapes* 5).

Yet up to this point there has been no in-depth analysis of the effect of critical reactions on either author, though it can be safely said that both considered the harsh negative reaction they received to be not only unwarranted but also unfair. This negativity also undoubtedly served to deflate their egos and to damage their self-image, causing a fluctuating reaction as they either defiantly denied the attack's credibility or submitted to humiliating acceptance of their failures. In King's case, his hostility and anger seem rather straightforward because he vented them in the prefaces and afterwords to his novels, sometimes even in the texts. The same cannot, however, be said of Steinbeck. While King's attitudes can be easily extrapolated by looking at novels such as *The Dark Half* and *Misery*, where his writer figures (presumably like King himself) struggle with the critics' perceived differentiation between classic and so-called popular fiction, Steinbeck's struggle seldom manifests itself in his texts.   Rather, his reactions to criticism appear in letters, interviews, and journals, and, unlike King's, his responses are more difficult to ascertain because they are inconsistent.

This essay, then, attempts an in-depth analysis of Steinbeck's comments in interviews and correspondence and suggests that Steinbeck's reactions, unlike King's, follow a developing pattern, a circular movement which reflects Steinbeck's inherent insecurity and low self-esteem as a person and as a professional. The pattern consists of four stages as Steinbeck matured from a naive and unpresuming young writer into a mistrusting and cynical older man. Initially believing that critics sincerely intended only to draw attention to serious flaws which needed to be corrected, Steinbeck, in his later years, changed his mind and began to believe that they were intentionally malicious, desiring to hurt and demean rather than to foster improvement.

As time went on, Steinbeck also realized that critics were even less perceptive than the general reading public, who lacked the educational background and credentials for engaging in literary analysis and interpretation. An examination of Steinbeck's own words shows an ever-building tension in his relationship with critics and reviewers. As the antagonism mounted, Steinbeck was forced to employ different techniques in his attempt to come to terms with his detractors, moving from an initial humble acceptance to hostility and antagonism. Steinbeck then feigned apathy or lack of interest before returning to an earlier self-deprecating mode that was accompanied by despair and waning confidence in his writing talent.

The first stage of Steinbeck's interaction with critics seems to have lasted from 1921 till the publication of *Tortilla Flat,* Steinbeck's first best-seller, in 1935. For example, in a 1924 letter to Carl Wilhelmson, a college classmate, Steinbeck wrote that all their "thinking ponderously and seeking and finding" resulted merely in "a glorified question mark."[3] Later he wrote,

"For every favorable criticism, I get four knocks on the head. Oh well, who cares?" (LIL 7, 8)

Generally, Steinbeck's rather puerile reaction to these "unwarranted" putdowns was to behave as though he did not care and was not depressed when his work was misunderstood. Yet other letters suggest that this apparently stolid approach was merely a front and that Steinbeck was indeed cognizant of the devastating effect negative critics were having on his production. In 1928 he wrote to his close friend, Carlton "Dook" Sheffield: "I shall write good novels, but hereafter I ride Pegasus with a saddle and martingale, for I am afraid he will rear and kick, and I am not the sure steady horseman I once was.. I do not take joy in the unmanageable horse anymore. I want a hackney of tried steadiness" (*LIL*, 12).

The literary allusion, of course, suggests that though he was originally an imaginative and innovative writer, Steinbeck had somehow been influenced by critics to rein in his fantastical "winged" ideas and to replace them with more commonplace ones, those associated with a less fanciful farm horse who is harnessed to the everyday, a tried and true steed who is trustworthy, but one who represents an artist who is not only unwilling to break tradition but who will also never soar into experimentation. Steinbeck was learning that taking chances was risky and that it was safer to follow the status quo as a writer than to endure the wrath of reviewers who were leery of artists who broke new ground.

After the publication of his first novel, *Cup of Gold*, in 1930, Steinbeck wrote his friend Amasa (Ted) Miller and suggested that the publishers had wrongly described the book and that the reviewers were misled by the jacket and cover blurb into thinking it was an adventure story. Initially, he thus tried to write off negative judgments by attributing them to such misunderstandings rather than his own artistic flaws.

It is evident that this way of dealing with critics was somewhat helpful in warding off Steinbeck's fear of failure and enabling him to recover from bouts of self-doubt. Thus, he states in a 1930 letter to a friend that "nobody seems to want my work. That doesn't injure me, but it must be having a definite effect on you that you are handling such a dud." But he can also state a few months later: "I shall be so good that I cannot be ignored" (*LIL* 26, 29). As time passed, the humble young man was gradually gaining confidence and putting aside his feelings of inadequacy. Witness this December letter of the same year to Amasa "Ted" Miller: "From my recent efforts, it has been borne to me that I am not capable of writing the very best yet. I have no doubt I shall be able to do so in the future, but at present, I cannot. It remains to be seen whether I can write the very worst (*LIL* 32).

Even though he was steadily improving at his craft, Steinbeck still had a lingering sense of insecurity about his writing.   He relates his growing depression at his "fallow" days: "I have had a couple of fallow days-- absolute disgust and lack of faith in my own work and inability to go on" (*LIL* 49).   Despite his denial that negative critical reactions affected his psyche, he wrote Amasa Miller: "I wonder you don't lose faith in my future. Everyone else does. For myself, I haven't brains enough to quit. Maybe you haven't brains enough to get out from under the wreck" (*LIL* 54). Later to Sheffield he continued to confess his latent feelings of inadequacy and fear of failure: "Now as always--humility and terror. Fear that the working of my pen cannot capture the grinding of my brain" (*LIL* 64).

In a 1933 letter to Wilhelmson, Steinbeck continued his admission of failure at his craft: "A couple of years ago I realized I was not the material of which great artists are made and that I was rather glad I wasn't" (*LIL* 87). Nevertheless, as he confided in Edith Wagner, he made every effort to "try to write what seems to me true. If it isn't true for other people, then it isn't good art. But I've only my own eyes to see with. I won't use the eyes of other people" (*LIL* 90).   Steinbeck was beginning to see, though only superficially at this point, that there was little evidence that critics offered competent readings of great literature. Though they claimed great expertise, Steinbeck now realized that they often had misconceptions about greatness and frequently made significant mistakes in interpreting and evaluating artistic success. He wrote to Mavis Macintosh, his editor: "I notice that a number of reviewers (what lice they are) complain that I deal particularly in the subnormal and the psychopathic. If said critics would inspect their neighbors within one block, they would find that I deal with the normal and the ordinary" (*LIL* 68).

After *To a God Unknown* appeared in 1933, he asserted that his work was far broader and deeper than it was usually conceived to be and said of the novel's reception, "It is probable that no one will know it for 200 years. It will be confused, analyzed, analogized, criticized, and none of our fine critics will know what is happening" (*TA* 260). Yet at the same time he demonstrated his vacillating attitude about its quality by writing to Mavis Macintosh:

> I think I told you in an earlier letter that the imperfections of the Unknown God had bothered me ever since I first submitted it for publication. In consequence of this uneasiness, your announcement of the book's failure to find a public is neither unwelcome nor unpleasant to me. . . . I shall rewrite it. . . . Whether my idea of excellence coincides with editors' ideas remains to be seen. Certainly I shall make no effort to "popularize" the

story. . . . Thank you for your help. I am an unprofitable client. *(LIL* 45-
46)

Despite his growing knowledge of the inadequacy of the critical response,
at this stage in his career he claimed to be "impervious to ridicule" and
tended to blame his disinterest in critical commentary on what may be
"simply dullness and stupidity" rather than on the misperceptions of the
critics themselves (*LIL* 92). Using the self-deprecating term "bum," stating
that his sister calls him a "fake," and admitting that his family was "ashamed:
of him, Steinbeck remarks about himself and his critics: "If I had the drive
of ridicule I might make something of myself" (*LIL* 94).

After the publication of *Tortilla Flat* in 1935, however, there appears to
be less self-doubt and humility in Steinbeck's correspondence as a second
stage of his interaction with critics begins. During this stage he began to
question the clarity of his plots and the framework of his writing. He even
considered the possibility that it might be necessary to spell things out more
clearly since so many reviewers seemed to miss what he considered to be
very obvious themes, allusions, and structures. Although he was frustrated
that critics seemed to approach his work with preconceived opinions or from
wrong angles (e. g., their suggestion that there was "an ideal communist or
a thoroughly damnable communist" whose views should have been
presented in *In Dubious Battle*), he declared that his "opposition caused him
to work well" (*LIL* 108), trying desperately to transform negatives into
positives.

When *Tortilla Flat* won the Commonwealth Club of California award
in 1935, Steinbeck felt as though deserved recognition had finally arrived,
but he still found it difficult to dismiss negative self-concepts as a writer.
Deciding not to attend the ceremony, he wrote to critic Joseph Henry
Jackson that his whole life had been "poisoned with egotism, a reverse
egotism, or course, beginning with self-consciousness" (*LIL* 119) and urged
the book reviewer to explain his absence since he felt somehow unworthy
of the honor. In what was to become a typical reaction to praise, Steinbeck
also downplayed his achievement, calling *Tortilla Flat* "a secondrate book,
written for relaxation" and wondering why it had caused "this fuss,"
marveling that "people are actually taking it seriously" (*LIL* 111).

By the publication of *In Dubious Battle* in 1936, this brief second stage
which had combined humility with a sense of challenge seemed to be
drawing to a close. Instead Steinbeck entered a third phase in which he
became increasingly hostile toward what he considered to be inexcusable:
the educated readers' lack of perception while so-called lay readers

manifested deeper understandings with relatively few prompts. Backing away from his earlier impulse to simplify or clarify his writing in order to make it more accessible, Steinbeck now seemed to abhor the concept of "spelling the message out." As his biographer, Jackson Benson, notes, Steinbeck came to believe that "art should be a mystery, and that mystery should not be diluted or dissipated by outside discussion or explanation" (*TA* 232). Soon he developed a pattern of refusing to comment about his intentions in fiction because "he feared it might contaminate his art and weaken its integrity" (*TA* 233). According to Benson, his tenet became "No matter how many people misunderstand or how often, an artist must keep his mouth shut" (*TA* 233).

Yet Steinbeck found it difficult not to react to what he considered misguided and uninformed reactions, especially Mary McCarthy's review of *In Dubious Battle* that, he maintained, only served to reveal her own ignorance and misunderstanding of the shaping influences and literary allusions which permeated its text. Steadily Steinbeck's reaction toward such negative reviews and criticism became angry and his replies cynical and charged with hostility. Benson notes that the critics who disturbed Steinbeck most were those who seemed to react with the "cocksure certainty of the parlor theoretician who never got his hands dirty." (*TA,* 324)

Steinbeck's move toward hostility was gradual and often veiled in wry, sarcastic humor. For example, in 1936 when *Of Mice and Men* was in its composition stages, Steinbeck wrote his agent Elizabeth Otis to inform her that the manuscript had been devoured by his setter pup, jokingly suggesting that "the poor little fellow may have been acting critically," an analogue to his critics who he felt arbitrarily devoured his artistic production and spat it out in little pieces (*LIL* 124). When the play version of the novella won the New York Critics Circle award, Steinbeck continued to use animal imagery to describe his relationship with reviewers, describing himself as "a little timid to be lying down with the lion" (*LIL* 164).

By the time *The Grapes of Wrath*[4] appeared in 1939, the negative press seemed to send Steinbeck into a returning sense of depression; unfortunately, his hostile replies in his correspondence also became less and less effective in protecting him from a feeling of failure and fear that "his success was a fluke and only temporary" (*TA* 331). His self-confidence fluctuated wildly after the publication of *GW*, even though he had correctly anticipated that critics would not be kind in their evaluations of the work. Unfortunately, as Benson points out, many of the attacks were directed at Steinbeck personally rather than at the text, and "of all novelists, he was probably the least able to shrug his shoulders and let the venom run off his back" (*TA* 418).

Certainly Steinbeck was aware of his vulnerability, and the one thing that sustained him was the fact that many lay readers of *GW* seemed to understand what more sophisticated reviewers missed. He wrote to Pascal Covici, his editor: "Do you notice that nearly every reviewer hates the general chapters? They hate to be told anything outright. . . .Fortunately I'm not writing for reviewers. . . .I think probably it is the usual revolt against something they aren't used to" (*LIL* 182-83). Similarly, in a letter to Elizabeth Otis he wrote: "Amazing that these critics don't seem know what that last chapter is about One says superficial and another sentimental, and it is neither. Well, I know that some people do understand it and that's enough" (*TA* 395)

The negative critical reception of *The Moon is Down* in 1942 and of *Cannery Row* in 1944 led Steinbeck to respond that "there is a time in every writer's career when the critics are gunning for him to whittle him down. This is my stage for that" (*LIL* 278). Set in Monterey, a town near Steinbeck's childhood home, *Cannery Row*, like *GW,* again rubbed native Californians the wrong way as many area residents saw the portrait of Mac and the boys, Doc, and the girls at the Palace Flophouse as derogatory and uncomplimentary to their hometowns.

Steinbeck wrote to Covici, lamenting that "the better people in town don't know whether they like *Cannery Row* or not. They are waiting to see what other people think. This attitude is always true of better people. The critics say at once that it is not true to nature and that it is in bad taste. In nature two things do not occur–the wheel and good taste. So what do they want" (*LIL* 278)? Later, he further confided in Covici: "What saddens me is the active hatred of writers and pseudowriters around here. . . . There is a deep and active jealousy out here that makes me very sad" (*LIL* 279-80).

As Steinbeck read the reviewers' comments, it became obvious that once again they had ignored much of his careful planning and layered meaning. Benson speculates that "in the long run what bothered him most was the failure of reviewers to get his point, to address the real issues of his books, which he saw as conceptual and philosophical" (*TA* 593). Such misunderstandings, in Benson's opinion, began to eat away at him, creating a troubled, restless, and unsure writer from what had already been a troubled, restless man.

Steinbeck was most frustrated that now reviewers were disappointed by his failure to produce another *GW* and that they failed to see beneath the surface of his comic novel serious social and moral commentary:

> Are they [critics] somehow the lowest common denominator? If in
> pictures, the thing must be slanted for the nine year old mind, in books
> they must be slanted for the critics and it seems to amount to the same
> thing. Far from being the sharpest readers, they are the dullest. . . . Don't
> you remember the years when those same critics were sneering at every
> book--the same books incidentally that they now remember with awe. No,
> I feel all of the old contempt for them and it is a good feeling. (*TA* 562,
> 563)

The publication of *The Wayward Bus* brought still further tension between
Steinbeck and his critics, but he was beginning to develop yet another way
to deal with the negative press—cultivating a belief that controversy created
higher sales and more discussion of issues. In a letter to Jack Wagner, he
wrote:

> I should never read reviews, good or bad. They just confuse me
> because they cancel each other out and end up by meaning nothing.
> I should let them alone. The book [*The Wayward Bus*] is getting
> good notices mostly here, although a couple of my congenital enemies
> are sniping. This is good for a book. The more arguments the better.
> (*LIL* 296)

Yet he was frustrated with the critics' inability to plumb the deeper levels
of meaning of any of his works: " I hope some time some people will
know what the *Bus* was about. Even with the lead [the literary allusion to
Everyman], they didn't discover" (*LIL* 297). Occasionally, however, his
anger resurfaced, despite his attempts to keep it under control. "There is so
much yapping in the world," he wrote. "The coyotes are at us all the time,
telling us who we are, what we should do and believe. The stinking little
parasitic minds that fasten screaming on us like pilot fish that fasten on a
shark, they contribute only drag" (*LIL* 359).

When the play/novella *Burning Bright* elicited personal attacks that
questioned his promise as an author of merit, Steinbeck attributed its
failure to the reviewers' lack of moral sensitivity and gave them credit for
bringing a renewed sense of vigor to his writing, for creating a controversy
that heightened rather than demeaned his reputation as a writer.

The final stage, bringing Steinbeck full circle back to his initial
depression and lack of confidence, occurred when his hostility became
more muted, and his excuses waned. Instead, he tried to be nonchalant and
apathetic in order to deceive himself into believing that he really didn't
care. Yet for a while hostility toward critics continued to surface

frequently, for unfortunately, the reviews of *East of Eden,* the book Steinbeck considered to be his masterpiece, were no better than those of his previous works. Once again Steinbeck was accused of writing in bad taste, of including irrelevant story material, and of being inconsistent in the creation of the personality traits of his major characters. On the question of taste, he responded: "Now good taste is a codification of manners and attitudes of the past. . . . Any writer who produced a book of unquestioned good taste has written a tasteless book, . . . of no excitement and surely of no originality" (LIL 436).

Still the reviewers of *East of Eden* again returned to the work of the past, offering it as measuring stick by which Steinbeck's achievements could be assessed. Although they had previously downgraded and deplored parts of *GW*, however, that novel had now become the watermark by which the entire Steinbeck canon would be evaluated. Steinbeck felt that *East of Eden* deserved to be valued on its own merits rather than on those of a book that had an entirely different purpose and was composed under entirely different circumstances. But in a career that had now spanned almost thirty years, he had found that the literary establishment had seldom understood him. By this point in his career, however, he had learned to deny his self-involvement as well as the pain such comments caused him. Instead he feigned apathy, often accompanied by self-justification for his determination to ignore critical comments or to see them as inconsequential and unhelpful.

When Viking reissued his short novels in a single volume, Steinbeck took the opportunity to lunch with six critics and to ask them to reflect on their previous comments after a period of time had passed. He shared the experience with Sheffield: "Recently I had lunch with six critics. They were men who had knocked each book as it came out. Reading the books again, they said they couldn't recall why they had gotten so mad. Harry Hansen said the books were so different one from another it used to make him mad because he thought it was a trick" (*LIL* 474).

Ironically, Steinbeck's complexity and variety had combined to work against him rather than in his favor. Further, since reviewers approached Steinbeck's work by intellectual analysis instead of by feeling as the ordinary, "sensitive" reader would, it became almost a given that the author and the critical community would never see eye to eye. When *Sweet Thursday* went to press in 1954, Steinbeck once again expressed his desire for at least minimal recognition by the accepted school of educated thought: "I wish just one critic would have found some of the very low keyed jokes which were placed for the highly educated," he said. " I suppose as usual, these will be only discovered by the illiterate" (*TA* 760).

Steinbeck's definition of the purpose of an author in a 1956 letter to Peter Benchley goes a long way toward explaining why the author took negative criticism so personally: "A man who writes a story is forced to put into it the best of his knowledge and the best of his feeling. . . . A writer out of loneliness is trying to communicate like a distant star sending signals. He isn't telling or teaching or ordering. Rather he seeks to establish a relationship of meaning, of feeling, of observing" (*LIL* 523). The desire to attain this intense personal relationship made perceived failure quite a serious matter. Yet Steinbeck coped by continuing to tell himself that no critical analysis really had credibility since all were biased by what the writer or the reviewer valued or considered an appropriate realm for literature.

When he published *The Short Reign of Pippin IV* the following year (1957), his subtle satire and wry humor again went unappreciated, causing him to strike back at "the searchers after secret meanings, the dour priesthood of obscurantist criticism and the devout traffic cops of literature" (*LIL* 538). Nevertheless, hostility became more and more difficult for Steinbeck to maintain. More and more often his reactions were dismissive rather than angry, as in a letter to Covice: "Back to critics--I have known for a long time that they are building their own structures which have little reference to mine. So I'm afraid I will go ahead and do my own work in my own way" (*TA* 650).

Such an attitude was supported by the realization that he was not the only writer who suffered from critical misunderstanding. After Russian Boris Pasternak was awarded the Nobel Prize in 1958, Steinbeck wrote to Stuart L. Hanson, director of Radio Free Europe, condemning the "poor official writers sitting in judgment on a book they are not allowed to read." Returning to his traditional animal imagery, he labeled them "the grounded vultures of art who having helped to clip their own wings are righteously outraged at Flight and contemptuous of Eagles. These are the sad ones at last, the crippled and distorted ones, and it is quite natural that they should be hostile toward one who under equal pressures did not succumb and did not fail" (*LIL* 602).

Unfortunately, ignoring, disparaging, or disregarding the critical community continued to function mostly as superficial defense mechanisms, and as his career drew to a close, Steinbeck seemed to return full circle, beginning to believe that indeed he was guilty of the charges laid against him and questioning whether he had any talent to defend. He was weary of being under attack and almost convinced that he was perhaps only a hack popular artist and not the great writer he had once thought himself to be. He wrote to Covici: " A writer and his work is and should be like a surly dog with a bone, suspicious of everyone, trusting no one, loving no one" (*LIL* 610).

Slowly he began to abandon projects as the negative ramifications began to accumulate and destroy his already shrinking ego. The depression which resulted for Steinbeck was heightened in 1958 after Alfred Kazin's evaluation of Peter Lisca's *The Wide World of John Steinbeck* appeared in the *New York Times Book Review*. Kazin labeled Steinbeck as a pastoral writer and bewailed "his lack of intellectual and creative resource" as well as "his relapse into sentimentality." Kazin's review was a completely damning indictment, suggesting that nothing in Steinbeck's canon after *GW* had any value. Kazin's influence in the literary world was, however, devastatingly injurious, and Benson suggests that Kazin's remarks somehow evolved into a simpleminded formula that other critics began to apply to Steinbeck.

Even his happy third marriage was insufficient to raise his spirits, but his significant accomplishments were still not over. He transferred the energy and ideas he had mustered for an abandoned work on the Arthurian translation and employed them in *The Winter of Our Discontent*, which was composed in record time from April to July 1960, the exact time frame of the novel itself. Again the work was experimental, shifting from first person to third person narrator and employing a wide range of literary allusions from the Old and New Testaments, Shakespeare's *Richard III*, Eliot's "The Wasteland" and the Arthurian Grail legend. In addition, many modern cultural referents suggest the demise of American moral integrity and the sad reality that lies, greed, and betrayal were now the cornerstones of this "free" society.

This time the critics' attack elicited the following response from Steinbeck: "The reviews of *Winter* have depressed me very much. They always do, even the favorable ones, but this time they have sunk me particularly. Of course, I know the book was vulnerable." He continued: "I don't think I'll read them right yet. I feel too badly about the good ones to rub my nose in the bad ones" (*LIL*, 698). In "Critics--From a Writer's Viewpoint" he expressed his confusion after reading these reviews: " In many cases one critic canceled out another; while the exponents of the new criticism wrote in a parochial language which was completely obscure to me. I became depressed, . . . for it seemed to me that there were no laws of criticism. Read all together one had an appalling sense of anarchy" (Tedlock and Wicker 48).

Although he claimed in another letter to Covici that he was "past the usual crisis of fighting back at critics" and called any response to his work "just a part of the rather tiresome quadrille. . . . [that] never changes," he seemed still to be desperately seeking for acceptance and recognition. Indeed, he cited one reviewer who "said a little sadly about *Winter*, 'I suppose, as usual, the faults we point out as making this book less than a work of art, will in the future turn out to be the factors of its excellence,'" as evidence that critics were finally beginning to see beyond their own noses (*LIL* 699).

As he mulled over and tried to classify reactions, Steinbeck ultimately concluded that his efforts at originality and his shifting employment of a variety of genres and styles were most responsible for his lack of approbation. His eclectic personality continued to revel in his use of versatility and change even though it only resulted in increased negativity from the literary establishment. Ironically, Steinbeck also felt that he was criticized because he enjoyed his work and dared to combine humor and pathos, comedy and tragedy. His claim to fame would be that he wrote truthfully: "I've tried to write the truth as I saw it and I have not held on to a truth when it became false" (*LIL* 710-11).

The final outrage that Steinbeck had to endure from the critical establishment occurred when he won the Nobel Prize in 1962. An editorial in *The New York Times* strongly suggested that he was an unworthy recipient, and the quarrel about his talents once again fomented. Steinbeck made one final reply in his own defense; not surprisingly, he used the platform of the Nobel Awards. He wrote to Bo Beskow: " I suppose you know of the attack on the award to me not only by *Time* magazine with which I have a longtime feud but also from the cutglass critics, that grey priesthood which defines literature and has little to do with reading. They have never liked me and now are really beside themselves with rage. It always surprises me that they care so much" (*TA* 917). He decided to use his acceptance speech, then, not only to define the goals of great writers but also to lash out at his detractors: "Literature was not promulgated by a pale and emasculated critical priesthood singing their liturgies in pale churches—nor is it a game for the cloistered elect, the tinhorn mendicants of lowcalorie despair" (Parini 447).

Refusing to be a "grateful and apologetic mouse" as he took his place on a world stage, Steinbeck wrote an acceptance speech that was designed to roar like a lion and to assert, as Benson puts it, that "good literature in his view had never been what a select few decided in their wisdom was good for the people, nor had it been in our society something that only a few with self-proclaimed special sensibilities could apprehend" (*TA* 985). Shortly before he received the prize, still further attacks surfaced, but the most cruel was Arthur Mizener's negative assessment of Steinbeck's career in "Does a Moral Vision of the Thirties Deserve a Nobel Prize?" in *The New York Times Book Review*, an article in which he mocked, faulted, disparaged and rejected Steinbeck's every accomplishment, concluding that "the Swedes had made a terrible error in judgment by honoring a writer whose "limited talent is, in his best books, watered down by tenth-rate philosophizing" (*TA* 923). Hurt by such critical attacks more deeply than he cared to admit, Steinbeck curbed his desire to fight back and undertook a journalistic assignment that almost precluded his writing more fiction.

In later years, Steinbeck increasingly found it best to regard negative criticism as reflective of the reviewer's personal bias. In a 1965 interview with Herbert Kretzmer, he said, "Literary critics really write about themselves. A critic is interested in his own work, his own career, and properly so. I don't care what is SAID about my books. I do care, however, what is THOUGHT about them. . . . I am an ordinary man, . . . scared and boastful and humble about my books. I love compliments, but I am not thrown by insults" (*CJS* 95). A similar dismissal was published after Steinbeck's death in 1968 in an interview that he had had with Ed Sheehan: "As for the outraged Mizeners and Kazins—forget it. I wonder, though, whether they realize how completely they describe not me but themselves. I have known for years that criticism describes the critic much more than the thing criticized" (*CJS* 101).

Finally he wrote in "Critics--From a Writer's Viewpoint" that the reading public should not forget "that the critic is primarily a writer himself and that his first interest lies in his own career. . . . He is prone to warp his piece in favor of his own cleverness" (Tedlock and Wicker, 48-49). Yet such glib dismissals were not always possible as cruel comments took their toll. As Steinbeck stated later in the same article, "Reading a course of reviews of a critic over a period gives a writer the idea that he started with nothing and got nowhere" (50).

Finally, the unassuming, humble young writer had come full circle. For Steinbeck as author, the minor accusations had combined with cruel words and misunderstandings to create an overwhelming accumulation of negatives which, though minor when compared with his public popularity and the complex nature of his messages, ultimately cowed his spirit and left him a defeated man and artist.

Though he had learned his craft well and was at times fairly confident of his talent, the incessant sniping eventually proved too much for him.

Although hostile replies were ineffective in quelling the critics, Steinbeck felt in the end that capitulation was his only alternative:

> I do hate the feeling of a hot breath down my neck. It doesn't bring out the best in me nor even the sweetest. . . . There are two distinct crafts, writing and writing for someone. The second requires a kind of second sight with which I do not seem to be gifted. . . . In writing for someone you must first, during and after, keep an invisible editor sitting on the typewriter shaking an admonitory finger in your face. It is a special business and one I don't seem to learn very easily. (*LIL* 446)

Now over thirty years following his death, the dilemma with his critics that Steinbeck faced remains current for Steinbeck scholars, who also have options: to humbly admit Steinbeck's flaws, to angrily attack misreadings, or to casually dismiss earlier negative reactions as missing the point or being uninformed by recent innovative approaches to literary interpretation.

It can now safely be said that early dismissals of Steinbeck as a hack or just as a popular writer have not stood the test of time. Although some highly influential members of the literary establishment have continued to promote Mizener's contention that none of Steinbeck's work after *GW* bears rereading and that even that novel offers too much third-rate philosophizing and sentimentality, the general reading public has continued to embrace his works warmly. Moreover, *Of Mice and Men*, *The Pearl* and *GW* remain staples of a high school education, and readers are still moved by Steinbeck's brilliant imagery, his complex and layered symbolism, and his moral commitment to reveal the truth about the human condition.

No doubt *The Steinbeck Question*, as Donald Noble labeled it in his 1993 collection of essays, will continue as future generations try to decide if Steinbeck's work is indeed art (classic fiction) or merely, as some would have us believe, banal entertainment. Steinbeck himself anticipated this dilemma in a letter to Pascal Covici, which was later reprinted in *The Journal of a Novel*. Here he envisioned a potential conversation between a writer and an editor. The editor has asked the author to justify parts of the book and has suggested numerous changes. As he enlists the aid of another editor and a proofreader in his attempts to convince the author, the conversation exposes the writer to various idiosyncrasies and inadequacies. Ironically, however, the author has observed their non sequiturs, recognizing that the demands for change have failed to take in one essential criteria: the reader, whose genius can transform what some might consider damp garbage into significant pearls of wisdom.

When Steinbeck's works are evaluated another decade hence, it is hoped that this criteria--readers and their response will be a part of the equation. For, unlike Harold Bloom,[5] who insisted that Steinbeck "aspired beyond his aesthetic means" and that "he fell into bathos in everything he wrote, even in *Of Mice and Men* and *The Grapes of Wrath*" (4), the responses of most readers would be more in accord with Covici's assessment in a February 12, 1958, letter to his friend:

> When I look back at the long list of your books I am truly astounded. And if you don't write another book, you have written your name in American literature for as long as the human race can read. For you, too, have the poetry, the compassion, the laughter and tears we find in Cervantes, and Dickens and Mark Twain. A reading of your work will always add something new to one's imagination and will always have something to say. (*TA* 961)

Steinbeck's own words regarding the worth of critical reception provide a fitting conclusion. Questioning the critics' role, Steinbeck offers them some guidelines, stipulating that they are neither "directors of writers" nor intermediaries "between writer and reader." He further dismisses the critic who wants to function as "a kind of traffic cop of literature," attempting to determine literary immortality. With tongue-in-cheek, he concludes wryly:

> It would be very interesting for a good and intelligent critic to exercise his craft on a body of work of his fellow critics. . . . I think it would be found that the product of a reviewer is not objective at all. . . . I don't think critics should change; only our attitude toward them. Poor things, nobody reviews them. (Tedlock and Wicker 50-51)

This essay is an original contribution to this text.

Notes

1. Benson, Jackson. *The True Adventures of John Steinbeck, Writer*. (New York: Viking, 1984). Hereafter references appear parenthetically in the text as *TA*.
2. Tedlock, E. W. and C. V. Wicker, eds. *Steinbeck and His Critics: A Record of Twenty-Five Years*. (Albuquerque: University of New Mexico Press, 1957). Hereafter references to this work will appear parenthetically in the text.
3. *Steinbeck: A Life in Letters* (posthumous, edited by Elaine Steinbeck and Robert Wallsten). (New York: Farrar, Straus and Giroux, 1976). Hereafter references to this work will appear parenthetically in the text.
4. *The Grapes of Wrath: Text and Criticism*. (New York: Penguin Books, 1997). References to this text will hereafter appear as *GW*.

5. Bloom, Harold, ed. *John Steinbeck's "The Grapes of Wrath.": Modern Critical Views*. (New York: Chelsea House Publishers, 1988). Hereafter references to this work will appear parenthetically in the text.

References

Benson, Jackson. *The True Adventures of John Steinbeck, Writer*. (New York: Viking, 1984).
Fench, Thomas, ed. *Conversations with John Steinbeck*. (Jackson and London: 1988).
King, Stephen. "Introduction: Myth Belief, Faith and Ripley's *Believe It Or Not!*" in *Nightmares and Dreamscapes*. (New York: Viking, 1993).
Steinbeck, Elaine and Robert Wallsten, eds. *Steinbeck:A Life in Letters*. (New York: Viking, 1975).
Sturz, Herbert. "Steinbeck on Critics: Writers Don't Need Further Humbling." *International Herald Tribune* (August 16, 1990), 7.
Tedlock, C.W., Jr. and C.D. Wicker, ed. *Steinbeck and His Critics: A Record of Twenty-Five Years*. (Albuquerque, N. M. : University of New Mexico Press, 1957).
Underwood, Tim and Chuck Miller, eds. *Bare Bones: Conversations on Terror with Stephen King*. (New York: Warner, 1989).

The Grapes of Wrath and the Literary Canon of American Universities in the Nineties

Mary M. Brown

In the spring of 1996 when I was preparing to write this chapter on the status of *The Grapes of Wrath* in the American literature canon of the 1990's, rock star Bruce Springsteen was touring America with his "Tom Joad" tour. Many were speculating that the success of the tour and of the album *The Ghost of Tom Joad* would help sell some copies of *The Grapes of Wrath*, the implication being that Springsteen's use of Steinbeck's character would engender interest in a book largely foreign to end-of-the-century teens and twenty-somethings. Even Steinbeck's family seemed grateful for the potential boost from Springsteen. An Entertainment News Service release reported that Steinbeck's son "thanked Springsteen [personally] for reviving the Joad character"; Steinbeck's widow was "honored" by the attention to *The Grapes of Wrath* from the rock star and by the parallels that Springsteen found between the plight of the book's Joads and that of more contemporary American immigrants. The title song of the album is a kind of lament by a first person narrator down on his luck--homeless, jobless, a part of a Southwest community made up largely of others in similar situations:

> The highway is alive tonight
> But nobody's kiddin' nobody about where it goes
> I'm sitting down here in the campfire light
> Searchin' for the ghost of Tom Joad

How the success of Springsteen's album and tour actually has affected sales of *The Grapes of Wrath* is undocumented, but even the speculation about its impact is telling: without the ephemeral benefit of a rock star's attention, the book is no longer seen as the staple of American high school and university education that it once was. A smaller percentage of American students of the 1990's have come to know Tom Joad by fulfilling a course requirement than in previous decades.

This is not to say that *The Grapes of Wrath* is no longer taught at all in American universities. In fact, perhaps it is taught more than many in academia perceive that it is taught. And there is little hard data on how much the book was taught earlier in the century after it won Steinbeck the Pulitzer Prize in 1940. (Perhaps it should be noted that many Pulitzer Prize winning books seldom or never make it to university course syllabi. Consider the 1936 winner, Harold Davis' *Honey in the Horn*; the 1940 winner, Margaret Wilson's *The Able McLaughlins*; and the 1972 winner, Wallace Stegne's *Angle of Repose*.) In 1989 when *The Grapes of Wrath* celebrated its fiftieth anniversary, numerous conferences (both scholarly and popular) were planned, and professors were more inclined to include the book in their course requirements than in a less prodigious year. But the overwhelming perception in university communities in the 1990's is that *The Grapes of Wrath* is a book that *used to be* taught regularly in American literature and American novel courses and automatically in twentieth century American novel classes. And that that position in the university curriculum has been usurped by a variety of other works.

For those of us who value the book, the question is why. And the answer is as complicated as debates on the canon itself. As Eric Cheyfitz writes in his 1995 article in *American Literature*, "Any history of American literary study must be, whether it admits it or not, polemical" (843). As this critical history has already established, debates on *The Grapes of Wrath* have been polemical since its publication in 1939, but the apparent decline in the position of *The Grapes of Wrath* in the American university canon is worth a careful and analytical exploration since it is clear that the canon will never be fixed and since it is also clear that adjustments in the canon are not necessarily good or irreversible.

I conducted a nonscientific survey by mail and also over the Internet, hoping to get syllabi and opinions about *The Grapes of Wrath* from literature professors at various institutions of higher education all over the country. I sent questionnaires to English department chairs at 150 institutions, trying to achieve geographical balance as well as balance in school size and type (including public and private institutions, renowned schools and schools I'd never heard of until I saw their names on an Internet list of American colleges and universities). In a letter accompanying the survey I asked department heads to distribute these questionnaires to members of their departments who teach courses in American literature or any course that might conceivably include *The Grapes of Wrath* as required or recommended reading. I also inquired over several academic bulletin boards and chat lists, soliciting comments from professors who teach courses in which *The Grapes of Wrath* might be used. Despite the common belief that the Internet is the center of communications in the nineties, my mailed questionnaires produced the most helpful information for me.

I received 119 completed questionnaires, sometimes four or five from the same institution where the department chair diligently copied my questionnaire and distributed it to every department member to whom it pertained. And I received nine responses from my Internet queries, several of them very detailed and helpful. The bottom line is that of those 128 respondents, 21 include *The Grapes of Wrath* in at least one course that they teach. I tend to think that respondents were more likely to pay attention to and return my mail survey, perhaps too blatantly entitled *The Grapes of Wrath* Survey, if they cared about the book and/or used it. And so I speculate that actually fewer than (and perhaps *far* fewer than) 20% of college professors who might teach the book actually do. The reasons for and against including the book in a particular course curriculum as expressed by those who responded were interesting and cause for reflection. Although there are variations on the theme, the reasons for NOT including *The Grapes of Wrath* in a course where it might be legitimately considered as a text can be broken into three categories: 1) The book is simply not good (or not good *enough* to warrant inclusion in a course syllabus) 2) The novel is dated and inappropriate for courses and students of the 90's and 3) The book is too long. And in many of the responses these reasons are intertwined in various combinations.

That some college professors argue that *The Grapes of Wrath* is unworthy of their courses should not surprise us. Negative criticism of the book has abounded since 1939. Some professors answering my query state it bluntly, calling the book "marginal," "mediocre," or "inferior." Emily Watts of the University of Illinois at Urbana-Champaign writes that she does "not believe Steinbeck to be of the first rank of 20th century writers" and

Roger Lundin of Wheaton College believes that Steinbeck has not "made the cut." Interestingly, Alan Wald of the University of Michigan writes that he has taught *The Grapes of Wrath* in the past "in a theory course to discuss how a mediocre work becomes both popular and canonized." Again, especially for those of us who admire the work, it is important to uncover and consider the specific criticisms leveled against the work, causing professors to classify it as "mediocre" or "inferior."

Many academics express the general negative critical opinion of *The Grapes of Wrath* that it is "sentimental" and so unsuited for the college curriculum. William Harmon and C. Hugh Holman's *A Handbook to Literature*, 7th edition, cites two definitions of "sentimentalism." The first is "an overindulgence in emotion, especially the conscious effort to induce emotion in order to enjoy it" and the second, "an optimistic overemphasis of the goodness of humanity" (474). Few of the respondents in my survey identified directly the branch of sentimentalism they believed *The Grapes of Wrath* to be guilty of, but several comments were pointed and others helpful in my speculations about the criticisms of the book.

Both the terms *overindulgence* and *overemphasis* suggest a judgment call that is, of course, at the basis of all evaluations of value and taste. One professor referred to the "cloyingly precious dialect" of the Okies in *The Grapes of Wrath*, a feature of the book that others find realistic and masterful. Whether one finds the following exchange from Chapter 22 "cloyingly precious" or regional and authentic may color an overall judgment of the book's quality and its suitability for serious literary study:

> Ruthie stared at the ground in embarrassment, and changed the subject.
> "They got toilets over there," she said. "White ones."
> "You been in there?" Ma demanded.
> "Me an' Winfiel'," she said; and then, treacherously, "Winfiel', he bust a toilet."
> Winfield turned red. He glared at Ruthie. "She pee'd in one," he said viciously.
> Ma was apprehensive. "Now what did you do? You show me." She forced them to the door and inside. "Now what'd you do?"
> Ruthie pointed. "It was a-hissin' and a-swishin'. Stopped now."
> "Show me what you done," Ma demanded.
> Winfield went reluctantly to the toilet. "I didn' push it hard," he said. "I jus had aholt of this here, an'--" The swish of water came again. He leaped.
> Ma threw back her head and laughed, while Ruthie and Winfield regarded her resentfully. "Tha's the way she works," Ma said. "I seen them before. When you finish, you push that." (312)

Here the Joad family's naivety, especially coupled with the extreme dialect, strikes some readers as an "overindulgence." And the intricate transcription suggests to them that Steinbeck was indeed consciously inviting a wholly emotional response. Some critics are similarly repelled by the intercalary chapters with the opinionated voice of a strongly emotional narrator, a voice which suggests to them that Steinbeck is too consciously attempting to move his readers and so has lost artistic integrity.

Even contemporary critics who celebrate the book do not dispute that Steinbeck himself was personally moved by the plight of the real life folks who inspired the Joads and the other fictional farm migrants of the thirties. John H. Timmerman, writing for *The Christian Century* in 1989, reminds us that in writing *L'Affaire Lettuceberg*, the precursor to *The Grapes of Wrath*, Steinbeck's anger was his motivation, the writing a purgation of it. But Steinbeck understood that anger alone was insufficient for a novel. He wanted readers to understand the heart and soul, the hopes and fears of these people, to empathize with them, rather than simply witness his outrage. (342) Timmerman goes on to explain that although Steinbeck destroyed the manuscript of *L'Affaire Lettuceberg*, the rewriting of what would become *The Grapes of Wrath* "nearly possessed the author" and "Steinbeck faced disconsolate moments when his best craft seemed unable to capture the raw truth of the human emotions" (342). Still, such authorial intensity is often viewed as the genius of a novel--is, indeed, viewed as the genius of *this* novel by many. There is a very thin line between sentimentalism and passion at the foundation of a literary work.

The intercalary chapters of the book are often at the center of discussions on where that line should be drawn. In these chapters the voice of the narrator is very strong (some would say *overly* intrusive) and does seem to appeal directly to reader emotions. These chapters interspersed throughout the work do not refer to the story of the Joad family; instead, they seem to make comment on the world, nature, society, the plight of the poor, on all humanity. Chapter three, for instance, traces a short history of a land turtle--not necessarily the turtle that Tom Joad takes home to his little brother, but a more anonymous, struggling turtle pitted against nature and the trafficked road. It is a short metaphoric glimpse of the travail of the oppressed, the underdog, and so, perhaps, tugs deliberately at our emotions without being centered in the context of the story. Other intercalary chapters are more overtly directive, focusing on the suffering of children, the unbearable realities of poverty and oppression. Critics might cite this final section of Chapter Nineteen, for instance:

> The men squatted on their hams, sharp-faced men, lean from hunger and hard from resisting it, sullen eyes and hard jaws. And the rich land was around them.
>
> D'ja hear about the kid in that fourth tent down?
>
> No, I jus' come in.
>
> Well, that kid's been a-cryin' in his sleep an' a-rollin' in his sleep. Them folks thought he got worms. So they give him a blaster, an' he died. It was what they call black-tongue the kid had. Comes from not gettin' good things to eat.
>
> Poor little fella.
>
> Yeah, but them folks can't bury him. Got to go to the county stone orchard.
>
> Well, hell.
>
> And hands went into pockets and little coins came out. In front of the tent a little heap of silver grew. And the family found it there. (248)

For some readers, this scenario, somewhat removed from the central story and its character development, is too consciously designed to create empathy, seems sentimental, a characteristic many college professors believe disqualifies it from inclusion in course syllabi.

In responding to my survey, Martin Bucco of Colorado State University adds another dimension to criticisms of the book's value. He acknowledges the book's "sentimentality," but still calls it a "masterpiece," suggesting that something in the book compensates for its flaws. He also goes one step further in identifying those flaws, adding that its "black-white fallacy is irritating at times." Other respondents alluded to Steinbeck's obvious bias, his empathy with the poor and his portrayal of those who benefit from the capitalistic system as black hats. Indeed, Steinbeck (again, often in the intercalary sections) often portrays capitalists, not as individuals, but as collectives, institutions, "banks" and "companies." Consider these two passages, the first from Chapter Five, the second from Chapter Twenty-One:

> But--you see, a bank or a company can't do that, because those creatures don't breathe air, don't eat side-meat. They create profits; they eat the interest on money. If they don't get it, they die the way you die without air, without side-meat. It is a sad thing, but it is so. It is just so. (32)
>
> And the companies, the banks worked at their own doom and they did not know it. The fields were fruitful, and starving men moved on the roads. The granaries were full and the children of the poor grew up rachitic, and the pustules of pellagra swelled on their sides. The great companies did not know that the line between hunger and anger is a thin line. And money that might have gone to wages went for gas, for guns, for

agents and spies, for blacklists, for drilling. On the highways the people moved like ants and searched for work, for food. And the anger began to ferment. (295)

Passages like these call to mind John Gardner's famous criticism of *The Grapes of Wrath* in *The Art of Fiction.* Gardner says that

> while Steinbeck knew all there was to know about Okies and the countless sorrows of their move to California to find work, he knew nothing about the California ranchers who employed and exploited them; he had no clue to, or interest in, their reasons for behaving as they did; and the result is that Steinbeck wrote not a great and firm novel but a disappointing melodrama in which complex good is pitted against unmitigated, unbelievable evil. Objectivity, fair-mindedness, the systematic pursuit of legitimate evaluation, these are some of the most highly touted values of university life, and even if--as is no doubt true--some professors are as guilty of simplification as John Steinbeck was, the very fact that these values are mouthed must have some effect on the alert student. (10)

Perhaps this is what John McElroy, Professor of English at the University of Arizona, was referring to when he said that although he had been very moved by this book in his twenties, he believes he would now find it "too doctrinaire in its views of capitalism." Similarly, several professors who took part in my survey referred to the book as "too romantic."

The charge of too much romanticism apparently stems not only from Steinbeck's individual vs. the establishment perspective, but also from what many see as his "optimistic overemphasis of the goodness of humanity" (Harmon & Holman 474). That particular optimism is masked by the fact Steinbeck sees also man's evil and has established a dichotomy between the rich (evil) and the poor (good). Some readers find the final, sacrificial gesture of Rose of Sharon to be unrealistic and out of character and thus Steinbeck's sentimental assertion of human magnanimity. Rose of Sharon, of course, is a Joad, a poor Okie, the mother of a stillborn infant whose father Connie has been defeated by a life of poverty, by the greed of the oppressive rich. She is one of the good guys and so ultimately behaves beneficently, despite forces working against that beneficence. Some find Steinbeck's celebration of the essential goodness of the poor contrary to artistic wisdom, as in his unabashed declaration at the end of Chapter Nineteen:

> Our people are good people; our people are kind people. Pray God some
> day kind people won't all be poor. Pray God some day a kid can eat.
> (248)

For many college professors this optimism about human nature and/or what
they see as Steinbeck's conscious manipulation of emotion constitutes
sentimentalism, a factor which for them eliminates the book as a college text.
Jane Tompkins of Duke University makes an interesting statement about the
book. She says that it is her guess that "*The Grapes of Wrath* might be
considered too sentimental for college teaching." Note that she does not
contend that the novel *is* too sentimental, only that it is *considered* to be. Dr.
Tompkins goes on to say that if she were teaching the modern American
novel (she's not) she "*would* teach it" and thinks "it's a great book." Dr.
Tompkins's comment raises interesting questions about the role of literary
reputation and who is responsible for establishing and perpetuating that
reputation, a topic that will be explored later in this essay.

The perceived sentimentalism of *The Grapes of Wrath* is not the only
value issue that keeps some professors from teaching the book. My survey
revealed that many college teachers see the book at "dated," rather than
classic and universal. Those professors cite the book's "limited relevance,"
its inappropriateness for contemporary students. Certainly many of those
faculty members who reported teaching the book use it in very specialized
courses, including but certainly not limited to these: Literature of the
American Southwest since 1900, Heritage of the West, Road Literature,
American Literature of the Thirties, American Social Issues, American
Fiction Between the Wars, 1918-1939. Furthermore, as might be expected,
the book is taught more often in states between Oklahoma and California
than in other parts of the country. However, Steve Garrison at the University
of Central Oklahoma, who teaches the book in his survey course of the
American novel from 1900-1940 says this in defense of his choice of the
novel:

> It is generally one of the favorite books in the class, though oddly not
> because of locale. (I don't get students telling me of their grandparents'
> travails.) I think they like the fact that the book paints in primary colors,
> so to speak. There's a simplicity to it that seems to be a welcome relief
> after *Light in August* and *The Day of the Locust*.

But J. Work of Colorado State University has had another experience and a
different opinion. He seems to be speaking for several of the respondents to

the survey when he reports that he has taught the book in the past but no longer does:

> For ten years or more, I have not sensed that students could make the novel relevant to their contemporary life and modern problems. It is, I think, too specifically sociological, too sharply focused on a certain combination of politics, economy, and national mindset. By the time one finishes lecturing on the dust bowl and the Okies, the students have lost interest in the characters and their motivations.

Similarly, Margaret J. Youce of August State University states *The Grapes of Wrath* is a "valuable artifact in our literary history," noting, however, that in her opinion its "message" and "method" are outdated. But, again, the disparity in opinion about the narrowness of breadth and the datedness or timelessness of *The Grapes of Wrath* is staggering.

Cynthia L. Walker, head of the Department of English at the University of Alaska, Fairbanks, sees it as such an "American novel that it certainly belongs in any U.S. curriculum." She also cites it as "one of the two or three books" in her 20th Century American Prose course that students like the best. Others also dispute the assertion that contemporary students do not relate to its setting or themes. Jean Wyrick of Colorado State University says simply that it is a "great novel" that "captures the despair, the hope, the political climate, in ways students can understand . . . extremely valuable for its style, 'voice,' and content." Nearly all of the responding professors who use the work made reference to their students' responses to it. John K. Sheriff of Bethel College in North Newton, Kansas, uses *The Grapes of Wrath* in Eng. 323, American Literature II, and finds "students interested in the characters, themes, and structuring devices of the work." W.D. Brown of Calvin College, who uses the novel in a course on Modern British and American Fiction, says directly that "students like the book very much."

But at work here might be the debate over the relationship between reader appeal and inherent literary value. Many academics see little relationship whatsoever between the two, finding it merely a rare and pleasant coincidence when the two coincide at all.

Also at work are other bigger cultural phenomena that have changed academia remarkably in the last decades. A report written by Clifford Adelman that the United States Department of Education issued late in 1995 gave some insight into what is really going on on college campuses by focusing on student transcripts. The study revealed declining student interest in modern languages and literatures and course selection based largely on professional (especially business) considerations (Franklin 6, 5).

The inevitable result of this is that universities must offer fewer courses in literature and/or consolidate previously existing course foci. This trend, by its nature, means that the range of works taught in any department is reduced, and so many books must be taught less frequently. Many who responded to my questionnaire alluded to this trend and its effect on *The Grapes of Wrath*. Joseph Brogunier, associate professor at the University of Maine, writes,

> I have taught Steinbeck's *The Grapes of Wrath*--years ago (maybe two decades ago) in the second semester of the senior-level American Novel course and at a time when this department still scheduled the American Novel as a two semester course. I haven't taught it since the American Novel became a one-semester, rapid "survey" course.

Certainly students' growing reluctance to take "impractical," elective courses in literature and the subsequent streamlining of literature department offerings have taken their toll on *The Grapes of Wrath*, as well as other significant novels in English or any other language. Several professors reported feeling compelled to teach *Steinbeck*, but, being limited by time and course offerings, choose only their personal favorite of his novels, in some cases *Of Mice and Men*, in others *East of Eden* or *The Winter of our Discontent*.

The other factor working against *The Grapes of Wrath* is what Roger Shattuck of Boston University has called "a calamity" which has "befallen the humanities . . . the invasion of politics" (70). In his article in *Civilization* (Sept/Oct 1995), Shattuck laments that in recent years other interests have usurped the desire to teach good literature in university English departments, namely, politics and theory (71). What Shattuck recognizes is undoubtedly connected to what is popularly known as *political correctness*, a phenomenon with many branches and a myriad of implications. For an instructor influenced by any of the branches of the movement, *The Grapes of Wrath* is not a likely choice of texts.

Feminists, (who often, according to Shattuck's theory, have as a first priority the teaching of *feminism*, rather than the teaching of literature), might well find Steinbeck offensive and *The Grapes of Wrath* antithetical to their first purposes. Although Rose of Sharon becomes an unlikely savior at the end of the book and Steinbeck's women more successfully survive than men, gender roles in the book are ostensibly rigid, and few feminists could justify teaching a novel that includes a passage like this in the first chapter:

Men stood by their fences and looked at the ruined corn, drying fast now, only a little green showing through the film of dust. The men were silent and they did not move often. And the women came out of the houses to stand beside their men--to feel whether this time the men would break. The women studied the men's faces secretly, for the corn could go, as long as something else remained. . . . Women and children knew deep in themselves that no misfortune was too great to bear if their men were whole. The women went into the houses to their work, and the children began to play, but cautiously at first. As the day went forward the sun became less red. It flared down on the dust-blanketed land. The men sat in the doorways of their houses; their hands were busy with sticks and little rocks. The men sat still--thinking--figuring. (3-4)

This is a passage that a radical feminist could teach only as evidence of the history and the level of gender oppression in America, a passage from a book to rail against and decry. And it is a passage that someone removed from feminist perspective and theory might avoid in order to protect him or herself from the criticisms of those in the center of the political correctness movement.

Similarly, at a time when fewer literature courses are offered, there is pressure on English departments and college professors in the 1990's to teach literature with strong ethnic connections. One respondent in my survey suggests that *The Grapes of Wrath* might be a fitting book for a course in WASP Lit. Though I recognize the tongue in her cheek, her comment strongly suggests the political climate in many American universities in this decade. Other respondents describe less overtly the prevailing climate and perhaps the pressure they are under to respond appropriately in that climate. Margo Lukens of the University of Maine writes,

I haven't taught it [*The Grapes of Wrath*], but I came very close to including it in my American novel course, ENG 445, a course for English majors. Instead, I ordered *Quicksand* and *Passing* by Nella Larson.

It seems significant and somewhat curious that one would teach *two* novels by the same black woman in a one semester course in an American novel course. But many respondents indicated teaching books like Louise Erdrich's *Tracks*, Toni Morrison's *The Bluest Eye*, and Alice Walker's *The Color Purple* in similar courses in which, one assumes, six to eight representative American novels constitute the course texts. The study of ethnicity (rather than of literature) may well be at the center of these courses. According to Shattuck, "It is not easy today to teach literature without a political or a theoretical package--a package that often itself becomes the content" (71). In such a climate, it becomes more unlikely for a book like *The Grapes of Wrath* to be a chosen text. But a few professors (like Shattuck) work in direct opposition of the trends. David Milofsky of Colorado State University writes that he teaches *The Grapes of Wrath* in his Modern American Fiction course specifically because "in these politically correct times, Steinbeck is neglected and because students today have very little sense of history."

One final explanation offered by professors who do not teach *Grapes of Wrath* is, perhaps, the saddest of all: it is too long. Again, the reason is more a comment on the state of higher education in the 1990's than it is a comment on *The Grapes of Wrath*. Early in the decade a Doonesbury comic strip (by Garry Trudeau) captured the atmosphere in many college literature classes today. A professor stands before his classroom saying that when he first taught this course (it happens to be a history course) twenty years earlier, he assigned seventeen books, seven of them *long* books. Three hundred students registered for the class. Ten years later, the professor goes on, only nine books were required, but class size was down to 110, and thirty of those students dropped the class. Today, the professor continues, he requires only three books, each under two hundred pages. It is only then that we see that *one* student sits in this classroom. He is making a "time-out" sign with his hands, saying, "*Three*? WHOA! Time out!"

The 473 pages of *The Grapes of Wrath* are apparently daunting to a majority of college students or at least to a majority of their professors. Ironically, others avoid the book because they still believe it to be a staple of the high school curriculum, an assumption whose accuracy this essay does not address, but which seems unlikely, given the attitude of college professors about the book's length. One college professor who actually teaches the book says that its "only limitation is its length--eats up quite a bit of my syllabus." For most instructors, that "limitation" is prohibitive. June Howard of the University of Michigan, who does not use *The Grapes of Wrath*, admits to subconscious qualms about the book because of its length:

> I have written about Steinbeck a bit and I do think the book "belongs" in the university curriculum. . . . I can easily imagine that I might teach the book sometime--I just don't happen to have done so. I should add that I suspect its length makes me reluctant to include it in an introductory course, and I don't teach advanced courses in the period.

Jeff Evans of the University of Maine expresses the sentiments of many who believe *The Grapes of Wrath* to be a first quality American novel and who worry about the state of American higher education: "It rarely appears in our curriculum--sadly, I suspect, because of its length."

The reasons are varied, but it does seem true that there is somewhat less interest in *The Grapes of Wrath* in the 1990's than in the past, certainly at least as a college text. During the decade (through July of 1998) the MLA index included only 63 articles mentioning the book. Perhaps the lack of attention to the book will change again now that in 1998 a Modern Language Association panel of scholars and writers has selected *The Grapes of Wrath* as 10th on their list of the best novels written in English in this century. It should be noted that of the nine novels coming in ahead of *The Grapes of Wrath*, only three were by American writers. One might suspect that this affirmation of value by a respected team might boost the book's reputation and so increase the attention it receives within academia. Then again, the panel's rankings may be of little significance. Almost as soon as the list was released, skepticism about its validity and value flooded the media, the most frequent criticism concerning the make up of the ten-member panel, which included only one woman and no minorities. Writing for *The New Yorker*, Louis Menand points out that the average age of the panel members was 68.7 (4). Syndicated columnist Donald Kaul, who found the list esoteric and funless, writes that the panel was comprised primarily of "nearly-dead white males." Proponents of political correctness assert that this panel certainly did not fit their requirements for making contemporary integrous judgments about works of literature. And it does not help their cause that 91 of the 100 novels on their list were written by men and only four were published after 1975. Menand sums up the opinion of a large segment of society (if not academia) this way: "This is not to say that the list is unrecognizable to anyone born after 1950. It's completely recognizable; these are the books your parents read." I believe Menand uses the word *read* as a past tense rather than a present tense verb here.

And so it is highly possible that despite the 1998 Modern Language Association list, the real position of *The Grapes of Wrath* in the American canon, indicated by how much it is read and how often it is assigned in the university curriculum, may continue to decline in the 21st century. The stream of what is taught can change directions, as indicated by the current prevalence of books like Kate Chopin's *The Awakening* and Zora Neale Hurston's *Their Eyes Were Watching God* on college course syllabi. These are novels that for years were completely ignored in universities. But one college professor's comment does not bode well for books like *The Grapes of Wrath*: "I've never read it, and so have never considered teaching it." When the current generation of college professors is replaced by another generation, many of whom have never read the book, the status of Steinbeck's work might well continue its decline. Springsteen's "Tom Joad" tour was short lived, its influence on popular reading choices minimal, I suspect. And so those of us who have experienced and long appreciated the value of *The Grapes of Wrath* can only hope that we have taught the book often enough and well enough to perpetuate its legacy.

This essay is an original contribution to this text.

References

Cheyfitz, Eric. "What Work Is There for Us To Do? American Literary Studies or Americasn Cultural Studies." *American Literature* 67.4 (Dec. 1995): 843-853.

Entertainment News Service. "'The Boss' meets Steinbeck, thanks to Tom Joad." *The Herald Bulletin*, Anderson, IN Jan 21, 1996: E5.

Franklin, Phyllis. "New Light on Undergraduate Course-Taking Patterns." *MLS Newsletter* (Spring 1996): 5-6.

Gardner, John. *The Art of Fiction*. New York: Vintage, 1983.

Harmon, William and C. Hugh Holman. *A Handbook to Literature*. Seventh Edition. Upper Saddle River, N.J.: Prentice Hall, 1996.

Kaul, Donald. "Pondering the List of Novels." *The Herald Bulletin*, Anderson, IN July 28, 1998: A10.

Menand, Louis. "Novels We Love." *The New Yorker* 3 Aug. 1998: 4-5.

Shattuck, Roger. "Standing Up for Literature." *Civilization* Sept/Oct 1995: 70-72.

Steinbeck, John. *The Grapes of Wrath*. New York: The Viking Press, 1939.

Timmerman, John. "*The Grapes of Wrath* Fifty Years Later." *Christian Century* 5 April 1989: 341-343.

The Enduring Values of John Steinbeck's Fiction: The University Student and *The Grapes of Wrath*

Kenneth Swan

The world has changed dramatically since Steinbeck wrote *The Grapes of Wrath* in the thirties. Our age is an age of affluence contrasted to a time in the novel of poverty and hostile environment. Ours is an age of internationalization contrasted to the local, the regional, and the provincial. Ours is an urban age contrasted to the rural and the agrarian; an age of education contrasted to the age of the unlearned and the uneducated; an age of technology and the computer contrasted to the backwoods and the unsophisticated, an age of science fiction contrasted to the realism of the Dust Bowl and the Great Depression. So why do the students of the nineties still read the fiction of John Steinbeck? Certainly, there is always the intriguing appeal of the long ago and far away, but *The Grapes of Wrath* does not fit well in the genre of the literature of nostalgia. Its realism is too brutal for that, and its naturalistic detail too discomforting in its vivid portrayal of the dehumanization of character and the destruction of the Joad family despite their heroism. So why are university students still intrigued with John Steinbeck? I asked that question of several of my students, and I discovered that there was a consensus in their responses and that they find enduring values that have broad appeal to today's university students.

Accustomed to an organizational structure involving plot development or character delineation, students are initially troubled with the organization of *The Grapes of Wrath* around situations rather than plot or character. Organized as it is against a backdrop of the panoramic and scenic, the detail, symbols, dramatization, and choric effects in *GW* are techniques designed for the portrayal of situation, not plot or character. Therefore, description often substitutes for narration. The successive situations--the drought in Oklahoma, the journey west on Highway 66, and the oppression and hardship in California--are panoramic and constitute the essential structure of the novel. These situations are basically scenes which must be depicted or described, not actions that must be narrated or dramatized. Students often note that Steinbeck's tendency toward panoramic vision makes this book (and others of his) highly memorable and easily adapted to film. The scenes are layered with images which are rich with realistic details and with creative imagination which appeal to the aesthetic sense of the student. Who can forget the stark images of Mule Graves creeping in the shadows of an abandoned house; of Grampa being buried in the dirt along the roadside; of the contempt of the men who spit and swear and say about the Joads, "They aint human"; of the displaced families in Hooverville looking desperately for work, any kind of work; of the bludgeoning death of Jim Casy, that gentle prophet; of the Joad truck mired in the mud swept by the flooding river; of the loss of Rosasharn's stillborn baby and the dramatic, symbolic nurturing of a starving, dying man? These images burn themselves into the mind and form a lasting memory. To students, these images are brutal but unforgettable.

Another enduring value of *The Grapes of Wrath* is its symbolic texture, its biblical parallels. Even though some of the parallels are transformed, the texture of this novel is rich with biblical symbols which strengthen the unity of the novel and enhance its thematic structure. Steinbeck's ability to select an archetypal situation and shape it into his own story dramatizes the universality of human behavior and the cyclical recurrence of human situations and human responses. Students observe the Biblical patterns in many of Steinbeck's works, including the disturbing parallel to Judas, the betrayer, in *The Winter of Our Discontent*; the multifaceted parallel to Cain and Abel in *East of Eden*; and in *The Grapes* of Wrath the dramatic parallel to the children of Israel, an impoverished people's leaving Egypt for the promised land. The Joads leave Oklahoma, where they have been victimized by circumstances beyond their control, and sojourn to a new land, led by a charismatic leader, Jim Casy.

Peter Lisca and Joseph Fontenrose have discussed these parallels at length. Fontenrose, for instance, states that the name Joad is meant to suggest Judah (75). Readers have long identified Jim Casy with Moses or with Jesus Christ. Certainly, John Steinbeck does not want the reader to miss these parallels since he appropriately selects a biblical phrase for the book's title, and he structures his story after the exodus of the Hebrews from Egypt to Canaan. As critics have pointed out, the drought, the journey, and the sojourn in California, the three main divisions of the book, follow the pattern of the biblical exodus of the children of Israel. At my university, where students are steeped in biblical literature, they often trace these biblical parallels in insightful papers which delineate the Joads as the chosen people who suffer oppression and denial in the land where they had lived for generations and who meet with hostility and conflict in the land of their destination. The unwritten code of the migrant camps is reminiscent of Mosiac law, and Rose of Sharon's stillborn child, set adrift upon a stream, reminds the reader of baby Moses floating in a basket made of bulrushes. Biblical parallels are extensive, providing depth and variety that enrich the fabric of the text and provide multiple levels of reading for the student who enjoys searching out the parallels, as inverted as they are at times.

The thematic structure of *The Grapes of Wrath* also offers considerable fascination for students because Steinbeck dramatizes a cluster of ideas which have less to do with social and economic causes and more to do with human worth, meaning, and value. The attention that Steinbeck gives to the idea of the transcendental unity of all humanity is a welcome contrast to today's emphasis on the individual and solitary. Understanding this concept of unity, commonalities, and responsibility constitutes the primary education of the Joad family as well as the chief message of Jim Casy. This concept offers the opportunity to introduce students to Victor Frankl as well, who maintains that America needs a Statue of Responsibility on the west coast to balance the Statue of Liberty on the east coast. The contentions of these two writers, both of whom are concerned with what it means to be truly human-- one a writer by profession and the other a Jewish psychiatrist who endured and survived the Nazi death camps during the Holocaust--work in concert with one another, their ideas reverberating, the one authenticating the other. And, painful as this pairing may be in showing human beings at their worst, it provides today's students a way of focusing on their own humanity. Like the Joads, to use Warren French's depiction, they are introduced to an "education of the heart."

French re-titles *The Grapes of Wrath* as "The Education of the Heart" and discusses the theme of universal brotherhood, as taught by Jim Casy, which in the course of the plot transforms the behavior of the Joads from ignorance and selfish clannishness to enlightenment and unity with others (107). In Casy's words, "a fella ain't got a soul of his own, but on'y a piece of a big one." This concept of spiritual unity, contrasting sharply to the physical reality of everything's falling apart, places the novel squarely in the tradition of the transcendental literature of Emerson, Thoreau, and Whitman (as Frederick Carpenter points out in "The Philosophical Joads"). This primary theme is one of the unifying forces within the novel and gives the work a level of meaning that engages the theoretical and intellectual. Other critics, such as Alfred Marks, interpret this theme in a biological or microcosmic sense (74). The individual is not only a part of a specific group but a part of the macrocosm of humanity. The Joad family members mold into a mass of migrating humanity.

A third thematic consideration is Casy's moral philosophy--"There ain't no sin and there ain't no virtue. There's just the stuff people do." Casy's rejection of absolute moral principles to judge the conduct of people leads him to a relativistic, humanistic view of life. Critics have made much of Steinbeck's non-teleological thought and his reluctance to think in cause-and-effect terms (Marks 77). Although the typical college student reading Steinbeck has read little literary criticism, Steinbeck's dramatization of the key ideas of transcendental unity, group identity, "is thinking," and moral ambiguity stimulate thoughtful responses from thoughtful students, who are led to reflect on their own place in relation to others.

Steinbeck's human sympathy for characters robbed of their human dignity in a hostile environment is readily evident, and students relate well to the underdog or victim, often with a strong sense of injustice. Even though the Joads are far removed in terms of time, place, and social position, they represent heroic losers, who despite their ignorance and narrowness develop in positive ways. In the novel, a contrast is established between the negative, naturalistic force of events that threaten the Joad family's physical survival, and the positive movement of the strength and beauty of the human spirit demonstrated as they accept, believe, and act out the spiritual vision of Jim Casy.   The Joads are not simply naturalistic victims of their environment, but they are heroic losers. They do suffer calamitous events which are destructive of almost everything that they value. They lose their land, Grampa and Granma die, they are out of work, always looking for a job, Noah and Connie wander off, the truck mires down in the mud, Rose of Sharon's baby is born dead, and the family is deeply fragmented. But, in faith and defiance, Ma Joad exclaims, "We are the people. We go on."

Steinbeck reveals a sense of compassion for their unfortunate plight. In like manner, students respond with identification and compassion. In comparison to student response to a Charles Dickens novel, there is not the sentimentality or deep sense of compassion as for Oliver, but there is a sense of moral outrage for the injustice done to the Joads: "They were hungry, and they were fierce. And they had hoped to find a home, and they found only hatred." Steinbeck's own ethos and sense of moral outrage often is expressed in objective terms within the interchapters which serve to reinforce his ideas and to unify the microcosm of the novel in its relation to the macrocosm. To this strong sense of outrage, students relate.

Another enduring value of *GW* for the American university student is the focus on the American scene and social criticism. The context of *The Grapes of Wrath* is America in the 30s, the Great Depression, the failure of farms in the Dust Bowl, and the consequent migration to California, the land of promise. A slice of history portraying the hardship and human cost of hard times forms the basis of this story. In addition to the American setting, Steinbeck comes to the novel with clusters of American values and attitudes. Carpenter, as has been noted, shows that the novel reflects typically American ideas and ideals--Jefferson's agrarianism, Emerson's self-reliance, Whitman's love of the masses, and William James' pragmatism (324-325). Certainly, the western migration, the dream of California as a land of promise, the individualism, the free market system, the emphasis on the rights of the worker, the raw conflict, and the turmoil, restlessness, and yearning of the American characters within the book make this novel a unique representation of our country at a specific time and place. Even the idealism of Jim Casy and the unfaltering hope of the Joads to find a better place hint at doctrine of Manifest Destiny, which spiritualizes the role which people play in shaping their future and the character of their country.

Yet Steinbeck does not let America off easy, and students are often startled by the social criticism, perhaps because it challenges their view of their nation. In *The Grapes of Wrath*, America is a chaotic place governed by greed, self-interest, and a relentless hunger for land and money. Steinbeck writes:

> Once California belonged to Mexico and its land to Mexicans; and a horde of tattered feverish Americans poured in. And such was their hunger for land that they took the land--stole Sutter's land, Guerrero's land. . . .And these things were possession, and possession was ownership. The Mexicans were weak and fed. They could not resist, because they wanted nothing in the world as ferociously as the Americans wanted land. (231)

Also, America is a place which exploits the labor and the labor market:

> Now farming became industry, and the owners followed Rome. . . . They imported slaves, although they did not call them slaves: Chinese,

> Japanese, Mexicans, Filipinos. They live on rice and beans, the business
> men said. They don't need much. They wouldn't know what to do with
> good wages. Why look how they live.. Why, look what they eat. And if
> they get funny--deport them. (232)

And America is a place of conflict, violence, and hatred. Steinbeck speaks
of the Okies who are "seven generations back Americans" and yet are hated
because they are impoverished, concluding that

> when property accumulates in too few hands it is taken away. And that
> companion fact: when a majority of the people are hungry and cold they
> will take by force what they need. And the little screaming fact that
> sounds through all history: repression works only to strengthen and knit
> the repressed. (238)

Another value of Steinbeck's fiction to which students relate is the
spiritual search for values and meaning. This observation is not surprising
because the most fundamental of all human problems is to discover the
meaning and value of life, to deal with the reality of evil, and to discern the
nature of man and God. This spiritual search is portrayed in characters such
as Jim Casy, who struggles with the hypocrisy within himself, his
responsibilities toward others, and his definition of the human soul. The
Joads move from selfishness to servanthood, a psychic journey typical of
much of Steinbeck's fiction. The servant-philosopher, Lee, in *East of Eden*,
for example, struggles with the reality of the human soul and the
interpretation of the biblical word 'Timshel.' This same novel prods the
conscience with the recurrent theme: Am I my brother's keeper? In *The
Winter of Our Discontent*, Ethan Allen Hawley, like Judas, follows his baser
animal nature and betrays his wife, his friend, and his boss, but finally in a
moment of regret and desperation, wills that his daughter not be corrupted
by evil as he has. In *The Grapes of Wrath*, Jim Casy serves as the seeker and
philosopher who interprets for the Joads not only the meaning of their
changing circumstances but their role and relationship to others. Actually,
he is more of a seeker than a preacher, but he has enormous influence,
especially on Tom Joad and Ma Joad. Through his death Tom Joad and
others are transformed, expanding a narrow, provincial concept of family to
include all humankind. His ideals and ideas, then, live on through others.
It is interesting to note, however, that typically, Steinbeck's philosophers are
seekers, not those with "the answer" or "the solution" to life's problems.

In addition to identification with this spiritual search, my students often
are puzzled by what Steinbeck's own philosophical position is and what he

really believes in terms of the meaning and value of life. Because Steinbeck subscribes to no orthodox system of beliefs, they are often frustrated in their search, for he proves to be an illusive and enigmatic author. For he himself is a seeker, and his belief system continues to shift throughout his lifetime. Is the author's philosophical position the same in *East of Eden* as in *The Grapes of Wrath*? Is Jim Casy Steinbeck's persona or spokesman in *The Grapes of Wrath*? Many critics think so. What about the servant philosopher Lee in *East of Eden*? Does his search reflect the philosophical search of the author? Are his conclusions the conclusions of the author? What is Steinbeck's own position concerning determinism and freedom? Why is Lee so jubilant in discovering that the word "timshel" may be interpreted 'thou mayest' rather than 'thou shalt'? These and other questions continue to tantalize the student of Steinbeck.

No novelist succeeds unless he is a skilled storyteller, a craftsman who creates a powerful story which lingers in the mind and forms a lasting memory. And my students find that one of the most enduring values of Steinbeck's fiction is that his stories are memorable. To read *The Grapes of Wrath* or *East of Eden* is not only to read two of Steinbeck's greatest novels but also to enter a time and place distinguished both by infinite detail and particularity as well as general truth and universality. Steinbeck says of his own writing, "My whole work drive has been aimed at making people understand each other." His typical approach is to create a contemporary story based on an ancient archetype, or a universal pattern of human behavior, and it is often this fusion of an ancient story with a modern one that makes his fiction so memorable.

In addition, Steinbeck's acute sense of the dramatic and cinematic infiltrates his texts, particularly at points of crisis or climax. Recall the ending of the story *The Flight* when Pepe, the boy-man pursued for killing a man and now trapped in the mountains, dramatically stands, unprotected, to face the consequences of his actions. Recall the final scene in *Of Mice and Men* with George and Lennie. George, fearful of what the vigilantes will do to Lennie when they catch him, takes the life of his friend, as he tenderly verbalizes their shared dreams and wishes. Recall the crisis of *East of Eden* when the scheming Cal takes his brother, the innocent Aron, to see their mother Kate, the madam of a brothel. Recall also the dramatic ending to *The Grapes of Wrath*, the extraordinary gesture of Rose of Sharon in saving a dying man. Steinbeck's use of the dramatic is heightened with symbolism and irony. His reversals of fortune border on the Sophoclean. When everything is lost--when there is nothing left to cling to--then there is a triumph of the human spirit, a glimpse into the meaning of things. My students relate well to this dramatic vision.

Critics have noted the infinite variety in the Steinbeck's work, and he says of his own writing,

> My experience in writing has followed an almost invariable pattern. Since by the process of writing a book I have outgrown that book, and since I like to write, I have not written two books alike. . . . If a writer likes to write, he will find satisfaction in endless experimentation with his medium, . . . techniques, arrangements of scenes, rhythms of words, rhythms of thought. (*Saturday Review*)

Peter Lisca speaks of Steinbeck's work as being remarkable not only for the variety but for the range of its "achievements in prose style as different as *In Dubious Battle* and *Tortilla Flat*; in structure as different as *The Pearl* and *The Grapes of Wrath*; in materials as different as *The Pastures of Heaven* and *Cannery Row*; in sentiment as different as *The Pearl* and *The Grapes of Wrath*" (293-294). While some critics have been offput by Steinbeck's thus refusing to be pigeonholed, my students respond positively to this wide range of prose styles.

Finally, Steinbeck's simplicity, imagination, and raw power in characterizing the elemental realities of the human heart in stories such as *The Red Pony* and *The Pearl*, short novels to which students are probably first introduced in high school, have left a memorable impact. When I ask, "How did you feel in response to reading this book? the invariable answer comes, "I felt sad." A simple answer but a good response. I have to admit that on my first reading of the plight of the Joads, the loss, the hatred, the suffering, the injustice, the dehumanization, I experienced anger and a deep sense of injustice. Students, too, often express an experience of a deep sense of anger and injustice in reading *The Grapes of Wrath*. Steinbeck plays to the elemental emotions, and my students identify with his powerful depiction of the human struggle.

Juliana Menges, a 1998 graduate of Taylor University, describes her experience with Steinbeck's fiction, maintaining that she finds herself attracted to his works because

> he seems to create elaborate puzzles to which there is not any one solution--the dimensions overlap and yet depend upon each other. Each time I read one of Steinbeck's books I understand more about the man himself and his intentions for the work. Steinbeck was not meant to be

neatly defined; instead, he transcends and soars above conventional definitions. He is not neat and tidy.

Nor is *The Grapes of Wrath* "neat and tidy." My students are challenged by its layers of meaning and quite willing to explore them, in part because they are in search of themselves, their own identity and meaning. Steinbeck's vivid depiction of time and place, then, is a powerful dramatization of a harsh era which rises above time and place. As a parable of the strength and beauty of the human spirit, it achieves universal value. Such a story will always appeal to readers regardless of time, place, and relentless change. My students have discovered in the Steinbeck aesthetic a consideration and enactment of those vital principles that remind us of our humanity. In his characters who have come to occupy a mythic place in the national identity, in his focus on the American scene that further tells us who we are, in his social criticism that takes us on a spiritual search and that gives us a glimpse of who we can be or should be, my students find a challenge for both mind and heart.

This essay is an original contribution to this text.

References

Astro, Richard. *John Steinbeck and Edward F. Ricketts.* Minneapolis: The University of Minnesota Press, 1973.

Carpenter, Frederick I. "The Philosophical Joads." *College English* 2 (January 1941): 324-325.

Fontenrose, Joseph. *John Steinbeck: An Introduction and Interpretation.* New York: Barnes and Noble, 1963.

French, Warren. *John Steinbeck.* New York: Twayne Publishers, 1961.

Lisca, Peter. *The Wide World of John Steinbeck.* New Brunswick, New Jersey: Rutgers University Press, 1958.

Marks, Lester Jay. *Thematic Design in the Novels of John Steinbeck.* The Hague: Mouton, 1969.

Menges, Juliana. "One Student's Response to Steinbeck." Taylor University, June 1998.

Steinbeck, John. "Critics, Critics Burning Bright." *The Saturday Review of Literature* 33 (11 Nov. 1950): 20-21.

Steinbeck, John. "Letter to Literary Agent." In *The Wide World of John Steinbeck* by Peter Lisca. January 1937.

Honoring an American Classic: Viking's 1989 Edition of John Steinbeck's *The Grapes of Wrath* (Review)

Linda C. Pelzer

Fifty years after its first publication on 14 April 1939, *The Grapes of Wrath* still gives voice to America's dispossessed. They may no longer be Okies set adrift by dust and Depression, but whether Hispanic migrants working the California fields or Midwestern farmers battling bankruptcy, their plight is no different from the Joads', and no less poignant. This is the point of Studs Terkel's moving and perceptive introduction to the fiftieth anniversary edition of John Steinbeck's masterpiece. This is the quality that accounts, perhaps, for the novel's continued ability to touch its readers' hearts and minds. When Tom Joad vows to "be there," "wherever they's a fight so hungry people can eat," "wherever they's a cop beatin' up a guy," his words resonate to the deep heart's core of our common humanity, moving us not only to feel the numbing poverty, the torturous suffering, the callous anonymity that constitute life for a vast American underclass but to recognize as well the quiet dignity with which they endure such indignities. Fifty, indeed sixty, years after its first publication, *The Grapes of Wrath* remains a powerful testament to human resilience and solidarity.

Steinbeck's epic tale of struggle and survival focuses on the Joads, a family of Oklahoma tenant farmers forced by natural disaster and economic exigency to make their way to California's migrant labor camps. Their odyssey is marked by violent death and slow starvation, by cruel indifference and calculated cruelty. Along the way, Grampa and Granma fall victim to the journey, and Rose of Sharon, a pregnant child bride, delivers a stillborn child. By the novel's end, Preacher Casey, the novel's moral center, has been murdered; Tom Joad, the novel's intellectual center, is on the run for killing a vigilante; and the flood-ravaged remnants of the Joad entourage, held together by Ma, the novel's spiritual center, must pull up stakes again, their dream of finding a new Eden as illusory as ever.

Such peril and privation, however, are certainly not unique to the Joads. In fact, their plight is shared by an entire social class, as Steinbeck makes clear through his use of the interchapters he called "generals." In the "generals," Steinbeck provides a context for the Joads' experience, background information about general American subjects such as the dust bowl and the tractor, the roadside diner and the used-car salesman. Such information is tangential to the Joads' story, mere digression, some would say, impeding the narrative flow (which it certainly does). Such information, however, delivered as counterpoint to the tale of an individual family, emphasizes the communal nature of the Joads' odyssey. "The one, the many, all heading in the same direction," notes Terkel. "The singular flows into the plural, the 'I' in the 'We'." Such information, moreover, fixes the Joads' experience in time and place, making it an American epic, a tale of national significance and, in its communitarian vision, a challenge to an economic-political system that seemed to have failed its people.

That vision of community lies at the heart of Steinbeck's novel. It echoes in the words of Tom and Casey. It is visible in the action of Ma, who intuitively reaches beyond her blood family to embrace the human family when, for example, on her departure from yet another camp she leaves behind for the less fortunate the remainder of a pot of stew. And it shines forth in Rose of Sharon's beatific suckling of a starving stranger in the novel's final scene (which some readers find excessive). Steinbeck's vision is "tribal," to use Terkel's word for it, intended to remind us of our common human needs and desires. "A fella ain't got a soul of his own, but only a piece of a big one," Tom says, echoing Casey's (and Steinbeck's vision), and knowledge of that transcendent soul ultimately redeems the Joads' struggle and gives meaning to their odyssey. For them, there can be no "tribal forgetting," another Terkel phrase. Nor can there be for *The Grapes of Wrath*'s readers fifty, even sixty, years later. As the title of Terkel's introduction asserts, "we still see their faces" in the dispossessed of our own communities, such is the power of Steinbeck's masterpiece.

Viking's fiftieth anniversary edition of *The Grapes of Wrath* certainly honors Steinbeck's sentiment and subjects. A handsome volume, its sepia-tone end papers reproduce the sheet music to "The Battle Hymn of the Republic," the source of the novel's title, and the text has been offset from the first printing. Terkel's introductory essay, moreover, is both an appreciation and expansion of this American classic. A champion of the worker in his own right, Terkel makes clear the subversiveness of the novel's social, political, and economic issues and argues for its artistic integrity. But above all, he reminds readers that Steinbeck's Okies are among us yet, that, indeed, they are us. Steinbeck would, I suspect, approve of such sentiments.

This review is an original contribution to this text.

The 1993 Everyman's Library Edition of John Steinbeck's *The Grapes of Wrath* (Review)

Barbara A. Heavilin

In the 1993 Everyman's Library edition of *The Grapes of Wrath,*[1] Brad Leithauser's Introduction begins with an inauspicious thesis: "In its tone, its methods, and the solutions it tenders for the social problems it documents--indeed, in its very willingness to tender solutions for colossal social problems--the book seems miles distant from most contemporary fiction" (v). Such a thesis promises little that is applicable to this novel because Steinbeck, like postmodern writers such as Toni Morrison, offers no solution for the problems of the Joads. Although the novel's final scene celebrates a triumph of the spirit, it leaves their problems squarely in the hands of the reader. As Morrison concluded *Jazz,* so Steinbeck might have concluded, "Say make me, remake me. You are free to do it and I am free to let you because look, look. Look where your hands are. Now"[2] (229).

Not surprisingly, in this comparison/contrast between *The Grapes of Wrath* and his vaguely conceptualized reference to "most contemporary fiction," Leithauser finds that this novel's "piece-by-piece construction" and "incremental pacing" bear the "smack of yesteryear" (v). Further, like Harold Bloom and Leslie Fiedler, he labels Steinbeck and his work as "middlebrow," interestingly choosing their terminology as he takes on their points of contention. Like them, too, he ridicules Steinbeck's handling of character, diction, dialogue, structure, and symbolism.

He holds up to ridicule also Steinbeck's obvious love and respect for his characters: "Steinbeck plays it straight. . .by respectfully allowing his Joads for six hundred pages to figger and innerduce and understan', to git a-sayin' and go a-billy-goatin.'" Nevertheless, he concedes that in the creation of these characters, Steinbeck has succeeded "in reaching the tender-hearted and the hard-hearted alike," the latter a reference to Dorothy Parker, a usually acerbic critic who reserved her highest praise for *The Grapes of Wrath* (vi).

Bearing the markings of early reviewers and critics who assert--to borrow Lisca's term--rather than thoughtfully assess and analyze, Leithauser assertively castigates *The Grapes of Wrath* as a work that does not "satisfy all the strictures of naturalism" (x) and Steinbeck himself as "a writer of such variable strengths and such uncertain instincts that any attempt at an epic novel would seem destined for failure" (xi).

Curiously, this acerbic tone does not carry throughout the review, for at times Leithauser takes on the tone (along with the well-taken points) of other critics. His discussion of Chapter Fifteen, to illustrate, is very close to Mary Ellen Caldwell's study of this chapter as central to this novel's thematic structure.[3] Similarly, his discussion of the novel's organic, thematic structure and the final scene, concluding that this novel is "all of a piece", echoes both Martha Heasley Cox's "The Conclusion of The Grapes of Wrath: Steinbeck's Conception and Execution"[4] and my "Hospitality, the Joads, and the Stranger Motif: Structural Symmetry in Steinbeck's *The Grapes of Wrath*"[5] This shift in tone and focus leads to a positive assessment of *GW* (and of this new publication of the Everyman's Library) as one of those books in which the reader is privileged to "behold . . . that little miracle of transformation by which, with just a bit of fleshing out, a stick figure becomes an Everyman" (xv-xvi).

But before arriving at this positive conclusion (that somehow does not seem sincere), Leithauser returns to his initial, negative tone and echoes some vague, poorly substantiated assertions of other critics, maintaining that "with *The Grapes of Wrath* . . . one is cheered to see an artist creating something far better--in view of his weaknesses--than anything one might realistically have expected" (xv).[6] These perceived "weaknesses," then, among them, according to Leithauser, a lack of "the wit and precision necessary for . . . poised irony," may account for what Leithauser describes as "Steinbeck's precipitous decline after *The Grapes of Wrath*." By his shifts in voice and tone as he parrots critical works that he does not credit, Leithauser leaves the reader wondering whether or not he actually read the novel itself before writing this introduction. However this may be, his inconsistencies serve to make the ending, playing on the Everyman's Library motif, seem facile and insincere even though the qualifier, "occasionally," shows that what at first seems to be a compliment is given grudgingly, withholding as much praise as it gives:

> The book occasionally offers one of the rarest and most gratifying pleasures that literature opens up to us. We behold in it that little miracle of transformation by which, with just a bit of fleshing out, a stick figure becomes an Everyman. (xvi)

This review is an original contribution to this text.

Notes

1. (New York: Alfred A. Knopf, 1993). Hereafter references to this work appear parenthetically in the text.
2. (New York: Alfred A. Knopf, 1992), 229.
3. "A New Consideration of the Intercalary Chapters in *The Grapes of Wrath,*" *Markham Review*, May 1973.
4. *San Jose Studies* (San Jose State University), 1 (November 1975).
5. *South Dakota Review*, 34.2 (Summer 1996), 192-205.
6. He also bemoans the opposite: "Most books by Steinbeck leave one unable to shake a regretful sense--in view of his many strengths--of how much better a writer he might have been" (xv).

The 1996 Library of America Edition of John Steinbeck's *"The Grapes of Wrath"* and Other Writings *1936–1941* (Review)

Barbara A. Heavilin

In one volume, together with *The Long Valley*, *The Log from the Sea of Cortez*, and *The Harvest Gypsies*, in 1996 the Library of America published the first unexpurgated edition of John Steinbeck's *The Grapes of Wrath*, described as follows:

> The text of *The Grapes of Wrath* has been newly edited based on Steinbeck's manuscript, typescript, and proofs. Many errors have been corrected and words omitted or misconstrued by his typist have been restored. (Front Flap)

Steinbeck scholar Robert DeMott, with Elaine Steinbeck as special consultant, provides "a newly researched chronology, notes, and an essay on textual selection." In addition, *The Harvest Gypsies*, "Steinbeck's 1936 investigative report on migrant workers which laid the groundwork for the novel, is included as an appendix." This volume provides both an indispensable beginning point for those interested in Steinbeck and an invaluable critical addition to the scholar's library. DeMott writes with the expertise and warmth of one whose scholarship has informed his thinking-- from an intimacy that only comes with long and close acquaintance.

The "newly researched chronology," for example, includes fascinating family lore:

> Paternal grandfather, John Adolph Grossteinbeck, a German cabinet-maker from Dusseldorf, moved to Jerusalem with his brother Frederic in 1854 and married Almira Dickson, daughter of Sarah Eldridge Dickson and evangelist Walter Dickson, Americans who has gone to the Holy Land to convert the Jews. (1031)

In function, this chronology is more like a biography in a nutshell than the usual chronicling of a novelist's passage points with dates of birth, death, marriages, publications, Nobel Prize, and the like.

In effect, it is more like a novella, at times even like a diary with Steinbeck's thoughts on a topic interjected when apropos, as though he were by the writer's and reader's side, commenting on his own life. Between the years of 1903 and 1909, DeMott writes, Steinbeck

> spends summers by the sea, . . . enjoys roaming in fields and along seashore, . . . learns to love gardening. . . . Receives a red Shetland pony named Jill . . . and cares for her himself. Home is full of books. . . . Begins reading books himself and especially enjoys Sir Thomas Malory's *Le Morte d'Arthur* (later writes, "The Bible and Shakespeare and *Pilgrim's Progress* belonged to everyone. But this was mine--secretly mine . . . Perhaps a passionate love for the English language opened to me from this one book"). (1031)

These antiphonal voices of DeMott and Steinbeck continue throughout the chronology--the essentially clipped tone of the chronicler offset by the authorial comments. In 1945, DeMott records,

> Troubled by resentment he has experienced in Monterey, writes to Covici: "There is no home coming [sic] nor any welcome. . . . Our old friends won't have us back." (1046)

The notes are similarly aesthetically pleasing as well as informative. Beginning with the account of Carol's (Steinbeck's first wife) choosing the title, to his instructions that Viking Press "print the 'Battle Hymn' on the endpapers of the first edition," to identifications of allusions, to authentication of some material, to notations of restoration of wording in the original manuscript (including a recording of some of the crossed-out material that Steinbeck decided not to include), these notes are a rich addition to the scholarly paraphernalia of *GW*.

The crossed-out material in itself reveals Steinbeck's steely determination to control his anger and his tone. For what is left unsaid shows that, like Toni Morrison, he wants to tell his story "the quiet way," as an objective observer compiling fact after fact, vignette after vignette in order to capture the essence of the experience of the dispossessed against the backdrop of a wealthy nation that is, for the most part, oblivious to the needs of the impoverished in the midst. DeMott identifies the "newspaper fella near the coast" as "Newspaper publisher William Randolph Hearst, . . . who in 1919 began building a private castle on 240,000 acres adjacent to the Pacific Ocean at San Simeon, California." But Steinbeck has crossed out the paragraph beginning "Hearst got a million acres, they say, an' the old houses all burned down 'fear somebody'd live in 'em." (1059)--evidently preferring the general to the specific in portraying a nation's greed.

The essay on textual selection documents both the process that delineates the steps in bringing the 1939 edition of *GW* to print and also that which shows the care with which this 1996 edition has been prepared and "corrected with reference to the original manuscript, typescript, and galleys," consulting also "Roy Simmonds' collation of the manuscript against the first edition" (1052). All of the changes from the 1939 text are listed at the end of the essay. The 1997 Viking edition of *GW* adopts the text of this Library of America edition.

Future scholars are indebted to the scholarly expertise of DeMott and the generous and devoted contribution of Elaine Steinbeck for this book that captures some of the essence of both the person and the persona of John Steinbeck and of *GW*, of which he wrote, "This book is my life." In a chapter by that title in his 1996 *Steinbeck's Typewriter: Essays on His Art*, DeMott expands on topics touched on in brief in this edition. Although I do not know which comes first in 1996--the Library of America edition or the book of essays on Steinbeck's art--nevertheless, the latter reads like a kind of sequel, an expansion of the first.

This review is an original contribution to this text.

Viking's 1997 Edition of John Steinbeck's "The Grapes of Wrath": Text and Criticism (Review)

Beverly K. Simpson

In the preface to Viking's second critical edition of John Steinbeck's *The Grapes of Wrath*, Peter Lisca states that

> what distinguishes this one novel is not only its greater authenticity of detail but also the genius of its author, who, avoiding mere propaganda, was able to raise those details and themes to the level of lasting art while muting none of the passionate human cry against injustice.[1]

Lisca maintains that "this second Viking Critical Library edition of the novel together with historical and critical materials enriches our appreciation of its greatness" (xi). The text in this revised edition "follows the Library of America edition of *The Grapes of Wrath*, . . . corrected with reference to the original manuscript, typescript, and galleys" (xix). The book begins with an introductory summary about Steinbeck's life and works and contains a four page chronology of Steinbeck's works and life. "A Note on the Text" records "by page and line number . . . transcription errors that have been corrected," "places where censored passages have been restored," and "typographical errors made in the first edition that have been corrected" (xix). Of particular interest is a map, "The Itinerary of the Joads," which details their journey from Oklahoma to California and includes page references to the text.

Following the text of the novel are "The Social Context," "The Creative Context," and "Criticism." "The Social Context" begins "with two essays . . . about the conditions depicted in the novel, and . . . continue[s] with another essay that samples reactions to the novel in Oklahoma" (xii). "The Creative Context," "consists of two essays, by major Steinbeck scholars, which set out the actual conditions under which the novel was conceived and written, and a letter by John Steinbeck himself, setting forth his intentions in writing the novel" (xii). "Criticism" offers, in chronological order, essays representing what the editors believe to be the more illuminating or provocative examinations of the novel down to the most recent approaches" (xii). The editors' introduction to this section presents a "history of critical reactions to the novel, highlighting the major trends" (xii). Other material of interest includes topics for discussion and papers and a selected bibliography.

In "California's Grapes of Wrath," Frank J. Taylor maintains that his investigation indicates that the conditions set forth in the novel do not hold up because nurses and sometimes doctors were available to the migrants (460). He claims also that "inquiry reveals that officers invade camps only when appealed to by health officers" (461). He does admit, however, that "a shanty- town or squatter camp . . . are [sic] frightful places . . . to live" (461).   In "California Pastoral," Carey McWilliams, attorney and Commissioner of Immigration and Housing for the state of California, relates several incidents reflecting the treatment of migrant workers in California and concludes that "Mr. Steinbeck, in *The Grapes of Wrath*, was not relying upon his imagination" (489). Completing this section is Martin Shockley's "The Reception of *The Grapes of Wrath* in Oklahoma." Shockley states, "There are, I should say, two main bodies of opinion, one that this is an honest, sympathetic, and artistically powerful presentation of economic, social, and human problems; the other, the great majority, that this is a vile, filthy book, an outsider's malicious attempt to smear the state of Oklahoma with outrageous lies," But he adds, "The latter opinion . . . is frequently accompanied by the remark: 'I haven't read a word of it, but I know it's all a dirty lie'" (500).

The third section of the book, "The Creative Context," begins with Jackson J. Benson's "The Background to the Composition of *The Grapes of Wrath*" in which he dispels the myth of Steinbeck's having traveled to "Oklahoma and then ma[d]e a trip back to California with a migrant family. He made four trips to the Central Valley, and on one occasion drove on from Bakersfield over the Tehachapi Mountains through the Mojave to the state line near Needles" (506). Secondly, Benson notes that "the Tom of the dedication does not refer to a real-life Tom Joad or to a migrant at all, but to Tom Collins, the manager of the Arvin Sanitary Camp." (506). Benson details Collins' expertise at dealing with the migrants and includes accounts of Steinbeck's and Collins's living and working amongst them (509). The Collins records, together with Steinbeck's own experience with Collins and the migrants furnishes background for *The Grapes of Wrath*. Benson further recounts how Collins and Steinbeck rescued "starving mothers and children during the flood at Visalia" (520). After that traumatic struggle, he started the novel over, with the "focus on the migrants themselves, rather than on his hatred of those who had persecuted them" (523).

In the second essay, "'Working Days and Hours': Steinbeck's Writing Of *The Grapes of Wrath*," Robert DeMott writes, "Between 1936 and 1938 Steinbeck's engagement with his material evolved through . . . four stages of writing," the final stage being *The Grapes of Wrath*, "which was written in one hundred days between late May and late October 1938" and was published on April 14, 1939 (527). DeMott chronicles Steinbeck's writing in excerpts taken from the diary Steinbeck kept during his writing of the novel. The third selection in this section is "Suggestions for an Interview with Joseph Henry Jackson," [which contains] the kind of questions and answers Steinbeck would prefer in such an interview" (540).

Section IV, "Criticism," includes an "Editor's Introduction: The Pattern of Criticism" focusing on the history of Steinbeck criticism, followed by ten articles on Steinbeck's work. The editors show that early reviews of *The Grapes of Wrath* "were emotional reactions to the social message of the novel" rather than an analysis of the book (548). This introduction provides a comprehensive overview of Steinbeck criticism, listing leading Steinbeck scholars and their contributions. "Literary critics have added to our under-standing and appreciation of what is certainly one of the great American novels," write the editors, but "this process is not yet complete" (561). "As you read the following essays," they suggest, "perhaps you will find that some particular point significant in your own understanding of the novel seems not to have been noticed by these critics. That will be the beginning of your own contribution," thus extending an invitation to future Steinbeck readers and scholars (561).

"The Philosophical Joads" by Frederic I. Carpenter posits the theory that for the first time in American literature in *The Grapes of Wrath*, the "mystical transcendentalism of Emerson reappears, and the earthy democracy of Whitman, and the pragmatic instrumentalism of William James and John Dewey" (563). In the second essay, "*The Grapes of Wrath* as Fiction," Peter Lisca focuses on Steinbeck's ingenious structuring of *The*

Grapes of Wrath. Two functions of the intercalary chapters, Lisca says, are "to amplify the pattern of action created by the Joad family" and to provide "such historical information as the development of land ownership in California, the consequent development of migrant labor, and certain economic aspects of the social lag" (574). "Steinbeck's great achievement in *The Grapes of Wrath*,"writes Lisca, "is that while minimizing what seem to be the most essential elements of fiction--plot and character--he was able to create a well-made and emotionally-compelling novel" (587).

In "Machines and Animals: Pervasive Motifs in *The Grapes of Wrath*, Robert J. Griffin and William A. Freedman suggest that "by their very pervasiveness," the machine and animal tropes "contribute significantly to the unity of the work," serving "to bind together the Joad chapters with those which generalize the meaning that the Joads' story illustrates" (600).

In "*The Grapes of Wrath* and the Esthetics of Indigence," John R. Reed claims that although the novel "was denounced as filthy, crude, and ill-made," it was "none of these" because "Steinbeck, through selection and restraint, transformed the potentially offensive details of indigent life into an esthetically sound artistic creation" (615). Patrick W. Shaw, in "Tom's Other Trip: Psycho-Physical Questing in *The Grapes of Wrath*" puts forth Tetsumaro Hayashi's summary in *Steinbeck's Travel Literature: Essays in Criticism* that shows Tom's journey as being '"never merely a passage from place to place, but an urgent quest for discovery'" (vi). Through his five-stage and five-state psychic journey, though Tom "does not literally discover the Eden that he and his family imagined, he does discover the enlightened state of awareness that is his salvation" (624).

The main focus of John J. Condor's "Steinbeck and Nature's Self: *The Grapes of Wrath*" is Steinbeck's harmonizing "freedom and determinism," and he suggests that Jim Casy "must translate the insight derived from . . . experience into ethical terms on the level of practical action" (632; 640). In "The American Joads," Louis Owens concludes that "the American Myth--the myth of this continent as the new Eden and the American as the new Adam--appear again and again throughout [Steinbeck's] fiction" (646). But in *The Grapes of Wrath*, he points out that "there is no Promised Land and nowhere else to go, no place for a Moses to lead his chosen people. The American myth of the Eden ever to the west is shattered, the dangers of the myth exposed. The new leader will be an everyman, a Tom Joad" (653).

In "The Ending of *The Grapes of Wrath: A Further Commentary*," John Ditsky observes that several Steinbeck scholars "have noted the eucharistic nature of Rose of Sharon's act," and he then reveals and examines the apotheosis by which this scene ascends "into the. . expressionistic (655). In

"Happy[?]-Wife-And-Motherdom": The Portrayal of Ma Joad in John Steinbeck's *The Grapes of Wrath*," Nellie Y. McKay reiterates "the centrality of women to the action" of the novel (664) while pointing out that Ma Joad "never achieves an identity of her own or recognizes the political reality of women's roles within a male-dominated system," that "she is never an individual in her own right" (665-666).

In "*The Grapes of Wrath*: Steinbeck And the Eternal Immigrant," (1993) Mimi Reisel Gladstein relates that "perhaps the theme of the eternal immigrant is another reason . . . the story of the Joads speaks to such varying audiences" (684). She points out that "Chapter 19 is one of the most clearly articulated instances in which Steinbeck's narrative demonstrates that he understood that the Oklahomans were more immigrant than migrant in the minds of his fellow Californians" (685). Gladstein explores the theme of "ethnophaulism" ("finding a derogatory term with which to label the new arrival") such as Okies (687). Because Steinbeck "shows that he understands the effects of this kind of name-calling," Gladstein states, this novel "speaks of me, an immigrant, who with my family experienced the pains and promise of immigration, an experience Steinbeck wrote of so tellingly in his story of the Joads" (688; 691).

The book closes with seven pages of "Topics for Discussion and Papers" and a selected bibliography. Such a comprehensive text with the three additional chapters provides the reader with a welcome overview of author, text, reactions, and criticism. The editors' chronicle the move from emotional reactions to *The Grapes of Wrath* to critical analysis. The varied, yet comprehensive, analysis of the critical response to *The Grapes of Wrath* encourages new Steinbeck readers/scholars to participate in this dialogue and submit their own contribution.

This review is an original contribution to this text.

Note

1. John Steinbeck, *The Grapes of Wrath: Text and Criticism*, 2nd ed. Edited by Peter Lisca with Kevin Hearle. (New York: Viking, 1997), xi. All page references hereafter will be cited parenthetically in the text.

Fermenting *The Grapes of Wrath:* From Violent Anger Distilling Sweet Concord

Michael Meyer

John Steinbeck's interest in Eastern thought, including the philosophy of Lao Tze and the precepts of Buddha, is now generally recognized by critics. Perhaps it also accounts for his wide popularity in such Asian nations as Korea, Thailand and Japan. Unfortunately, in the years that have passed since 1978 when Peter Lisca traced this Eastern influence on *Cannery Row* and John Ditsky similarly discussed *East of Eden* and the East, little has been done to connect Oriental tenets of belief with other texts in the Steinbeck canon.

Yet a consideration of the impact that Taoist philosophy may have had on Steinbeck's writing indicates that books other than *Cannery Row* and *East of Eden* have been informed by Eastern principles. In fact, Robert DeMott has determined in *Steinbeck's Reading* that a copy of the *Tao Teh Ching* was available to Steinbeck in the lab of his close friend, Ed Ricketts. Finally, Steinbeck's tendency to rewrite or reinterpret classics such as *Everyman* (*The Wayward Bus*), King Arthur (*Tortilla Flat*), Shakespeare (*The Winter of Our Discontent*), and the Bible (*East of Eden, The Grapes of Wrath*) makes it intriguingly possible that he may also have embedded Eastern precepts in his texts--especially the thought of Lao Tze in *The Way*—in particular, duality, the yin and yang balance, the principles of creative quietude, and rejection of materialism.

Since Steinbeck once wrote to Pascal Covici that there are five layers of meaning in *GW (LIL 178)*, it does not seem far-fetched to suggest that allusions to Lao Tze are a fruitful avenue of discussion of these levels.   For example, Tze's insistence on non-violence as the ultimate way to conquer and subdue one's enemies appears frequently in *The Grapes of Wrath*. To illustrate, in Stanzas 2 (39) Lao Tze says:

> In olden times, these attained unity:
> Heaven attained unity,
> And thereby became pure
> Earth attained unity,
> and thereby became tranquil,
> The spirits attained unity,
> And thereby became divine.
> The valley attained unity,
> And thereby became full
> Feudal lords and kings attained unity
> And thereby all was put right.

Through animal symbols, tropes, parallel characters, historical events, and plot, *GW* progressively and repetitively communicates this message of the Tao. For example, this Taoist virtue of unity is suggested by the characters who must become "pure . . . tranquil . . . divine [and] . . .full" (*Tao Teh Ching* 2(39), after which all will be put right, and they will have attained a full understanding of life. Since Steinbeck realizes that such a goal is ultimately unattainable, however, he portrays his characters on a continuing journey to full understanding and consistently suggests the difficulty involved in the attainment of unity by portraying their trip as hazardous–a slow, tedious, and repetitive process.

The very earliest pages of the novel indicate that its hero, Tom Joad, is hardly an advocate of non-violence or a follower of The Way—quite the contrary, for he is on parole from McAlester State Prison after being imprisoned for murder. As Tom relates his past to the nosy truck driver with whom he hitches a ride, he reveals his violent past when he smashed the head of Herb Turnbull during a barroom brawl. He acknowledges his guilt but maintains he acted in self-defense, reluctant to relate full details of the crime. In prison he has learned to keep his "nose clean." He tells the trucker, "I'm just tryin' to get along without shovin' nobody around" (*GW* 16, 13). But beneath the surface, his anger still rages.

Successfully repressing his violent tendency to strike out physically, Tom is still hostile, regarding the driver's prying questions with increasing annoyance, pictured in his crushing the grasshopper's head—a detail graphically parallel to his killing Turnbull (*GW* 16). In stark contrast, the truck driver seems to recognize the sanctity of all life as he carefully guides a bee into the air stream and lets it blow out the window.

On their journey along Route 66 from Oklahoma to the supposed "Eden" of California, the Joads themselves will eventually be forced to admit the futility of violence. In each of their confrontations, one or another of the Joads must exorcise hatred and murderous thoughts, refuse to succumb to the human propensity for evil, and learn the difficult lesson of the universal brotherhood of all things. The "Jesus meek" side of Tom (29) must take precedence over his Cain-like, murderous tendencies. As Lao Tze puts it:

Nonbeing penetrates nonspace
Hence I know the advantages of non-action
The doctrine without words,
The advantage of nonaction –
Few under heaven can realize these! (*Tao Teh Ching* 6, 43)

Tom himself ultimately represents a human struggle not only to practice sisterhood and brotherhood with human beings but also to respect all of God's creatures as part of the unity of an ideal society.

Tom's encounter with Jim Casy provides a first option in dealing with a society that increasingly espouses violence, that of escape. As Casy describes his own isolation, Tom sees the potential of merely running away from his destructive nature. But instead of seeking to escape, Casy acknowledges his need to lead others to an understanding of a concept that is new to him, just beginning to develop in his own consciousness—a gospel of love. As Casy develops this new philosophy for daily living, his actions bear a striking resemblance to those advocated by Lao Tze, whose teaching requires of his followers a reformed attitude. As he prescribes new tenets for living, like a disciple, Tom listens carefully and mulls over wisdom that proclaims, "Pure and still, / one can put things right everywhere under heaven" (Tao 8, [45]).

When they meet Muley Graves, the Taoist tenet of non-violence is again examined. The name "Muley" is significant because it appropriately suggests stubbornness, and the last name, "Graves," is significant because his own espousal of violence will bring death. As he recounts the story of another Okie, Willy Feeley, who violently bulldozes and demolishes the homesteads of his friends and neighbors, readers once again see how murderous hate fuels humanity's destructive bent. In self-interest, some destroy others, even those who are not their enemies, but their neighbors about whose welfare they should be concerned. When Feeley resorts to violence to maintain his own life, he creates more violence, not a solution.   Consequently, self-centeredness and greed damages all of society. As Lao Tze reminds his readers, "Abiding in softness is called strength / Use your light to return to insight, / Be not an inheritor of personal calamity" (*Tao*, 15 (32)).

Echoing intercalary chapter 5's relation of Jo Davis' boy who crushes houses like bugs (echoing also Tom Joad's crushing the grasshopper's head and contrasting to the truck driver's gently releasing the bee), the sixth chapter underscores America's problem with violence—not only during the era of the Dust Bowl, but also before and since. "Fella gets use' to a way of thinkin', it's hard to leave," says Casy (*GW* 53). Steinbeck seems to suggest here that America's long history of violence begins as a way of life in the early years of settlement and has somehow come to seem normal and perhaps even frighteningly comfortable to the nation's citizens.

Not surprisingly, then, Tom Joad, a typical inheritor of this tradition, ignores the tenets of non-violence promoted by Lao Tze as he recounts once again his "eye-for-an-eye" attitude in the killing of Herb Turnbull. As Tom discusses the ineffectiveness of prisons as corrective institutions designed to repress violent crimes, Steinbeck again stresses the tenet that violence merely breeds more violence.   Forced incarceration does not cure crime--it fosters it by breeding anger and resentment. In fact, prison is described as a "thing that started way to hell an' gone back, an' nobody seems to be able to stop her, an' nobody got sense enough to change her" (*GW* 58). Violence proliferates, and its rewards are questionable. Muley, for example, believes Willie Feeley to be "mad" because he says, "What happens to other folks is their look-out" (*GW* 58).   Espousing a similarly destructive attitude, Muley maintains that he has changed from being "mean like a wolf" to being "mean like a weasel"--analogies offering no high expectations for human actions.

Steinbeck's oblique allusion to the feud of the Hatfields and McCoys, an actual historical occurrence which seems to have been raised to mythological significance by the later 1930's, reminds the reader that such family vs. family violence has become a part of America's traditions, perhaps even a national icon (*GW* 56).   Certainly such "brotherly" hatred is also evident in the Civil War, to which Steinbeck alludes in the title, reminding readers that brother has fought brother in the past and will continue to do so.

Unlike Casy, then, who through contemplation discovers a new way, Muley presents Tom with another option for Americans who are fed up with their violent heritage. They can become isolates, hiding, escaping the truth, refusing to acknowledge the evil of their past. But Casy's time in the wilderness has shown that this method is ineffective.

As Tom returns to his own homestead, there are still further lessons to be learned about employing violence to combat violence. Again Steinbeck relies on actual historical material from the 30's to make his point. Ma's concern for Tom's addiction to violence is shown in her relation of the story of Purty Boy Floyd, a story appearing periodically in the narrative to illustrate the tragic effect of violence on the individual. In Floyd's case, uncontrolled anger and a vicious temper result in "a walkin' chunk of mean-mad" (*GW* 78). Repression does not cure Purty Boy: it merely makes him madder and eventually destroys him completely.

In addition to this historical allusion, a similar lesson is offered in the description of Pa's violently wresting Noah from his mother's womb. Driven by fear of the unknown, Pa is also described by Steinbeck as "mad" with apprehension. (*GW* 80). His violent reaction results in a twisted, warped skull for his first-born child and emotional consequences far beyond a physical scarring. Well aware of the double meaning of "mad," Steinbeck denotes anger as well as insanity, thus suggesting that all violence is insane.

Illustration upon illustration follows, each indicating the futility and destructiveness of a hostile nature. For example, Granpa also mentions the McCoy / Hatfield feud, reiterating Muley's speech and recalling once again the hereditary nature of violent solutions to problems. "He just done what I'd do," he says, adding, "You lay down your sights anywheres near Tommy, an' I'll take it an' ram it up your ass." (*GW* 81). This thoughtless defense of violence is followed almost immediately by Casy's epic speech about the great OverSoul, an espousal of holiness, oneness, unity. Tom must contemplate each speech in turn--evaluating, blending, and balancing opposite, mutually contradicting views. For Casy maintains that "it on'y got unholy when one mis'able little fella got the bit in the teeth an' run off his own way, kickin' and draggin' an' fightin'. Fella like that bust the holiness" (*GW* 83). And Lao Tze similarly instructs his followers to

Act through non-action,
Handle affairs through non-interference. . . .
Repay resentment with integrity. (*Tao Teh Ching*, 25 (63))

Casy suggests also the merits of working together for a common good, implying a mutual responsibility, an acceptance of the role of a brother's or sister's keeper. Although Tom does not fully understand the import of Casy's speech at this point, the seeds have been sown, and they will soon begin to germinate. Meanwhile, the recurring hints of the negative consequences of violence become more subtle, underlying and offsetting an increased emphasis on the Joads' hopes of renewal and resurrection in the promised land of California. As the family journey continues, however, symbols and parallels flesh out the message of non-violence.

With the tedious demands and requirements of the road, it is not surprising that tempers flare and anger surfaces as the Joads travel across the Dust Bowl toward an approaching desert. They encounter those who also evaluate the way society deals with those whom they label enemies. Some assess the so-called "normality" of violence and find it decidedly abnormal. The gas station attendant from chapter 13 is just one example. This unnamed character surprisingly practices brotherhood, helping his desperate customers even when they are spiteful and abusive. But this attendant is woeful and whines about the heartlessness he sees daily--yet another way of dealing with violence, by lamenting its existence, hoping that it will disappear. But he tries to be brotherly by offering the Joads water and by letting them barter possessions for gas, a step in the right direction.

The Joads' journey toward a discovery of a new way continues with their meeting the Wilsons and by Granpa's death.   The Wilsons exemplify the new type of brotherhood continuously advocated by the novel: that all human beings are our brothers and sisters. The kindness and generosity of the Wilsons in the Joads' time of trouble suggests that a new pattern based on Casy's principle of brotherhood and sisterhood is developing. Like Lao Tze, Tom (with the rest of the Joads) discovers that "the more he does for others, the more he has himself. The more he gives to others the more his own bounty increases" (*Tao Teh Ching* 31(81)). When Tom writes "Blessed is he whose transgressions are forgiven" to mark Granpa's grave, it is implied that such a premise must guide the Joads as they continue to discover a new and different approach to living. Past sins must be overlooked and wiped away. The hostility of the past must be rejected and be replaced by a realization of the oneness of all humankind.

Ironically, this new life will not bring a new land of milk and honey which the Joads are literally anticipating as they travel dusty Route 66. Instead, it will mean a spiritual transformation as the family adopts a new philosophy about how to live with and relate to others. As the intercalary chapters suggest by expanding the scope of the novel from one family to the nation as a whole, the direction of the Joads must move away from "I" and toward "we," away from hatred and hostility and toward love and cooperation. The story of Mae, the waitress, and her generosity to an unnamed Okie family illustrates such a changed society. By giving, Mae does not lose: instead, she receives abundantly as the truckers leave her sizable tips to offset her generosity. Steinbeck thus pictures the way a non-violent, cooperative society may work.

As the journey progresses, the Joads continue to practice and develop their dawning realization that all human beings are their sisters and brothers. In a process that begins when the Joads invite Casy to join them on their journey and share their food, the family now embraces and befriends the Wilsons and sees the value of traveling together and mutually sharing responsibilities. By returning the favors that strangers so willingly have given them, the Joads discover how reciprocal brotherhood is. Not all strangers need to be seen as threatening "others"; instead they can be friends who journey together, assisting each other. As the Wilsons share their quilt and tent and Al repairs their broken-down car, there is a parallel to Muley's sharing his freshly caught rabbit with Tom and Casy: "I ain't got no choice in the matter . . . what I mean is, if a fella's got somepin' to eat and another fella's hungry–why, the first fella ain't got no choice (*GW* 51-52).

But Steinbeck's recurrent insistence on the message of brotherhood through parallel plot situations and intercalary chapter events suggests that convincing the Joads to change will not be easy. Despite non-listeners, however, *The Grapes of Wrath* persists in warning about what will ensue should hostility continue to be the norm. And Casy offers hope for a change: "They's gonna come a thing that's gonna change the whole country (*GW* 174).

Like the gas station attendant before him, the one-eyed man at the junkyard practices brotherhood at least to an extent. But his generosity in offering help and reasonably priced car parts to Tom and Al is as much motivated by his own feelings of inferiority and his desire to get back at his boss as it is by love for his fellow human beings.

As they return to the family after reasonably obtaining from this generous, one-eyed wrecking yard attendant the needed parts and a flashlight in addition, Al demonstrates a continuing attraction to violence as he swerves to hit a cat crossing the road. Here Steinbeck portrays a violation of the precepts of Lao Tze, that is, the oneness of all: "When a man is sparing of his body in caring / for all under heaven, / Then all under heaven can be delivered to him" (*Tao Teh Ching*, 57 (13)). The destruction of the cat is vicious and cruel; indeed, it demonstrates a basic inclination toward evil rather than good. As Al crushes a jackrabbit under the Ford's wheels, as the truck driver swerves to hit the land turtle, and as the Joads' dog is flattened by a speeding car, the portrayals reveal a violence that evokes pleasure rather than revulsion. And such animal symbols are yet another way to make a Taoist statement": such "uncaring" is not a desirable attribute for human beings.

In Ma Joad, however, is an example, not of "uncaring," but of "caring." Although Ma's confrontation with the California policeman has the potential for violence, she only threatens aggressive behavior, ultimately refraining from hostility as she has done previously shown when she threatened Pa and Tom with a jack handle when they spoke of breaking up the family (*GW* 169, 120, 214). Perhaps one of the earliest of converts to non-violence, Ma recognizes that the human family, the people, are far more important than the individual entity. As Casy remarks, "There's a woman so great with love--she scares me" (*GW* 229).

When the Joads reach California, one of their first stops is Hooverville, a group of lean-to shacks constructed by other desperate migrants. In this place they again confront violence that breeds loss and sadness. The "bull-simple" man (278) and the woman whose hand is shattered by the deputy's gunshot both indicate the destructiveness of retribution and hate. Here Tom learns from Floyd Knowles and Casy the futility of fighting back. When Tom threatens retribution should anyone harm him, Floyd responds, "You're nuts. . . . Won't be no good in that [murder]." Later he says: "Don't hit no cops. That's jus' suicide. Be Bull-simple," and he reassures the Tom that non-action is not the same as no action: "Don't you worry. We're doin' somepin', on'y we ain't stickin' our necks out" (*GW* 247, 248). By implication, then, strength can be found in banding together, not in retribution.

But this new pattern or way of life is slow to arrive. For Al brags to Floyd about Tom's having "killed a fella" and warns him not to "fool" with Tom because "He don't take nothin' from nobody." Tom's instinctive and reckless striking back at enemies, however, is set against

Casy's sacrificial submission as he is arrested in Tom's place, covering for him by stating that he, not Tom, hit the deputy. Casy's willingness to be arrested and imprisoned demonstrates that, although he subjects himself to those in authority, he is still a man of action, willing to enact his faith. Although he is innocent, like Christ, he will suffer for the people he loves in order to [re]form a higher society.

Reflecting on the occurrence later, the Joads deplore the violence of the "law." Appalled by its negativity, Tom says, "They're a'workin' away at our spirit. They're a'tryin' to make us cringe and crawl like a whipped bitch. They're tryin' to break us" (278). Ma reminds him that "he has to keep clear" and resist his tendency to violence. In this personal test, Ma forcibly restrains from him from fighting back: "His hand crept down and felt the jack handle. Ma caught his arm and held it powerfully" (278). The difficulty of attaining Lao Tze's tenet of non-violence is portrayed as, for the first time, the hardened Tom cries, his "hard smothered sobbing" evidence of the challenges posed by practicing restraint. Ma reassures him that this time he has chosen the right path: "Don' you mind. You done good. You done jus' good" (280).

Still, Tom does not fully realize Lao Tze's principle of non-violence. Though he has seen others demonstrate their developing understanding of this new premise, Tom's conversion is still to come. But before that momentous event occurs, he observes others who engage in a "still better way," a way similar to that advocated by Lao Tze. For example, the Wallace family's sharing of breakfast and work demonstrates the values of sharing and working together. Unselfishly, the Wallaces find joy in sharing with others. Similarly, the Weedpatch Camp is run by tenets of cooperation and caring for others.

This camp is also the site for the initiation of another Joad into the ineffectuality of violence. When confronted by a number of camp children playing croquet, Ruthie tries to force her way into a game: "Ruthie sprang at her, slapped her, pushed her and wrested the mallet from her hand." No doubt influenced by her family's almost intuitive belief in the power of violence, she shouts, "I **says I** [bold mine] was gonna play." Everything backfires, however, as the other children do let her play—alone, "like [they] done with Ralph last week" (317). They set down their mallets in a simulation of the forthcoming boycott the migrant workers will organize against the fruit-growers, and Ruthie's violence has been met with an immovable passive resistance.

As the main narrative pictures the Joads' encounters with violence, so the intercalary chapters assess the moral and social failures of violence in America. As these chapters depict the gatherings of representative migrants, they reveal America's growth as it is set off by a violent past, including the eviction of Native Americans so that invaders could prosper. The depiction of the death of an Indian brave in chapter 23 shows that the slaughter of a human being brings no joy. The migrant story teller reiterates the connections among all living things, comparing the brave's death to the random killing of a cock pheasant, the meaningless destruction of beauty and life: "You pick him up–bloody and twisted," he says, "and [you realize] you spoiled somepin' better'n you, and you spoiled somepin' in yaself and you can't never fix it up" (326). The violence that the Okies have deplored in the banks, therefore, is the same as the violence that they themselves have employed in taking land from its previous owners. They, too, are guilty of cultivating the fruits of aggression in order to satisfy their personal search for property and possession—negative examples of Lao Tze's tenet of non-violence: "Weapons are not instruments of the superior man. / Weapons are instruments of evil omen, / to be used only when there is no other choice" (*Tao Teh Ching*, 75 (31)).

The dance at the Weedpatch camp, in contrast, provides a positive example of Lao Tze's precepts. Outsiders plot to start a fight and to bring a perverted "justice" to bear on the migrants. Discovering the plot, the camp chairman discourages violence, quelling Unit 3's representative suggestion to "squash the hell out of them." (Note the similarity to the death of the grasshopper, the murder of Herb Turnbull, to Muley's desire to brain Willie Feeley, and to the crushing of rabbits, snakes, cats and turtles on Route 66.) Houston states:

> "No. . . . That's what they want. No, sir. If they can git a fight goin',
> then they can run in the cops an' say we ain't orderly. . . . Don't you let
> nothing happen, Willie. . . . Don' you hurt them fellas--Don' you use
> no stick nor no knife or arn or nothing like that." (331-32)

Thus the instigators of the fight are surrounded by camp men, whose sheer number is enough to stop the threat of hostility.

This incident and Black's Hat's story of an Akron, Ohio, turkey shoot at which 5,000 mountain men marched with shouldered guns, intimidating, without directly threatening, a rubber company that is trying to "run the union right outa Akron" suggest an enlightened community that embraces a new philosophy like that of Casy (345). The practice of returning evil for evil, therefore, is shown to be no longer a necessarily hereditary and inescapable given. As the Joads' stay at the Weedpatch Camp comes to a close, the values of working together, of practicing brotherhood, and of espousing Jesus Meek rather than Purty Boy Floyd have been clearly established. Yet the difficulty of establishing and practicing such an ideal is revealed when Winfield, the youngest Joad, lashes out at a young boy who has called his family "Okies."

Tom observes the penultimate example of violence and passive resistance in chapter 26 when the Joads seek work at the Hooper Ranch where Casy is a strike organizer—a position that brings martyrdom. Doing what he believes must be done, Casy sacrifices his very life in the interest of fairness and justice, not attempting to save himself from the crushing skull blow which ends his life. Dying, he reiterates Christ's words: "You don' know what you're a-doin" (386). Espousing brotherhood and abjuring harm—even in self-defense, Casy exemplifies a higher way.

Just as Simon Peter cuts off the ear of the high priest's servant, so Tom impulsively crushes the killer/officer's skull, reenacting his murder of Herb Turnbull, again meeting violence with violence. As other critics have argued, Tom thus returns full circle to the book's beginning as he once again kills a man. Yet this second murder, though similar, has had a different motivation–concern for another. Ma tells him, "It's awright. I wisht you didn' do it. I wisht you wasn' there. But you done what you had to do. I can't read no fault on you" (392). Whereas violence is deplored, therefore, it may not be entirely escapable. In the Weedpatch Camp, Houston worries that it somehow manages to infiltrate and threaten all happiness:

> "I like this here. Folks gits along nice; an' God Awmighty, why can't they let us do it 'stead of keepin' us miserable an' puttin' us in jail? I swear to God that they gonna push us into fightin' if they don't quit a'worryin' us." (334)

After Casy's death Tom accepts the consequences of his crime–he must go undercover, disappear, be hunted. Marked with a permanent head wound (a Cain sign of a hereditary addiction to anger and violence), Tom goes into exile (also like Cain), even buried for a time in a cave. Accepting Casy's mantel, preaching a new Gospel of brotherhood, Tom finds his place in the Over-Soul, which Casy has suggested as a possibility quite early in the novel. In a final conversation with Ma, Tom observes the unity of all things:

Then it don' matter. Then I'll be all aroun' in the dark. I'll be ever'where—wherever you look. Wherever they's a fight so hungry people can eat, I'll be there. Wherever they's a cop beatin' up a guy, I'll be there. If Casy knowed, why, I'll be in the way guys yell when they're mad an'—I'll be in the way kids laugh when they're hungry an' they know supper's ready. An' when our folks eat the stuff they raise an' live in the houses they build--why, I'll be there. (419)

Though he has elsewhere observed many role models for non-violence, Tom has not previously accepted this goal as his own. Now he understands the paradox of the strength that lies in non-violence and the weakness that underlies violence.

The Joad family, representative of the people who go on, has been exposed to the tenets of non-violence continuously as it seeks a new life. But this new life demands a new way to live, a rejection of old ways no longer appropriate. A practitioner of this new faith even before it can clearly be articulated, throughout the novel, Ma reaches out to others in generosity: first to Casy, then the Wilsons, then the Hooverville children, the Weedpatch camp residents, and finally to the Wainwrights. She stands in sharp contrast to American images of macho strength and also to Lao Tze's view of the feminine qualities embodied in yin as being weaker than the masculine yang.   Yet Lao Tze urges;   "Know masculinity, / Maintain femininity" (*Tao Teh Ching*, 72(28)). Although maintaining such a balance between polar opposites is difficult, believers must strive mightily to attain the brotherhood and unity such a balance will foster. In Ma, then, is the paradigm of Lao Tze's balanced man— the one who sees and copes with the paradoxical nature of yin and yang, of strength residing in apparent weakness.

These tenets of Eastern thought portrayed over and over in *GW* provide an overview of a spirit of non-violence that Lao Tze advocated nearly three centuries before Christ. In the nearly sixty years that have passed since the novel appeared in print, this connection has gone largely unexplored. Steinbeck, an inscrutable intellectual, often complained that critics missed a great deal of his carefully worked out intentions, pointing out that this novel has "five layers." Much remains to be discovered in the various "layers" of *The Grapes of Wrath*, and it is probable that still more tenets of the Old Master lie beneath the pages of other Steinbeck texts. Like ripe grapes ready for the fermenting vat, they are waiting to be distilled by those who want to sip the knowledge of an American

Master and to taste some of the sweetness of the wine of truth to be found in the tenets of a great Chinese philosopher.

This essay is an original contribution to this text.

References

Steinbeck, John. *"The Grapes of Wrath": Text and Criticism.* Ed. Peter Lisca, updated with Kevin Hearle (New York: Penguin Books, 1997).

Tzu, Lao. *Tao Te Ching: The Classic Book of Integrity and the Way.* Trans. Victor H. Mair. (New York: Bantam Books, 1990).

Selected Bibliography

Beyond the sometimes resplendent—and perhaps almost erotic—
property of books and allure of manuscripts, there is the sad knowledge
that print-based lists, bibliographies, and catalogs, by their very nature are outdated—
and therefore forever incomplete—
as soon as they are published. With that awareness
the Sisyphean absurdity surrounding the compiler's task begins to emerge.
--Robert DeMott in *Steinbeck's Typewriter*

PRIMARY WORKS

Fiction

Cup of Gold. New York: Robert McBride, 1929.
The Pastures of Heaven. New York: Brewer, Warren & Putnam, 1932.
To a God Unknown. New York: Robert O. Ballou, 1933.
Tortilla Flat. New York: Covici-Friede, 1935.
In Dubious Battle. New York: Covici-Friede, 1936.
Of Mice and Men. New York: Covici-Friede, 1937.
The Long Valley. New York: Viking Press, 1938.
The Grapes of Wrath. New York: Viking Press, 1939.
The Moon Is Down. New York: Viking Press, 1942.
The Red Pony. Illustrations by Wesley Dennis. New York: Viking Press, 1945.
Cannery Row. New York: Viking Press, 1945.
The Wayward Bus. New York: Viking Press, 1947.
The Pearl. Drawings by Jose Clemente Orozco. New York: Viking Press, 1947.
Burning Bright: A Play in Story Form. New York: Viking Press, 1950.
East of Eden. New York: Viking Press, 1952.
Sweet Thursday. New York: Viking Press, 1954.
The Short Reign of Pippin IV: A Fabrication. New York: Viking Press, 1957.
The Winter of Our Discontent. New York: Viking Press, 1961.

The Acts of King Arthur and His Noble Knights. Ed. Chase Horton. New York: Farrar, Styraus & Giroux, 1976.
Uncollected Stories of John Steinbeck. Ed. Kiyoshi Nakayama. Tokyo: Nan' un-do Company, 1986.

Nonfiction

Their Blood Is Strong. San Francisco: Simon J. Lubin Society, 1938.
Sea of Cortez: A Leisurely Journal of Travel and Research. New York: Viking Press, 1941.
Bombs Away: The Story of a Bomber Team. New York: Viking Press, 1942.
A Russian Journal. New York: Viking Press, 1948.
The Log from the "Sea of Cortez." New York: Viking Press, 1951.
Once There Was a War. New York: Viking Press, 1958.
Travels with Charley in Search of America. New York: Viking Press, 1962.
Speech Accepting the Nobel Prize for Literature. New York: Viking Press, 1962.
America and Americans. New York: Viking Press, 1966.
Selected Essays of John Steinbeck. Eds. Hidekazu Hirose and Koyoshi Nakayama. Tokyo: Shinozaki Shorin Press, 1983.
The Harvest Gypsies: On the Road to "The Grapes of Wrath." Berkeley, CA: Heyday Books, 1988.

Letters and Journals

Journal of a Novel: The "East of Eden" Letters. New York: Viking Press, 1969.
Steinbeck: A Life in Letters. Eds. Elaine Steinbeck and Robert Wallsten. New York: Viking Penguin Inc., 1975.
Letters to Elizabeth: A Selection of Letters from John Steinbeck to Elizabeth Otis. Eds. Florian J. Shasky and Susan F. Riggs. San Francisco: Book Club of California, 1978.
Fensch, Thomas. *Steinbeck and Covici: The Story of a Friendship.* Middlebury, VT: Paul S. Eriksson, 1979.
Working Days: The Journals of "The Grapes of Wrath," 1938-1941. Ed. Robert DeMott. New York: Viking Press, 1989.

SECONDARY WORKS

Bibliographies

DeMott, Robert. *John Steinbeck: A Checklist of Books By and About.* Bradenton, FL: Opuscula Press, 1987.
Goldstone, Adrian, and John R. Payne. *John Steinbeck: A Bibliographical Catalogue of the Adrian H. Goldstone Collection.* Austin, TX: Humanities Research Center, 1974.
Harmon, Robert B. *Steinbeck Bibliographies: An Annotated Guide.* Metuchen, NJ: Scarecrow Press, 1987.
___. *"The Grapes of Wrath": A Fifty Year Bibliographical Survey.* With John F. Early. San Jose, CA: Steinbeck Research Center, 1990.

___. *John Steinbeck: Annotated Guide to Biographical Sources.* Lanham, MD: Scarecrow Press, 1967.

Hayashi, Tetsumaro. *John Steinbeck: A Concise Bibliography (1930-1963).* Metuchen, NJ: Scarecrow Press, 1967.

___. *A New Steinbeck Bibliography, 1927-1971.* Metuchen, NJ: Scarecrow Press, 1973.

___. *A New Steinbeck Bibliography. Supplement 1: 1971-1981.* Metuchen, NJ: Scarecrow Press, 1983.

Research Guides

Hayashi, Tetsumaro, ed. *Steinbeck Criticism: A Review of Book-Length Studies (1939-1973).* Steinbeck Monograph Series, no. 4. Muncie, IN: John Steinbeck Society of America/Ball State University, 1974.

___. *A Student's Guide to Steinbeck's Literature: Primary and Secondary Sources.* Steinbeck Bibliography Series, no. 1. Muncie, IN: Steinbeck Research Institute/Ball State University, 1986.

___, and Beverly K. Simpson, comps. *John Steinbeck: Dissertation Abstracts and Research Opportunities.* Metuchen, NJ: Scarecrow Press, 1994.

Railsback, Brian. *The John Steinbeck Encyclopedia.* Westport, CT: Greenwood Press, forthcoming.

Books and Monographs

Astro, Richard. *John Steinbeck and Edward F. Ricketts: The Shaping of a Novelist.* Minneapolis: University of Minnesota Press, 1973.

Burrows, Michael. *John Steinbeck and His Films.* St. Austell, Cornwall, England: Primestyle, 1970.

Chada, Rajni. *Social Realism in the Novels of John Steinbeck.* New Delhi, India: Harman Publishing House, 1990.

DeMott, Robert. *Steinbeck's Reading: A Catalogue of Books Owned and Borrowed.* Garland Reference Library of the Humanities, vol 246. New York: Garland Publishing, 1984.

___. *Steinbeck's Typewriter: Essays on His Art.* Troy, New York: The Whitson Publishing Company, 1996.

Ditsky, John. *John Steinbeck: Life, Work, and Criticism.* Fredericton, New Brunswick: York Press, 1985.

Fontenrose, Joseph. *John Steinbeck: An Introduction and Interpretation.* American Authors and Critics Series. New York: Barnes and Noble, 1963.

French, Warren. *Film Guide to "The Grapes of Wrath."* Indiana University Press Filmguide Series. Bloomington: University of Indiana Press, 1973.

___. *John Steinbeck's Fiction Revisited.* Twayne's United States Author Series, no. 638. New York: Twayne Publishers, 1994.

Gannett, Lewis. *John Steinbeck: Personal and Bibliographical Notes.* New York: Viking Press, 1939.

Gladstein, Mimi Reisel. *The Indestructible Woman in the Works of Faulkner, Hemingway, and Steinbeck.* Studies in Modern Literature, no. 45. Ann Arbor, MI: UMI Research Press 1986.

Jain, Sunita. *Steinbeck's Concept of Man: A Critical Study of His Novels.* New Delhi, India: New Statesman Publishing, 1979.

Levant, Howard. *The Novels of John Steinbeck: A Critical Study.* Columbia: University of Missouri Press, 1974.

Lisca, Peter. *The Wide World of John Steinbeck.* New Brunswick, NJ: Rutgers University Press, 1958.

___. *John Steinbeck: Nature and Myth.* New York: Thomas Y. Crowell, 1978.

Marks, Lester. *Thematic Design in the Novels of John Steinbeck.* Studies in American Literature, vol. 11. The Hague: Mouton, 1969.

Moore, Harry Thornton. *The Novels of John Steinbeck: A First Critical Study.* Chicago: Normandie House, 1939.

Owens, Louis. *John Steinbeck's Re-Vision of America.* Athens: University of Georgia Press, 1985.

___. *"The Grapes of Wrath": Trouble in the Promised Land.* Twayne's Masterwork Studies, no. 27. Boston: Twayne Publishers, 1989.

Railsback, Brian E. *Parallel Expeditions: Charles Darwin and the Art of John Steinbeck.* Moscow: University of Idaho Press, 1995.

Satyanarayana, M. R. *John Steinbeck: A Study in the Theme of Compassion.* Hyderabad, India: Osmania University Press, 1977.

Shillinglaw, Susan, ed. *"The Grapes of Wrath": A Special Issue.* Proceedings from "The Grapes of Wrath, 1939-1989: An Interdisciplinary Forum," March 16-18, 1989, San Jose State University. *San Jose Studies* XVI. 1 (1990).

Shimomura, Noboru. *A Study of John Steinbeck: Mysticism in His Novels.* Tokyo: Hokuseido Press, 1982.

Simmonds, Roy S. *Steinbeck's Literary Achievement.* Steinbeck Monograph Series, no. 6. Muncie, IN: John Steinbeck Society of America/Ball State University, 1976.

Sreenivasan, K. *John Steinbeck: A Study of His Novels.* Trivandrum, India: College Book House, 1980.

Timmerman, John H. *John Steinbeck's Fiction: The Aesthetics of the Road Taken.* Norman: University of Oklahoma Press, 1986.

Collections of Essays

Bloom, Harold, ed. *John Steinbeck's "The Grapes of Wrath."* Modern Critical Interpretations Series. New York: Chelsea House Publishers, 1988.

Davis, Robert Con, ed. *Twentieth Century Interpretations of "The Grapes of Wrath."* Englewood Cliffs, NJ: Prentice Hall, 1982.

Ditsky, John, ed. *Critical Essays on "The Grapes of Wrath."* Critical Essays on Modern Literature Series. Boxton: G. K. Hall, 1989.

Donohue, Agnes, McNeill, ed. *A Casebook on "The Grapes of Wrath."* New York: Thomas Y. Crowell, 1968.

French, Warren, ed. *A Companion to "The Grapes of Wrath."* New York: Viking Press, 1963.

Hayashi, Tetsumaro, ed. *A Study Guide to Steinbeck: A Handbook to His Major Works.* Metuchen, NJ: Scarecrow Press, 1974.

___. and Kenneth D. Swan, eds. *Steinbeck's Prophetic Vision of America.* Proceedings of the Bicentennial Steinbeck Seminar. Upland, IN: Taylor University for the John Steinbeck society of America, 1976.

___. *Steinbeck's Women: Essays in Criticism.* Steinbeck Monograph Series, no. 10. Muncie, IN: John Steinbeck Society of America/Ball State University, 1980.

___. *Steinbeck's "The Grapes of Wrath": Essays in Criticism.* Steinbeck Essay Series, no. 3. Muncie, IN: Steinbeck Research Institute/Ball State University, 1990.

___. *Steinbeck's Literary Dimension: A Guide to Comparative Studies, Series II.* Metuchen, NJ: Scarecrow Press, 1991.

___. *John Steinbeck: The Years of Greatness, 1936-1939.* Proceedings of the Third International Steinbeck Congress, Honolulu, HI, May 1991. Tuscaloosa: University of Alabama Press, 1993.

___. *A New Study Guide to Steinbeck: Major Works, with Critical Explications.* Metuchen, NJ: Scarecrow Press, 1993.

Lewis, Cliff, and Carroll Britch, eds. *Rediscovering Steinbeck--Revisionist Views of His Art, Politics, and Intellect.* Studies in American Literature, vol. 3. Lewiston, NY: Edwin Mellen Press, 1989.

Nakayama, Kiyoshi, Scott Pugh, and Shigeharu Yana, eds., *Steinbeck: Asian Perspectives.* Proceedings of the Third International Steinbeck Congress, Honolulu, HI, May 1991. Osaka, Japan: Osaka Kyoiku Tosho, 1992.

Noble, Donald R., ed. *The Steinbeck Question: New Essays in Criticism.* Troy, NY: Whitston Publishing, 1993.

Sharma, R. K., ed. *Indian Responses to Steinbeck: Essays Presented to Warren French.* Jaipur, India: Rachana Prakashan, 1984.

Tedlock, E. W., and C. V. Wicker, eds. *Steinbeck and His Critics: A Record of Twenty-Five Years.* Albuquerque: University of New Mexico Press, 1957.

Wyatt, David, ed. *New Essays on "The Grapes of Wrath."* The American Novel Series. New York: Cambridge University Press, 1990.

Yano, Shigeru, Tetsumaro Hayashi, Richard F. Peterson, and Yasuo Hashiguchi, eds. *John Steinbeck: From Salinas to the World.* Proceedings of the Second International Steinbeck Congress, Salinas, CA, August 1984. Tokyo: Gaku Shobo Press, 1986.

Journals

The Steinbeck Collector (San Jose, CA), 1 (August 1979)-4 (April 1981).

Steinbeck Newsletter (San Jose State University), 1 (Fall 1987)-present.

Steinbeck Quarterly (Ball State University), 1 (Spring 1968)-26 (Summer-Fall 1993).

Review

White, Ray Lewis. "*The Grapes of Wrath* and the Critics of 1939." Resources for American Literary Study 13 (2) (Autumn 1983), 134-64--contains documentation and excerpts from "108 American reviews. . .from 1939" (134).

Essays

Bristol, Horace. "John Steinbeck and *The Grapes of Wrath.*" *Steinbeck Newsletter* (Fall 1988): 6-8.

Browning, Chris. "Grape Symbolism in *The Grapes of Wrath.*" *Discourse* XI (Winter 1968): 129-40.

Cassuto, David. "Turning Wine into Water: Water as Privileged Signifier in *The Grapes of Wrath.*" *Papers on Language and Literature: A Journal for Scholars and Critics of Language and Literature* 29.1 (1993): 67-95.

Davis, Robert Murray. "The World of John Steinbeck's Joads." *World Literature Today: A Literary Quarterly of the University of Oklahoma* 64.3 (1990): 401-404.

Dircks, Phyllis T. "Steinbeck's Statement on the Inner Chapters of *The Grapes of Wrath*." *Steinbeck Quarterly* 24.3-4 (1991): 86-94.

Ek, Grete. "A 'Speaking Picture' in John Steinbeck's *The Grapes of Wrath*." *American Studies in Scandinavia* 10 (1978): 111-15.

Evans, Thomas G. "Impersonal Dilemmas: The Collision of Modernist and Popular Traditions in Two Political Novels, *The Grapes of Wrath* and *Ragtime*." *South Atlantic Review* 52.1 (1987): 71-85.

Gladstein, Mimi R. "Ma Joad and Pilar: Significantly Similar." *Steinbeck Quarterly* 14.3-4 (1981): 93-104.

"*The Grapes of Wrath*." *Columbia Literary History of the United States*. Ed. Emory Elliott, 726, 753-54, 859, 864, 868. New York: Columbia University Press, 1988.

Greene, Suzanne Ellery. "*The Grapes of Wrath*." *Books for Pleasure: Popular Fiction, 1914-1945*, 116, 120, 125, 127-28, 138-39, 143-45, 151-52. Bowling Green, OH: Bowling Green University Popular Press, 1974.

Haslam, Gerald. "*The Grapes of Wrath*: A Book That Stretched My Soul" and "What about the Okies?" *The Other California: The Great Central Valley in Life and Letters*, 87-95, 105-23. Reno: University of Nevada Press, 1994.

Hayashi, Tetsumaro. "Steinbeck's Use of Old Testament Motifs in *The Grapes of Wrath*." *Kyushu American Literature* 29 (1988): 1-11.

Hearle, Kevin. "Sturges and *The Grapes of Wrath*: 'Sullivan's Travels' as Documentary Comedy." *Steinbeck Newsletter* (Summer 1994): 5-7.

Heavilin, Barbara A. "Hospitality, the Joads, and the Stranger Motif: Structural Symmetry in John Steinbeck's *The Grapes of Wrath*." *South Dakota Review* 29.2 (1991): 142-52.

Henderson, George. "John Steinbeck's Spatial Imagination in *The Grapes of Wrath*." *California History* 68.4 (1989): 210-23.

Hunter, J. P. "Steinbeck's Wine of Affirmation in *The Grapes of Wrath*." *Essays in Modern Literature*. Ed. Richard E. Langford, Guy Owen, William Taylor, 76-89. Deland, FL: Stetson University Press, 1963.

Kaida, Koichi. "The Cave Experience in *The Grapes of Wrath*." *Kyushu American Literature* 28 (1987): 67-69.

Krim, Arthur. "Fruchte des Zorns: *The Grapes of Wrath* in Wartime Germany." *Steinbeck Newsletter* (Summer 1994): 1-4.

___. "John Steinbeck and Highway 66." *Steinbeck Newsletter* (Summer 1991): 8-9.

___. Lorentz, Pare. "*The Grapes of Wrath*." *Movies 1927-1941: Lorentz on Film*. Norman: University of Oklahoma Press, 1986.

Lucius, Ramona. "Let There Be Darkness: Reversed Symbols of Light and Dark in *The Grapes of Wrath*." *Pleiades* 12.1 (1991): 50-58.

McCarthy, Paul Eugene. "The Joads and Other Rural Families in Depression Fiction." *South Dakota Review* 19.3 (1981): 51-68.

Maine, Barry. "Steinbeck's Debt to Dos Passos." *Steinbeck Quarterly* 23:1-2 (1990): 17-26.

Motley, Warren. "From Patriarchy to Matriarchy: Ma Joad's Role in *The Grapes of Wrath*." *American Literature* 54.3 (1982): 397-412.

Mullen, Patrick B. "American Folklife and *The Grapes of Wrath*." *Journal of American Culture* 1.4 (1978): 742-43.

Owens, Louis, and Hector Torres. "Dialogic Structure and Levels of Discourse in Steinbeck's *The Grapes of Wrath.*" *Arizona Quarterly* 45.4 (1989): 75-94.

Rombold, Tamara. "Biblical Inversion in *The Grapes of Wrath.*" College Literature 14.2 (1987): 146-66.

Salter, Christopher L. "John Steinbeck's *The Grapes of Wrath* as a Primer for Cultural Geography." *Humanistic Geography and Literature: Essays on the Experience of Place*, 142-58. London: Croom Helm, 1981; Totowa, NJ: Barnes and Noble, 1981.

Slade, Leonard A. "The Use of Biblical Allusions in *The Grapes of Wrath.*" *College Language Association Journal* XI (March 1968): 241-47.

Terkel, Studs. "The Dust Bowl Revisited: 'We Still See Their Faces.'" *San Francisco Review of Books* 13 (Spring 1989): 24, 29.

Timmerman, John H. "The Squatters' Circle in *The Grapes of Wrath.*" *Studies in American Fiction* 17.2 (1989): 203-11.

Werlock, Abby H. P. "Poor Whites: Joads and Snopeses." *San Jose Studies* 18.1 (1992): 61-71.

White, Ray Lewis. "The Grapes of Wrath and the Critics of 1939." *Resources for American Literary Study* 13.2(Autumn 1983): 134-64.

Worster, Donald. "I Never Knowed They Was Anything Like Her." *Rivers of Empire: Water, Aridity and the Growth of the American West*, 213-33. New York: Pantheon, 1985.

Wyatt, David. "Steinbeck's Lost Gardens." *The Fall into Eden: Landscape and Imagination in California.* New York: Cambridge University Press, 1986.

Index

About the Editor

BARBARA A. HEAVILIN is Associate Professor of English at Taylor University.

ISBN 0-313-29990-0

EAN

9 780313 299902

HARDCOVER BAR CODE